DAT

MESSAGES

A Reader in Human Communication

Third Edition

MESSAGES

A Reader in Human Communication

THIRD EDITION

Edited by

Sanford B. Weinberg
University of Connecticut

Random House
New York

to Ellie and Seymour, who
help in so many ways

Third Edition
987654321
Copyright © 1974, 1978, 1980 by Random House, Inc.

Manufactured in the United States of America

Library of Congress Cataloging in Publication Data

Main entry under title:

Messages, a reader in human communication.

  First-2d editions edited by J. M. Civikly.
  Includes bibliographies.
  1. Communication—Addresses, essays, lectures.
I. Weinberg, Sanford B. II. Civikly, Jean M., comp.
Messages, a reader in human communication.
P90.C565 1979   301.14   79-18993
ISBN 0-394-32431-5

Cover: Lawrence Daniels & Friends, Inc.

Permissions Acknowledgments

Aristotle, from *Rhetoric and Poetics,* translated by Rhys Roberts, pp. 24–27. Copyright © 1954 by Random House, Inc. Reprinted by permission of Oxford University Press and Random House, Inc.

George R. Bach and Peter Wyden, "The Language of Love: Communications Fights," from *The Intimate Enemy,* pp. 118–137. Copyright © 1968, 1969 by George R. Bach and Peter Wyden. Reprinted by permission of William Morrow & Company.

John E. Baird, Jr. and Sanford B. Weinberg, "Leadership," from *Communication: The Essence of Group Synergy.* Reprinted by permission of William C. Brown Company Publishers, Dubuque, Iowa.

Ross Buck, "Nonverbal Communication of Emotions in Humans," from *Human Motivation and Emotion.* Copyright © 1976 by John Wiley & Sons, Inc. Reprinted by permission of John Wiley & Sons, Inc.

Donald Byker and Loren J. Anderson, "The Classical Bases for Improving Communication," from *Communication as Identification,* pp. 23–28. Copyright © 1975 by Donald Byker and Loren J. Anderson. Reprinted by permission of Harper & Row, Publishers, Inc.

C. William Colburn and Sanford B. Weinberg, from *Modcom: Modules in Speech Communication: An Orientation to Listening and Audience Analysis.* Copyright © 1976 by Science Research Associates, Inc. Reprinted by permission of the publisher.

Arthur M. Coon, "Brainstorming—A Creative Problem-Solving Technique," from *Journal of Communication,* vol. 7, no. 3 (1957), pp. 111–118. Reprinted by permission of the International Communication Association.

Joseph A. DeVito, "Universals of Language," from *The Interpersonal Communication Book,* pp. 234–238. Copyright © 1976 by Joseph A. DeVito. Reprinted by permission of Harper & Row, Publishers, Inc.

Jack R. Gibb, "Defensive Communication," from *Journal of Communication,* vol. 11, no. 3 (1961), pp. 141–148. Reprinted by permission of the author and the International Communication Association.

Gary Gumpert, "The Rise of Mini-Comm," from *Journal of Communication,* vol. 20, no. 3 (1970), pp. 280–290. Reprinted by permission of the author and the International Communication Association.

Nicholas Johnson, "The Careening of America: Caution: Television Watching May Be Hazardous to Your Mental Health," from *The Humanist,* July/August 1972. Reprinted by permission.

Sidney M. Jourard, "Self-Disclosure: The Scientist's Portal to Man's Soul," from *The Transparent Self,* 2nd ed. Copyright © 1971 by Litton Educational Publishing, Inc. Reprinted by permission of D. Van Nostrand Company.

John W. Keltner, "Private Speaking to Public Speaking," from *Interpersonal Speech-Communication, Elements and Structures.* Copyright © 1970 by Wadsworth Publishing Company, Inc., Belmont, California. Reprinted by permission of the publisher.

Mark L. Knapp, "The Role of Nonverbal Communication in the Classroom," from *Theory into Practice,* College of Education, The Ohio State University, vol. 10, no. 4 (1971), pp. 243–247. Reprinted by permission of the publisher.

Cheris Kramer, "Folk-Linguistics: Wishy-Washy Mommy Talk," from *Psychology Today,* June 1974, pp. 82–85. Copyright © 1974 by Ziff-Davis Publishing Company. Reprinted from *Psychology Today* Magazine.

Albert Mehrabian, "Communication Without Words," from *Psychology Today,* September 1968, pp. 53–55. Copyright © 1968 by Ziff-Davis Publishing Company. Reprinted from *Psychology Today* Magazine.

Thomas R. Nilsen, "Ethical Problems in Communication," from *Ethics of Speech Communication,* 2nd ed. Copyright © 1974 by The Bobbs-Merrill Company, Inc. Reprinted by permission of the publisher.

Andrea L. Rich, abridgement of "Interracial Implications of Nonverbal Communication," from *Interracial Communication.* Copyright © 1974 by Andrea L. Rich. Reprinted by permission of Harper & Row, Publishers, Inc.

W. P. Robinson, "Functions of Language," from *Language and Social Behavior,* pp. 34, 57–58, 58–59, 64, 67–71, 72–73. Copyright © 1972 by W. P. Robinson. Reprinted by permission of Penguin Books Ltd.

Larry A. Samovar and Richard E. Porter, "Communicating Interculturally," from *Intercultural Communication: A Reader,* 2nd ed. Copyright © 1976 by Wadsworth Publishing Company, Inc., Belmont, California. Reprinted by permission of the publisher.

William C. Schutz, "The Postulate of Interpersonal Needs," from *The Interpersonal Underworld.* Copyright © 1966 by Science and Behavior Books, Inc., Palo Alto, California. Reprinted by permission of the author and the publisher.

John Steward and Gary D'Angelo, "Responsive Listening," from *Together: Communicating Interpersonally,* pp. 186, 191–195, 198–199. Copyright © 1975 by Addison-Wesley Publishing Company, Inc., Reading, Massachusetts. Reprinted with permission.

Charles J. Stewart and William B. Cash, Jr., "An Introduction to Interviewing," from *Interviewing: Principles and Practices.* Reprinted by permission of William C. Brown Company Publishers, Dubuque, Iowa.

"My dear fellow," said Sherlock Holmes, as we sat on either side of the fire in his lodging at Baker Street, "life is infinitely stranger than anything which the mind of man could invent. We would not dare to conceive the things which are really mere commonplaces of existence."

A CASE OF IDENTITY

In many senses, the scholar is like the detective. Both employ the tools of deductive reasoning, of investigation, and of healthy skepticism. Students of communication are no exception. They must carefully discover hidden clues, intricately piece those clues together into complex relationships, and make the tricky distinction between false leads and genuine hopes. The result, too, makes an interesting parallel. While we are not pursuing sinister criminals and insidious masterminds, we are seeking the answers to questions just as elusive and mysterious.

In this book you will find a collection of clues: articles that each contain small pieces of the whole story of communication. By carefully analyzing the clues and integrating each finding, you can deduce a great deal about the fundamental nature of communication.

Since we are employing the methods of the detective in an effort to study communication, it seems appropriate to call upon the master from time to time for guidance and encouragement. Each part therefore begins with a quotation from one of the famous cases of the world's foremost detective, Sherlock Holmes. Special thanks are due Dr. John Watson, who, under the pseudonym of Arthur Conan Doyle, chronicled these cases and, incidentally, recorded Holmes's own theories about communication. It is hoped that these quotations provide a focus, an inspiration, a guide, and, perhaps, an entertainment.

This third edition of *Messages* represents a continuation of the principles that led to the success of each previous edition. Articles have been selected according to criteria of timeliness, readability, and general educational value. They constitute a collection representing the current status of the communication field and the direction in which it is moving.

The articles are arranged in parts designed for each of use in the classroom. The book begins with an examination of the theoretical underpinnings of the field and then expands in ever-widening circles of interaction through the special natures of verbal and nonverbal communication, the intrapersonal setting, the interpersonal situation, groups and organizations, public communication, the mass media, and the intercultural setting.

Several pedagogical devices should simplify classroom use. The introduction themselves give the parts perspective and direction. Each part introduction includes objectives of studying the individual articles, including the understanding of key concepts. Discussion questions and exercises offer the instructor great flexibility in presenting and utilizing the selections.

The third edition of *Messages* reflects an expansion of horizon and a continued update of approach. As education theory hovers on the brink of a return to basics, we have added an entirely new section on public speaking. This new collection of articles offers an audience viewpoint as well as a speaker orientation and is suited to a general survey course in communication as well as a more traditionally designed performance course.

The addition of several articles dealing with organizational communication also reflects a broadening of interest. According to feedback received from a number of reviewers and adopters, career-centered students are looking to courses in organizational communication as preparation for the business world. In response, departments of communication are including the field in their introductory and upper-level courses.

The updating process involved the dual goals of adding contemporary, readable articles while retaining some of the classic pieces that should be read by all communication students. The result is a collection of articles largely dating from the 1970s but including a selection from Aristotle's *The Rhetoric* (in a sense, as contemporary today as when it was first written) and several old articles that still represent the state of the field. In most parts the articles have been reordered to reflect a progression of difficulty in reading level and vocabulary as well as a progression of concepts.

As you might note from the above modifications, I have tried to maintain the successful elements of the previous *Messages* editions wherever possible. The change in editorship reflects not a change in direction but rather the addition of a new perspective. Special thanks therefore go to Jean Civikly for constructing the foundation upon which I tried to build.

Acknowledgments

The nature of a "reader" text is such that the reviewers who suggest and help to evaluate the articles included serve a very important function, in many ways shaping the final form of the book. I would therefore like to specifically thank Robert Gaines, Larry Erlich, Patricia Fleming, Jerry Anderson, Theodore Hopf, and Jon Blubaugh, who constituted the panel of advisers for this project.

Permissions are often issued by publishers after little or no consultation with authors. It is therefore fitting here to publicly thank those individuals whose thoughts, research efforts, and writings form the content of *Messages*. Their contributions are the best examples of our discipline's contributions to the state of knowledge about communication. And, perhaps of equal importance, these contributors stand in that elite body of scholars who can clearly and concisely tell us what they have discovered.

The exercises materials have been tested in a basic course at the University of Connecticut and ought to prove useful to both students and instructors. All the many teaching assistants who employed and evaluated them of course deserve a note of thanks and a special commendation for honesty and courage under often hostile fire. Carla Mond, who helped compile the comments from battle-scarred testers and who personally designed some of the most successful exercises, deserves an Oak Leaf Cluster with full honors.

Finally, publishers' editors can range from being a great help to being a great hinderance. In any case, they rarely receive—and often do not desire—much credit for the result. Occasionally an editor reaches beyond the "help" range by adding his or her own innovative ideas, suggestions, and approaches. I think that in this case Richard Garretson, of Random House, deserves special mention: He was a great help in all stages of the project and is a fine person to work with.

Contents

PART ONE

An Overview: Theories and Strategies

Our visitor bore every mark of being an average, commonplace British tradesman, obese, pompous, and slow. He wore rather baggy gray shepherd's check trousers, a not over-clean black frock-coat, unbuttoned in the front, and a drab waistcoat with a heavy brass Albert chain, and a square piece of metal dangling down as an ornament. A frayed top hat and a faded brown overcoat with a wrinkled velvet collar lay upon a chair beside him. Altogether, look as I would, there was nothing remarkable about the man save his blazing red head and expression of extreme chagrin and discontent upon his features.

Sherlock Holmes' quick eye took in my occupation, and he shook his head with a smile as he noticed my questioning glances. 'Beyond the obvious facts that he has at some time done manual labor, that he takes snuff, that he is a Freemason, that he has been in China, and that he has done a considerable amount of writing lately, I can deduce nothing else.'

THE RED-HEADED LEAGUE

How can the same situation, complete with the same messages, convey such different kinds and depths of interpretation to the great detective and to his friend Dr. Watson? Is communication such a vague subject that it is dependent solely upon the intuitive or deductive powers of the recipients? Can the process of information exchange be so unreliable as to produce such varying impressions?

Despite the differences in reception here, communication can be studied as a science, complete with postulates and relationships that will explain the process of exchange and the problems that might be blocking Watson's reception. By looking at the two major communication channels (verbal and nonverbal) in a variety of situations (intrapersonal, interpersonal, group and organizational, public, mass, and cross cultural), we will see how that process leads to successful human interaction.

A general overview will provide the kinds of clues any Sherlock welcomes. While generalities may vary in specific situations, what are the principles we can expect to find consistently operating? C. David Mortensen provides the first link in his discussion of "Communication Postulates." He describes the general nature of communication in much the same way as a master detective might describe the general nature of a crime: communication is dynamic, proactive, irreversible, interactive, and contextual. Here, then, is a framework upon which to hang further conclusions.

Ah, how easy a detective's job would be if all suspects were open and honest! In communication, too, complexity is added by disguise and deception. Jack Gibb adds to the framework of our investigation by discussing this guile in his article "Defensive Communication." He suggests an alternative motive in communication: information exchange may not be the only "role of communication" to be considered!

Every framework, of course, requires a foundation. Just as Holmes bases his investigations upon the theory of logic, so Schramm provides the classic model for understanding communication. He explains "How Communication Works" in terms of a series of interactive postulates and propositions, supporting the structure provided by Gibb and Mortensen.

And how would a detective function without a sense of right and wrong? Certainly the question of ethics enters into every pursuit, both in crime and in communication. Thomas Nilsen provides the ethical tools necessary to evaluate and apply the framework created. The problems and solutions he identifies will permeate our entire investigation.

With the tools acquired in these four articles, we will be able to begin an examination of the case of communication, leading eventually to an understanding of the modus operandi of the successful communicator.

"Quick, Watson! The game's afoot!"

OBJECTIVES

After carefully reading these four articles you should be able to define the following key terms:

communication   (Mortensen)
dynamic change
irreversibility
proactive
transaction
interactive
contextual
sociocultural background

defensive climates   (Gibb)
supportive climates

descriptive speech
evaluative speech
problem orientation

source　　　　　　　　　　(Schramm)
message
designation
encoder
signal
decoder
interpreter
field of experience
feedback

ethics　　　　　　　　　　(Nilsen)
values

And:

1. Explain and illustrate each of the five postulates of the transactional approach to communication: (a) communication is dynamic; (b) communication is irreversible; (c) communication is proactive; (d) communication is interactive; and (e) communication is contextual (Mortensen)
2. Describe and illustrate the six defensive categories of communication in a common communication situation. (Gibb)
3. For each of the categories described in (2), describe and illustrate a corresponding supportive climate. (Gibb)
4. Apply the model suggested by Schramm to a common conversational situation. Illustrate each element with a specific example. (Schramm)
5. Describe a major ethical issue for each of the following communication situations: political speech, protest demonstration, intimate interpersonal interaction, news broadcast, and advertisement. (Nilsen)

One

Communication Postulates

C. David Mortensen

Discovering the meaning of the term *communication* is not unlike the problem of defining any abstract concept. In conventional usage, abstract terms such as *education, motivation, behavior,* and *perception* seem clear enough, though their precise boundaries are not. Sometimes, however, conventional usage is inadequate. Until recently, for example, few would have thought to question the conventional use of the terms *life* and *death.* The distinction perhaps is all too clear. And yet with the advances in medical science, it is now possible to sustain life artificially, often for extended periods of time, in the hope of miraculous recovery. Furthermore, the possibility of transplanting vital organs heightens the difficulties of weighing matters of life and death. Since the time and circumstances in which life can be sustained are only vaguely known, each situation requires a medical authority to make a somewhat arbitrary decision in determining the final irrevocable moment when death occurs.

The need for greater precision is inherent in all scientific enterprises. In the case of the term *communication,* few would have qualms about saying that it occurs whenever people attempt to use the power of spoken or written words to influence others. And yet here is where the difficulties occur. Does our common-sense notion mean that communication is limited solely to human activity? Do machines communicate? Is all communication a matter of using spoken or written words? What is meant by the idea of *influence?* Must the influence be intentional? If so, what about overheard or accidental speech that nonetheless modifies the behavior of a bystander? Is all thinking to be regarded as communication?

These questions may appear to be a trivial exercise in pedantry. But the willingness to engage in such preliminary concerns is necessary to avoid terminological confusion and to gain insights that transcend intuition and common sense. Moreover, without some attention to definitional matters, the study of communication can all too easily proliferate to an ever-widening range of activities until it encompasses all human experience and goes even beyond to the realm of machines and lower animals in a regression line that eventually rules out nothing. Still, the business of finding a workable conception of communication is not without its hazards. The term can be conceived so broadly that it loses value as a scientific object of study. Conversely, if defined too narrowly, it can be reduced to a trivial and inconsequential concern. In short, we cannot escape the somewhat arbitrary risks inherent in definition. Furthermore, another type of risk occurs if we search for a highly compartmentalized definition, one that categorically and arbitrarily decides what communication is and what it is not. Little wonder that the attempts to evolve a universally acceptable definition of communication have resulted only in a proliferation of conflicting notions! Over ninety-five have appeared in print, according to one account (Dance, 1970). The most fruitful alternative to an exhaustive and exclusive definition is one that specifies the conditions deemed necessary for an act of communication to be said to occur. The concern, then, is with *fundamental attributes* rather than with an exhaustive and definitive description. These fundamental aspects or conditions can best be surveyed within the framework of a single broadly conceived postulate: *Communication occurs whenever persons attribute significance to message-related behavior.*

This broad conception implies a number of supporting assumptions and postulates. The concept of *transaction* calls attention to a way of looking at reality. It views events as dynamic, on-going, a process of interacting forces in a state of constant change. The forces are not static; they cannot be properly understood as unchanging or fixed elements in time and space. As Berlo (1960) insisted, happenings do not have "*a* beginning, *an* end, *a* fixed sequence of events [p. 24]." A communicative transaction changes, as Dance (1967) observed, in the very act of examining it. No single particular operates apart from the totality of forces at work in the event itself. Changes in any one aspect of the process invariably affect all other constituent aspects of behavior. This transactional orientation calls attention to several secondary postulates.

Communication Is Dynamic

There are any number of ways to conceive of a process of change. The simplest and least satisfactory is to think of change as synonymous with movement or activity, an unbroken sequence in which the operation of any one element, A, effects changes in B which in turn effect further changes in C and so on. Such a click-clack, mechanistic notion of change impoverishes the concept of communication by reducing it to the activity and chance we associate with conveyer belts, a falling line of dominoes, or the clatter of billiard balls on a pool table. In sharp contrast is the more complex notion of *dynamic change,* one in which an indefinitely large number of particulars interact in a reciprocal and continuous manner. Each successively smaller level of activity is itself a composite of interacting elements. An example is the activity of the nervous system. In reference to the complex interacting forces at work within the nervous system, Lashley (1954) wrote:

> Theories of neuron interaction must be couched, not in terms of the activity of individual cells, but in terms of mass relations among the cells. Even the simplest bit of behavior requires the integrated action of millions of neurons; . . . I have come to believe that almost every nerve cell in the cerebral cortex may be excited in every activity. . . . Differential behavior is determined by the combination of cells acting together rather than by cells which participate only in particular bits of behavior [p. 116].

Another level of dynamic change takes place in perception, of which Platt (1968) commented:

> Our perception-process goes over continuously into our larger manipula-
> tion of the world around us. We do not think of perception as manipula-
> tion, because the brain somehow organizes our ever-changing visual
> observation-fields into a continuous seen-and-remembered "stable
> world," and because simple passive observation, even with moving eye-
> balls, changes the objects and relations of this "stable world" very little,
> so that we think of it as unaffected by our observation; but manipulation
> it is, nevertheless, manipulation by the electrical signals in the out-going
> nerves, by the motion of the eyeballs, and finally by the hands [p. 96].

The difference between static and dynamic conceptions of change is like the
difference between adjusting light in a room with a light switch and with a
rheostat. The former permits only an all-or-nothing change, whereas a rheostat
allows a gradation of change much like the dimming of house lights in a
theater. Yet even the rheostat grossly oversimplifies. For the level at which
change occurs in human interaction is not one of isolated particulars, or even
of combinations of elements; rather, it occurs at the most inclusive level of
consciousness—the sense each party has of the total event. Above all, we must
resist the temptation to think of change in a tangible sense as we would a
physical thing. Communication simply is not analogous to a process where
something changes as it is "passed" or "transferred" from one person or setting
to another. It is less misleading to think of communication as an occurrence,
a happening, rather than something that exists in and of itself.

Finally, dynamic change implies a transaction that is not static, yet through
all the fluctuations maintains its stability and identity. There is a certain
evolving, elastic quality to the experience of communicating with another
human being. The act is constantly taking new shape, but only in a state of
equilibrium that changes along lines which are consistent with the immediate
expectations and past experience of the respective parties. The sequence may
change the participants in some discernible way, but never in ways that are
completely foreign to what has already taken place. As Kelley (1963) stated,
"If one is to understand the course of the stream of consciousness, he must
do more than chart its head waters; he must know the terrain through which
it runs and the volume of the flood which may cut out new channels or erode
old ones [p. 83]." Somehow, in ways not well understood, man seeks change
and novelty in ways that do not undermine his stability or feelings of identity
and uniqueness.

Communication Is Irreversible

The concept of irreversibility has a direct heritage in the adage which insists
that a man can't step in the same river twice: the very act changes the man
and the river. The past influences one's sense of the present and what is
anticipated about the future. And yet the past can never be reconstructed or
reclaimed. It was the irreversible and irretrievable succession of events that

Thomas Wolfe underscored in his classic novel *You Can't Go Home Again.* The transactional, flowlike qualities of communication may be taken literally as truth. Research on perception suggests that human beings do not perceive at any single time; in the stream of consciousness there is no literal sense of the instant, no sharp beginning or sharp ending, no lines of demarcation in what we perceive of the physical world. In operational terms, Platt (1968) insisted that there is no direct past or future, only the present instant; he likened this to a "rowboat anchoring in a flowing river, which may bear the gashes of the past logs that have floated by but which never experiences any part of the river except where it is. In such a system, the only moment of decision and change, the only time there is, is now [p. 84]." Whyte (1954) compared time to a line running "through each succeeding wakeful hour of the individual's past life. . . . Time's strip of film runs forward, never backward, even when resurrected from the past. It seems to proceed again at time's own unchanged pace [p. 117]." Human experience flows, in the words of Barnlund (1970), as a stream, in a "single direction leaving behind it a permanent record of man's communicative experience [p. 93]."

Irreversibility assumes that people engaged in communication can only go forward from one state to the next. It also gives import to the spontaneity of the existing moment of experience and to the accumulative significance of what unfolds. As communication ebbs and flows, its content and meaning ever widen. Each phase of the on-going sequence helps to define the meaning assigned to each succeeding aspect of what is said and done. Seen in this light, no statement, however repetitious, can be regarded as pure redundancy. Somehow, repetition of even the same signal alters the larger significance of the exchange. Once the transaction begins, there can be no retreat, no fresh start, no way to begin all over again.

Communication Is Proactive

When a person engages in an act of communication, he does so totally; nothing less than his entire dynamic as a person and his total, immediate field of experience is involved. This recognition complicates matters. At once it contradicts images that reduce communication to an exercise in translation or to any action that ensures agreement between what is said and what is understood. The immediate implication is that communicative behavior cannot be understood properly apart from the psychological and social determinants of individual behavior generally—and we shall be concerned with perception, motives, emotions, beliefs, and feelings later on. But for now, let us emphasize that this link between the transaction of communication and the psychological processes does not imply that *any* behavior automatically qualifies as communication. Rather, *there are certain communicative aspects in all social situations, and these bear most directly on the interaction of the respective parties.*

It is somewhat fashionable today to explain human behavior in images that presuppose man to be a passive respondent to stimuli. This passive, or *reactive,* model is held in particularly high esteem by adherents of stimulus-response paradigms and certain learning theories, and by students of the mass media who are prone to think of society as an undifferentiated mass of inert respondents who wait to be altered in predetermined ways by all-powerful manipulators of advertising, brainwashing, and hidden persuasion. The following statement by Meerloo (1968) summarizes the reactive approach:

> Our technical means of communication, especially the press, radio, movies, and TV, *have gradually exerted a peculiar weakening influence on people's critical capacities.* Too much sensational imagery, reading and hearing is offered to our senses. The feast is too rich for our stomachs. *We lose all sense of proportion.* Advertising continually insinuates dissatisfaction with the products we have at hand. We are living in the richest country in the world. Yet we are daily urged to feel most deprived. Television *hypnotizes* us in our own living rooms. *We feel trapped in a web of technical communications* with their confusing and conflicting persuasions and *we cannot escape.*
>
> Technical devices of advertising and propaganda—those new media with their paradoxical messages—*gradually break down our barriers of criticism.* Glued to the TV screen, *people become passive and apathetic,* and compulsively want to drink in the overabundance of communications like greedy babes with a bottle. We are all a little bit *slave* to the great television hypnosis. Instead of looking inward and reviewing our thoughts and meditations, *we are held in a vise* by a screen that dribbles away our time [p. 84, italics added].

What such a reactive image ignores is the tremendous capacity of the human organism to select, amplify, and manipulate the signals that assault his senses. It ignores the fact that people engaged in communication are *proactive* because they enter the transaction totally. Sensory data are not so much arranged and stamped into categories as they are amplified, selected, and transferred into patterns that fit the expectations of the individual. The notion of man as a detached bystander, an objective and dispassionate reader of the environment, is nothing more than a convenient artifact. Among living creatures man is the most spectacular example of an agent who amplifies his every activity, first in the way he perceives it, and then in the way he modifies his environment. The man-made world is, in the words of Platt (1968), a world that is increasingly "what we have seen, studied and shaped ourselves." As a consequence, we construe the environment in ways that make it ever more docile and manageable.

The intricate activity of the brain is further testimony to the proactive dimension of communication. The brain does not suddenly become inert simply because no immediate physical stimuli demand instantaneous and focused attention. Here are Langer's (1942) comments about the brain:

> If it were, indeed, a vast and intricate telephone exchange, then it should be quiescent when the rest of the organism sleeps. . . . Instead of that, it

goes right on manufacturing ideas—streams and deluges of ideas, that the sleeper is not using to *think* with about anything. But the brain is following its own law; it is actively translating experience into symbols, in fulfillment of a basic need to do so [p. 33].

Man, to be sure, reacts to his surroundings; and in doing so he, in turn, acts upon the environment—by constructing meaning, assigning significance, ruling out, distorting some items, adding others, and ordering the stream of conscious thought by rules and tactics largely unique to his own chemistry.

It is a rare social situation that does not extract from its participants a measure of active commitment, a sense of vested interest in what is said and done. Even when the psychological stakes seem trivial, the minimal needs to preserve identity and self-esteem are there. Furthermore, the very act of expressing one's views serves to heighten the stakes; when others react in approval or indifference, hostility or accord, the sense of personal involvement is intensified. And, we shall discover, once the interaction moves to topics that are highly ego-involving, there is no way to retreat from the lines of self-defense and personal influence. Indeed, in the marketplace of social contact, few can for long remain passive, inert spectators or detached bystanders.

Communication Is Interactive

The cycle from self to world and back again has no sharply defined boundaries, for the human organism does not live as a self-contained, set-off entity. The minimum condition for communication is a more or less constant monitoring of the two realms of experience, the physical and the symbolic. As we said earlier, no event in our physical world has any self-contained or proper significance; nor, for that matter, does activity within us. Meaning occurs, rather, when we interpret or assign significance to the objects of our experience. However, assignment of meaning cannot be properly understood apart from the constant succession of interacting forces that influence us, both internally and externally. As Kelley (1963) wrote:

> A person can be a witness to a tremendous parade of episodes, and yet, if he fails to keep making something out of them, or if he waits until they have occurred before he attempts to reconstrue them, he gains little in the way of experience from having been around when they happened. It is not what happens around him that makes a man experienced; it is the successive construing and reconstruing of what happens, as it happens, that enriches the experience of his life [p. 73].

The term *interaction* suggests a reciprocal influence. In matters of communication this mutual influence may take place on two fronts. One is an individual, or *intrapersonal,* level, where a person assigns significance to messages apart from the presence of another person. The second form of interaction is *interpersonal;* it takes place between two or more parties and consists of a complex process whereby each maintains a shared frame of reference, or coorientation. It is important not to think of either form of interaction—intrapersonal or interpersonal—as the discrete action of particulars working under separate power; nor even to think of them as balancing elements in causal connection. The notion of interaction entails the far more complex idea of *interdependence* —a mutual influencing process among countless factors, each functioning conjointly so that changes in any one set of forces affect the operations of all other constituent activity in a total field of experience (Sereno and Mortensen, 1970).

The concept of interaction has important implications for our ideas of what a message is. For instance, if there is no way to divorce events from their assigned significance, then clearly a message cannot be reduced to a static entity, words on a page or sounds that have their own built-in or proper sense, much like the fixed barter values of coins. Conversely, when viewed in a functional perspective, *a message consists of whatever unit of behavior serves to link the parties of communication.* This behavior may be *verbal* (as in the case of writing and conversation) or *nonverbal* (such as gestures, eye contact, and facial expression). To qualify as a verbal or nonverbal message cue, the behavior must fulfill two requirements. First, it must be available for inspection. Unnoticed or unattended aspects of joint behavior do not constitute a functioning message. Second, the behavior must be interpreted as significant by at least one of the parties. Consequently, that which constitutes a message cue for one person may not function as one for others. In a situation where only one person is present—where a person writes a letter, for example—the two criteria of availability of cues and assigned significance apply as they would in the situation where two or more communicants are present. Hence, behavior constitutes a message when it is verbal or nonverbal, personal or public, shared by all or only by some.

Communication Is Contextual

Communication never takes place in a vacuum; it is not a "pure" process, devoid of background or situational overtones; it always requires at least one's minimal sensitivity to immediate physical surroundings, an awareness of setting or place that in turn influences the ebb and flow of what is regarded as personally significant. To be sure, the context of communication comprises physical characteristics—seating arrangement, color and light, physical space, and the like—but it is much more than the sense of these physical things. It includes the less tangible matter of atmosphere and ambiance, of *sociocultural background*.

Situational factors, we will find, do much to define the emotional and expressive overtones of what is said and done. Context may engender a sense of psychological comfort and warmth, an inviting and congenial atmosphere, or one of threat, distance, and detachment. Often the exact meaning of what is said cannot be separated from the significance of the immediate context.

Watzlawick (1967) illustrated the impact of context by citing the following incident described by Lorenz (1952, p. 43):

> In the garden of a country house, in plain view of passers-by on the sidewalk outside, a bearded man can be observed dragging himself, crouching, round the meadow, in figures of eight, glancing constantly over his shoulder and quacking without interruption. This is how the ethologist Konrad Lorenz describes his necessary behavior during one of imprinting experiments with ducklings, after he had substituted himself for their mother. "I was congratulating myself," he writes, "on the obedience and exactitude with which my ducklings came waddling after me, when I suddenly looked up and saw the garden fence framed by a row of dead-white faces: a group of tourists was standing at the fence and staring horrified in my direction." The ducklings were hidden in the tall grass, and all the tourists saw was totally unexplainable, indeed insane, behavior [p. 20].

Our concern with the context of communication will also include what Brockriede (1968) calls the "encompassing situation," an elaborate set of implicit conventions and rules imposed on an individual's behavior in given *types* of social situations. The distinction between *immediate* and *encompassing context* is largely one of inclusiveness. The impact of a particular social situation—of a neighborhood police station, record store, or tavern—constitutes, an immediate context for communication, whereas one's image of police stations, record stores, and taverns corresponds to the influence of an encompassing context.

The impact of context, therefore, is never exhausted by one's immediate surroundings alone. Context is a fascinating and elusive concept that can be extended to apply to ever-widening levels of inclusiveness which eventually embrace all social and cultural milieux.

REFERENCES

BARNLUND, D. C. "A Transactional Model of Communication," in K. K. Sereno and C. D. Mortensen (eds.), *Foundations of Communication Theory.* New York: Harper & Row (1970).

BERLO, D. K. *The Process of Communication.* New York: Holt (1960).

BROCKRIEDE, W. E. "Dimensions of the Concept of Rhetoric." *The Quarterly Journal of Speech,* 54:1–12 (1968).

DANCE, F. E. "Toward a Theory of Human Communication," in *Human Communication Theory.* New York: Holt (1967).

DANCE, F. E. "The 'Concept' of Communication." *The Journal of Communication,* 20:201–210 (1970).

KELLEY, G. A. *A Theory of Personality.* New York: Norton (1963).

LANGER, S. *Philosophy in a New Key.* New York: New American Library, Mentor (1942).

LASHLEY, K. As cited in W. R. Ashby, "The Application of Cybernetics to Psychiatry," *Journal of Mental Science,* 100:114–124 (1954).

LORENZ, K. Z. *Solomon's Ring.* London: Methuen (1952).

MEERLOO, J. A. "From Persuasion to Brainwashing: Some Clinical Variations in Persuasion and Suggestion," in C. E. Larson and F. E. Dance (eds.), *Perspectives on Communication.* Milwaukee: Speech Communication Center (1968).

PLATT, J. R. "The Two Faces of Perception," in B. Rothblatt (ed.), *Changing Perspectives on Man.* Chicago: University of Chicago Press (1968).

SERENO, K. K., and C. D. MORTENSEN (eds.). *Foundations of Communication Research.* New York: Harper & Row (1970).

WATZLAWICK, P., J. BEAVIN, and D. JACKSON. *The Pragmatics of Human Communication.* New York: Norton (1967).

WHYTE, L. L. *Accent on Form.* New York: Harper & Row (1954).

Two

Defensive Communication

Jack R. Gibb

One way to understand communication is to view it as a people process rather than as a language process. If one is to make fundamental improvements in communication, he must make changes in interpersonal relationships. One possible type of alteration—and the one with which this paper is concerned—is that of reducing the degree of defensiveness.

Defensive behavior is defined as that behavior which occurs when an individual perceives threat or anticipates threat in the group. The person who behaves defensively, even though he also gives some attention to the common task, devotes an appreciable portion of his energy to defending himself. Besides talking about the topic, he thinks about how he appears to others, how he may be seen more favorably, how he may win, dominate, impress, or escape punishment, and/or how he may avoid or mitigate a perceived or an anticipated attack.

Such inner feelings and outward acts tend to create similarly defensive postures in others, and if unchecked, the ensuing circular response becomes increasingly destructive. Defensive behavior, in short, engenders defensive listening, and this in turn produces postural, facial, and verbal cues which raise the defense level of the original communicator.

Defense arousal prevents the listener from concentrating upon the message. Not only do defensive communicators send off multiple value, motive, and affect cues, but also defensive recipients distort what they receive. As a person becomes more and more defensive, he becomes less and less able to perceive accurately the motives, the values, and the emotions of the sender. My analyses of tape-recorded discussions revealed that increases in defensive behavior were correlated positively with losses in efficiency in communication.[1] Specifically, distortions became greater when defensive states existed in the groups.

The converse, moreover, also is true. The more "supportive" or defense reductive the climate, the less the receiver reads into the communication distorted loadings which arise from projections of his own anxieties, motives, and concerns. As defenses are reduced, the receivers become better able to concentrate upon the structure, the content, and the cognitive meanings of the message.

In working over an eight-year period with recordings of discussions occurring in varied settings, I developed the six pairs of defensive and supportive categories presented in Table 1. Behavior which a listener perceives as possessing any of the characteristics listed in the left-hand column arouses defensiveness, whereas that which he interprets as having any of the qualities designated as supportive reduces defensive feelings. The degree to which these reactions occur depends upon the personal level of defensiveness and upon the general climate in the group at the time.[2]

Speech or other behavior which appears evaluative increases defensiveness. If by expression, manner of speech, tone of voice, or verbal content the sender seems to be evaluating or judging the listener, then the receiver goes on guard. Of course, other factors may inhibit the reaction. If the listener thought that the speaker regarded him as an equal and was being open and spontaneous, for example, the evaluativeness in a message would be neutralized and perhaps not even perceived. This same principle applies equally to the other five categories of potentially defense-producing climates. The six sets are interactive.

Because our attitudes toward other persons are frequently, and often necessarily, evaluative, expressions which the defensive person will regard as nonjudgmental are hard to frame. Even the simplest question usually conveys the answer that the sender wishes or implies the response that would fit into his value system. A mother, for example, immediately following an earth tremor that shook the house, sought for her small son with the question: "Bobby, where are you?" The timid and plaintive "Mommy, I didn't do it" indicated how Bobby's chronic mild defensiveness predisposed him to react with a

TABLE 1

Categories of Behavior Characteristic of Supportive and Defensive Climates in Small Groups

Defensive Climates	*Supportive Climates*
1. Evaluation	1. Description
2. Control	2. Problem Orientation
3. Strategy	3. Spontaneity
4. Neutrality	4. Empathy
5. Superiority	5. Equality
6. Certainty	6. Provisionalism

projection of his own guilt and in the context of his chronic assumption that questions are full of accusation.

Anyone who has attempted to train professionals to use information-seeking speech with neutral effect appreciates how difficult it is to teach a person to say even the simple "Who did that?" without being seen as accusing. Speech is so frequently judgmental that there is a reality base for the defensive interpretations which are so common.

When insecure, group members are particularly likely to place blame, to see others as fitting into categories of good or bad, to make moral judgments of their colleagues, and to question the value, motive, and affect loadings of the speech which they hear. Since value loadings imply a judgment of others, a belief that the standards of the speaker differ from his own causes the listener to become defensive.

Descriptive speech, in contrast to that which is evaluative, tends to arouse a minimum of uneasiness. Speech acts which the listener perceives as genuine requests for information or as material with neutral loadings are descriptive. Specifically, presentations of feelings, events, perceptions, or processes which do not ask or imply that the receiver change behavior or attitude are minimally defense producing. The difficulty in avoiding overtone is illustrated by the problems of news reporters in writing stories about unions, Communists, Negroes, and religious activities without tipping off the "party" line of the newspaper. One can often tell from the opening words in a news article which side the newspaper's editorial policy favors.

Speech which is used to control the listener evokes resistance. In most of our social intercourse someone is trying to do something to someone else—to change an attitude, to influence behavior, or to restrict the field of activity. The degree to which attempts to control produce defensiveness depends upon the openness of the effort, for a suspicion that hidden motives exist heightens resistance. For this reason, attempts of nondirective therapists and progressive educators to refrain from imposing a set of values, a point of view, or a problem solution upon the receivers meet with many barriers. Since the norm is control, noncontrollers must earn the perceptions that their efforts have no hidden motives. A bombardment of persuasive "messages" in the fields of politics, education, special causes, advertising, religion, medicine, industrial relations, and guidance has bred cynical and paranoid responses in listeners.

Implicit.in all atempts to alter another person is the assumption by the change agent that the person to be altered is inadequate. That the speaker secretly views the listener as ignorant, unable to make his own decisions, uninformed, immature, unwise, or possessed of wrong or inadequate attitudes is a subconscious perception which gives the latter a valid base for defensive reactions.

Methods of control are many and varied. Legalistic insistence on detail, restrictive regulations and policies, conformity norms, and all laws are among the methods. Gestures, facial expressions, other forms of nonverbal communication, and even such simple acts as holding a door open in a particular manner are means of imposing one's will upon another and hence are potential sources of resistance.

Problem orientation, on the other hand, is the antithesis of persuasion. When the sender communicates a desire to collaborate in defining a mutual problem and in seeking its solution, he tends to create the same problem orientation in the listener, and of greater importance, he implies that he has no predetermined solution, attitude, or method to impose. Such behavior is permissive in that it allows the receiver to set his own goals, make his own decisions, and evaluate his own progress—or to share with the sender in doing so. The exact methods of attaining permissiveness are not known, but they must involve a constellation of cues, and they certainly go beyond mere verbal assurances that the communicator has no hidden desires to exercise control.

When the sender is perceived as engaged in a stratagem involving ambiguous and multiple motivations, the receiver becomes defensive. No one wishes to be a guinea pig, a role player, or an impressed actor, and no one likes to be the victim of some hidden motivation. That which is concealed also may appear larger than it really is, with the degree of defensiveness of the listener determining the perceived size of the suppressed element. The intense reaction of the reading audience to the material in the *Hidden Persuaders* [by Vance Packard, 1957] indicates the prevalence of defensive reactions to multiple motivations behind strategy. Group members who are seen as "taking a role," as feigning emotion, as toying with their colleagues, as withholding information, or as having special sources of data are especially resented. One participant once complained that another was "using a listening technique" on him!

A large part of the adverse reaction to much of the so-called human relations training is a feeling against what are perceived as gimmicks and tricks to fool or to "involve" people, to make a person think he is making his own decision, or to make the listener feel that the sender is genuinely interested in him as a person. Particularly violent reactions occur when it appears that someone is trying to make a stratagem appear spontaneous. One person has reported a boss who incurred resentment by habitually using the gimmick of "spontaneously" looking at his watch and saying, "My gosh, look at the time—I must run to an appointment." The belief was that the boss would create less irritation by honestly asking to be excused.

Similarly, the deliberate assumption of guilelessness and natural simplicity is especially resented. Monitoring the tapes of feedback and evaluation sessions in training groups indicates the surprising extent to which members perceive the strategies of their colleagues. This perceptual clarity may be quite shocking to the strategist, who usually feels that he has cleverly hidden the motivational aura around the gimmick.

This aversion to deceit may account for one's resistance to politicians who are suspected of behind-the-scenes planning to get his vote, to psychologists whose listening apparently is motivated by more than the manifest or content-level interest in his behavior, or to the sophisticated, smooth, or clever person whose "oneupmanship" is marked with guile. In training groups the role-flexible person frequently is resented because his changes in behavior are perceived as strategic maneuvers.

In contrast, behavior which appears to be spontaneous and free of deception is defense reductive. If the communicator is seen as having a clean id, as having uncomplicated motivations, as being straightforward and honest, and as behaving spontaneously in response to the situation, he is likely to arouse minimal defense.

When neutrality in speech appears to the listener to indicate a lack of concern for his welfare, he becomes defensive. Group members usually desire to be perceived as valued persons, as individuals of special worth, and as objects of concern and affection. The clinical, detached, person-as-an-object-of-study attitude on the part of many psychologist-trainees is resented by group members. Speech with low affect that communicates little warmth or caring is in such contrast with the affect-laden speech in social situations that it sometimes communicates rejection.

Communication that conveys empathy for the feelings and respect for the worth of the listener, however, is particularly supportive and defense reductive. Reassurance results when a message indicates that the speaker identifies himself with the listener's problems, shares his feelings, and accepts his emotional reactions at face value. Abortive efforts to deny the legitimacy of the receiver's emotions by assuring the receiver that he need not feel bad, that he should not feel rejected, or that he is overly anxious, though often intended as support giving, may impress the listener as lack of acceptance. The combination of understanding and empathizing with the other person's emotions with no accompanying effort to change him apparently is supportive at a high level.

The importance of gestural behavioral cues in communicating empathy should be mentioned. Apparently spontaneous facial and bodily evidences of concern are often interpreted as especially valid evidence of deep-level acceptance.

When a person communicates to another that he feels superior in position, power, wealth, intellectual ability, physical characteristics, or other ways, he arouses defensiveness. Here, as with the other sources of disturbance, whatever arouses feelings of inadequacy causes the listener to center upon the affect loading of the statement rather than upon the cognitive elements. The receiver then reacts by not hearing the message, by forgetting it, by competing with the sender, or by becoming jealous of him.

The person who is perceived as feeling superior communicates that he is not willing to enter into a shared problem-solving relationship, that he probably does not desire feedback, that he does not require help, and/or that he will be likely to try to reduce the power, the status, or the worth of the receiver.

Many ways exist for creating the atmosphere that the sender feels himself equal to the listener. Defenses are reduced when one perceives the sender as being willing to enter into participative planning with mutual trust and respect. Differences in talent, ability, worth, appearance, status, and power often exist, but the low defense communicator seems to attach little importance to these distinctions.

The effects of dogmatism in producing defensiveness are well known. Those who seem to know the answers, to require no additional data, and to regard themselves as teachers rather than as co-workers tend to put others on guard. Moreover, in my experiment, listeners often perceived manifest expressions of certainty as connoting inward feelings of inferiority. They saw the dogmatic individual as needing to be right, as wanting to win an argument rather than solve a problem, and as seeing his ideas as truths to be defended. This kind of behavior often was associated with acts which others regarded as attempts to exercise control. People who were "right" seemed to have low tolerance for members who were "wrong"—that is, those who did not agree with the sender.

One reduces the defensiveness of the listener when he communicates that he is willing to experiment with his own behavior, attitudes, and ideas. The person who appears to be taking provisional attitudes, to be investigating issues rather than taking sides on them, to be problem solving rather than debating, and to be willing to experiment and explore tends to communicate that the listener may have some control over the shared quest or the investigation of the ideas. If a person is genuinely searching for information and data, he does not resent help or company along the way.

Conclusion

The implications of the above material for the parent, the teacher, the manager, the administrator, or the therapist are fairly obvious. Arousing defensiveness interferes with communication and thus makes it difficult—and sometimes impossible—for anyone to convey ideas clearly and to move effectively toward the solution of therapeutic, educational, or managerial problems.

NOTES

1. J. R. GIBB, "Defense Level and Influence Potential in Small Groups," in L. Petrullo and B. M. Bass (eds.), *Leadership and Interpersonal Behavior* (New York, 1961), pp. 66–81.
2. J. R. GIBB, "Sociopsychological Processes of Group Instruction," in N. B. Henry (ed.), *The Dynamics of Instructional Groups* (Fifty-ninth Yearbook of the National Society for the Study of Education, Part II, 1960), pp. 115–135.

Three

How Communication Works

Wilbur Schramm

Communication always requires at least three elements—the source, the message, and the destination. A *source* may be an individual (speaking, writing, drawing, gesturing) or a communication organization (like a newspaper, publishing house, television station, or motion picture studio). The *message* may be in the form of ink on paper, sound waves in the air, impulses in an electric current, a wave of the hand, a flag in the air, or any other signal capable of being interpreted meaningfully. The *destination* may be an *individual* listening, watching, or reading; or a member of a *group,* such as a discussion group, a lecture audience, a football crowd, or a mob; or an individual member of the particular group we call the *mass audience,* such as the reader of a newspaper or a viewer of television.

Now what happens when the source tries to build up this "commonness" with his intended receiver? First, the source encodes his message. That is, he takes the information or feeling he wants to share and puts it into a form that can be transmitted. The "pictures in our heads" can't be transmitted until they are coded. When they are coded into spoken words, they can be transmitted easily and effectively, but they can't travel very far unless radio carries them. If they are coded into written words, they go more slowly than spoken words, but they go farther and last longer. Indeed, some messages long outlive their senders—the *Iliad,* for instance; the Gettysburg address; Chartres cathedral. Once coded and sent, a message is quite free of its sender, and what it does is beyond the power of the sender to change. Every writer feels a sense of helplessness when he finally commits his story or his poem to print; you doubtless feel the same way when you mail an important letter. Will it reach the right person? Will he understand it as you intend him to? Will he respond as you want him to? For in order to complete the act of communication the message must be decoded. And there is good reason, as we shall see, for the sender to wonder whether his receiver will really be in tune with him, whether the message will be interpreted without distortion, whether the "picture in the head" of the receiver will bear any resemblance to that in the head of the sender.

We are talking about something very like a radio or telephone circuit. In fact, it is perfectly possible to draw a picture of the human communication system that way:

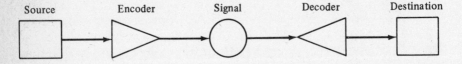

Source   Encoder   Signal   Decoder   Destination

Substitute "microphone" for encoder, and "earphone" for decoder and you are talking about electronic communication. Consider that the "source" and "encoder" are one person, "decoder" and "destination" are another, and the signal is language, and you are talking about human communication.

Now it is perfectly possible by looking at those diagrams to predict how such a system will work. For one thing, such a system can be no stronger than its weakest link. In engineering terms, there may be filtering or distortion at any stage. In human terms, if the source does not have adequate or clear information; if the message is not encoded fully, accurately, effectively in transmittable signs; if these are not transmitted fast enough and accurately enough, despite interference and competition, to the desired receiver; if the message is not decoded in a pattern that corresponds to the encoding; and finally, if the destination is unable to handle the decoded message so as to produce the desired response—then, obviously, the system is working at less than top efficiency. When we realize that *all* these steps must be accomplished with relatively high efficiency if any communication is to be successful, the everyday act of explaining something to a stranger, or writing a letter, seems a minor miracle.

A system like this will have a maximum capacity for handling information and this will depend on the separate capacities of each unit on the chain—for example, the capacity of the channel (how fast can one talk?) or the capacity of the encoder (can your student understand something explained quickly?). If the coding is good (for example, no unnecessary words) the capacity of the channel can be approached, but it can never be exceeded. You can readily see that one of the great skills of communication will lie in knowing how near capacity to operate a channel.

This is partly determined for us by the nature of the language. English, like every other language, has its sequences of words and sounds governed by certain probabilities. If it were organized so that no set of probabilities governed the likelihood that certain words would follow certain other words (for example, that a noun would follow an adjective, or that "States" or "Nations" would follow "United") then we would have nonsense. As a matter of fact, we can calculate the relative amount of freedom open to us in writing any language. For English, the freedom is about 50 per cent. (Incidentally, this is about the required amount of freedom to enable us to construct interesting crossword puzzles. Shannon has estimated that if we had about 70 per cent freedom, we could construct three-dimensional crossword puzzles. If we had only 20 per cent, crossword puzzle making would not be worthwhile.)

So much for language *redundancy,* as communication theorists call it, meaning the percentage of the message which is not open to free choice. But there is also the communicator's redundancy, and this is an important aspect of constructing a message. For if we think our audience may have a hard time understanding the message, we can deliberately introduce more redundancy; we can repeat (just as the radio operator on a ship may send "SOS" over and over again to make sure it is heard and decoded), or we can give examples and analogies. In other words, we always have to choose between transmitting more information in a given time, or transmitting less and repeating more in the hope of being better understood. And as you know, it is often a delicate choice, because too slow a rate will bore an audience, whereas too fast a rate may confuse them.

Perhaps the most important thing about such a system is one we have been talking about all too glibly—the fact that receiver and sender must be in tune. This is clear enough in the case of a radio transmitter and receiver, but somewhat more complicated when it means that a human receiver must be able to understand a human sender.

Let us redraw our diagram in very simple form, like this:

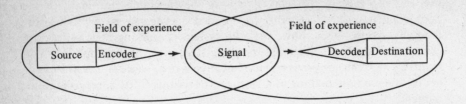

Think of those circles as the accumulated experience of the two individuals trying to communicate. The source can encode, and the destination can decode, only in terms of the experience each has had. If we have never learned any Russian, we can neither code nor decode in that language. If an African tribesman has never seen or heard of an airplane, he can only decode the sight of a plane in terms of whatever experience he has had. The plane may seem to him to be a bird and the aviator a god borne on wings. If the circles have a large area in common, then communication is easy. If the circles do not meet —if there has been no common *experience*—then communication is impossible. If the circles have only a small area in common—that is, if the experiences of source and destination have been strikingly unlike—then it is going to be very difficult to get an intended meaning across from one to the other. This is the difficulty we face when a non-science-trained person tries to read Einstein, or when we try to communicate with another culture much different from ours.

The source, then, tries to encode in such a way as to make it easy for the destination to tune in the message—to relate it to parts of his experience which are much like those of the source. What does he have to work with?

Messages are made up of signs. A sign is a signal that stands for something in experience. The word "dog" is a sign that stands for our generalized experience with dogs. The word would be meaningless to a person who came from a dog-less island and had never read of or heard of a dog. But most of us have learned that word by association, just as we learn most signs. Someone called our attention to an animal, and said "dog." When we learned the word, it produced in us much the same response as the object it stood for. That is, when we heard "dog" we could recall the appearance of dogs, their sound, their feel, perhaps their smell. But there is an important difference between the sign and the object: the sign always represents the object at a reduced level of cues. By this we mean simply that the sign will not call forth all the responses that the object itself will call forth. The sign "dog," for example, will probably not call forth in us the same wariness or attention a strange dog might attract if it wandered into our presence. This is the price we pay for portability in language. We have a sign system that we can use in place of the less portable originals (for example, Margaret Mitchell could re-create the burning of Atlanta in a novel, and a photograph could transport world-wide the appearance of a bursting atomic bomb), but our sign system is merely a kind of shorthand.

The coder has to be able to write the shorthand, the decoder to read it. And no two persons have learned exactly the same system. For example, a person who has known only Arctic huskies will not have learned exactly the same meaning for the shorthand sign "dog" as will a person who comes from a city where he has known only pekes and poms.

We have come now to a point where we need to tinker a little more with our diagram of the communication process. It is obvious that each person in the communication process is both an encoder and a decoder. He receives and transmits. He must be able to write a readable shorthand, and to read other people's shorthand. Therefore, it is possible to describe either sender or receiver in a human communication system thus:

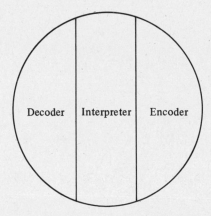

What happens when a signal comes to you? Remember that it comes in the form of a sign. If you have learned the sign, you have learned certain responses with it. We can call these mediatory responses, because they mediate what happens to the message in your nervous system. These responses are the *meaning* the sign has for you. They are learned from experience, as we said, but they are affected by the state of your organism at the moment. For example, if you are hungry, a picture of a steak may not arouse exactly the same response in you as when you are overfed.

But subject to these effects, the mediatory responses will then determine what you do about the sign. For you have learned other sets of reactions connected to the mediatory responses. A sign that means a certain thing to you will start certain other processes in your nerves and muscles. A sign that means "fire," for example, will certainly trigger off some activity in you. A sign that means you are in danger may start the process in your nerves and muscles that makes you say "help!" In other words, the meaning that results from your decoding of a sign will start you *en*coding. Exactly *what* you encode will depend on your choice of the responses available in the situation and connected with the meaning.

Whether this encoding actually results in some overt communication or action depends partly on the barriers in the way. You may think it better to keep silent. And if an action does occur, the nature of the action will also depend on the avenues for action available to you and the barriers in your way. The code of your group may not sanction the action you want to take. The meaning of a sign may make you want to hit the person who has said it, but he may be too big, or you may be in the wrong social situation. You may merely ignore him, or "look murder at him," or say something nasty about him to someone else.

But whatever the exact result, this is the process in which you are constantly engaged. You are constantly decoding signs from your environment, interpreting these signs, and encoding something as a result. In fact, it is misleading to think of the communication process as starting somewhere and ending somewhere. It is really endless. We are little switchboard centers handling and rerouting the great endless current of communication. We can accurately think of communication as passing through us—changed, to be sure, by our interpretations, our habits, our abilities and capabilities, but the input still being reflected in the output.

We need now to add another element to our description of the communication process. Consider what happens in a conversation between two people. One is constantly communicating back to the other, thus:

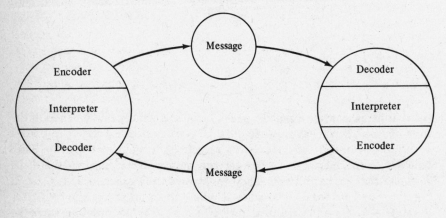

The return process is called *feedback,* and plays a very important part in communication because it tells us how our messages are being interpreted. Does the hearer say, "Yes, yes, that's right," as we try to persuade him? Does he nod his head in agreement? Does a puzzled frown appear on his forehead? Does he look away as though he were losing interest? All these are feedback. So is a letter to the editor of a newspaper, protesting an editorial. So is an answer to a letter. So is the applause of a lecture audience. An experienced communicator is attentive to feedback, and constantly modifies his messages in light of what he observes in or hears from his audience.

At least one other example of feedback, also, is familiar to all of us. We get feedback from our own messages. That is, we hear our own voices and can correct mispronunciations. We see the words we have written on paper, and can correct misspellings or change the style. When we do that, here is what is happening:

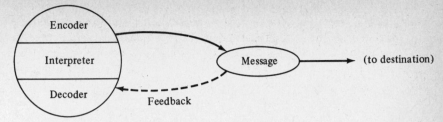

It is clear that in any kind of communication we rarely send out messages in a single channel, and this is the final element we must add to our account of the communication process. When you speak to me, the sound waves from your voice are the primary message. But there are others: the expression on your face, your gestures, the relation of a given message to past messages. Even the primary message conveys information on several levels. It gives me words to decode. It emphasizes certain words above others. It presents the words in a pattern of intonation and timing which contributes to the total meaning. The quality of your voice (deep, high, shrill, rasping, rich, thin, loud, soft) itself carries information about you and what you are saying.

This multiple channel situation exists even in printed mass communication, where the channels are perhaps most restricted. Meaning is conveyed, not only by the words in a news item, but also by the size of the headline, the position on the page and the page in the paper, the association with pictures, the use of boldface and other typographical devices. All these tell us something about the item. Thus we can visualize the typical channel of communication, not as a simple telegraph circuit, in which current does or does not flow, but rather as a sort of coaxial cable in which many signals flow in parallel from source toward the destination.

These parallel relationships are complex, but you can see their general pattern. A communicator can emphasize a point by adding as many parallel messages as he feels are deserved. If he is communicating by speaking, he can stress a word, pause just before it, say it with a rising inflection, gesture while he says it, look earnestly at his audience. Or he can keep all the signals parallel —except *one*. He can speak solemnly, but wink, as Lowell Thomas sometimes does. He can stress a word in a way that makes it mean something else—for example, "That's a *fine* job you did!" And by so doing he conveys secondary meanings of sarcasm or humor or doubt.

The same thing can be done with printed prose, with broadcast, with television or films. The secondary channels of the sight-sound media are especially rich. I am reminded of a skillful but deadly job done entirely with secondary channels on a certain political candidate. A sidewalk interview program was filmed to run in local theaters. Ostensibly it was a completely impartial program. An equal number of followers of each candidate were interviewed—first, one who favored Candidate A, then one who favored Candidate B, and so on. They were asked exactly the same questions and said about the same things, although on opposite sides of the political fence, of course. But there was one interesting difference. Whereas the supporters of Candidate A were ordinary folks, not outstandingly attractive or impressive, the followers of Candidate B who were chosen to be interviewed invariably had something slightly wrong with them. They looked wildeyed, or they stuttered, or they wore unpressed suits. The extra meaning was communicated. Need I say which candidate won?

But this is the process by which communication works, whether it is mass communication, or communication in a group, or communication between individuals.

Four

Ethical Problems in Communication

Thomas R. Nilsen

An Ethical Orientation

As a subject of study ethics deals with questions of right and wrong conduct, of the good and the bad, and of moral obligation. In one sense we all know a good deal about such questions, but in another sense we know very little. Without any formal study of ethics we can all point to or describe many acts we would unhesitatingly call wrong, and others we would call right. We all feel there are some things we *ought* to do, and some things we *ought not* do. We ought to help people we encounter who are in need; we ought to keep our promises, be helpful, civil, and avoid hurting others. We ought not cheat, slander, deceive, or otherwise injure another human being. In short, we feel we ought to do what is right, and we ought not do what is wrong.

We are aware, however, that it is often difficult to decide whether an act or statement is morally right or wrong. We are frequently unsure of ourselves when trying to decide what is, in a given case, the right, or good, or better thing to say or do. For instance, is it wrong to tell a lie to avoid hurting someone's feelings? To be honest, must we tell the "whole truth" about what we are talking about? If we present only "facts," are we being truthful? Is it wrong to break a window or two in order to call attention to what we are saying about an important social problem that people in authority seem to be ignoring? Is it wrong to use obscene language when our intentions are good (even if the obscene language offends some people)? If we are selling something, whether an artifact or an idea, ought we tell about its weaknesses as well as its strengths? Ought we to go out of our way to say or do the right thing? Can we really know, in most cases, what is the morally right thing to do or say? . . .

The questions raised above suggest that ethical questions are not confined to issues of great moment, but arise constantly in our day-to-day living, whenever the behavior—verbal or nonverbal—of one person affects the well-being of another. The philosopher Ralph Barton Perry states, "The moral drama opens only when interest meets interest; when the path of one unit of life is crossed by that of another."[1] Most human actions, then, are part of a moral drama, since almost everything said or done by one person touches the life of another. From the small courtesies that make human relations more pleasant to the supreme sacrifice of one life for another, what one human being does affects the well-being of others. The eloquent phrases of an inspired leader may energize a nation; a thoughtless remark may injure the feelings of a sensitive child. Over the whole range of human life, words have their impact on people for good or ill. . . .

Ethical Problems in Communication

When we think about the "ethics of speech," what probably first comes to mind is political campaigns and quasi-political protests and demonstrations. This is not surprising, since in a democratic society political campaigns are an essential and recurring feature of national life, from the election of the village mayor to the election of the nation's President. And where traditional political processes fail to meet the needs of significant groups in society—as they see these needs—extrapolitical means are used, and since their success is in large part dependent on the attention they get, such tactics are employed as will get the most of it.

In citizen political action the interests of literally hundreds of different social, economic, labor, and professional organizations are involved, and so too is the personal success of the competing politicians. In other words, the stakes are high for the many and diverse individuals and groups taking part; and with it all, the opportunities for deception and guile, for manipulation and influence peddling, are endless. Moreover, our political tradition has legitimized a kind of public symbolic infighting and given license to accusation, exaggeration, and partisanship such as is rarely tolerated outside the political arena.

Even though we may discount much of the "campaign oratory," we are faced with the fact that in political campaigns significant issues are often avoided or oversimplified and attention-getting but minor issues are often exaggerated. Vague fears are heightened, fears of the culprits of the season, whether they be fascists or communists, capitalists or labor leaders, student activists or revolutionary professors. A political slogan or "formula" is sought which captivates public interest and creates a sense of common purpose, yet does not raise serious questions about difficult problems.

A thoughtful and humane person cannot but feel grave doubts about whether this is the way to decide who will have the power to make war or peace, to decide whether we will feed our hungry and clothe our poor, whether we will put men to work. Is this the way to develop informed and critical citizens who can make intelligent choices?

Where the well-being of many is so vitally involved, our ethical common sense tells us that it is morally wrong to evade issues, to present highly biased and misleading information, to oversimplify problems, and to place the success of a political party above the opportunity for genuine choice on the part of the voters. Where such important decisions are to be made, there is, we cannot but feel, a moral obligation to have more respect for truth, more honesty and candor in the discussion of issues, and more selfless interest in the public good.

However, when we consider some other factors, such as the practical problems faced by the candidate, we may be less certain in our moral criticism. If a candidate were to attempt to discuss the intricacies of policy, would he lose the interest of his audience? Would he open himself to objections and criticisms to which he would have no opportunity to reply? Moreover, if he did not talk about those things of most interest to each particular group of listeners, in terms familiar to them, would they listen? If he did not try to reassure the voters of his common humanity and sincerity, thus enabling them to identify with him, could he be elected?

These questions do not lessen the moral obligations of the candidate; they do not change the ethical issues. They do, however, remind us how difficult it is to know what is the most morally right thing to do or say in a given case. Campaign speaking and the public-relations activity that goes with it are important to the democratic process. Such speaking provides at least some basis upon which voters can have confidence in their choice of a leader, and some basis upon which to approve or disapprove the general directions of public policy. To say and do that which best serves the public good is difficult indeed, especially under the pressures of a campaign.

As mentioned above, when the ordinary and accepted political processes appear to be dominated by vested interests and the existing institutions are seen as unresponsive to the needs of significant numbers of people, other methods of social change are sought. Recent years have seen a particularly active period of protest against inadequately responsive and allegedly inhumane institutions —educational, political, legal, economic—and there has been violent outcry for greater opportunity and equality. Protest has taken many forms, from peaceful sit-ins, teach-ins, mass meetings, and boycotts, to mass confrontations, traffic-disrupting marches, and physical attacks on property and persons. The speaking has varied as greatly, from the religiously oriented exhortations to nonviolent resistance of Martin Luther King, Jr., to the virulent, often obscene and profane denunciations and attacks of some of the more radical leaders of such groups as the SDS, the Weathermen, and the early Black Panthers. The earlier protest urged legal and political action in the accepted tradition; the later and more radical protest often repudiated the traditional legal and political methods in favor of demands backed by coercive power.

The protest movement in the large has had as its goal the eradication of social injustice. It has not always been clear that some of the more militant leadership has been so committed. Inevitably it seems that a social movement seeking radical changes attracts to it individuals of such extreme views and temperament that they distort the aims and actions of the movement itself.

The problem of achieving greater equality and justice is made more difficult by other types of extremists, those who seem to oppose all social change. Whether to preserve their own vested interests—economic, political, or cultural—or because of religious or other ideological conviction, they condemn virtually all social legislation or cultural change, most of which is seen as the machinations of a diabolical communism. For many people such right-wing extremism gains a certain validity with its appeal to tradition, religious fundamentalism, and the preservation of law and order.

It is easy to become morally indignant, and not without reason, when groups flout established authority and custom and seem to foster a disrespect for law and normal democratic political procedures which the majority feel to be the very bases of their social, political, and economic security. But when one sees the disparity between rich and poor, black and white, privileged and underprivileged, and when the political processes are seen as radically favoring the white and the affluent (as can be seen in tax laws, selective law enforcement, partisan legislation) it is not surprising that the disadvantaged—and those in deep sympathy with them—should seek to force social change. The built-in bias in legal codes and political processes leans toward the preservation of existing legal, political, and economic relationships; and the inertia of a culture preserves its values even though the natural and technological environment may be changed. Where the disparity, the discrimination, the disadvantage is arbitrary, it is hard to condemn the aggression that stems from the frustration of those who feel outraged and see normal avenues of change as blocked.

At the same time, however, it is difficult to countenance actions that seem to endanger the very institutions which make constructive social change possible—which make possible the greater realization of the goals of equality and justice. Thus we live with an ethical dilemma that man has faced, in all probability, since organized society has existed.

Although political campaigns and organized protest are spectacular examples of public communication that raise ethical questions, such campaigns and protests do come and go. There are other significant public communications, however, with which we are unremittingly confronted through the mass media: advertising, news, entertainment of every description, preaching, and pressure-group propaganda.

Advertisements too often mislead by implying much more than they explicitly claim. They appeal to vanity and cupidity; they play on the emotions surrounding the need to have the approving attention of others. Advertisements sometimes display and glamorize products that are demonstrably harmful. In their endless appeal to self-glorification and aggrandizement they distort our sense of values.

Newspaper reporting is often extremely biased; some events and issues are ignored or suppressed while others are exaggerated, with little regard for the need for public understanding. Often headlines are lurid, stories and pictures are sensationalized, and privacy is invaded. The responsibility for informing the public is neglected.

Television programs feature crime and violence; the gun is too often the ultimate arbiter of disputes. Many shows are puerile, their production guided almost solely by the money to be made in pandering to the lowest common denominator of public taste. Responsibility for public enlightenment and cultural development is all but ignored. The commentator who arouses serious economic and political controversy, however enlightening, is likely to be replaced by the safe and innocuous television personality who avoids confronting his listeners with significant discussion.

Here, as in the case of political speaking, the ethical issues are complex. The freedoms to make, to buy and sell, within broad limits, are freedoms important to a democratic society. Advertising, with all its faults, is important to a free economy. If a free economy is important to democracy, then it would appear that advertising should not be entirely eliminated. Although there is little doubt that some advertising is unethical, who can decide at what point it becomes morally wrong? How far could we go in restricting advertising without doing more harm than good? So too with respect to the communications of the press, radio, and television. At what point would restrictions and regulations make such inroads on the freedom of expression as to weaken democratic processes and undermine basic values? As much as we may lament the low standards of communication in the mass media and their failure to meet the moral obligations of public service, we must recognize that the ethical problems involved do not admit of easy answers.

There are other sources of questionable public communication. Throughout our society there are hundreds of partisan voices vying to be heard and to influence the thought and action of citizens. Every profession, every trade, almost every interest has its national and local organizations which seek to serve the interests of its members through building favorable public attitudes and influencing public policy. Every ideology, every political, social, economic, and religious persuasion, seeks to influence and proselytize. In the work of these groups there are varying degrees of public service, but there is also much that is highly partisan and self-seeking.

It is part of our heritage of beliefs, however, that such competing groups, when free to pursue their own ends, will in the long run contribute to the public good. If the competition is open, it is believed, those groups will win support which have the most to offer, and the public good will best be served. That there is truth in this is attested to by the success of our own society, in which freedom to pursue individual and group interests has been unparalleled. It is also true, however, that the exhortations and propaganda of these groups often severely distort the truth through their highly biased selection of facts and interpretations of events. Often public confusion results from the conflicting claims and demands, as, for example, in the demands of business and labor. In the case of more extreme groups, such as those of the extreme political right and left, not only do they create confusion, but worse, they sow suspicion of and create hatred toward whatever groups or individuals hold differing views.

Whatever abuses of the right of free speech may occur, we still do not want to restrict the right of people to organize in pursuit of their interests and to express themselves freely. Ethical questions cannot help arising, however, if we have any commitment to the basic values of our culture. The question is not whether freedom of speech and association serve our values: Such a freedom is at the very foundation of those values. The question is whether the wide-spread abuse of the freedom endangers the freedom itself by eroding the conditions that make it possible. Do extreme bias, marked lack of objectivity, disregard of sound evidence and reasoning, and crass self-interest undermine the democratic process, create disrespect for and intolerance of differing opinions, and militate against respect for the individual?

A relatively new—in terms of effectiveness—set of pressure groups has begun competing for the attention of government and society. The recent upsurge of action on the part of ethnic minorities has brought new and often strident voices into the public discourse. Where such ethnic and culturally disadvantaged minorities are concerned, their problem has been to find a voice that can and will be heard. Theirs is less a seeking of special privilege than a seeking to share the privileges they see as their due as citizens of an affluent society, to share the advantages deemed legitimate for the average member of the cultural majority. And these are not merely material advantages, but the right to be thought of and acted toward as a complete human being and citizen, without discrimination of any kind. Where there exists bias, overstatement, ethnocentricism, bitterness, or virulence, these must be viewed in the light of the peculiar circumstances of the group. This, of course, should be done for all individuals and groups, we see the need more clearly, however, where disadvantaged minorities are concerned.

It is not only in public discourse, in political campaigns, in the use of the mass media, or in the exhortations and machinations of pressure groups that ethical problems in communication are to be found. In our day-to-day interactions with others we affect them with our words in countless ways. We touch their lives by our small talk, our courtesies, explanations, instructions, entreaties, commands, words of endearment or resentment, approval or rebuke. Words as expressions of thought and feeling are instruments of action. With them we are constantly and inevitably doing things to people. Thus there is even an ethical problem in the way we use speech in our everyday lives: a failure to speak when someone needs encouragement; a hasty response that suggests indifference; an arbitrary order that wounds someone's ego; a seemingly innocent remark that hurts someone's pride; a word of disapproval in a context that magnifies the disapprobation; gossip; a half-truth, or the full truth at the wrong time or place. We cannot, of course, know at all times what effect our words will have, and sometimes a well-intentioned statement causes comeone to suffer. It is not always easy to say the right thing.

This brief reflection on the ethical problems of speech should remind us of how pervasive they are and how difficult of resolution. It should also remind us that we do have a common background of values in the light of which we can make ethical judgments. Very likely there has been, thus far in this discussion, a reasonably adequate meeting of minds between reader and writer on what is morally questionable in communication and what is morally desirable, and on how difficult it sometimes is to decide which is which. If we were to make judgments about specific instances, however, we would doubtless find ourselves in disagreement very quickly.

. . .

Ethics and Speech

Our concern is with the ethics of speech. Every act of speech is essentially a social act, influencing the attitudes or behavior of others. Therefore, rather than attempt to divide communication into moral and nonmoral, we will think of every communicative act as having an ethical component—as carrying some degree of ethical charge. Virtually every act of speech, then, involves an ethical obligation.

Speech communication is related to so many facets of man's life that a comprehensive view of man and a far-reaching ethical concern are necessary to an adequate ethic of speech. Melvin Rader's statement on the requirements of an ethic complete enough to serve man is helpful:

> The real subject of value is the person-in-society, and this social personality, as a dynamic focus of interests, is the whole man. Only an ethics that does justice to every essential side of human nature, as both individual and social, as mind and body, as thinking and feeling, and desiring, is complete and complex enough to be the basis of valid ideals.[2]

Our goal as individuals and as members of groups ought to be to act in our personal relationships with others, and through whatever public agencies are available to us, to contribute directly and indirectly to doing "justice to every essential side of human nature."

Morally right speech, like any morally right behavior, is that which contributes to the well-being of others, to their fulfillment as human beings. Ethical principles, to be valid guides to morally right speech, must be based on considerations of the effects of speech on every side of man's nature that it touches.

It is helpful to think of the ethical requirements of speech communication as falling into two broad, but overlapping, categories: those growing out of the area of formal public address, and those that arise in the informal communications of group discussion and interpersonal relations. The same basic values underlie each category, but they are served in somewhat different ways.

In public discourse, where relationships are relatively impersonal and the issues public, the good is served by communications that preserve and strengthen the processes of democracy, that provide adequate information, diversity of views, and knowledge of alternative choices and their possible consequences. It is served by communications that provide significant debate, applying rational thought to controversial issues, recognizing at the same time the importance and relevance of feeling and personal commitment. Further, the good is served by communications that foster freedom of expression and constructive criticism, that set an example of quality in speech content, in language use, and in fair play and civility.

In informal and interpersonal communications our values are served by speech that respects similar standards. But in interpersonal communication, where the impact of personality on personality is more direct and immediate, there are additional concerns. It is in such communications that we most fully share the human condition. The personality is served by speech which preserves the dignity and integrity of the individual ego, which make possible the optimum sharing of thought and feeling, the experience of belonging and acceptance, and which fosters cooperation and mutual respect. If these aspects of interpersonal communication are not ordinarily thought of as having a significant ethical component, it is because we have lacked a sufficiently inclusive sense of moral obligation.

As we have noted, there is general agreement on our basic values and on our ethical principles when stated broadly. There is often disagreement on the application of general principles to specific actions. This is as it should be. We do not, and cannot, all see a situation from the same perspective. Moreover, the conditions of life are constantly changing, and values must be reinterpreted and principles adapted if they are to be applied constructively to new situations. Society receives its most important ethical dividends not from rigid ethical prescriptions, but from the struggles of men to reconcile their ethical conflicts. In this process light is shed on the different interests affected and their claims to consideration, and on the various factors that enter into each unique ethical problem. The resulting compromise is more likely to preserve the dignity and integrity of the individual than an arbitrarily applied moral prescription.

NOTES

1. RALPH BARTON PERRY, *The Moral Economy* (New York: Scribner, 1909), p. 13.
2. MELVIN RADER, *Ethics and the Human Community* (New York: Holt, 1965), p. 435.

PART ONE

An Overview: Theories and Strategies

Experiences and Discussions

1. What is the practical value of determining general principles of communication? Will the development of such theories have any real influence upon individuals and societies? Has communication changed because of the communication theory derived thus far? Has your communication behavior changed since reading these four articles?
2. Select a sample of ten persons, and ask each to define "communication." What elements do the ten definitions share? How do they differ?
3. Were the ten people selected in (2) defensive? How could you have modified your interview to make them more defensive? Less defen-

sive? What characteristics are you using to judge the degree of their defensiveness?

4. During a three-hour block of television viewing, record or summarize all commercial advertisements. How many do you consider ethical? What values are you employing in your decision? Were any sexist? Racist? Purposely distorting? Misleading? For "unethical" products?

5. Try the following values clarification exercise: Draw two circles on a blank piece of paper. Use the first as a pie graph, and cut it into portions representing your major priorities or concerns in life, for example, you might label one-half "career," one-quarter "social," and two-eighths each "friends" and "religion." Be as specific or general as you like, using as many slices as you require.

   Now, on the second circle, divide another pie into slices representing the division of your communication time. Do you spend the most time in "career-oriented" communication, such as classes? Or in communication with or about friendship relations?

   Compare the two graphs. Do they help you to put your values into perspective? Do these values suggest any ethical considerations or judgments? Are your values typical of those of your peers? Of those of society as a whole? Of your values over a period of time?

For Further Reading

ADLER, RON, and NEIL TOWNE. *Looking Out, Looking In.* 2nd ed. New York: Holt, 1978.

   Written in a highly personal and readable style, this introductory text begins the analysis of communication with a look at the self and at perception. Rather than review as many aspects of communication as they can, the authors select several communication styles for their focus: defensive communication, conflict, nonverbal communication, and interpersonal listening. The book also includes short readings, poems, and exercises which accent the written text.

BARKER, LARRY L., and ROBERT K. KIBLER (eds.). *Speech Communication Behavior: Perspective and Principles.* Englewood Cliffs, N.J.: Prentice-Hall, 1971.

   This book is composed of both original essays and selected readings by noted scholars on seven aspects of communication behavior. Each section contains objectives and discussion questions to help you analyze such topics as persuasion and attitude change, the acquisition of communication behaviors, physiological principles, and transracial communication.

DEVITO, JOSEPH A. (ed.). *Communication.* Rev. ed. Englewood Cliffs, N.J.: Prentice-Hall, 1976.

   A well-chosen collection of twenty-eight readings offering a variety of articles on communication processes, messages, sources, and receivers. The combination of classic and contemporary writings provides a foundation for both the theoretical and practical aspects of communication. This new edition includes readings on self-perception and intercultural communication and greater emphasis on the intrapersonal and interpersonal dimensions.

LEE, IRVING, and LAURA LEE. *Handling Barriers in Communication.* New York: Harper and Row, 1957.

Two manuals in one—a workbook which contains both a discussion section and a readings section. The cases illustrate communication barriers involved in jumping to conclusions, giving and getting information, making corrections, and being closed-minded. The analysis of everyday thinking, speaking, and behaving should stimulate your investigation of similar behaviors in your own encounters.

MCCROSKEY, JAMES C., and LAWRENCE R. WHEELESS. *Introduction to Human Communication.* Boston: Allyn and Bacon, 1976.

This book provides research on communication behaviors often neglected in introductory texts. Discussion topics include human communication and change, the motivation to communicate, communication apprehension, personality variables and communication, interaction versus transaction, interpersonal confirmation, and information processing.

MINNICK, WAYNE C. *The Art of Persuasion.* 2nd ed. Boston: Houghton Mifflin, 1969.

In addition to offering a comprehensive analysis of the components of persuasion, the author also considers the ethical dimensions of influencing attitudes and behaviors.

NILSEN, THOMAS R. *Ethics of Speech Communication.* Indianapolis: Bobbs-Merrill, 1974.

Nilsen discusses the importance of ethics for all levels of communication, intrapersonal to intercultural. Topics of particular interest include ethical considerations in protests and social confrontations, the issue of majority and minority rights, omission of information, advertising responsibilities, ambiguous responses, and telling the truth.

PART TWO

Verbal Messages: The Symbolic Channel

"I beg that you will draw your chair up to the fire, and favour me with some details as to your case."

"It is no ordinary one."

"None of those which come to me are. I am the last court of appeal."

"And yet I question, sir, whether in all your experience you have ever listened to a more mysterious and inexplicable chain of events than those which have happened in my own family."

"You fill me with interest," said Holmes. "Pray give us the essential facts from the commencement, and I can afterwards question you as to those details which seem to be most important."

THE FIVE ORANGE PIPS

With that introduction, Sherlock urges his new client to engage in verbal communication, that most commonly and potentially most fruitful form of human interaction. Certainly, throughout any investigation of communication, verbal interaction is a major focus of the study. The words chosen and the interpreted meaning of those words have significant influences upon the way a message is received and interpreted.

Unlike other organisms, humans regularly and extensively utilize symbolic interaction as a means of expressing thoughts. Our communication is commonly characterized by words, or verbal symbols, that can carry many hidden meanings. The *word* "burglar," for example, does not wear a mask, carry a blackjack, and sneak down dark alleys. The image conveyed, though, may have these qualities, at least in the minds of some people. If you are a sneak thief, of course, the image produced by "burglar" might be an inspiration: a person who is brave, bold, and cunning. The image conveyed by a word is not universal; it depends largely upon the interpretation of the receiver.

There are some "Universals of Language," though, as Joseph DeVito explains. They are universals not of interpretation but rather of structure. DeVito suggests sixteen principles shared by all languages.

All verbal codes have common goals: limiting ambiguity, forcing norm conformity, regulating interaction, revealing hidden meanings—just as diverse legal systems may share the goal of promoting justice. W. P. Robinson discusses these and other functions of the verbal channel, suggesting that it is something of a police force in the communication process.

The police force can easily deal with clear infractions and overt problems, but more difficulties occur with the subtleties and ambiguities of a situation. John Condon suggests that these complexities are dealt with in communication through a hybrid of the verbal and nonverbal channels termed ''paralanguage'': the inflection, pitch, and nuance that might clarify and modify the verbal message.

Acting together, it seems that the elements of verbal channel provide a series of regulations and guidelines for maximizing clarity of interaction.

OBJECTIVES

After carefully reading these three articles you should be able to define the following key terms:

vocal-auditory   (DeVito)
broadcast transmission
directional reception
specialization
semanticity
rapid fading
interchangeability
arbitrariness
duality of patterning
total feedback
discreteness
displacement
productivity
cultural transmission
reflexiveness
prevarication
learnability

norm   (Robinson)
affect
emitter

paralanguage   (Condon)
metacommunication
phatic communion

blocking
instrumental communication
affective communication
catharsis
magic
ritual

And:

1. Illustrate DeVito's sixteen universals using the English language as an example (DeVito).
2. Compare the way the sixteen principles are involved in the English language and in a human nonlanguage system, such as mathematics, semaphores or chess (DeVito).
3. Describe the characteristics of an emitter, including emotional states, personality, and social identity (Robinson).
4. Describe the eight functions of language listed by Condon (Condon).
5. List three examples of the "magic" function of language related to your experience in a university setting (Condon).

Five

Universals of Language

Joseph A. DeVito

Perhaps the best way to understand language and verbal interaction is to focus on those characteristics that are universal—those characteristics that all human languages possess in common. These characteristics or universals define what language is, how it is constructed, and what its potentials and limitations are. In all we shall distinguish sixteen such universals, following the work of the linguist Charles Hockett.

Vocal-Auditory Channel

To say that human language is vocal-auditory means that its signals are combinations of sounds produced by the respiratory system and received by the auditory system. Not all signals so produced, however, constitute language; paralinguistic features, such as volume, intonation, and vocal quality, are not included in the domain of language proper.

That human language makes use of the vocal-auditory channel is an obvious but not necessary fact. Gestural or tactile systems could conceivably evolve to a point where they would serve many of the communicative functions now served by the vocal-auditory channel. In fact, they have not; these nonverbal systems serve primarily to supplement the messages of the vocal-auditory channel. The advantage that this channel provides should be clear if one imagines what communication limited to other channels would be like. With a gestural system, for example, communication in the dark, or around corners, or when working with our hands, or with someone not looking directly at us would be impossible. Tactile systems are even more limiting.

Broadcast Transmission and Directional Reception

This feature follows from the nature of the channel used. Broadcast transmission points to the public nature of language; sounds are emitted and can be received by anyone within earshot, by enemies as well as by friends. Directional reception refers to the fact that the emitted sounds serve to localize the source; upon hearing a sound one can detect its location. Although it is true that one can whisper so that others will not hear, or "throw" one's voice so that receivers will not be able to tell where the sounds originate, in general, human language can be heard by anyone, regardless of the intended receiver, and indicates the location of the source.

Specialization

A specialized communication system, according to Hockett, is one whose "direct energetic consequences are biologically irrelevant." Human language serves only one major purpose—to communicate. It does not aid any biological functions. On the other hand, a panting dog communicates information as to its presence and perhaps about its internal state. But the panting itself serves the biological function of temperature regulation. The fact that communication accompanies or results from this behavior is only incidental.

Semanticity

As already indicated, language signals refer to things in the real world; they have referents. Not all signals have such referents, of course; it would be difficult, for example, to find the referents of such terms as *mermaid* or *or.* Yet for the most part, language symbols have some connection, however arbitrarily established, with the real world.

Rapid Fading

Speech sounds fade rapidly; they are evanescent. They must be received immediately after they are emitted or else not received at all. Although mechanical devices now enable sound to be preserved much as writing is preserved, this is not a characteristic of human language. Rather, these are extralinguistic means of storing information, aiding memory, and so forth. Of course, all signals fade; written symbols and even symbols carved in rock are not permanent. It relative terms, however, speech signals are probably the least permanent of all communicative media.

Interchangeability

Any human being can serve as both sender and receiver—the roles are interchangeable. Human beings are *transceivers.* Exceptions to this property are not in the nature of language but in the nature of certain individuals. The person who cannot speak or hear obviously cannot exchange roles as can most individuals. These limitations are not a function of language but of certain physiological or psychological dysfunctions of the individual. Similarly, infants cannot function as both senders and receivers in the same way as adults. This, too, is not a function of language but of the maturational level of the individual. In some languages of the world there are different codes for men and women: certain words are restricted to males and others to females. This, too, is not so much a linguistic as it is a cultural feature. Both men and women are capable of using the other's code; when directly quoting a member of the opposite sex, for example, the appropriate code is used. The restriction is imposed by society, not by language.

Arbitrariness

Language signals are arbitrary; they do not possess any of the physical properties or characteristics of the things for which they stand. The word *wine* is no more tasty than the word *sand,* nor is the latter any less wet.

Opposed to arbitrariness is *iconicity.* Iconic signals do bear resemblance to their referents. A line drawing of a person is iconic in representing the body parts in proper relation to each other. But it is arbitrary in representing the texture and thickness of the anatomical structures.

Both arbitrariness and iconicity are relative. For example, a line drawing is more arbitrary than is a black and white photograph, which is more arbitrary than a color photograph. Paralinguistic features (volume, rate, rhythm) are more iconic than are the features normally classified as belonging to language. Rate, for example, may vary directly with emotional arousal and hence would be iconic. But the sound of the word *fast* is not actually fast.

Duality of Patterning

Human language is composed of two levels: the level of the smallest differentiating, but meaningless, elements (called cenemes) and the level of the smallest meaningful combinations of these elements (called pleremes). In human language cenemes correspond to phonemes (roughly, individual sounds) and pleremes to morphemes (roughly, the smallest meaningful combinations of sounds).

According to Hockett, it is characteristic of systems possessing significant duality of patterning to have a relatively small number of cenemes and an extremely large number of possible pleremes. Human language clearly evidences significant duality in this sense; there are relatively few phonemes but a great many morphemes.

Total Feedback

This feature enables senders to receive their own messages. Speakers receive what they send primarily by auditory feedback, although kinesthetic and proprioceptive feedback can also be involved. This is not to say that the sources receive their messages in the same way as do receivers or that they receive all and only what the receivers do. Because the senders also hear their voices through bone conduction, as well as by ear, they sound different to themselves than they do to others.

Discreteness

This universal can probably best be explained by first noting its opposite: continuousness. A continuous signal contains no sharp divisions; vocal volume is probably a good example. In reality there is no sharp break between loud and soft, for example, but only gradual changes. A discrete system, on the other hand, does contain sharp divisions. For example, the sounds /t/ and /d/ differ in the feature of voiceness (the vibration or lack of vibration of the vocal cords). By pronouncing "time" and "dime" while holding your hand against your throat, you will notice that there is vibration of the vocal cords on "dime" but not on "time." Although voiceness is, in reality, a continuous variable, the sound is heard as either /t/ or /d/ and not as one midway between /t/ and /d/, regardless of how much voicing is used.

Displacement

Human language can be used to talk about things which are remote in both time and space; one can talk about the past and future as easily as the present. And one can talk about things one has not, does not, and will not ever perceive —about mermaids and unicorns, about supernatural beings from other planets, about talking animals. One can talk about the unreal as well as the real, the imaginary as well as the actual.

Productivity

Utterances in human language, with only trivial exceptions, are novel; each utterance is generated anew. The rules of grammar have already imposed certain restrictions on the way in which sentences may be generated, so complete productivity, in regard to form at least, does not exist. One can, however, talk about a vast number of different things and can even coin new words for new ideas and concepts. Whether human language imposes any restrictions on what can be communicated is an interesting, though probably unanswerable, question.

Cultural or Traditional Transmission

The form of any particular human language is traditionally transmitted. The child raised by English speakers learns English as a native speaker, regardless of the language of his or her biological parents. The genetic endowment pertains to human language in general rather than to any specific human language.

Reflexiveness

Human language can be used to refer to itself. That is, we can use language to talk about people and events in the world, but we can also use language to talk about language itself—much as we are doing right now. Language used to talk about language is referred to as *metalanguage*

Prevarication

As a consequence of semanticity, displacement, and productivity, speakers of human languages can lie. In any system that does not possess these three features lying would be impossible. Although animal lovers are fond of telling about their pets who try to fool them, it appears that "lying" is extremely rare in animals.

Learnability

Any human language can be learned by any normal human being. It might be added that this is only true at particular times in the life of the human. One cannot learn a language as a native after a certain age. This feature is best interpreted to refer to the equal learnability of all human languages—no one language should present any greater difficulty for a child than any other language.

These sixteen features or universals do not, of course, exhaust the characteristics of language. Taken together, however, they should serve to clarify how human language is made up, and what some of its potentials and limitations are. Further, these features, taken together as a definition of human language, should enable you to distinguish human language from all other communication systems, whether these are animal systems, such as the language of the bee or the dolphin, or man-made systems, such as the language of semaphore, chess, or mathematics.

SOURCES

For universals of language I relied on the work of Charles F. Hockett, particularly his "The Problem of Universals in Language," in J. H. Greenberg, ed., *Universals of Language* (Cambridge, Mass.: M.I.T. Press, 1963) and "The Origin of Speech," *Scientific American* 203(1960):89–96. The concepts of language universals are most thoroughly surveyed in Greenberg's *Universals of Language.* Most of the material, however, presumes a rather thorough knowledge of linguistics.

Portions of the material in this unit were adapted from my *The Psychology of Speech and Language: An Introduction to Psycholinguistics* (New York: Random House, 1970).

Six

Functions of Language

W. P. Robinson

The Interaction of Language and Social Setting

With disarming and charming Quixotic flourish, Hymes (1967) has suggested that the term SPEAKING can itself serve as a comprehensive mnemonic to remind any investigator of the components associated with variations in speaking. They are:

(S) Setting or scene
(P) Participants or personnel
(E) Ends as (i) objectives and (ii) outcomes
(A) Art characteristics
(K) Key
(I) Instrumentalities, both (i) channel and (ii) code
(N) Norms of interaction and interpretation
(G) Genre

Not surprisingly the English language is not so accommodating to Hymes's ingenuity that he can select labels whose meanings are self-evident. "Setting" and "participants" are clear and appropriate. Under "ends" are included both purpose and functions, manifest and latent: purpose referring to intentions of participants or organizers, function to what actually transpires. The two may coincide but may not. "Art characteristics" is unfortunate, covering as it does both the "form of a message" and its "topic," and unintentionally but apparently relegating topic to a low level of importance. "Key" distinguishes the tone, manner or spirit in which an act is performed, e.g. joking, solemn, gracious, etc. "Instrumentalities" refers both to channel of transmission, itself combining speech versus writing and telephone versus face to face, while "code" means language in the sense of Chinese versus English, with the additional rider that sub-code or variety, e.g. American English, Pakistani English, BBC English, will also be a necessary further sub-division. By "norms," Hymes intends specific rules like using an appropriate volume and not interrupting a speaker. "Genre" classifies the type of speech act, namely, prayer, lecture, or sales talk.

. . .

Verbal Behaviour as a Means of Avoiding Other Problems

It is alleged that some teenagers, and some not-so-teenagers, plug themselves into continuous transistorized music to save themselves from thinking. This allegation can be supported superficially by casual interviewing and, although not yet systematically investigated, it seems evident that self-selected exposure to patterned sequences of stimulation of various sorts can be used to delay or avoid dealing with problems. Talking to oneself, writing, and conversation with other people are among such devices, along with drugs, alcohol, watching television or playing bridge. A virgin field of study and likely to be a fertile one insofar as the incidence of such activities may well be high in contemporary industrialized societies.

. . .

Conformity to Norms

"There is a time to speak and a time to keep silence." The rules governing the occasions for silence and speech differ from culture to culture, but all cultures will have such rules. In our society these norms will differ from group to group and from situation to situation. Quaker meetings for worship can enjoy an hour's silence; the House of Commons commonly does not. Railway carriages in the south of England have a reputation for respecting privacy; silences of short duration at parties represent failure. Radio stations apparently have to confine their periods of silence to seconds rather than minutes to avoid questioning phone calls.

It is easy to conceive of situations where the person who can talk is at a premium: post-funeral breakfasts, meetings of strangers, reunion dinners, hospital visiting, and so on. It can be a relief to have someone present who will keep talking regardless of topic, interest or even propriety. But these settings are not the only ones where sustained verbal activity is required. When was a newspaper last published with a column blank except for a notice announcing that there was insufficient news to fill the space that day? How often does an "expert" interviewed on television or radio admit that he has nothing to say in reply to a question posed? As a personal and inadequate investigation it is masochistically instructive to be honest and say, "I'm too ignorant of the facts to venture an opinion" in reply to requests for views about international events. Our norms appear to dictate that an opinion be offered in reply to a request for one, and to admit that one's knowledge is inadequate may be as socially maladroit as to inquire too deeply into the evidence underpinning the opinions of others. Breaking conventions is often an illuminating way of testing their force.

We can go a little further and ask how often pupils in any educational organization admit they do not understand or even know when they do not? How often, on the other hand, do they feel constrained to offer some answer, perhaps successfully "psyching" out (another American contribution to the English language) the teacher and saying or writing what he approves of? Informed pessimists might argue that this is the commonest influence on pupils' products, that a student's main problem is to evoke certain responses from teachers or peers and that understanding the subject matter has a low place in the scale of priorities. For example, a university student submitting an essay could have a hierachy of priorities. The essay must cover four foolscap sides; the writing should be almost legible; the prose should be in reasonably acceptable English; it should cite references; it should be sprinkled with the appropriate jargon—and it must be done by Thursday. The logical structure of the arguments may have less importance, and that what is written should have a correspondence to a construction of reality relevant to the topic (referential function) almost none.

. . .

Encounter Regulation

Goffman (1963) and Argyle (1969) in particular have recently opened up this problem lying at the heart of social psychology: how do two people initiate an interaction, maintain and close it. Several lines of research have been sparked off, including Schegloff's (1968) analysis of the sequence rules governing telephone conversations and Kendon's (1967) work on how people switch the conversational roles of speaker and listener. In many situations, non-verbal as well as verbal cues are relevant to these activities, and role relationships will be relevant to the choice of forms made.

Any language will probably have a finite number of items that can be used to attract attention, to greet, and to take leave, and there will be norms relating to the order in which events should occur, which items go together, and what choices of particular items mean. "Hallo Jane" may occur in different situations from "Jane Hallo!" "Watcha sir!" may be an uncommon compound greeting, while "Watcha!," "Hi!," "Hallo!" and "Good morning!" may convey different meanings. In the switching of conversational roles, direct questions, the use of intonation in unfinished sentences, and head and eye movements may serve to help switch roles smoothly. The use of these devices will be evaluated not only in terms of whether encounters occur and proceed smoothly, but also in terms of appropriateness to the role relationship of the participants.

. . .

Regulation of Self

Behaviour and Affect

Unlike speech regulating the behaviour of others, that which is used to control one's own behaviour has no unique label. "Talking to oneself" is inadequate, both because it might be premature to eliminate from consideration covert as opposed to audible speech, and because simple talking may involve other functions such as encouraging oneself (affective instrumental) or giving a commentary of ongoing action (referential).

While there have been studies of this regulatory function in developing children (e.g. Luria, 1961), adults have been left alone. There are no reported studies of how housewives attempt to control their cake-baking or gardeners their rose-pruning. We cannot say with what frequency "talking to oneself" has an apparent instructional component and, if it has, what its formal characteristics are. This is particularly unfortunate. It would be illuminating to know just what form the grammatical structure of the speech takes. Does it simply omit explicit references to features of the environment already understood, and therefore involve an extreme degree of contextual presupposition? Or is it "telegraphic" in the ways in which the speech of very young children is, that is omitting as many function words as possible and relying on the order of selected lexical items to convey the essence of the message?

Without the necessary empirical evidence it would be hazardous to venture guesses about what differences found might mean. Could it be that the structures are commonly intermediate forms between the "deep structures" (Chomsky, 1965) and their ultimate vocal realization? With so little knowledge of the facts of the matter we cannot readily offer answers to questions about any possible increases in efficiency a person might achieve through overt speaking to himself.

Studies with young children have led Luria to suggest a three-stage process in the development of the regulatory function: an initial one in which speech has no relevance, a second in which it accentuates the vigour of an ongoing activity, and a third in which the semantic value of the language units used becomes relevant. For example, a child at the intermediate stage with his hand poised to push a button will respond positively whether he says to himself "Press!" or "Don't press!," and while "Press twice!" will yield one push, "Press! Press!" will yield two. Claims to obtain such results (Luria, 1961; Lyublinskaya, 1957) date from a period when Russian psychologists were prone to present their supportive evidence in an illustrative and piecemeal fashion, so that other investigators could not critically examine the methodology or stages between premises and conclusions of arguments. Jarvis (1964), after most carefully piecing together fragments of information to recreate and elaborate one of Luria's most quoted investigations, found no evidence to support the results reported. Random results can be obtained by bad experimentation, but such a criticism would not appear to have substance in relation to Jarvis's work. The field itself is wide open. Klein (1964) has been able to show that speech to self declines with age, but that within that constraint, task-relevant mutterings increase and task-irrelevant speech decreases. There is variation among children, but high talkers do not appear to be either more or less successful at puzzles or button-pushing tasks than low talkers, although not all his results were random.

Both Jarvis and Klein suggest that certain parent-child variables may be relevant to how much children do talk to themselves, but they are not specific. Maybe highly dependent children being socialized out of close attachment to their mothers talk to themselves to reassure themselves: talking could substitute for whistling when you are afraid in the dark. Whether or not, and if so how much, speech-for-self is controlling affect rather than sensori-motor skills, and whether it works, we do not yet know.

We have already mentioned that we do not know what linguistic structures are used, whether or not there is a high incidence of imperatives and modal verbs, whether a large amount of presupposition and abbreviation is present or what.

As with behaviour, so it is with affect. We have no idea whether we can induce affective states merely by verbal autoinstruction.

Regulation of Others

Behaviour

As with the regulation of encounters, our language does afford us lexical items like "command" and "request" which refer to activities involved in the regulation of the behaviour of others. Norms may require that among certain groups of people only a limited number of linguistic forms are likely to be efficient and polite, but the total range of possibilities for speakers of the language is likely to be greater. Soskin and John mention six verbally based ways of attempting to borrow a coat, but not all would convey the same meaning regardless of context or manner of delivery. People could evaluate these means not only in terms of politeness, but also in terms of probability of being understood. This is one reason for suggesting that it may be useful to distinguish between primitive and other linguistic forms. Imperative and interrogative forms used to give orders and ask questions and which include verbs of action as a focus are the immediately obvious candidates for primitive forms associated with controlling others. The modal verbs (must, need, ought, should) in combination with verbs of action would appear to be another set of primitives which enable a differentiation among reasons for the action being taken, although these enter a child's speech repertoire some time after requests and commands.

But in what sense are these forms more primitive? No doubt many a linguist would bring charges that this sort of view reveals a fundamental misunderstanding of the way language works. Utterances mean what people agree that they mean. It is true that a fine analysis of the constituents and their relationships in any proverb will not reveal the meaning of the idiom, any more than dictionary definitions will increase the chances of someone understanding "Get up them apples!" However we can trace the derivation of the use of "apples," so that knowledge of the system of Cockney rhyming slang (stairs —pears—apples and pears—apples) reveals how a more primitive form is changed. The system could not work the other way round. The same style of argument can be brought forward for claiming that the use of "Brrh!" or "That coat looks warm" as indirect requests or commands—and we do call them "indirect"—are derivatives. Their primitive functions are respectively to express your coldness or to make a statement about an attribute of a coat.

The issue of "primitiveness" could probably be put to weak empirical tests if anyone wished to do so. One test would be to have a random sample of adult speakers judge what examples of each form meant. If a wide range of people judge the primitive form more unequivocally comprehensible, then its greater universality would suggest that particular sub-cultures have invented derived forms. Another test would involve comparisons of children at different stages of development. Provided that their utterances are based on the construction of sentences from their constituent elements rather than imitation of total utterances picked up from adults who use only the alleged derived forms, children should learn to use and understand primitive forms before they learn the derived ones.

Whether or not the verbal behaviour as a means of direct control is effective can be evaluated against the listener's comprehension, one strong test of which would be his obedience or disobedience. Reasons for not obeying could stem from a variety of sources other than a failure to understand, while failures to grasp the commanding force of some of the indirect forms mentioned by Soskin and John might indicate an ignorance of norms peculiar to a sub-culture. It would in fact be interesting to know whether or not some of the indirect requests can be readily discriminated from the forms having the more obvious function, e.g. does "Brrh!" as a comment differ from "Brrh!" as a request by virtue of non-verbal, para- or extralinguistic features?

. . .

Expression of Affect

One set of vocal features often ignored in teaching second languages are the indigenous forms of grunting, snorting, laughing, and enthusing. Insofar as these expressive features are not unmodified innate responses to certain stimuli, then they are linked to or are part of verbal behaviour. The various expressive noises are perhaps minimal forms of utterances which can use words in exclamation or swearing, but their variety and efficacy remain unexamined.

Characteristics of Emitter: Marking of Emotional States; Personality and Social Identity

A person's speech may indicate how he is feeling, what sort of personality he has, who he is. Certain speech patterns are indicators of demographic characteristics such as age, sex, occupation, amount and type of education, nation or region of origin. There may also be links with personality, that is, relatively enduring characteristics referred to with words like intelligence, extraversion, neuroticism or psychotism. There are paralinguistic and linguistic features that signal ongoing emotional states. For social identity, although we cannot at present describe regional accents with great precision, a trained and well-informed phonetician can apparently emulate the example of Professor Higgins, at least to the level of county and town in England and can probably carry his detection more finely still, provided the necessary information is available. Grammatical and lexical choices, along with peculiar meanings for special structures and items, may similarly contribute to identification, although precise details have not been tabulated. The casual observations of Nancy Mitford were expressed as distinctions between U and non-U English—the lexical choices of glass/mirror, pudding/sweet, lavatory/toilet, napkin/serviette and others marking off the lower middle class from those of a higher station. Unfortunately once the distinctive features are exposed, people aspiring to a certain identity may be able to incorporate them into their speech. Speech may reveal preferred identity as much as real identity, but here our concern is with noting relationships between the verbal and non-verbal rather than with deciding whether wolves are wearing their own clothes.

REFERENCES

ARGYLE, M. *Social Interaction.* New York: Atherton Press, 1969.

CHOMSKY, N. *Aspects of a Theory of Syntax.* Cambridge, Mass.: M.I.T. Press, 1965.

GOFFMAN, E. *Behavior in Public Places.* New York: Free Press, 1963.

HYMES, D. "Models of the interaction of language and social setting," *Journal of Social Issues,* 1967, *23,* 8–28.

JARVIS, P. E. "The effect of self-administered verbal instruction on simple sensory-motor performance in children." Ann Arbor, Mich.: University Microfilms, Inc., 1964, 64-9238.

KENDON, A. "Some functions of gaze direction in social interaction," *Acta Psychologica,* 1967, *26,* 22–63.

KLEIN, W. L. "An investigation of the speech-for-self of children." New York: University of Rochester, doctoral dissertation, 1964.

LURIA, A. R. *The Role of Speech in the Regulation of Normal and Abnormal Behavior.* New York: Pergamon Press, 1961.

LYUBLINSKAYA, A. A. "The development of children's speech and thought," in B. Simon (ed.), *Psychology in the Soviet Union.* London: Routledge and Kegan Paul, 1957.

SCHEGLOFF, E. A. "Sequencing in conversational openings," *American Anthropologist,* 1968, *70,* 1075–95.

SOSKIN, W. F., and JOHN, V. "The study of spontaneous talk," in R. G. Barker (ed.), *The Stream of Behavior,* New York: Appleton-Century-Crofts, 1963.

Seven

When People Talk with People

John C. Condon

Years ago, a popular phonograph record produced by Stan Freberg presented a short conversation between two persons, Marsha and John. The conversation began like this:

"John—"

"Marsha . . ."

"John . . ."

"Marsha . . ."

"John . . ."

"Marsha . . ."

(Using the above dialogue as a basis, the clever reader can extrapolate the entire three-minute conversation.)

The printed form does not convey what the recording artists did with only two words. They were able to indicate differences in meaning by speaking the words with varied inflections and in different tones of voice. In fact, so skillful was the performance that several radio stations banned the harmless record from the air as "too suggestive."

The vocal variations on a theme of two words illustrate two simple but very important points about communication: (1) that the spoken word can have many different intended and interpreted meanings depending upon *how* it is said; and (2) that a phrase or even a single word can serve many functions depending upon its context and the way in which it is expressed. The sensitive conversant, the diplomat, the therapist are well aware of the many purposes of communication that any word or phrase may serve, and yet this awareness is frequently ignored when persons give too much attention to conventional semantics of word-thing relationships. Without such an awareness we must either disregard much, perhaps most, of everyday conversation, or we are likely to totally misinterpret the conversational meaning of all that talk.

Paralanguage and Metacommunication

In everyday communication there are always more than words that pass between persons. There are also cues that indicate to the persons how the spoken words are to be interpreted. One writer[1] has suggested we interpret all verbal messages on two levels: the *report,* what might be considered the "literal meaning" of the words, and the *command,* which is the apparent purpose or intention or function of those words. Thus the John-Marsha dialogue on paper appears to be a repetition of reports, but because of the varying inflection, loudness, and tone of voice, as well as the spoken words preceding and following each "John" or "Marsha," we seem to have a great number of different commands.

Leo Rosten in his delightful book, *The Joys of Yiddish,*[2] presents a treasury of similar examples, suggesting that part of the richness of Yiddish lies in the many meanings of some words as determined by a "Yiddish tone of voice." He tells the story of a Russian man who received a telegram from his wife which read: DOCTOR SAYS OPERATE OPERATE. The husband then cabled back immediately this telegram: DOCTOR SAYS OPERATE OPER-ATE. This exchange aroused the suspicions of the authorities who immediately investigated to see if this was some secret code. But the husband protested that the authorities were misreading the telegram; clearly what they said was: "Doctor says operate. *Operate?*" And the reply: "Doctor says operate, *operate!*"

The general name given to meaningful differences in tone of voice, inflection, rate, pitch, volume, and so forth is *paralanguage.* In ordinary face-to-face conversation, however, even paralanguage describes only a part of all that is communicated to give particular interpretations (or to suggest particular intentions) to any given expression. The social setting (a cocktail party or a funeral), the vast array of nonverbal cues (facial expression, hair style, clothing, eye behavior, posture, distance between the people conversing, and gestures), and even the difference between what we expect to hear and what we think we hear all render apparently similar reports into apparently different commands. Some writers have called all such aspects of communication *metacommunication.* (We should note that metacommunication is sometimes used with quite different meanings, including the technical language used for analyzing communication.)

As mentioned earlier, most of traditional semantic studies and even a large portion of general semantics literature have so stressed the word-thing relationship (the semantic dimension in Morris's three-part scheme) and have relied so much on printed or written words that paralinguistic and functional considerations of meaning have been overlooked. But unless we pay attention to these concerns we will run into the same kind of problem that foreign language students face when they are too literal minded about the language they are studying, reporting one's state of health when asked, "How are you?" or, in Japan, giving an honest answer to the question, "Where are you going?" Viewed one way, the two questions seem completely different; viewed *functionally,* the two "questions" mean about the same thing: "Hello."

Phatic Communion

Small talk, uninspired greetings, and idle chatter are among the description of a fundamental type of communication that Bronislaw Malinowski called *phatic communion.* To show that we welcome communication, that we are friendly, or that we at least acknowledge the presence of another person, we exchange words. In English we do not have special words for this function of communication, though phatic communion tends to be rather unimaginative. We say, "How are you?" or "Hello," or "Nice day." There may be variations based on geography ("Howdy!") or familiarity ("Hi ya, Baby!") or specific conditions ("Cold enough for ya?"). Whatever the words, the speaker is saying, in effect, "I see you and I am friendly." The channels of communication are opened.

In phatic communion, the specific words exchanged are not important. This is illustrated in the story of a U.S. businessman who, while traveling to Europe for the first time, finds himself seated across from a Frenchman at lunch. Neither speaks the other's language, but each smiles a greeting. As the wine is served, the Frenchman raises his glass and gesturing to the American says, *"Bon appétit!"* The American does not understand and replies, "Ginzberg." No other words are exchanged at lunch. That evening at dinner, the two again sit at the same table and again the Frenchman greets the American with the wine, saying, *"Bon appétit!"* to which the American replies "Ginzberg." The waiter notices this peculiar exchange and, after dinner, calls the American aside to explain that "the Frenchman is not giving his name—he is wishing you a good appetite; he is saying that he hopes you enjoy your meal." The following day the American seeks out the Frenchman at lunch, wishing to correct his error. At the first opportunity the American raises his glass and says, *"Bon appétit!"* To which the Frenchman proudly replies, "Ginzberg."

Although in this story the ignorance of a common language made more significant communication impossible, it was the exchange of simple words like *Bon appétit* (and *Ginzberg*) that broke the tension of silence and expressed friendship. Without the small talk first there can be no "big talk" later.

The only rule that seems to apply to phatic communion is that the "subject" of the communication be such that each party can say something about it. That is why everybody talks about the weather. The important thing is to talk—and this is why so much of phatic communion begins with a question, for a question requires a reply.

We do not request specific information in phatic communion and we are not expected to reply with precision or accuracy. If we are greeted with a "How are you?" we do not reply as we might if our doctor asked the question. When we are precise the result is likely to be humorous, as when James Thurber was once asked, "How's your wife?" and replied, "Compared to *what?*"

Specific information is sought in one kind of greeting, however. Members of secret organizations sometimes speak in code when they meet to determine whether each knows the password, special handshake, or other symbol. If the answer to the secret question is not precise, then the other is not regarded as a brother Mason or sister Theta or whatever, and subsequent communication will be prevented. Such coded phatic communion dates from times when members of such organizations might be persecuted if discovered. Among some "secret organizations" today, the reverse seems to be true. The coded greeting is often expressed loudly, more for the benefit of the outsiders than for the "secret" members. Phatic communion is usually the most casual, even careless, form of communication. The stories of persons passing through receiving lines and saying something like "I just killed my mother-in-law," which is met with a smile and a "Fine, I hope you're enjoying yourself" are well known. They illustrate what little significance is attached to phatic communion, so little that the speaker is not even listened to. In such extreme cases, however, we may wonder to what extent the channels of communicaiton have been opened after that exchange of noises. In any case, it seems that we prefer some noise to no noise.

Blocking of Communication

A second function of communication is the opposite of the first. Just as we rarely open a conversation with "I see you and I am friendly," when this may be the real "message" of our greeting, we rarely prevent further communication by saying directly, "I don't want to talk to you anymore." This is said sometimes, to be sure. But there are more sophisticated ways that we have mastered.

There are the dismissal reactions "Ha!" "That's crazy!" "Yeah, I'll bet!" and so forth. Whether the speaker intends these to block communication or whether they merely function in this way is often difficult to determine. In either case it takes but a few well chosen reactions to end a conversation—and a few more to end a friendship.

Then there are the guarded utterances of verbal grunts that seem to show a lack of interest in speaker or subject: "Oh, really?" "I see—," "Indeed," or "Hmm."

These brief snips of uninterested responses will end a conversation, and often large hunks of verbiage will achieve the same end. Either the language seems to say nothing or it is so difficult to decipher that it does not seem worth the effort. A favorite technique of naughty children, students taking examinations, and some U.S. Senators is to talk on and on about anything irrelevant to the subject at hand.

Recording-Transmitting Functions

One definition of teaching goes something like this: "Teaching is the transmission of the professor's notes into the students' notebooks without their having passed through the minds of either." A few years ago it was reported that a professor at a large midwestern college put his lectures on tape and had the tape recorder sent into his classroom and played every day. Weeks later, when he stopped into the room to see if all was going well, he found, on each student's desk, another machine recording the lectures. Allowing for the hyperboles here, these stories illustrate a basic function of communication, where the individual performs like a precise and self-contained transmitting and recording machine.

In one sense, all communication is a process of transmitting some information that is received by another. This is one definition of communication. But as we note the variety of ways in which we can describe the kind and purpose of a message sent, the category of transmitting-recording seems insufficient. The category is useful only for the most neutral exchanges of information, messages without intent to be instrumental, compliment the listener, let off steam, and so on. Thus, asking when the next bus leaves and being told; asking what time it is, and being told; reporting or hearing the news, weather, classroom lectures, and so on, all might be examples of this function of communication.

Instrumental Communication

When we say something and something happens as the result of our speaking, then our comments have been instrumental in causing that event to happen. The instrumental function of communication is one of its most common purposes. We request a secretary to type three copies of a letter. We ask a friend at dinner to pass the butter. We order a salesman out of the house.

The category of instrumental communication is loose enough to allow for several kinds of statements. There are statements that are clearly instrumental in their wording, for which the result correlates with the language. If we say "Shut the door" and the door is then shut, we may assume that the noise we made was influential in the shutting of the door. There are also statements for which the results cannot be so easily attributed to our utterances. If on a day planned for a picnic it is raining and so we sing, "Rain, rain go away"—and the rain does stop—it would be immodest to assume that our words caused that action. Much of prayer has been traditionally instrumental, and if the faithful believe that some prayers "have been answered," we could say that for these people the prayer was an instrumental communication. We will touch on this subject again when we discuss ritual and the magic function of communication.

Some statements are instrumental in intent of effect, but are not phrased as such. For example, if you want the salt passed to you, you may request it directly (instrumental) or you might comment that the food needs salt (transmitting information). If a wife wants a new fur coat, she may request it directly or she may comment on how well dressed her husband seems, especially when compared to her (apparently an effective technique). One instrumental request may result in a different instrumental action, as when commercial airlines do not ask passengers to stop smoking but to "observe the no smoking sign."

One characteristic of some instrumental statements is a faint resemblance between manner of speaking and the requested action itself. One sometimes speaks as if his words *were* instruments, as a belaying pin or rawhide whip are instruments. The voice (see metacommunication) does its best to imitate the desired action, as do voices instrumentally cheering at a football game, "Push 'em back, push 'em back, w-a-a-a-a-y back!"

Affective Communication

Communication in which the message is the emotional feelings of the speaker toward a listener is known as *affective communication*. Compliments, praise and flattery, and also snide and cutting remarks may be so classified.

There are affective elements in many of the functions of communication. Phatic communion may contain praise, as when old friends greet by saying, "You're looking great!" As noted in the previous section, instrumental purposes are often best served through affective communication, too.

It seems to be part of the woman's role in our society to use more affective communication than does the opposite sex. Where tradition has not given women authority in all situations, women have had to achieve their goals indirectly. And this indirection may be reflected in instrumental desires disguised in affective language. The wife who says to her husband, "You look so handsome all dressed up," might be requesting a new wardrobe for herself or be asking to go out to dinner, rather than just complimenting her husband.

The nonaffective language of fact and description or the language of clear and explicit requests need not be any more desirable than it is common in interpersonal communications. We admire and respect the clarity of the scientist in writing his report, but we may find him less explicit during his courtship. Perhaps the reason is that whereas the scientist communicates to himself and to others pursuing one goal, the diplomats or the lovers may not be sure they are pursuing the same goal.

A study of the social gestures of dating, which I once made in an attempt to discover what was "meant" when a man held the door for his date or failed to open the door, and so on, certainly indicated this. Each sex had its own mythology for the purpose of the gesture. To the woman, the man performed the task out of respect for Woman. To the man, he performed the task because he "had to" if he was going to get anywhere. Again, the man's purpose even in the nonverbal language was far more instrumental than the woman's. If the words and actions were more specific, it would not be possible for the sexes to maintain their mutual self-delusion.

Affective language is also *convincing* language. In many cases a person would not do something if asked to do it directly; he would be too aware of reasons that he might not be able to accept. We seem to prefer to do things we think we want to do, not things we are told to do. There is a story of an experiment performed by a university class on its professor. The class set out as a group to apply simple learning theory (reward-punishment) on the professor in order to force him to do something he would not ordinarily do and certainly not do if requested. The emotional rewards and "punishments," though nonverbal in this case, are comparable to the use of affective language for instrumental purposes. The class decided it would try to move the professor into a corner from which he would deliver his lectures. The reinforcement was of the kind professors like best, interested expressions on student faces, passionate note taking at his every word, smiles at his whimsy and laughter at his wit. These responses, when appropriate, were made whenever the professor moved in the direction of the desired corner. When he moved in the other direction the class responded with looks of boredom, gazing out the windows, shuffling of feet, and the other academic behaviors one has rehearsed since childhood. As the story goes, by the end of the semester the professor was, indeed, giving his lectures from the corner of the room.

Although this story may be apocryphal, affective communication in a variety of situations does "move" the listener in a way that direct requests would not. The salesman knows it ("I'll make a special deal just for you"), the professor knows it ("I'm sure that your studies of Artaud and Beckett have led you to ask . . ."), the lover knows it. Most persons recognize the influence of words on the ego. ("I'm sure that *you*, dear reader, are very sensitive to the communication process. . . .") To make another person feel good (or bad) through language is a rather common and vital function of communication.

It is possible to characterize attitudes of speakers toward their listeners on the basis of instrumental-affective content. One unpublished study[3] of Mexican attitudes toward male and female members of the Holy Family discovered that the language used toward male statues in a church was almost entirely instrumental in content, whereas the language used before the statue of the Virgin was highly affective. This distinction mirrored the differences in language used by children toward their parents in the average Mexican home. It is possible that degrees of anger, hostility, authority, and so on, can be measured by the comparative content of instrumental and affective language in our everyday expressions.

Many criticisms of the U.S. visitor or resident abroad have their basis in a lack of affective communication and a preponderance of instrumental communication. As a pragmatic people, we may have a cultural tendency to "get down to business," to be impersonal. Former Secretary of State John Foster Dulles is often quoted in Latin America as having said with some pride that "the U.S. does not have friends; it has interests." If others are treated as "interests" when they are more accustomed to being treated as "brothers" or at least "cousins," surely they will resent the change. The nonaffective communication may be honest, fair, sincere. But to one who does not expect it, the communication is cold, unfeeling, mechanical.

"Better understanding through communication" is a popular slogan. Too often what is meant is an improvement in semantics, an increase in the clarity of what we *mean.* We must not forget the affective aspects of communication, and must strive for an increase in the interpersonal attraction that we *feel.*

Catharsis

When you are angry or disturbed or hurt, physically or mentally, probably you give expression to your feelings. It is curious that expressions, which could be as personal as the feelings that evoke them, are rather stylized and predictable within the language. Words like *ouch!* or *oh!* are spoken by a people who speak English, whereas our neighbors who speak Spanish will say *ay!* when they express a comparable feeling. Grunts may be the only universal expression of catharsis.

When pain or frustration is sufficient, our cathartic expression becomes more obviously symbolic. We move from the "ouch!" to words that might be used in other ways, most often words that are socially disapproved of. We swear or curse or substitute words that sound something like the popular curses we long ago learned were "adult" and special. We find that different kinds of expressions for releasing tension are appropriate among different ages and occupations. A sailor who is angry is not expected to say "Oh, goodness me!" and an angry nun is not expected to sound like a sailor.

It is safe cultural generalization that in most societies of the world, the sex roles and expectations are clearly, symbolically, distinguished between males and females. They dress differently, play different games as children, walk differently, and are expected to assume different social roles. They are also expected to talk differently. In the United States and in a few other parts of the world, however, sex differences have tended to be diminished. The late 1960s saw a rise in unisex fashions in clothing as well as the passing of many laws designed to break this distinction (labeled "discrimination") in employment, membership in organizations, and so on. It also was a period when many words, particularly those most frequently associated with cathartic expressions (swearing, exclamations, and so on) went unisex. (It is significant that some women were free to swear like men, not the other way around.) It was often reported that during protest marches and speeches that characterized this period, policemen would become most upset by the taunts of women, particularly college-age women. The explanation was simply that most policemen come from backgrounds where the sex-role distinction, including language style, was still an important distinction, and therefore when girls used some choice "male" epithets to taunt the police they seemed to be threatening the whole social and moral order.

The physical stimulus finds expression in a symbol. This symbol eventually ceases to stand for, directly, anything in the outside world except an attitude toward whatever produced it. We move from physical sensation to verbal assault on that sensation ("damn it!") to mere release of tension.

The idea of cursing a situation dates to times when the belief in magic language was more common. There was a time when "God damn you" was meant as a magic curse to bring about suffering. The transference into such symbols was a step above the infantile reaction of actually attacking the offending person or object. Children may be observed to run into a wall and then physically retaliate against the wall, kicking it and saying "you mean old wall." But when the child's father runs into the wall and says "damn it!" (or, if the child is there, "darn it!") he probably is not talking to the wall. He is simply relieving his tension in symbols that have long evolved from their literal meaning.

Because expressions of catharsis have no referential meaning, any word may serve the cathartic function. Probably each person has some favorite expressions for releasing anger. If you were to prepare a list of cathartic expressions, ranking them according to the degree of tension to be released, you might find it an easy task, too, which indicates that there are personal favorites for a hierarchy of catharsis. The meaning of any of these expressions is to be found in what they do for us, not in a dictionary or in what they do for anybody else. Through repetition we give our select swear words added significance, so that with each new experience and repeated expression we may recall the release of tension from past experiences.

If you have studied another language, you may have learned the kinds of swear words that are most common in that language. In the literal translation they may not seem to "do much for you." Obviously, they cannot, for they have not yet come to be associated with the experiences that give them meaning. This same observation might be made for all words, but the language of catharsis, associated with the strongest of emotions, is the most extreme example of the general principle.

Magic[4]

The belief in the magic power of words exists in all cultures and takes the form of superstitions, instrumental curses, aspects of most religions, and minor forms of wishful thinking. At the root of the attitude of magic is the assumption that words are part of the thing to which they refer and, often, that words precede the "thing" (such as expressed in the Bible, "In the beginning was the Word"). Another quality of the magic attitude of words is that words "stand for things" in the sense that a friend "stands for" a bride or groom in a marriage by proxy. With this belief it follows that one can alter a thing by altering its word. If I write your name on a piece of paper and burn it, you, too, will burn, or at least suffer pain. Words, in the magical interpretation, must be treated with the same care as one would treat what the words stand for.

A common example of the belief in word-magic is the hesitancy to speak of possible dangers. If, on an airplane, you remark about the possibility of crashing, fellow passengers may turn on you as if your utterance of the possibility might just cause that to happen. In some cases, of course, it may be simply that others do not wish to think of unpleasant things; but the manner and intensity of the reply often indicates a very real fear of the words. If the belief in a magic function of communication seems immature (that is, not at all what *you* would think or do), ask yourself whether in a plane, you ever avoided such "thoughts" or whether you ever thought "we will not crash, we will not crash." For better or for worse, the belief that thinking or saying words will have some effect on what the words stand for is an example of the magic function of communication.

In many religions the magic function of language is still present. One would expect this of any institution that is centuries old and seeks to conserve the language and ritual of the past. The distinction between transubstantiation and consubstantiation of the Roman Catholic and Protestant sects is, in part, the difference in attitude toward the magic function of language. Do the bread and wine *become* the body and blood of Christ, or do they merely symbolize the body and blood? There are other examples in religions. The Anglican and Roman Catholic faiths retain rituals for the exorcising of spirits from a haunted house. One may wish to make a distinction between these examples and examples of words that call for the intercession of a divine spirit (such as prayers of petition) where the effect is produced not by the utterance of the words but by the action upon the words by another being. The difference is the difference between Ali Baba saying "Open Sesame!" (and having the cave door open because of the magic in the words) and having the words heard by a god who then opens the door. In the latter case we have an example of instrumental communication.[5]

Symbols associated with persons have long been recognized for their magical associations. Personal names have been regarded as "part of the person," so that what is done to the name results in affecting the person. (Elements of this attitude are still very common today, as when parents give their child the name of somebody important to them so that the child will be like his namesake.) The magical attitude toward personal names requires that these names not be taken in vain or, in some cases, not even uttered.

Here the name is never a mere symbol, but is part of the personal property of its bearer; property which is exclusively and jealously reserved to him. . . . Georg von der Gabelentz, in his book on the science of language, mentions the edict of a Chinese emperor of the third century B.C. whereby a pronoun in the first person, that had been legitimately in popular use, was henceforth reserved to him alone. . . . It is said of the Eskimos that for them man consists of three elements—body, soul, and name. And in Egypt, too, we find a similar conception, for there the physical body of man was thought to be accompanied, on the one hand by his Ka, or double, and on the other, by his name, as a sort of spiritual double. . . . Under Roman law a slave had no legal name, because he could not function as a legal person.[6]

Cassirer points out, too, that this attitude toward personal names was held by the early Christians, and hence today Christians still say "In Jesus' name" instead of "In Christ."

The belief in the magic function of language is based on assumptions that are quite opposed to the discipline of semantics, which regards words as conventional and convenient and without necessary associations with persons or objects in themselves. There is a sense, however, in which words do have "power." Words have the "power" to limit our thought, for example, though this is a different sense of the word "power." With rumor, with labels that evoke signal reactions, and with labels we try to live up to, we see some effects of the "power" of words. Such powers, however, are not magical, for they are not to be found *in* the words. Rather, the powers are social, and thus they are effective only to the degree that we accept our language without evaluation and respond to words without evaluation. When we understand and evaluate our language habits this social magic spell of words is broken.

Ritual

The scene is a Senate Subcommittee hearingroom on October 1, 1963. A sixty-year-old convicted murderer, Joseph M. Valachi, calmly reports to the investigators some of the history and methods of the crime organization known as Cosa Nostra. According to the press reports, the witness appeared comfortable throughout his testimony until he described his induction into the organization. Emanuel Perlmutter[7] of the *New York Times* reports:

> Valachi said he had been taken into a large room, where 30 or 35 men were sitting at a long table.
> "There was a gun and a knife on the table," Valachi testified. "I sat at the edge. They sat me down next to Maranzaro. I repeated some words in Sicilian after him." . . .
> "You live by the gun and knife, and die by the gun and knife." . . .
> The witness said Maranzaro had then given him a piece of paper that was set afire in his hand.
> "I repeated in Sicilian, 'This is the way I burn if I betray the organization.' " . . .
> Valachi said the men at the table then "threw out a number," with each man holding up any number of fingers from one to five. The total was taken. Starting with Maranzaro, the sum was then counted off around the table. The man on whom the final number fell was designated as Valachi's "godfather" in the family. Valachi said the lot had fallen to Bonanno.
> The witness said that he had then had his finger pricked by a needle held by Bonanno to show he was united to Bonanno by blood. Afterward,

Valachi continued, all those present joined hands in a bond to the organization.

Valachi said he was given two rules in Cosa Nostra that night—one concerning allegiance to it and another a promise not to possess another member's wife, sister or daughter.

For the first time, the witness grew grim. "This is the worst thing I can do, to tell about the ceremony," he said. "This is my doom, telling it to you and the press."

If the ceremony Valachi described seems strange to us, stranger still is the fear of his "doom" caused by revealing that secret. For a tough-minded criminal who reported that for him "killing was like breathing," who gave evidence about the methods and men of the Cosa Nostra, why should the most fearful disclosure be his report of some remote and grisly rite performed years ago? The answer to that question is part of the answer to why some rituals affect almost all of us.

Few organizations or institutions have rituals quite like the Cosa Nostra. The language of the rituals of secret organizations, social fraternities, lodges, and some religious or political organizations is kept secret, known only to their members. But the language of other rituals—patriotic, religious, academic, and so on—is not kept private. Nevertheless, an oath of allegiance or a communal prayer can affect the nervous system as no statement of fact or judgment can.

Ritual is sometimes described as the behavioral part of a mythology. The mythology may be for almost any purpose, but consistently it emphasizes a sense of community among its members and a sense of permanence. To participate in a ritual is to participate in a community, often one that claims a tradition of centuries. The sense of timelessness is quite important. When the anthropologist asks the primitive why he performs a certain ritual, the answer might be, "because our ancestors have always done this." If in the modern-day United States our sense of tradition is a short one, we may find the same comfort in rituals realizing that we as individuals have always said the pledge or sung the hymn.

Comparatively speaking, the United States has never been overly enthusiastic about most rituals; many of our most important cultural values conflict with the values of ritual. Ritual celebrates permanence, while the U.S. values have stressed change; rituals celebrate the community while Americans extoll individualism and "going it alone." Ritual is rooted in the past; Americans are more concerned with the future. Nevertheless there has been a rise in the ritual function of communication for a least a sizable portion of the American public, particularly among the younger members. Indeed, part of what has come to be celebrated in some rituals might be considered as "youth," and yet another part of the ritual function has been to celebrate a youthful community as distinct from "the older generation," "the establishment," "the straight people," or whatever the ousiders happened to be called. In dress and hair styles, certainly in language and in music, in rallying figures (most notably among rock musicians), a kind of community was established. The "coming together" in marches, street protests, rock festivals like Woodstock, at religious revivals ("the Jesus freaks") was most remarkable. Apart from the apparent content of these events, which appears to be quite diverse, there is a common element which might best be described in terms of ritual satisfaction.

There appears to be little that is instrumental in the performance of a ritual, with some notable exceptions. Sociologist Robert Merton has noted that activities originally conceived as instrumental often become transmuted into ends in themselves. What was originally obtained through certain words or acts is no longer needed or desired. If at one time meat had to be prepared in a certain way to avoid contamination, meat may still be prepared in such a way because "that's the way our ancestors have always done it." If certain prayers were recited with the hope of rewards, the same prayers may be repeated even though a congregation no longer expects those rewards. In many, perhaps most, cases, a new mythology will develop to explain certain words and actions of a ritual. It is not clear whether rituals continue to exist by virtue of constant repetition or whether the participants in a ritual feel that some ends are being served.

Three characteristics of most rituals are most important: the rituals must be performed with others (immediately or symbolically present); they must be performed on some occasion; and they must be performed with special care to details.

This last characteristic makes ritual somewhat different from other forms of communication. Many children have difficulty with the high-level abstractions and archaic language often present in ritual. The usual vocabulary of children contains few high-level abstractions. But a child will learn to imitate or approximate the sounds of the rituals in which he finds himself participating. Frequently these words become translated in his own vocabulary without conflict. My niece and nephew, when very young, sang their favorite Christmas carol in church. The boy concluded "Silent Night" with the words "Sleep in heavenly beans." "No," his sister corrected, "not beans, peas."

Most of us have associations with aspects of some rituals from our earliest memories. Perhaps you have had the sudden awareness of what some words you have been saying all your life were really supposed to be. It can be both a startling and amusing realization. But it is one that characterizes a form of communication in which repetition of certain words over an expanse of time is most important.

For some persons, part of the appeal of ritual may be the pleasure of solemnly repeating words that seem to have no referent; this may evoke a mood of mystery for such persons. Other persons may find a deep satisfaction in discovering the meaning of what they have been saying for years. Such attitudes, if they exist, would seem to be unhealthy, not only as regards an understanding of the purpose of language but also for the significance of the ritual itself.

There are other characteristics of ritual that make it distinct from other functions of language in communication. One of these is the sublimation function of ritual. Through ritual, a person may symbolically take part in an event that would exclude his actual participation. During wartime, rituals tend to become more common and more significant. The displaying of the flag, the reciting of the pledge of allegiance, even the rationing of food and gasoline are ways of symbolically participating in the war effort. Or, to take a happier example, during a football game the fans who wish to help their team may better do so by cheering than by assisting on the field. It is common, for example, that at the kick-off the fans will go "ssssssspooooom!" as if their noise will help to carry the ball farther down field.

Some rituals last longer than their mythologies. At a time when some persons begin to question religious beliefs, they may find it relatively easier to "lose the faith" than to lose the habit of prayer or church attendance on certain holy days. A sense of compulsiveness frequently attends ritual, and a sense of guilt may enter when ritual has gone. As a nation becomes what is called a "nontraditional society" the rituals that are a part of the tradition die. This finds expression as "alienation," the subject of many books, dramas, and films of recent years. It may also explain, in part, the current attraction for many philosophies of the "absurd." If a society's stability has been largely dependent on ritual and the rituals fall, it is an easy out to label the world as "absurd."

A final point should be made and emphasized. That is that what was intended for some purpose other than ritual can take on a ritual function. This may be a healthy addition to some other instrumental purpose, or it may be unhealthy if it substitutes for that other purpose. An example of the former might be the lasting effect of the Civil Rights March on Washington of 1963. No legislation was passed as a direct result of the march, but there was produced an important sense of community among white and Black that had not been exhibited so dramatically before.

Conventions of many kinds, political, social, and academic, many times serve more of a ritual function than the function of exchanging information or achieving some instrumental goal. To see the participants cheer or clap as the speaker speaks the holy jargon and drops the right names at the right time is amusing and a little sad at the same time. What is called a report may better serve as an incantation. No group can maintain itself without strong cohesiveness, it is true. But if the main result of the group's effort is only cohesiveness, then surely we have the origins of a new ritual.

On Saying What You Mean, and Meaning What You Say

Semanticists are sometimes thought to desire complete honesty of expression, directness, and "No beating around the bush." An understanding of the many purposes of communication should dispel that view. We use language for too many purposes and find ourselves forced to make some comment in too many difficult situations to hold to such a goal. Simple friendship, not to mention diplomacy and tact, prohibits us from always saying what we are thinking.

Suppose, for example, some friends are in a drama. You attend the opening-night performance, which is, as accurately as you can judge it, a real turkey. Then, as you leave the theater you encounter your friends and the director. Do you say what you are thinking and maybe hurt a friendship? Do you betray your critical integrity? No. Assuming that you cannot avoid comment, you equivocate, you speak in ambiguities. The popular expressions for this moment of untruth are many: (to the director): "Well, you've done it again!"; (to the actors): "You should have been in the audience!"; (to the elderly bystander who may be the dean, the director's father, or the playwright): "It was an unforgettable evening!"

If you feel that the potential ridicule of these expressions is too strong, you may equivocate further with the always safe "Congratulations!"

One may protest that these comments, however deft, are still lies and should not be excused. I think, however, that to so regard them is to confuse standards of different functions of communication. Affective communication directed to the emotional responses of the listener does not require the accuracy, even of judgments, that the transmission of specific information does. The purpose is often friendship, not a critical evaluation. Often it is much more important to tell a person that you like his tie, coat, smile, voice, and so on, than to be bound by some standards of judgment which would severely limit your affective communications. A kind or friendly remark often does more for human understanding than a diplomatic silence or a hundred "honest" judgments.

To be aware of the many functions of communication is to be alive and sensitive to the most basic of human needs. As our needs for bodily health and comfort are met, we become more aware of (and create new) needs for symbolic health and comfort. To be loved or respected, to help others, to feel trust —the list could be elaborated greatly—becomes extremely important. Each communication situation both reveals our frailty and offers some promise for support.

NOTES

1. PAUL WATZLAWICK, et al., *The Pragmatics of Human Communication* (New York: W. W. Norton, 1967), Ch. 2.
2. LEO ROSTEN, *The Joys of Yiddish* (London: Penguin Books, 1968).
3. CYNTHIA NELSON, "Saints and Sinners: Parallels in the Sex-Role Differentiation in the Family of Saints and in the Family of Man in a Mexican Peasant Village" (mimeographed, N.D.).
4. SUSANNE LANGER includes the magic function of language as part of "ritual." She writes, "Magic . . . is not a method, but a language; it is part and parcel of that greater phenomenon, ritual, which is the language of religion." (*Philosophy in a New Key* [Cambridge: Harvard University Press, 1942], p. 39.) Although this may have a historical basis, and although magic and ritual are also clearly related today, I find it useful to make a distinction between the two.
5. Some students are unimpressed by the distinction.

6. ERNST CASSIRER, *Language and Myth* (New York: Dover Publications, N.D.), pp. 50–51.
7. EMANUEL PERLMUTTER, "Valachi Names 5 as Crime Chiefs in New York Area," *New York Times,* October 2, 1963, p. 28.

PART TWO
Verbal Messages
Experiences and Discussions

1. What are some examples of nonhuman language? How do such languages differ from human language in terms of the sixteen characteristics discussed by DeVito? Which characteristics are most similar in both human and nonhuman languages? Which are most dissimilar?
2. Create a twenty-word language that is new and use it to communicate with someone. Does your language have characteristics that are not explained by the sixteen universals discussed by DeVito? For example, should rapid fading of speech sounds be perceived as a limiting feature of human language? Is your new language specialized? Arbitrary? Reflexive? Learnable? Can you apply the feature of displacement to your language? Can you lie in your language?
3. Observe the linguistic behavior of a young child. Record the age of the child in years and months and the child's utterances.
4. Review the eight functions of communication discussed by Condon in respect to your daily communicative experiences. Which functions would you choose as most important or necessary for effective interpersonal relationships? Which functions do you use the most? Which the least?
5. In his discussion on "saying what you mean and meaning what you say," Condon distinguishes between an individual's accuracy in evaluating others and the concern for keeping friendships and not offending others. Describe a situation in which you are torn between being accurate and not offending someone you like. Do you feel comfortable in such situations? How do you respond? How would Condon resolve this conflict?
6. Robinson, in his discussion of conformity to norms, writes that "breaking conventions is often an illuminating way of testing their force." Select a norm of speaking for a specific situation (e.g., a job interview, a class discussion, a conversation with another person), and break the expected verbal behavior norm. What types of reactions do you notice? What do these reactions indicate about the power and force of that speaking norm?

7. Observe a conversation between two people. Record the language norms that occur as the conversational roles switch and at the close of the conversation. Do these norms differ according to the topic of conversation? According to the relationship of the two people? According to the age and sex of the two people? If so, in what ways?

For Further Reading

CAIRNS, HELEN S., and CHARLES E. CAIRNS. *Psycholinguistics: A Cognitive View of Language.* New York: Holt, 1976.

The authors provide an introductory yet thorough analysis of the cognitive view of language, which is the most widely accepted explanation of language today. The book is divided into two parts. The first section, dealing with linguistic competence, provides information on the basics of transformational grammar and analyzes the syntactic, semantic, and phonological components of human communication. The second section, dealing with linguistic performance, focuses on specific areas of study in psycholinguistics, including research on speech perception, semantic processing, and language acquisition.

CONDON, JOHN C., JR. *Semantics and Communication.* 2nd ed. New York: Macmillan, 1975.

In this second edition, Condon stresses changes in language use from 1965 to 1975, along with the social, cultural, and political changes of these years. Other topics include language and time, language and culture, and language in varying contexts.

DALE, PHILLIP S. *Language Development: Structure and Function.* Hinsdale, Ill.: Dryden, 1972.

Addressed to students who are studying the development of language, this book provides information on the structure of language and theories of language acquisition. Also included are selected readings (edited) to illustrate the issues in each chapter. Dale includes chapters on the social aspects of language: dialects, Black English, and educational applications. Overall, this is a good introduction to the study of language.

DEVITO, JOSEPH A. *Language: Concepts and Processes.* Englewood Cliffs, N.J.: Prentice-Hall, 1973.

This collection of twenty-six articles covers language forms and functions ("The Language of Responsibility," "The Sounds of Silence"), language and thought ("The Language of Prejudice"), and language and communication ("The Semantics of the Generation Gap"). Highly recommended for articles relevant to contemporary social issues.

DIVESTA, FRANCIS J. *Language, Learning and Cognitive Processes.* Monterey, Calif.: Wadsworth, 1974.

In this brief and simple text, DiVesta discusses language and a vari-

ety of topics related to educational theories and practices. Areas
discussed include the role of language in cognitive development,
concept learning, and language in social contexts.

WOOD, BARBARA S. *Children and Communication: Verbal and Nonverbal
Language Development.* Englewood Cliffs, N.J.: Prentice-Hall, 1976.
In this much needed text, Wood deals with the verbal and nonverbal
processes of development and how intrapersonal and interpersonal
forces facilitate these processes. Of particular interest is the focus on
communication situations and strategies of the child. A final section
of the text discusses instructional activities that aim to "increase the
repertoire of communication strategies that can be used by children
in dealing with critical communication situations."

PART THREE

Nonverbal Messages: The Other Channels

"I'll tell you one thing that might help you in the case," he continued, turning to the two detectives, "There has been murder done, and the murderer was a man. He was more than six feet high, was in the prime of life, had small feet for his height, wore coarse, square-toed boots and smoked a Trichinopoly cigar. He came here with his victim in a four-wheeled cab, which was drawn by a horse with three old shoes and one new one on his off foreleg. In all probability, the murderer had a florid face, and the fingernails of his right hand were remarkably long. These are only a few indications, but they may assist you."

A STUDY IN SCARLET

So saying, Sherlock Holmes astounded the detectives of Scotland Yard by demonstrating his uncanny ability to receive and interpret nonverbal communication.

Just as the solution to a crime often hinges upon the interpretation of subtle clues, so the communication process may rely upon the less formal and more ambiguous channel of nonverbal communication. At times, nonverbal messages may serve to reinforce verbal meanings. At other times, however, verbal and nonverbal signals are in conflict. Our folklore suggests that nonverbal clues may be more accurate, too: we look into the eyes of a suspect to determine whether or not he/she is lying.

Nonverbal communication has been a hotly pursued area of research in recent years, and the results have generally been both valuable and frustrating. So many factors overlap and interact that the tangled web, becoming increasingly more visible, is still twisted and confused. Despite these severe methodological handicaps, however, researchers in nonverbal communication have made great progress in tracking their prey. They have begun now to define, measure, and study a multitude of kinds of nonverbal communication.

The nonverbal channel is, of course, a major communication system. As such, it is subject to the laws and postulates suggested earlier by Mortensen and Gibb.

But what of the conflicting evidence, of the situation in which the verbal and nonverbal channels provide contradictory messages? In a classic article, Albert Mehrabian deals with this double bind and argues that the detective ought to look to the situation to resolve such problems.

Following that advice, Mark Knapp closes in upon the classroom situation, carefully pursuing all leads to discover the effect of proxemics, attire, body movement, eye contact, and vocality upon the processes of learning and interaction. Knapp detects a strong nonverbal influence here: pervasive, but not sinister.

As an example of kinds of cases in this field, Ross Buck stalks the elusive role of emotion in communication. After painstaking investigation, Buck unravels the characteristics of individuals able to accurately determine the emotion of a sender and describes the personality traits of these powerful receivers of nonverbal messages.

Together, these selections provide a glimpse at the range of nonverbal factors and variables. The importance of nonverbal elements in specific situations will further underscore the significance of nonverbal communication in the process of information exchange.

OBJECTIVES

After carefully reading these four articles you should be able to define the following key terms:

timing	(Mehrabian)
immediacy	
distance	
facial expression	
posture	
double bind	
space	(Knapp)
attire	
body movement	
eye contact	
voice	
kinesics	(Buck)
proxemics	
paralanguage	

And:

1. Compare verbal and nonverbal communication, relating both to Mortensen's communication postulates (Rosenfeld and Civikly).

2. Describe four factors of interaction that might provide nonverbal cues about the situation or speakers (Mehrabian).
3. Discuss the link between schizophrenia and nonverbal communication. Consider the double-bind theory and its implications for nonschizophrenic persons (Mehrabian).
4. Analyze nonverbal communication in a classroom setting, using the criteria suggested by Knapp (Knapp).
5. Based upon Knapp's discussion, design an ideal "learning box" for a college classroom (Knapp).
6. Describe the Landis experiment on nonverbal communication. Evaluate the experimental methodology employed (Buck).

Eight

Communication without Words

Albert Mehrabian

Suppose you are sitting in my office listening to me describe some research I have done on communication. I tell you that feelings are communicated less by the words a person uses than by certain nonverbal means—that, for example, the verbal part of a spoken message has considerably less effect on whether a listener feels liked or disliked than a speaker's facial expression or tone of voice.

So far so good. But suppose I add, "In fact, we've worked out a formula that shows exactly how much each of these components contributes to the effect of the message as a whole. It goes like this: Total Impact = .07 verbal + .38 vocal + .55 facial."

What would you say to *that?* Perhaps you would smile good-naturedly and say, with some feeling, "Baloney!" Or perhaps you would frown and remark acidly, "Isn't science grand." My own response to the first answer would probably be to smile back: the facial part of your message, at least, was positive (55 per cent of the total). The second answer might make me uncomfortable: only the verbal part was positive (seven per cent).

The point here is not only that my reactions would lend credence to the formula but that most listeners would have mixed feelings about my statement. People like to see science march on, but they tend to resent its intrusion into an "art" like the communication of feelings, just as they find analytical and quantitative approaches to the study of personality cold, mechanistic and unacceptable.

The psychologist himself is sometimes plagued by the feeling that he is trying to put a rainbow into a bottle. Fascinated by a complicated and emotionally rich human situation, he begins to study it, only to find in the course of his research that he has destroyed part of the mystique that originally intrigued and involved him. But despite a certain nostalgia for earlier, more intuitive approaches, one must acknowledge that concrete experimental data have added a great deal to our understanding of how feelings are communicated. In fact, as I hope to show, analytical and intuitive findings do not so much conflict as complement each other.

It is indeed difficult to know what another person really feels. He says one thing and does another; he seems to mean something but we have an uneasy feeling it isn't true. The early psychoanalysts, facing this problem of inconsistencies and ambiguities in a person's communications, attempted to resolve it through the concepts of the conscious and the unconscious. They assumed that contradictory messages meant a conflict between superficial, deceitful, or erroneous feelings on the one hand and true attitudes and feelings on the other. Their role, then, was to help the client separate the wheat from the chaff.

The question was, how could this be done? Some analysts insisted that inferring the client's unconscious wishes was a completely intuitive process. Others thought that some nonverbal behavior, such as posture, position and movement, could be used in a more objective way to discover the client's feelings. A favorite technique of Frieda Fromm-Reichmann, for example, was to imitate a client's posture herself in order to obtain some feeling for what he was experiencing.

Thus began the gradual shift away from the idea that communication is primarily verbal, and that the verbal message includes distortions or ambiguities due to unobservable motives that only experts can discover.

Language, though, can be used to communicate almost anything. By comparison, nonverbal behavior is very limited in range. Usually, it is used to communicate feelings, likings and preferences, and it customarily reinforces or contradicts the feelings that are communicated verbally. Less often, it adds a new dimension of sorts to a verbal message, as when a salesman describes his product to a client and simultaneously conveys, nonverbally, the impression that he likes the client.

A great many forms of nonverbal behavior can communicate feelings: touching, facial expression, tone of voice, spatial distance from the addressee, relaxation of posture, rate of speech, number of errors in speech. Some of these are generally recognized as informative. Untrained adults and children easily infer that they are liked or disliked from certain facial expressions, from whether (and how) someone touches them, and from a speaker's tone of voice. Other behavior, such as posture, has a more subtle effect. A listener may sense how someone feels about him from the way the person sits while talking to him, but he may have trouble identifying precisely what his impression comes from.

Correct intuitive judgments of the feelings or attitudes of others are especially difficult when different degrees of feeling, or contradictory kinds of feeling, are expressed simultaneously through different forms of behavior. As I have pointed out, there is a distinction between verbal and vocal information (vocal information being what is lost when speech is written down—intonation, tone, stress, length and frequency of pauses, and so on), and the two kinds of information do not always communicate the same feeling. This distinction, which has been recognized for some time, has shed new light on certain types of communication. Sarcasm, for example, can be defined as a message in which the information transmitted vocally contradicts the information transmitted verbally. Usually the verbal information is positive and the vocal is negative, as in "Isn't science grand."

Through the use of an electronic filter, it is possible to measure the degree of liking communicated vocally. What the filter does is eliminate the higher frequencies of recorded speech, so that words are unintelligible but most vocal qualities remain. (For women's speech, we eliminate frequencies higher than about 200 cycles per second; for men, frequencies over about 100 cycles per second.) When people are asked to judge the degree of liking conveyed by the filtered speech, they perform the task rather easily and with a significant amount of agreement.

This method allows us to find out, in a given message, just how inconsistent the information communicated in words and the information communicated vocally really are. We ask one group to judge the amount of liking conveyed by a transcription of what was said, the verbal part of the message. A second group judges the vocal component, and a third group judges the impact of the complete recorded message. In one study of this sort we found that, when the verbal and vocal components of a message agree (both positive or both negative), the message as a whole is judged a little more positive or a little more negative than either component by itself. But when vocal information contradicts verbal, vocal wins out. If someone calls you "honey" in a nasty tone of voice, you are likely to feel disliked; it is also possible to say "I hate you" in a way that conveys exactly the opposite feeling.

Besides the verbal and vocal characteristics of speech, there are other, more subtle, signals of meaning in a spoken message. For example, everyone makes mistakes when he talks—unnecessary repetitions, stutterings, the omission of parts of words, incomplete sentences, "ums" and "ahs." In a number of studies of speech errors, George Mahl of Yale University has found that errors become more frequent as the speaker's discomfort or anxiety increases. It might be interesting to apply this index in an attempt to detect deceit (though on some occasions it might be risky: confidence men are notoriously smooth talkers).

Timing is also highly informative. How long does a speaker allow silent periods to last, and how long does he wait before he answers his partner? How long do his utterances tend to be? How often does he interrupt his partner, or wait an inappropriately long time before speaking? Joseph Matarazzo and his colleagues at the University of Oregon have found that each of these speech habits is stable from person to person, and each tells something about the speaker's personality and about his feelings toward and status in relation to his partner.

Utterance duration, for example, is a very stable quality in a person's speech; about 30 seconds long on the average. But when someone talks to a partner whose status is higher than his own, the more the high-status person nods his head the longer the speaker's utterances become. If the high-status person changes his own customary speech pattern toward longer or shorter utterances, the lower-status person will change his own speech in the same direction. If the high-status person often interrupts the speaker, or creates long silences, the speaker is likely to become quite uncomfortable. These are things that can be observed outside the laboratory as well as under experimental conditions. If you have an employee who makes you uneasy and seems not to respect you, watch him the next time you talk to him—perhaps he is failing to follow the customary low-status pattern.

Immediacy or directness is another good source of information about feelings. We use more distant forms of communication when the act of communicating is undesirable or uncomfortable. For example, some people would rather transmit discontent with an employee's work through a third party than do it themselves, and some find it easier to communicate negative feelings in writing than by telephone or face to face.

Distance can show a negative attitude toward the message itself, as well as toward the act of delivering it. Certain forms of speech are more distant than others, and they show fewer positive feelings for the subject referred to. A speaker might say "Those people need help," which is more distant than "These people need help," which is in turn even more distant than "These people need our help." Or he might say "Sam and I have been having dinner," which has less immediacy then "Sam and I are having dinner."

Facial expression, touching, gestures, self-manipulation (such as scratching), changes in body position, and head movements—all these express a person's positive and negative attitudes, both at the moment and in general, and many reflect status relationships as well. Movements of the limbs and head, for example, not only indicate one's attitude toward a specific set of circumstances but relate to how dominant, and how anxious, one generally tends to be in social situations. Gross changes in body position, such as shifting in the chair, may show negative feelings toward the person one is talking to. They may also be cues: "It's your turn to talk," or "I'm about to get out of here, so finish what you're saying."

Posture is used to indicate both liking and status. The more a person leans toward his addressee, the more positively he feels about him. Relaxation of posture is a good indicator of both attitude and status, and one that we have been able to measure quite precisely. Three categories have been established for relaxation in a seated position: Least relaxation is indicated by muscular tension in the hands and rigidity of posture; moderate relaxation is indicated by a forward lean of about 20 degrees and a sideways lean of less than 10 degrees, a curved back, and for women, an open arm position; and extreme relaxation is indicated by a reclining angle greater than 20 degrees and a sideways lean greater than 10 degrees.

Our findings suggest that a speaker relaxes either very little or a great deal when he dislikes the person he is talking to, and to a moderate degree when he likes his companion. It seems that extreme tension occurs with threatening addressees, and extreme relaxation with nonthreatening, disliked addressees. In particular, men tend to become tense when talking to other men whom they dislike; on the other hand, women talking to men *or* women and men talking to women show dislike through extreme relaxation. As for status, people relax most with a low-status addressee, second-most with a peer, and least with someone of higher status than their own. Body orientation also shows status: in both sexes, it is least direct toward women with low status and most direct toward disliked men of high status. In part, body orientation seems to be determined by whether one regards one's partner as threatening.

The more you like a person, the more time you are likely to spend looking into his eyes as you talk to him. Standing close to your partner and facing him directly (which makes eyes contact easier) also indicate positive feelings. And you are likely to stand or sit closer to your peers than you do to addressees whose status is either lower or higher than yours.

What I have said so far has been based on research studies performed, for the most part, with college students from the middle and upper-middle classes. One interesting question about communication, however, concerns young children from lower socioeconomic levels. Are these children, as some have suggested, more responsive to implicit channels of communication than middle- and upper-class children are?

Morton Wiener and his colleagues at Clark University had a group of middle- and lower-class children play learning games in which the reward for learning was praise. The child's responsiveness to the verbal and vocal parts of the praise-reward was measured by how much he learned. Praise came in two forms: the objective words "right" and "correct," and the more affective or evaluative words, "good" and "fine." All four words were spoken sometimes in a positive tone of voice and sometimes neutrally.

Positive intonation proved to have a dramatic effect on the learning rate of the lower-class group. They learned much faster when the vocal part of the message was positive than when it was neutral. Positive intonation affected the middle-class group as well, but not nearly as much.

If children of lower socioeconomic groups are more responsive to facial expression, posture and touch as well as to vocal communication, that fact could have interesting applications to elementary education. For example, teachers could be explicitly trained to be aware of, and to use, the forms of praise (nonverbal or verbal) that would be likely to have the greatest effect on their particular students.

Another application of experimental data on communication is to the interpretation and treatment of schizophrenia. The literature on schizophrenia has for some time emphasized that parents of schizophrenic children give off contradictory signals simultaneously. Perhaps the parent tells the child in words that he loves him, but his posture conveys a negative attitude. According to the "double-bind" theory of schizophrenia, the child who perceives simultaneous contradictory feelings in his parent does not know how to react: should he respond to the positive part of the message, or to the negative? If he is frequently placed in this paralyzing situation, he may learn to respond with contradictory communications of his own. The boy who sends a birthday card to his mother and signs it "Napoleon" says that he likes his mother and yet denies that he is the one who likes her.

In an attempt to determine whether parents of disturbed children really do emit more inconsistent messages about their feelings than other parents do, my colleagues and I have compared what these parents communicate verbally and vocally with what they show through posture. We interviewed parents of moderately and quite severely disturbed children, in the presence of the child, about the child's problem. The interview was video-recorded without the parents' knowledge, so that we could analyze their behavior later on. Our measurements supplied both the amount of inconsistency between the parents' verbal-vocal and postural communications, and the total amount of liking that the parents communicated.

According to the double-bind theory, the parents of the more disturbed children should have behaved more inconsistently than the parents of the less disturbed children. This was not confirmed: there was no significant difference between the two groups. However, the *total amount* of positive feeling communicated by parents of the more disturbed children was less than that communicated by the other group.

This suggests that (1) negative communications toward disturbed children. occur because the child is a problem and therefore elicits them, or (2) the negative attitude precedes the child's disturbance. It may also be that both factors operate together, in a vicious circle.

If so, one way to break the cycle is for the therapist to create situations in which the parent can have better feelings toward the child. A more positive attitude from the parent may make the child more responsive to his directives, and the spiral may begin to move up instead of down. In our own work with disturbed children, this kind of procedure has been used to good effect.

If one puts one's mind to it, one can think of a great many other applications for the findings I have described, though not all of them concern serious problems. Politicians, for example, are careful to maintain eye contact with the television camera when they speak, but they are not always careful about how they sit when they debate another candidate of, presumably, equal status.

Public relations men might find a use for some of the subtler signals of feeling. So might Don Juans. And so might ordinary people, who could try watching other people's signals and changing their own, for fun at a party or in a spirit of experimentation at home. I trust that does not strike you as a cold, manipulative suggestion, indicating dislike for the human race. I assure you that, if you had more than a transcription of words to judge from (seven per cent of total message), it would not.

Nine

The Role of Nonverbal Communication in the Classroom

Mark L. Knapp

The teaching-learning process is essentially a communication event. Teachers and students alike are concerned with obtaining a desired response and the measure of their success is whether they obtain it. With this premise as a basis, many researchers have investigated communication behavior in classroom settings. In addition, many teacher training programs have stressed the importance of communication principles as integral to effective teaching. However, until recently such endeavors have been almost exclusively concerned with the spoken and written word.

Another means of communication, information and influence—one that has been generally neglected by researchers—is nonverbal communication. Of course nonverbal behavior is only a part of the total process of communication, but in order to understand the total process we must understand all the operating systems. It is the intent of this article to expose readers to the scope of the subject by highlighting some research on nonverbal communication conducted in educational settings.

Research Highlights

Obviously, one of the teacher's main goals is to increase the intellectual sophistication of the student. Can nonverbal cues assist in such a process? According to a study conducted by Rosenthal and Jacobson[1] and reported in their book, *Pygmalion in the Classroom,* nonverbal cues may play a significant role. In this study elementary pupils were given IQ tests prior to entering school. Some of these students were labeled randomly (not according to scores) as high scorers on an "intellectual blooming test" which suggested they would show unusual intellectual development in the following year. Teachers were given this information. IQ tests given at the end of the school year showed a sharp rise in the scores of the randomly labeled "intellectual bloomers." Although this study did not isolate and examine specific influential nonverbal cues, we can assume that teacher expectations for these special students caused them to engage in a wide range of verbal and nonverbal behaviors which helped the child to learn. Facial expression, touch, gesture, vocal tone, posture, spatial positioning, and a host of other nonverbal variables used in conjunction with verbal cues seem to have been highly influential.

The Learning Box

Numerous experimental deviations from traditional classroom architecture and interior design are being tried, but for the most part America's classrooms remain rectangular in shape, with a row of wide windows along one side, seats arranged in rows perpendicular to the windows (and frequently permanently attached to the floor), and a desk or table facing rows of chairs. The learning environment is often characterized further by poor lighting or acoustics, temperature that is too hot or too cold, outside construction noises, banging radiators, electrical outlets that do not work, gloomy, dull, or distracting color schemes and unpleasant odors. Any of these features, if it interferes with obtaining a learning response, is a barrier to effective communication.

Although there are some data available which would suggest that "unattractive" environments negatively affect interpersonal responses, very little empirical research is available showing the relationship between various kinds of learning environments and student-teacher behavior. Sommer's study[2] of the effects of different classroom arrangements on student verbal output or participation is an exception and of particular relevance here. The most unpleasant of the six types of rooms studied by Sommer included a windowless room and a laboratory room—complete with Bunsen burners, bottles and gas valves. Subjects attempting student-teacher dialog in these rooms frequently tried to change rooms or hold classes outside. In seminar rooms (movable chairs arranged in a horseshoe) the range of participation was more limited than in other rooms, but the length of participation was higher. The presence of windows in the classroom did not seem to alter the amount of participation significantly. In seminar rooms, most participation came from those sitting directly opposite the instructor and the two chairs on either side of the instructor were generally avoided by students—even when all other chairs were filled. When students did occupy the chairs on either side of the instructor they usually were silent throughout the class period. In typical straight row classroom settings, it seemed students sitting within eye contact range of the instructor participated more; students sitting in the center sections of each row participated more; participation tended to decrease from front to back; and participation decreased as class size increased. We should be quick to note that such findings are often qualified by other variables—e.g., when interested students sit in locations other than those which provide maximum visual contact. Sommer concludes his observations on the classroom environment by saying:

> At the present time, teachers are hindered by their insensitivity to and fatalistic acceptance of the classroom environment. Teachers must be "turned on" to their environment lest their pupils develop this same sort of fatalism.[3]

Space and Learning

Closely related to these findings on architectural and environmental factors are the factors of space and territory relationships—studied frequently outside the classroom but frequently ignored as areas of research within the classroom. We know, for instance, that we often stake out certain areas and objects as "our" territory and react aggressively to perceived invasions of it. With the increase of overcrowding in classrooms the question of diminishing territorial limits and increasing territorial violations seems a natural subject for investigation.

Students and their teachers engage in a variety of one-to-one conversations in which spatial relationships may be revealing. We know, for instance, that conversational space varies depending on the cultural background, the relationship of the interactants, the topic being discussed, and the personal and attitudinal characteristics of the two parties. Leopold's work[4] demonstrates how the anticipated attitude toward the same general topic can influence conversational distance. Students entering a room were given comments indicating stress ("Your grade is poor and you have not done your best"), praise ("You are doing very well and Mr. Leopold wants to talk with you further"), or neutrality ("Mr. Leopold is interested in your feelings about the introductory course"). Students anticipating a negative attitude sat furthest from the experimenter and those given praise sat closest.

Attire and Appearance for Learning

Just as it is assumed that environment often structures interpersonal and learning responses, many teachers and administrators assume also that dress has a significant impact. Many school systems even have a formal "dress code." During the last ten years we have read about or experienced an abundance of instances in which students have been expelled for wearing armbands, miniskirts, slacks, hot pants, long hair, beards, mustaches, peace symbols, and a host of other garments, styles and artifacts. Although we know such attire will have an influence on interpersonal communication, its exact role in classroom behavior is unknown. Rules are based on the attitudes and beliefs of those making them—not on empirical research.

A more fruitful body of literature is available on the effects of one's general attractiveness. For instance, some research shows that mere physical attractiveness may be influential in creating a social contact situation—i.e., whether one is sought out. It may have some bearing on whether one is able to persuade or manipulate others, and it may be an important factor in the selection of dating and marriage partners. A direct investigation of the concept of attractiveness and its influence in classroom interaction was conducted by Singer.[5] His research gives some empirical validation to a phenomenon well known on an intuitive level to professors and students alike for some time—that some females may use physical attractiveness as a manipulative device to obtain higher grades from college professors. Pictures of 192 freshman girls were rated on an attractiveness scale by 40 faculty members; each picture was rated five times. When these ratings were compared with grade point averages and birth order, Singer concluded that there was a positive relationship between first born attractive girls and grade point averages. When he obtained observational data on the actual behavior of these girls and some paper and pencil self-report data, he found that attractive first born girls tend to sit in the front of the room, come up more frequently after class, and make appointments to see the instructor during office hours more often. This "exhibiting" behavior would then cause professors to be more likely to remember them and give them the benefit of the doubt on grades. Was the girls' behavior intentional or was it merely a matter of luck? Follow-up studies showed that such girls have more accurate information about their body measurements, are more accurate in stating the norms of the ideal female figure, and are more likely to distort their measurements toward the ideal norms. Singer interprets this data, together with scores on a test [designed to uncover] Machiavellianism, as supporting his hypothesis that there is manipulative intent.

Body Movements in the Classroom

Although body movement has been a major area of nonverbal communication research, its specific manifestations in American classrooms have been neglected. Some of the most relevant research for teachers has been done in the areas of "liking" behavior and status behavior. For instance, our body positions and movements seem to help us indicate liking and disliking for other communicators. Mehrabian[6] found that the arms akimbo position by standing communicators seems to be used with greater frequency when interacting with disliked persons than with liked. Both males and females felt that a person leaning backward from them had a more negative attitude than the same person leaning forward. Rosenfeld's experiment[7] helps us identify approval seekers. Smiles, head nodding, and a generally higher level of gestural activity characterized those trying to win the approval of others. According to Reece and Whitman[8] a "warm" person's nonverbal behavior was perceived as a shift in posture toward the other person, a smile, direct eye contact, and hands remaining still.

Status also seems to be associated with certain body movements and positions. In standing positions, shoulder orientation seems to be more direct when facing a high status addressee, regardless of the attitude toward him. Again, the arms akimbo position is more likely to be used when one is talking to a person seen as having a lower status than one's own. It is interesting to speculate on the many conscious and unconscious ways in which teachers exhibit status cues when talking to students.

Theoretically, a teacher can use the facial expressions and gestures of students as a barometer indicating whether lecture material is being understood. However, Jecker et al.[9] found that experienced teachers were little better than novices in judging whether children had understood on the basis of facial and gestural cues alone.

Reporting such research is difficult because the final interpretation needs to be considered in context. That is, while a given configuration of nonverbal cues may seem to convey a certain feeling, we must be aware that the same configuration may take on a completely different meaning if it occurs in a context in which such behaviors are neutralized, added to, or cancelled by other factors.

Looking and Learning

Another frequently researched area outside the specific context of the classroom is the role of eye contact in communication. While anecdotal evidence is plentiful for classroom application, empirical research has not been done so we must again deviate from our original intention to cover only studies of classroom behavior. Research on eye contact reveals several occasions when eye contact is likely to occur and when it is not. A brief review will help us understand some familiar classroom behaviors.

Eye contact occurs when we want to signal that the communication channel is open. Students who avoid eye contact of teachers when a question is asked may be saying: "I don't know the answer; I don't want to be called on; if my eyes meet the eyes of the instructor, I am almost obligated to interact because I am saying the channel is open." Thus, this student acts very busy taking notes, rearranging his books and papers, dropping a pencil, etc.

Eye contact tends to occur following the end of an utterance—particularly when we are seeking feedback on how the utterance was received. Although we usually look more while listening than when speaking, the presentation of cognitively difficult materials will magnify this phenomenon greatly. The picture of the professor staring out the window while trying to state a particularly difficult concept to his class is a familiar one.

The fact that we tend to look at those things which are rewarding to us helps to explain the differential looking behavior of students who are criticized versus those who are praised by their teachers. It may also explain why it is so difficult to obtain dynamic student-to-student discussions in classes with straight row seating. How long can you be rewarded for talking to the back of someone's head?

Eye contact may also act as a psychological manipulator of physical distance. In large classes where the physical distance between communicators is too far, eye contact may help to psychologically reduce this distance.

Eye contact of extended duration can also be used to indicate aggressiveness or create anxiety in others. On the other hand, competition, dislike, tension, or a recent deception may cause a decrease in eye contact. Eye avoidance in this case may act as an insulator against threats or discovery. In one experiment students induced to cheat tried to avoid eye contact when interviewed about it later.[10]

The Voice and Learning

Although the study of vocal cues has been mainly concerned with judgments of personality and emotions, perhaps the most pertinent body of literature for teachers concerns the influence of vocal cues on listener comprehension and attitude change.

Several studies indicate that moderately poor vocal behaviors (hoarseness, nasality, stuttering) do not interfere significantly with a listener's comprehension. This may have implications for teacher training programs based on the assumption that only teachers who speak a fluent standard American dialect will be "good" teachers. Other evidence tells us that if we use variety in volume, pitch, and rate we may increase our chances of achieving audience comprehension of our speeches or lectures. Nonfluencies do not seem to affect attitude, but listeners appear to make some decisions about a speaker's credibility solely on the basis of wordless samples—and credibility can have a profound effect on teaching effectiveness.

Obviously, our total reaction to the other person is colored by cues received from his vocal tones. Sometimes it is the major source of influence. Take, for example, the case of a student inquiring about his work in a particular course.

The teacher replies, "Oh, your work has been fine up to this point." But the vocal tones make it clear to the student that there is considerable doubt about the excellence of his work. Any researcher recording responses in classrooms for an interaction analysis must be very sensitive to the vocal tones because the words alone may not fully reflect the intended meaning.

One final note. Any attempt to analyze the nonverbal aspects of classroom situations must also be concerned with the verbal dimensions. They are not discrete categories; they work together. Nonverbal cues may reinforce, contradict, complement, substitute for, accent, or help to regulate the flow of verbal communication. A grossly distorted analysis of the total process of communication would result if one neglected either of the two systems.

NOTES

1. R. ROSENTHAL and L. JACOBSON, *Pygmalion in the Classrroom* (New York: Holt, Rinehart and Winston, 1968).
2. R. SOMMER, *Personal Space* (Englewood Cliffs, N.J.: Prentice Hall, 1969).
3. Ibid., p. 119.
4. W. E. LEOPOLD, "Psychological Distance in a Dyadic Interview," Unpublished Ph.D. dissertation, University of North Dakota, 1963.
5. J. E. SINGER, "The Use of Manipulative Strategies: Machiavellianism and Attractiveness," *Sociometry* 27 (1964): 128–51.
6. A. MEHRABIAN, "Significance of Posture and Position in the Communication of Attitude and Status Relationships," *Psychological Bulletin* 71 (1969): 359–72.
7. H. ROSENFELD, "Instrumental Affiliative Functions of Facial and Gestural Expressions," *Journal of Personality and Social Psychology* 4 (1966): 65–72.
8. M. REECE and R. WHITMAN, "Expressive Movements, Warmth, and Verbal Reinforcement," *Journal of Abnormal and Social Psychology* 64 (1962): 234–36.
9. J. JECKER; N. MACCOBY; M. BREITROSE; and E. ROSE, "Teacher Accuracy in Assessing Cognitive Visual Feedback from Students," *Journal of Applied Psychology* 48 (1964): 393–97.
10. R. EUXLINE; J. THIBAUT; C. B. HICKEY; and P. GUMPERT, "Visual Interaction in Relation to Machiavellianism and an Unethical Act," in *Studies in Machiavellianism* by P. Christie and F. Geis (New York: Academic Press, 1970).

Ten

Nonverbal Communication of Emotion

Ross Buck

It is not possible here to give a comprehensive review of the large and rapidly growing literature of human nonverbal behavior, but some attempt should be made to indicate its scope. We shall concentrate on studies of the nonverbal communication of emotion by means of facial expression in humans. It should be noted that the communicative and social-regulatory functions of a wide variety of other human nonverbal behaviors have been pointed out in recent years. Duncan (1969) has suggested that the three nonverbal modalities which have received the most attention include the following: *Kinesics* is the study of body movements such as facial expressions, gestures, eye movements, posture, and so forth. The great current interest in kinesics is traceable in large part to the pioneering studies of Birdwhistell (1970). *Proxemics* is the study of the social and personal use of space . . . (cf. Hall, 1959; 1966; Sommer, 1969). *Paralanguage* includes voice qualities, nonfluencies of speech, and non-language sounds like yawning and grunting.

Behaviors in all of these categories are believed to be involved in the smooth regulation of human social behavior, although they may or may not be concerned with emotion or affect. For example, Weiner, Devoe, Rubinow, and Geller (1972) have discussed the role of nonverbal behavior in the flow of verbal communication. As a part of their analysis they hypthesize about the function of the orientation of the palms of the hands of a person who is speaking:

> Palms up is equivalent to uncertainty or to "I think" or "I believe" or "It seems to me" in a verbal statement, and adds for the addressee the message that the issue need not be pursued since uncertainty is indicated. Palms down indicates an assertion with the speaker again communicating that the subject matter is not open to question—equivalent verbal statements are "clearly," "absolutely," without doubt," etc. Palms out (i.e. facing toward the addressee) is a statement of assertion and is equivalent to the statement, "I shall say it" or "Don't interrupt." (Weiner et al., 1972, p. 211).

The reader might like to evaluate the validity of these hypotheses by his own observations.

The study of all of these kinds of nonverbal behavior will undoubtedly add to the understanding and appreciation of the complexities of human communication and interaction. We must restrict our present attention, however, to the communication of emotion by means of facial expressions and gestures.

Studies of Facial Expressions and Gestures

Early Studies

It is natural to inquire about the extent to which the experiments on monkeys have implications about human social behavior. It seems reasonable to expect that the ability to send and receive nonverbal messages is important in human social behavior as well.

The experimental investigation of the facial-gestural expression of affect in man began in the 1920s. In 1929 Landis published a classic experiment. Landis photographed his subjects as they went through a series of 17 situations, which included looking at pornographic pictures, smelling ammonia, listening to music, decapitating a live rat, receiving a strong electric shock, telling a lie, looking at pictures of people with skin diseases, and so forth. He selected the more expressive photographs and asked 42 judges to describe the emotion being portrayed and the situation that might have evoked it. He reported that the emotions and situations described by the observers were completely irrelevant to the actual situations and introspective reports of the subjects. He concluded that it is impossible to name an emotion accurately on the basis of facial expression alone.

The negative results of Landis and some other early investigators unfortunately tended to depress interest in the area (cf. Ekman, Friesen, and Ellsworth, 1972). However, it now appears that these negative findings were due to inappropriate experimental methodology. Ekman et al. (1972) have summarized a number of criticisms of Landis' experiment and other early studies. For example, they note that Landis' subjects may have been motivated to inhibit and mask the natural facial display of emotion. Landis' subjects knew they were being photographed and knew that Landis was interested in facial expression. In fact, their faces were marked with burnt cork to facilitate the measurement of facial movements, and every time they made a facial movement, Landis took a picture of them. On top of this, all of Landis' subjects knew him personally. It is perhaps not surprising that they did not behave naturally in such a situation.

Landis' situation may have been so stressful that it masked any differential effects of the 17 tasks. Landis felt that the different tasks should elicit disgust, astonishment, sexual excitement, and anger, but the effect of the experimental situation itself may have overwhelmed such differences. Also, as Ekman et al. point out, many of Landis' subjects showed frequent smiles. Landis was sure that they were not feeling happy, and he saw the smiles as evidence that the smile is a meaningless expression. However, these smiles could have indicated embarrassment or stress. A motion picture of the subjects showing the facial context of the smiles might have made this clear.

More recent experiments have established beyond doubt that significant communication of affect through facial expression occurs in humans.

PART THREE

Nonverbal Messages: The Other Channels

Experiences and Discussions

1. Create a double-bind situation with someone you know very well. Note the person's reaction and the communication channel he or she relied upon—the verbal, the nonverbal, or the vocal. You might try this several times with different persons and then tally your observations about channel reliance.

2. Consider your nonverbal behavior (keep a log for two hours), and determine if Mehrabian's equation for the total impact of a message (0.07 verbal + 0.38 vocal + 0.55 facial) is appropriate for you. Are there other nonverbal behaviors you would include or would prefer to Mehrabian's? List your behaviors and write an equation for the total impact of messages you send.

3. Compare seating arrangements in different classrooms you attend and student participation in each class. Which areas are most active? Which are least active? How do your observations compare with those reported by Sommer?

4. Select a person who you feel is an outstanding teacher. Describe this teacher according to the nonverbal-behavior criteria discussed by Knapp.

5. How do you react when verbal and nonverbal messages conflict? Do you always rely on verbal cues? On nonverbals? Do you seek clarifying feedback? What should other people do if they perceive conflict between your verbal and nonverbal messages?

6. Are you a good nonverbal receiver? Do you find yourself able to clearly perceive emotions on the basis of nonverbal communication? Make a list of the varying emotions verbal feedback proves you have accurately detected in the past week. How many times in the past week have you misread an emotion cue?

7. How do animals communicate nonverbally? Can a dog, cat, or other pet accurately send messages? How large a nonverbal vocabulary does a dog have? How accurately can a dog or cat receive nonverbally? How do dogs communicate with other dogs?

For Further Reading

BIRDWHISTELL, RAY L. *Kinesics and Context: Essays on Body Motion Communication.* Philadelphia: University of Pennsylvania Press, 1970. This collection of twenty-eight essays and lectures deals with various aspects of how body movements communicate. Of particular interest are Birdwhistell's thoughts and research on body movement and family relationships, the use of gestures, and the differences in movements by persons in various geographic regions. A large part of the book presents the coding system and methodology developed by the author, a pioneer in nonverbal-communication research.

"The Challenge of Nonverbal Awareness." Special issue of *Theory into Practice,* 1971, *10* (4). Columbus, Ohio: Ohio State University, College of Education.

This is a special journal issue devoted to nonverbal communication in the classroom. It is an excellent collection of articles which introduces the forces operating in the classroom on a nonverbal level. Topics include teacher and student nonverbal bahavior, affective education, and coding systems for recording nonverbal behavior.

EKMAN, PAUL, and V. FRIESEN. *Unmaskiing the Face.* Englewood Cliffs, N.J.: Prentice-Hall, 1975.

The introduction to this popular book tells it all: "This book is about faces and feelings." After providing research findings on facial expressions and emotions, Ekman and Friesen move on to a practical, workbook approach for practicing and checking your own facial expressions and detecting facial deceit. They deal with six specific emotions (surprise, fear, anger, happiness, sadness, and disgust) and provide numerous photos as guides.

————, ————, and PHOEBE ELLSWORTH. *Emotion in the Human Face.* New York: Permagon, 1972.

This is a more advanced text than *Unmasking the Face.* It provides a comprehensive review of research on facial expressions and emotions. The authors cover conceptual problems in the research (for example, what emotion is and if facial expressions can be controlled or disguised). The book deals with the methodological problems of selecting samples of persons, emotions, and category labels and deciding on methods for recording the expressions. A final section poses seven research questions and describes findings to date. Questions range from "What emotional categories can observers judge from facial behavior?" to "What are the similarities and differences in facial behavior across cultures?" Recommended for students interested in advanced study of research in facial expression.

LEATHERS, DALE G. *Nonverbal Communication Systems.* Boston: Allyn and Bacon, 1976.

This book deals with various elements of the nonverbal-communication process. Specifically, it includes kinesics; proxemics in the proximate and urban environments; the artifactual, vocalic, tactile, and olfactory communication systems. Also included are a section on telepathic communication systems and a discussion on observing, classifying, and measuring the quality of nonverbal communication.

MEHRABIAN, ALBERT. *Silent Messages.* Belmont, Calif.: Wadsworth, 1971.

This relatively brief book offers a theoretical analysis of the dimensions of human attitudes and nonverbal behavior. Mehrabian offers three "metaphors" for the study of nonverbal behavior: immediacy, potency, and responsiveness. After discussing various social styles and double-bind messages, Mehrabian suggests a variety of applications: advertising, political campaigns, social alienation, and romance.

SOMMER, ROBERT. *Tight Spaces: Hard Architecture and How to Humanize It.* Englewood Cliffs, N.J.: Prentice-Hall, 1974.

With the belief that form must follow function, Sommer looks at the problems of physical structures and social institutions: classrooms, airport terminals, even the zoo. Photos serve to illustrate Sommer's concerns about social responsibility in the way we structure our buildings and create soft architectural designs.

WEITZ, SHIRLEY. *Nonverbal Communication: Readings with Commentary.* New York: Oxford University Press, 1974.

Intended for advanced study, this collection of twenty-two readings analyzes nonverbal behavior from viewpoints of psychology, sociology, and communication. The following aspects of nonverbal behavior are included: facial and eye expression, vocal expression, body movement and gestures, spatial behavior, and multichannel communication.

PART FOUR

Intrapersonal Communication

In the dim light of the lamp I saw him sitting there, an old briar pipe between his lips, his eyes fixed vacantly upon the corner of the ceiling, the blue smoke curling up from him, silent, motionless, with the light shining upon his strong-set aquiline features. So he sat as I dropped off to sleep, and so he sat when a sudden ejaculation caused me to wake up, and I found the summer sun shining into the apartment. The pipe was still between his lips, the smoke still curled upward, and the room was full of a dense tobacco haze, but nothing remained of the head of shag which I had seen upon the previous night.

THE MAN WITH THE TWISTED LIP

When we are lost in silent contemplation or worrying over choice of words in a heated argument communication within self plays a key role in the process.

The questions of who we are and how we shall communicate about ourselves to others stand at the foundation of any investigation into the realm of intrapersonal communication. "There *is* a risk in growing, any act of communication begins with a thought in the sender's conscious or subconscious mind." write Ron Adler and Neil Towne, "but it's important to remember that you *do* have a choice, and in this sense you're responsible for being the kind of person you are." With that responsibility clearly placed, it is possible to follow the clues of verbal and nonverbal communication in the intrapersonal setting and determine here how the communication process functions.

Of course, intrapersonal communication does not exist in isolation. Even through his intrapersonal smoky haze, Holmes influences Watson and so communicates with him. Kenneth Gergen looks at this intra-interpersonal link and examines the influence of self-perception upon the ways in which others perceive you. Your self-concept may well be the message others read.

How is that self-concept communicated? Sidney Jourard suggests the medium is self-disclosure, the act of self-revelation. The cry of success that breaks Watson's sleep and signals the conclusion of Holmes' contemplation may well be the initial gesture in the chain of communication. The evidence suggests that communication may originate with a willingness to disclose a thought and hence shape the random signals being broadcast into a meaningful message.

Whether or not you agree with the suppositions of Jourard and Gergen, clearly intrapersonal communication is the logical situation in which to start if we are to deduce the characteristics of communication.

OBJECTIVES

After carefully reading these three articles you should be able to define the following terms:

self-concept	(Adler and Towne)
self-awareness	
self-fulfilling prophecy	
self-esteem	(Gergen)
unconditional regard	
evaluation accuracy	
conditional regard	
self-disclosure	(Jourard)
expressive role	
instrumental role	

And:

1. Identify the messages sent by your body which indicate specific needs and emotions (Adler and Towne).
2. Identify common "family messages" that can affect your self-concept (Adler and Towne).
3. Describe what is meant by "self-fulfilling prophecy." Use an example to show how self-fulfilling prophecy relates to self-concept (Adler and Towne).
4. Discuss four explanations of the relationship between regard for self and regard for others (Gergen).
5. Explain "conditional regard" and "unconditional regard" and give examples of each (Gergen).
6. Describe the relationship between attraction to a person and evaluations received from that person about oneself (Gergen).
7. Predict the changes in attraction that would occur according to the esteem-enhancement effect and the accuracy effect (Gergen).

8. Explain why Jourard writes that "the self is unique in all of nature" (Jourard).
9. Explain how persons learn about acceptable self-disclosure (Jourard).
10. Describe the general characteristics and results of Jourard's research with the Self-Disclosure Questionnaire for family, friends, and peers (Jourard).

Eleven

Self-Awareness: Communication Begins with Me

Ron Adler and Neil Towne

How Are You Now?

The first step in increasing your self-understanding is to look at how closely you're in touch with your emotions. Before you can communicate your feelings to others you have to be aware of them yourself—this seems obvious. Yet strange as it may sound to say it, there are probably times when you can't seem to sort out for certain just *how* you feel. If a friend lets you down when you were counting on him, are you angry, or is your real feeling one of disappointment? If someone you know gets a job or a grade you wanted, are you jealous of her or mad at yourself? It's questions like these that we want to take a look at now.

Why is it that people sometimes have such trouble recognizing how they feel? This doesn't seem to be a problem we're born with. If you've spent any time with babies or young children you know that for them there's no gap between feeling and acting. When a one-year-old is happy she laughs, not just with her face but with her whole body. When she feels pain she cries, and when she's angry you know it right away. Children this age don't follow the feel-think-act pattern that's so common with grown-ups; instead it seems that they just *are.*

What happens to get in the way of this easy expression of feelings? Part of the gap between thinking and feeling almost certainly comes from the lessons we learn while growing up. Usually without being aware of it, and almost inevitably, adults send message after message telling a child which emotions are acceptable and which aren't. In a house where angry words are taboo, the child gets the idea that anger is a "not o.k." thing. If sex is never discussed except with great discomfort, then the child will learn to stop talking about —and even stop consciously feeling—emotions that center around the body. If the parents only talk about trivial subjects and never share their deeper feelings, the child's conversation and thinking will tend to follow the same path.

Kids don't stop getting angry, having sexual thoughts, or intense feelings; emotions can't be turned off or on at will like water from a faucet. But because we're taught that certain feelings aren't o.k., we do learn to push them out of our consciousness so that pretty soon they become hard to recognize.

As we said earlier, this lack of spontaneity in expressing feelings can become a real problem as we grow up. But what can you do if you want to get more closely in touch with your emotions? When you're not sure how you feel, one thing you can do is analyze yourself. Are you really happy in your job, or should you look for a new one? You can list all the reasons for each decision. Do you really love him or her? (It's possible to think this one to death.) Sometimes after analyzing yourself this way it's likely that you wind up even more confused than when you began. You start trying to figure out all the ways you *could* be feeling or you ask yourself how you *should* feel, but you never really come up with a satisfying answer.

Fortunately there's another, often better, way to get in touch with those unclear emotions. Unlike the approaches we've been used to, this one relies very little on your intellect. Instead of thinking about how you are, all you need to do with this technique is to listen, to pay attention to your own body. By becoming aware of the messages it sends, you can often find out more clearly what's really going on between you and other people.

. . .

Avoiding the messages your body sends is one way to deal with the needs these messages signal. But you can also use your awareness to learn which parts of your life need change: which unpleasant things need to deal with, and which pleasant things are worth working for. For example, maybe you'll find that you're not happy in a situation you always thought was fine. One friend of ours began focusing on her internal messages and learned that every time she returned to the city from a vacation she felt a tremendous empty feeling in the pit of her stomach. From what she'd already learned about herself she knew that this sensation always accompanied things she dreaded; and once aware of this knowledge she realized that she was much happier in the country. Now she's trying to find a way to make the move she knows is right for her.

Another student of ours had a very high paying job in sales and always claimed to love his work until he became aware of a tightness in his throat every time he was trying hard to close a deal. This sensation made it clear to him that he'd been acting against his real feelings by persuading his customers to buy products he wasn't sure they needed. Once he got in touch with this fact by listening to his internal messages, our friend managed to change jobs, and now he has a position selling a product in which he has more faith.

Once you learn to listen to it, this inner sense can become almost like a warning signal that tells you what important changes you need to make. Are you happy with your present crowd of friends, or are you just pretending? Is there something that needs to be said which you've been holding back from an important person? Do you sometimes say things you don't really believe? Let your body tell you.

Your Self-Concept: How it Was Formed

From listening to your body you know better which social situations you enjoy and which ones make you uncomfortable, what kind of people you like and dislike, and the way you feel about yourself.

But how did you get to be the person you are? If you're an extrovert who seeks out others, what made you this way? If you're shy and unsure of yourself, how did you come to be like this? One way to answer these questions is to say that you were born the way you are, that it's a question of heredity. There's some truth to this, but to a great degree your personality is also shaped by the way you *think* you are. And the way you think you are was shaped by how people treated you while you were growing up.

When a child is born, he is socially a kind of blank slate. He has barely any ability to think and no experience to rely on; most of his time is spent eating and sleeping. But even at this time the way he's treated begins to give him a feeling about his worth. Some of the earliest messages he receives about himself come from

> Being hugged, cuddled, and kissed
> Being fed when hungry
> Receiving attention whenever he cries
> Being rocked to sleep

By all these actions the child's parents communicate their love and concern for him; if he could speak he might say "They really care about me. . . . I must be a pretty good person."

On the other hand, some children aren't so lucky. Because their parents either don't know much about raising kids or don't care, they send other kinds of messages to their child by the ways they treat him:

> Not feeding him when he's hungry
> Ignoring his crying
> Not touching him very much
> Not talking to or paying much attention to him

If a child who was treated this way could talk, he might say about himself "They don't care about me. . . . I'm no good."

As the child grows older and learns to use language, the kinds of messages he gets about who he is increase:

> Big boys don't cry.
> He's Daddy's little helper
> You didn't tell Mommy you had to go potty. That's naughty.
> She's not the scholar in the family.
> Mommies don't like little girls who don't mind.
> Daddy thinks you're the best baby in the whole world.
> Nobody in this family is musical, so she didn't stand a chance.
> If you cared anything about your mother you'd stop.

Children are trusting souls and believe these messages, especially since they have hardly any other way of learning about themselves at first. And so the child's feelings about himself slowly grow, shaped by what he hears about himself. By the time he's a year old he's already begun to develop these feelings, and by the time he's four or five he has such a consistent and strong opinion of himself—whether good or bad—that it's very hard to change it. This way we feel about ourselves is called our *self-concept.*

. . .

A Self-Fulfilling Prophecy

As you develop, you get a certain picture of how you are, and it's likely you act in a way that fits this picture. Other people shape your self-concept and others can change it, but the tendency to protect even an unrealistic image of yourself is a strong one.

Have you ever known persons with a low opinion of themselves? Maybe they were quite intelligent, but because they were constantly compared with especially bright brothers or sisters they grew up feeling stupid. Or maybe when they were younger they were teased by other children about some physical trait, such as wearing glasses or being overweight. Even though their self-concept wasn't very realistic, it may have hung on over the years so that even today they're unsure of themselves, carrying around a mental self-portrait in which they appear ugly or stupid or some other way.

And the sad thing is that when someone believes so strongly in this picture of himself, it becomes true. A person who thinks of himself as a poor student can find plenty of excuses for not doing well in his classes. After all, isn't that what poor students are supposed to do? Somebody who sees herself as shy isn't likely to start a conversation or ask a question in class. And so, the person with a poor self-concept ends up living up to his own low expectations, even though he could be much happier if he'd let himself.

This kind of example illustrates the tendency people have to keep their behavior consistent with their self-concept. We act in a way that fits the picture we hold of ourselves and then that picture becomes truth, but only because we made it so. In this sense, the self-concept becomes a self-fulfilling prophecy.

This self-fulfilling prophecy is a real block to any kind of change. It's strange, but once we develop a poor opinion of ourselves we'll defend it, even though we're unhappy. This is why you sometimes hear people say they're *not* smart, interesting, fun or whatever, almost as if they don't want to believe what you've told them.

. . .

The Self-Concept in Process

The way you are is not fixed—you're changing all the time. This may sound obvious, but it's very important in terms of your communication because it means that you're not going to be the same person forever: You *can* change.

Certainly your body is constantly changing. You're not the same person today as you were yesterday. You're a day older. Your heart has beat about 100,000 times more. Your hair and fingernails have grown slightly; you've been able to become stronger or weaker, heavier or lighter, healthier or more sickly, more in or out of physical shape. And all these things change the kind of person you are.

Do you feel you're fat? If this genuinely bothers you, you can go on a diet. Do you see yourself as unattractive? You can change your hair style, get a tan, buy some new clothes. Are you clumsy? You can be more careful and build up your coordination by practice. If you're not happy with yourself, you *can* change—if you really want to! You're not doomed to be the same person you were in the past.

What's true for your body also goes for other parts of your self-concept. Ask yourself this question: "Are you basing your present self-concept on outdated information?" Maybe you think you're a poor date because of something that happened a long time ago and isn't true any more. Maybe you think of yourself as a caterpillar when you've really become a butterfly! You aren't the same person you were!

Suppose that in the past you've been reluctant to meet strangers. You've been noticing someone in your class whom you'd like to know better, but because of some fears from your past—your old self-concept—you haven't done anything for fear of getting the brush-off. What are you going to do now? You have at least two choices: either you can make your old self-concept a self-fulfilling prophecy and not do anything, or you can take a chance and try being a new you. The worst thing that can happen is that you won't get anywhere with the person, in which case you're not worse off than before. And look what you stand to gain!

We're not saying that it's easy to change habits that may have been going on for a lifetime. Somehow it's comfortable to feel that you're the same person, not changing all the time. The future seems more predictable this way, even if it's less exciting than you'd like. And sometimes others want you to stay the same too. Why do you suppose a certain insurance company chooses a picture of the Rock of Gibraltar as their company symbol?

So there *is* a risk in growing. It's a frightening thing to break out of an old habit, even one that you know is wrong for you, and become a new person. To change or stay the same is a big decision, but it's important to remember that you *do* have a choice, and in this sense you're responsible for being the kind of person you are. It's up to you.

Twelve

Social Attraction and the Self

Kenneth J. Gergen

Persons may love or hate each other for a variety of reasons, but fundamental to the feelings we have for others are the feelings we have for ourselves. Depending on our self-esteem we may be predisposed not only to feel certain ways about others in general, but also to respond favorably or unfavorably to their actions toward us. Let us take a closer look at each of these dispositions.

Self-Esteem and the Acceptance of Others

The noted psychoanalyst Erich Fromm was one of the first to observe the close connection between a person's evaluations of self and his feelings for others (1939). For Fromm, "Hatred against oneself is inseparable from hatred against others." On the basis of this observation, he considered low self-esteem, or excessive feelings of humility, to be a form of neurosis. Years later, Carl Rogers (1959) noted a similar phenomenon in many of his patients. Those who felt least capable of reaching their goals found it hardest to accept people around them.

. . .

If self-esteem and esteem for others are indeed correlated, as the evidence suggests, we must ask why this should be so. Fromm has suggested that both feelings for self and feelings for others are based on the same set of childhood learning experiences. When children have been treated hostilely and their freedom has been spitefully curtailed, they develop a "character conditioned hatred" toward both self and others. Unfortunately, Fromm does not complete his argument by specifying exactly why this disposition should include both self and others. If a child has received continuous hostility from his parents and peers, a negative reaction to himself is quite likely to result from reflected appraisal. At the same time that he learns to dislike himself, he develops hatred for his parents and/or his peers. His subsequent dislike for other people may constitute a generalization from earlier experiences. On a subjective level the feeling might be, "I have always been treated badly, so what reason is there to suspect that others will be different?"

Rogers (1959) explains the relationship between self-esteem and acceptance of others in a slightly different way. For Rogers the regard received from others may be of two types: *conditional or unconditional.* Conditional regard is dependent on one's meeting the other's criteria of evaluation in order to be accepted; failure to meet his criteria leads to rejection. In contrast, unconditional regard is not dependent on the other's criteria of the evaluation. One is prized not for what he does but for his intrinsic value as a human being. Rogers observes that when regard is conditional, the person begins to evaluate himself conditionally —finding himself acceptable only if he meets certain criteria. When self-evaluation is conditional, the person defends against seeing himself in certain ways. He may distort his perception of self, avoid noticing certain of his actions, and, most important, be more defensive in social relationships. Since others may "show him up for what he is," he may avoid close contact or discredit their views. In effect, others are viewed as threats. Rogers, logically, is much opposed to the use of conditional regard in human relationships.

Another explanation of the relationship between regard for self and regard for others is that the person who feels inferior may not wish to admit to himself that others have positive attributes. To acknowledge others' superiority is to suffer through social comparison; to see them as inferior is to boost one's self-esteem. Through biased scanning one can always find shortcomings in others and in this way show himself that he is really not so bad after all.

Finally, there is a generalized tendency, when we have little clear information about another person, to assume that he is like ourselves. If we feel afraid when walking on a darkened street, we assume that this is probably normal and that most others would feel the same way. Similarly, the person low in self-esteem may make certain assumptions about others' "true characteristics," assumptions that differ from those made by the person with high self-esteem. Which of these various factors produce the generally observed relationship between self-love and love for others and to what degree each is influential are questions for future research. Let us turn now to an aspect of attraction that has been more extensively studied.

Reactions to Others' Evaluations of Self

Feelings toward self may not only influence our generalized feelings toward others, but may also predispose us to react in specific ways to their behavior and evaluations of us. Typically, people tend to be attracted to those who evaluate them positively and to dislike those who appraise them negatively. There is considerable research to support this proposition; one example is a study by Jones, Gergen, and Davis (1962) in which undergraduate males were interviewed by advanced graduate students. After the interview half of the subjects learned that the graduate interviewer had a very positive opinion of them, while the other half learned that he disapproved of many of their personal characteristics. Subjects then evaluated the interviewer on a variety of dimensions. The results were clear: those receiving positive appraisals were overwhelmingly more positive in their evaluations of the interviewer.

People are apt to incorporate positive facts about themselves more readily than negative facts, that they may accumulate goods in order to perceive themselves as superior to others, and that they tend to identify more completely with their roles when they receive positive reactions from others. All these observations point to the fact that self-esteem is all-important to the individual. Events or persons boosting one's esteem are gratifying and those which reduce it are abhorred. Rogers (1959) has spoken of a "basic need for self regard," a need that leads one to seek the regard of others. He has noted that in some clinical cases seeking the esteem of others seems more powerful a motive than physiological needs.

There is good reason to suspect that one's need for self-esteem develops in childhood. Essentially, it seems to depend on the close and frequent association between the reduction of physiological needs and feelings of being valuable. At the same time that a child is being fed he is also receiving the secondary message that he is valued. He may be fondled and caressed as an infant and may receive warm looks and affectionate talk as he grows older. He may be tickled when the wet, cold diaper is removed from his body and patted when a blanket is put over him to keep him warm. More subtly, by the very act of alleviating physical discomfort or increasing bodily pleasure, the other communicates to the child that he is esteemed.

The feeling of being valued or esteemed may be intrinsically neutral in tone. However, because of its frequent and continuous association with physical drive reduction, tactile pleasure, and the reduction of pain, it comes to have a learned value. An animal will seek out a chamber in which it has been fed long after the reward of food is no longer available, or it will expend great effort to escape a chamber in which it has been shocked long after the shock has been terminated. The animal acquires the motivation for stimuli that have been associated with basic states of pleasure or pain. In the same way, human feelings of being valuable have been associated with more basic states of pleasure and feelings of being valueless with states of pain or discomfort. As a result, the person learns to seek out the feeling of being esteemed for its own sake and to avoid the feeling of being valueless. To feel esteem for self is akin to one's most basic experience of well-being—the childhood experiences of being supported and nurtured by a benevolent environment. To be without esteem is symbolic of one's basic anguish in an unpredictable and uncontrollable world.

It follows from our discussion thus far that the more positive the appraisal we receive from another, the greater our attraction for him. However, let us turn to a study by Deutsch and Solomon (1959) and see how well this proposition holds up. In this experiment subjects worked together in groups to complete a difficult task. At a certain point in the procedure, each subject was given information indicating how much he had helped or hindered the group in reaching their goal. At random, half the subjects received information indicating that theirs had been one of the most outstanding contributions (success condition), while the other half learned that they had turned in the poorest performance in the group (failure condition). Although each subject received this information privately, he was led to believe that the others also knew of his rating. This manipulation was designed to create two groups, one with a temporary feeling of enhanced self-esteem and the other with a diminished regard for self.

. . .

Subjects who have succeeded (high self-esteem) react much as we have discussed. They are much more attracted to the person who appraises them positively than they are to a critic. But upon closer examination of the results we see another effect not previously accounted for. When subjects have failed (low self-esteem), they are more attracted to the critic than to the admirer. How can we account for this curious finding?

The one central feature of the condition in which low-esteem subjects are criticized is that the appraiser has been accurate in his judgment. When subjects fail and are praised, the appraiser has been grossly inaccurate in his estimates. It may be said, then, that *evaluation accuracy* plays an important role in our feelings toward someone who has appraised us. We may appreciate an accurate evaluator for several reasons. For one thing, he typically gives us information about ourselves that we can utilize. If we feel he is inaccurate in his estimates of us, he is irrelevant to our concern with developing a realistic and useful picture of self. Secondly, the credibility of the appraiser suffers when he is inaccurate. The inaccurate appraiser seems untrustworthy and possibly stupid. In addition, we are more likely to see the inaccurate appraiser as lacking in personalism. He may seem less attuned to us as persons and possibly influenced by ulterior motives. For a male to tell a female she is "beautiful" when she is feeling particularly unattractive may raise considerable suspicion about his motives. Additional research by Backman and Second (1962) further highlights the importance of accuracy. In a study of friendship in a sorority, they found that girls preferred to do things with others who most agreed with their appraisals of themselves.

But we have yet to deal with the major paradox. What do we feel toward a person who evaluates us much more positively than we typically evaluate ourselves? On the one hand, the more positive the other's evaluation, the more gratifying to our needs for esteem. On the other hand, the greater the difference between self-evaluation and the other's evaluation of self, the less the perceived accuracy. In effect, these two processes tend to work against each other. The one predicts greater attraction as the other's evaluation becomes more positive (an esteem-enhancement effect), while the other predicts less attraction (an accuracy effect). Are we destined to accept the flatterer or sycophant who feeds our needs for esteem? Or must we forsake personal happiness in order to reject false praise? How is this conflict resolved?

It seems wise not to search for a universal answer to this question, that is, for a solution holding under all conditions. Rather, the specific conditions of a relationship may be all important. Certain conditions or factors may cause self-enhancement effects to predominate; other conditions may cause accuracy effects to hold sway. Five factors may be particularly important.

Characteristics of the Evaluator

As we pointed out, part of the reason for disliking an inaccurate evaluator is that his inaccuracy reflects on his character. In particular, he may seem "stupid," "impersonal," or "driven by ulterior motives." It thus follows that any factors reinforcing such characterizations should enhance accuracy effects (reducing attraction) and offset the positive effects of esteem gratification.

An experiment by Dickoff (1961) nicely demonstrates this point. Undergraduate women participated in an interview procedure in which they were to be evaluated by a graduate student. One group of subjects found that the graduate student-evaluator (an experimental accomplice) agreed with their own evaluations of self very closely, while a second group found that the evaluator's appraisals of them were considerably more positive than their own self-ratings. Half the subjects in each of these groups were further told that it was the evaluator's task to be as honest as possible in her appraisals. The remaining half, however, were told that the graduate student wanted them to volunteer for an additional experiment—in other words, her motives for evaluating the subject were made to appear suspect. After the procedure subjects were asked to rate the evaluator. The results were clear: when the evaluator's motives seemed honest (that is, she could be trusted), subjects liked her much more when she had a high (but inflated) view of them. In contrast, when the evaluator's motives were suspect, there was no increase in attraction as she became more flattering. In fact, there was a tendency for her to be liked less when she was flattering than when her appraisals corresponded to the subjects' own self-estimates.

Characteristics of the Evaluation: Conditional versus Unconditional

Evaluations received from others vary in a number of ways. Of particular importance is the distinction between conditional versus unconditional appraisals. The folk-rock singer Bob Dylan once wrote a song in which he addressed a young lady with a long list of things he wasn't setting out to do. He was not there to "analyze her," "criticize her," or "make eyes at her." All he wished was to be her "friend." Dylan's song captures the essence of unconditional evaluations as contrasted to conditional evaluation. Conditional evaluations are tied to specific characteristics or behavior. As we explained earlier, the person is evaluated positively or liked because of specific things that he does or is capable of doing. By implication he would not be acceptable if he did not do these things. Grading systems consist of conditional evaluations and, unfortunately, so do many love or friendship relations. Unconditional approval is effusive and expresses generalized good-will, a positive feeling that exists without regard to the person's specific behavior. As in the Dylan song, the simple expression of friendship is unconditional; the positive feelings do not depend on a series of activities that the person might be called on to perform.

Both conditional and unconditional evaluations may enhance one's self-esteem. Receiving hugs and kisses after winning a race may be as gratifying as receiving an unsolicited expression of warmth. However, our orientations are not the same for both; we do not look to both for the same thing. With conditional evaluations, a higher premium is placed on accuracy. Such evaluations inform us that we have performed well or poorly and knowledge of the success of performance may be useful on future occasions. In matters of friendship, companionship, or love, however, unconditional evaluations are usually more relevant. Here we may not wish the other's evaluations to depend on our performance at the moment. In such instances, attraction to the other should increase as he is more positive toward us. Accuracy should be a minor concern.

Characteristics of the Situation: The Demand for Accuracy

Certain situations place a strong premium on being accurate about oneself. It would be unprofitable to enter a beauty contest without others' honest evaluations of one's talents and appearance or to set out to save a drowning man without an accurate estimate of one's own ability to swim. When rewards and punishments are contingent on accuracy, the person should be less attracted to inaccurate appraisals from others. As Pepitone (1967) has suggested, this set toward accuracy may account for the Deutsch and Solomon result discussed above. The task on which subjects were caused to succeed or fail involved their abilities to form accurate impressions. The situation emphasized the importance of being accurate; therefore, subjects may have been especially inclined to reject inaccurate appraisals of themselves by others.

The Need for Self-Esteem

People clearly differ in the extent to which they fulfill their need for self-esteem. Although social approval is readily available to some persons, others may be chronically impoverished. Success or failure may also affect our esteem needs at any moment. If we fail, our esteem is temporarily lowered and our need is greater. When one's esteem needs are unfulfilled, the approval of others becomes particularly valuable. It is the person most deficient in self-esteem who most exerts himself to obtain it. Most touching is the individual so lacking the love or affection of others that his grasping demands stifle precisely those who might be able to fulfill his needs.

One's need for self-esteem has a direct bearing on his reaction to others' evaluations. The person who is deprived of support, either chronically or at one particular time, should be most gratified by a positive evaluation. For him, evaluation accuracy should have little importance. When his esteem is high, he should be less attracted to one who evaluates him positively and unrealistically.

. . .

Functional Value of Relevant Concepts

Concepts differ in their functional value to the person. Holding the concept of himself as "intelligent" may render a person less vulnerable to others' attacks and allow him to engage in social relations without anxiety. Other concepts, such as "great grandson" may be less generally important; these are used less often in achieving goals. It seems quite likely that for concepts of great functional value, self-enhancement is preeminent. When it is important for a person to see himself in a certain way, receiving strong support (even if inaccurate) for this self-view may well yield attraction. On the other hand, if the aspect of self has little value to the person, praise is less gratifying and accuracy considerations may have greater weight. This reasoning leads to the conclusion that the more important a particular self-view is to the person, the more susceptible he is to the inflated and flattering remarks of others. But empirical evidence to support this is needed.

To summarize, positive evaluations from others often produce conflict. Because such evaluations boost esteem, we may be attracted to the evaluator. But to the extent that these same evaluations exceed our current estimate of self, they also seem inaccurate and the evaluator is then disliked. The relative strength of these opposing tendencies will depend on a variety of factors. Factors reducing the evaluator's credibility or personalism will reduce attraction. When conditional evaluations are at stake, accuracy will be more valued than when unconditional evaluations are desired. If the situation is one in which rewards are contingent on being accurate about self, accuracy effects will dominate. Persons whose need for esteem is great will also be more appreciative of another's positive evaluation. Finally, the greater the functional value of a particular self-view to the person, the greater his appreciation of positive appraisal.

REFERENCES

BACKMAN, C. W., and SECORD, P. F. The self and role selection. In C. Gordon & K. J. Gergen (eds.), *The self in social interaction.* Vol. 1. New York: Wiley, 1968.

DEUTSCH, M., and SOLOMON, L. Reactions to evaluations by others as influenced by self evaluations. *Sociometry,* 1959, 22, 93–112.

DICKOFF, H. Reactions to evaluations by another person as a function of self evaluation and the interaction context. Unpublished doctoral dissertation, Duke University, 1961.

FROMM, E. Selfishness and self love. *Psychiatry,* 1939, 2, 507–523. (Also reprinted in Gordon and Gergen.)

JONES, E. E., GERGEN, K. J., and DAVIS, K. Some reactions to being approved or disapproved as a person. *Psychological Monographs,* 1962, 76 (whole No. 521).

PEPITONE, A. Some conceptual and empirical problems of consistency models. In S. Feldman (ed.), *Cognitive consistency.* New York: Academic Press, 1967.

ROGERS, C. Therapy, personality and interpersonal relationships. In S. Koch (ed.), *Psychology: A study of a science.* Vol. III. New York: McGraw-Hill, 1959. (Outstanding statement of relationship between self-regard and mental disorder.)

Thirteen

Self-Disclosure: The Scientist's Portal to Man's Soul

Sidney M. Jourard

The soul of which poets speak, and which philosophers and theologians concern themselves with, is now operationally defined by psychologists and called the Self. That the soul, or self, is real, in the sense of existing, few can doubt. At least few would doubt its reality when we define the self as the subjective side of man—that which is private and personal, which he experiences immediately and spontaneously. Of course, what we term "self" has correlates—neurophysiological correlates and environmental stimuli. Doubtless too, the self—feelings, wishes, memories, thoughts, dreams, etc.—is lawful as well. But the self is unique in all of nature, though it is a part of nature. It is unique in this respect: Any other part of nature passively submits to the inquiry of the investigator who is after the facts. Man's self, as near as we now know, can never be known to any save the experiencing individual unless the individual man unequivocably co-operates and *makes his self known.* In short, man must consent; if we would know his self, he must *want* to tell us. If he doesn't wish to tell us of his self, we can torture him, browbeat him, tempt him, even make incisive psychoanalytic guesses; but unless he wishes to make his self known, we will of course never know it. However shrewd our guesses might be about a man's self, when we guess about a man's self, we never know whether we are correct until he says, and means it, "You're right." Moreover, we don't know for a certainty whether he means it.

This line of thinking should make us despair of ever subjecting man's soul to scientific scrutiny, except for one thing. It is unlikely that the *act* of self-disclosure follows laws—perhaps the laws of reinforcement (cf. Skinner, 1953). I believe that I may have stumbled upon a key to the lock of the portal to man's soul. So far, the key barely fits the lock; it doesn't always work; it needs to be made more precise, of course. But it is such an obvious kind of key, and it has been lying around unnoticed for such a long time, that I wonder why no one ever picked it up to try it out for size.

What is this key? It is the study of what information a person will tell another person about himself, or, more technically, about his *self.* I call the key—or portal, it doesn't really matter, since we are mixing metaphors—self-disclosure. Through my self-disclosure, I let others know my soul. They can know it, really know it, only as I make it known. In fact, I am beginning to suspect that I can't even know *my own soul* except as I disclose it. I suspect that I will know myself "for real" at the exact moment that I have succeeded in making it known through my disclosure to another person.

Let us look for a moment at the act of disclosing something about one's self to another person, a simple statement such as one's name, age, weight, height, what one did with whom yesterday, or the relating of a dream. A little introspection will verify that even simple, factual disclosures of this sort can often be matters that are fraught with anxiety. Whence the anxiety? Cameron and Magaret (1951) have a section in their excellent treatise on *Behavior Pathology* which is concerned with what they call behavioral duplicity. They point out that dissemblance is learned early in life by all of us. As children we *are,* and we *act,* our real selves. We say what we think, we scream for what we want, we tell what we did. These spontaneous disclosures meet variable consequences—some disclosures are ignored, some rewarded, and some punished. Doubtless in accordance with the laws of reinforcement, we learn early to withhold certain disclosures because of the painful consequences to which they lead. We are punished, in our society, not only for what we actually do, but also for what we think, feel, or want. Very soon, then, the growing child learns to display a highly expurgated version of his self to others. I have coined the term "public self" (Jourard, 1958) to refer to the concept of oneself which one *wants* others to believe. We monitor, censor our behavior and disclosures in order to construct in the mind of the other person a concept of ourselves which we want him to have. Obviously, our assorted public selves are not always accurate portrayals of our real selves. In fact, it often comes to pass —perhaps as a socially patterned defect (Fromm, 1955)—that our public selves become so estranged from our real selves that the net consequence is self-alienation: we no longer know our real selves. Our disclosures reflect, not our spontaneous feelings, thoughts, and wishes, but rather pretended experience which will avoid punishment and win unearned approval. We say that we feel things we do not feel. We say that we did things we did not do. We say that we believe things we do not believe. When self-alienation, which I believe is the consequence of what I call pseudo-self-disclosure, has proceeded far enough, the individual loses his soul, literally. Or, we may say he has sold his soul, his real self, in order to purchase popularity, his mother's affection, or a promotion in the firm.

Self-disclosure, then, entails courage—the kind of courage that Paul Tillich (1952) had in mind in writing his book *The Courage to Be.* I would paraphrase that title to read, *The Courage to Be Known,* since Being always occurs in a social context. Since I seem to be in a paraphrasing frame of mind, let me modify some other well-known sayings. The Delphic Oracle advised, "Know Thyself"; I would say "Make Thyself Known, and then Thou wilt Know Thyself." Shakespeare is the source of, "And this above all, to thine own self be true, and . . . thou cans't not then be false to any man." Let me re-state it, "And this above all, to any other man be true, and thou cans't not then be false to thyself."

What, after all, is the situation called psychotherapy, but a situation wherein one person, the patient—alienated from himself, troubled—starts to disclose his self to the other person, the therapist. Then he "blocks," he resists. The therapist uses his skill to overcome the resistance, thus promoting more self-disclosure. Whether or not psychotherapy works as well as nothing or any-thing, as Eysenck (1952) seems to believe (I do not really believe he really believes this), of one thing we can be sure: At the conclusion of a series of psychotherapeutic sessions, the therapist knows more about his patient's self than he knew at the beginning. Possibly, too, the patient knows more about his own self at that time too. What he does with this knowledge is of course another cup of tea.

Does it come as a shock that, in the studies conducted at Chicago by Rogers (1954) into the effects of psychotherapy, that after umpteen hours of therapy, the therapist could guess the self-description of his patient better than he could at the outset of therapy? It is a case of the therapist being taught by the patient's self-disclosures of what manner of a man the patient believes he is. Should we assert that empathy is facilitated by self-disclosure? Let's ask the question, "How do we obtain an accurate concept of another man's experienc-ing?" We can guess his experience on the basis of interpretations of such things as facial cues; we can indulge in assimilative projection, imagine how we would feel in that situation, and then assume that that in fact is what the other man *is* at the moment. A more effective way of obtaining an accurate concept of the man's experiencing is to ask him what he is thinking and feeling. If he tells us honestly, there we have it: the basis for perfect empathy.

I could go on in this vein, but I had better not. I have some data that I would like to share with you. Let me tell you of a method we have been using to study self-disclosure, and some findings. Then, I shall conclude with some plans, or rather hopes that I have for further investigation.

A few years ago, I was puzzling about Karen Horney's (1950) concept of the "real self." I wondered how to adapt this concept for purposes of research. Out of this thinking came the idea that the kind of personal data we all put down on an application form when we are applying for a job might have the makings of a research tool. Some application forms, labeled "confidential," ask for amazingly detailed data about oneself. I asked myself, "Whom would an applicant tell these things to besides his prospective employer or teacher?" And then I was off. I started itemizing classes of information about oneself which could only be known by another person through direct verbal telling. After much fiddling this way and that, I wound up with a 60-item question-naire listing 10 items of information in each of 6 categories, which I called Aspects of Self. I devised an answer sheet with rows corresponding to the items, and columns headed by Target-Persons. To start with, I arbitrarily selected Mother, Father, Male Friend, and Female Friend and/or Spouse as Target-Persons. Subjects were asked to indicate whether or not they had made information about each item known to each of the Target-Persons. Those devotees of analysis of variance can see the making of a colossal pot of data to be unscrambled with that method. After all, we had four or five Target-Persons and six Aspects of Self; our subjects could be classified endlessly (male-female, Negro-white, good-bad, etc.); and not the least, we had individ-ual differences to look into.

My colleague Paul Lasakow and I tested several hundred subjects with this simple instrument, and we selected smaller subsamples for particular analyses. Here are some of the things that we found. Men do not disclose as much about themselves, generally, as women. White subjects of both sexes disclose more, generally, than Negro subjects of comparable social class and educational level. For the age range we studied: white females disclose most to mother and girl friend, and least to father and boy friend; Negro females follow a similar pattern. White males disclose in about equivalent amount to both parents and male friend, and significantly less to female friend. Negro males disclose most to their mothers, and comparatively little, if at all, to father, male friend, or female friend.

Married subjects, of course, disclose most to their spouse. With regard to other target-persons, such as both parents and the same-sex friend, female married subjects disclose more than male married subjects, though there is no sex difference in disclosure to the spouse. I am led to suspect that males are relatively unknown to and by anyone until they marry, while women are better known. In fact, it seems that women are both the givers and the receivers of subjective data. Women know more, and tell more, about people's selves than men do. This doubtless, is part of their "expressive role" in social systems, in contrast with the male "instrumental role." It staggers me a little when I think of the stupendous amount of private and personal "self-data" that women have at their disposal. Men know the facts of nature, but women know the facts about men and women!

In connection with the theme of marriage, we are led, of course, to love. Married subjects, male and female, disclose less to their parents and friends than unmarried subjects of comparable age. What they have taken away from these folks, in the way of self-disclosure, they give unto their spouses. In this respect, they more or less follow the biblical injunction which holds that in marriage one should forsake all others. However, while our young married females obeyed the spirit of this injunction, they did not obey its letter— Momma was still disclosed to more than other target-persons. But we have more direct data than this, concerned with the relation between love and self-disclosure. Questionnaires measuring the feelings of a group of young female subjects toward their mothers and fathers produced scores that correlated substantially with self-disclosure to mother and father. In other words, when one loves or likes one's parents, one will make oneself known to them; not otherwise. Of course, psychotherapists are familiar with this fact; self-disclosure gets dammed up in their patients with every twinge of negative transference. And it is influenced by both positive and negative *counter*transference. But I am led to propose that when poets speak of love as a case of giving one's heart and soul to another, they are speaking, among other things, of this prosaic thing, self-disclosure.

Here is an interesting finding. Married police officers were compared with young married college males on self-disclosure to Wife and to Closest Male Friend. Compared with the college boys, the police officers were tight-lipped. Their wives and friends knew virtually nothing about them. Is this paranoia? An occupational pattern?

I am beginning to formulate a rather crude hypothesis about self-disclosure, one which is strongly suggested by certain patterns in our data. Let me state it rather dogmatically, so that it can be more readily tested. Speaking generally, we see in our data that our subjects disclose more to their family than to non-family members, and excepting the married subject, more to their own sex than to the opposite sex; and they disclose more to their age-peers than to their elders or youngers. In other words, the subjects tended to disclose more about themselves to people who *resembled them in various ways* than to people who differed from them. This leads me to propose that disclosure of self is a byproduct, among other things, of the perception or belief that the other, the target-person, is similar to the self. Probably the similarity which is crucial is similarity in *values*. We disclose ourselves when we are pretty sure that the target-person will evaluate our disclosures and react to them as we do ourselves (within certain limits).

Another finding of a general nature is obvious and was expected. The aspects of self were differentially disclosed. Obviously, some kinds of information about ourselves are easier to disclose than others. Psychotherapists are familiar with this fact, as were Kurt Lewin (1948) and, more recently, Marie Rickers-Ovsiankina (1956).

Where to follow this self-disclosure next? There are many avenues, not the least in importance being efforts to refine our instrument, which at present is very crude. But we can explore many general hypotheses in a broad spadework operation—age changes, social class, and many group comparisons. We can explore content systematically for its varying ease of disclosure. We can investigate, even map, interpersonal relationships, lending a depth dimension to sociometry. I'm of course interested in the mental health implications of self-disclosure.

Let me comment a little about self-disclosure and mental health. I really don't know which is cause and which is effect here; perhaps it doesn't matter. I have some evidence that the relationship between the two variables is curvilinear—too much or too little self-disclosure betokens disturbance in self and in interpersonal relationships, while some as yet undetermined amount under specified conditions is synonymous with mental health. I believe that self-disclosure is the obverse of repression and self-alienation. The man who is alienated from his fellows is alienated from himself. Alienated man is not known by his fellows, he doesn't know himself, and he doesn't know his fellows. Self-disclosure appears to be one means, perhaps the most direct, by which self-alienation is transformed into self-realization. Man hides much of his real self—his experience—behind an iron curtain. Our evidence shows that this iron curtain melts like wax when it is exposed to the warm breath of love.

I will conclude by sharing with you some less scientific aspects of the study of self-disclosure. Another man's self is an utterly fascinating datum. We spend much of our time in our daily life speculating about the other person's self; we have to in order to interact with him. Our purposes in securing knowledge of the other man's self vary, of course, but it is not difficult to see how one could become a student of others' selves for the love of the game. If I seem repetitious, enthusiastic, or both, I am like the guitar-player who, daily, for 20 years, sat with a one-string guitar, holding the same fret, plucking the same sound. One day his wife said, with surprise, "Dear, I noticed on TV today that a man was playing a guitar, but it had six strings, and the man kept moving his hands around, and making lots of different sounds—not like you." Her husband said, "Don't worry about him, dear. He's still huntin' the right note, and I already found it."

REFERENCES

CAMERON, N., and MAGARET, ANN. *Behavior Pathology.* Boston: Houghton Mifflin, 1951.

EYSENCK, H. J. "The Effects of Psychotherapy: An Evaluation." *Journal of Consulting Psychology,* 1952, *16,* 319–324.

FROMM, E. *The Sane Society.* New York: Holt, Rinehart and Winston, 1955.

HORNEY, K. *Neurosis and Human Growth.* New York: Norton, 1950.

JOURARD, S. M. *Personal Adjustment: An Approach Through the Study of Healthy Personality.* New York: Macmillan, 1958 (2nd ed., 1963).

LEWIN, K. "Some Social-Psychological Differences Between the United States and Germany." In Lewin, K. (ed.), *Resolving Social Conflicts: Selected Papers on Group Dynamics, 1935–1946.* New York: Harper and Row, 1948.

RICKERS-OVSIANKINA, MARIA. "Social Accessibility in Three Age Groups." *Psychological Reports,* 1956, *2,* 283–294.

ROGERS, C. R., and DYMOND, R. F. *Psychotherapy and Personality Change.* Chicago: University of Chicago Press, 1954.

SKINNER, B. F. *Science and Human Behavior.* New York: Macmillan, 1953.

TILLICH, P. *The Courage to Be.* New Haven, Conn.: Yale University Press, 1952.

PART FOUR

Intrapersonal Communication

Experiences and Discussions

1. Think back on your childhood and list all the family sayings, proverbs, warnings, and scoldings you can recall. Some examples might be "Frank has first choice—he's the oldest" or "You work for your pay and earn your way to the top." How do you think these early messages affected you? Do you do things today that may be a result of these messages? How do the messages change as you grow older? We all use and react to such messages, no matter what our age—only the

format changes. What are some messages you give to and receive from people with whom you interact daily?

2. Keep a diary of how you are feeling: good and bad days, ugly and attractive days, high- and low-mood days. Note the changes and see if there is any pattern to your feelings. If there is a pattern, how might you handle it?

3. How do you view yourself? Make a list of people in your past and present ("significant others") who contribute to the maintenance or increase of your self-esteem. Now make a list of people in your past or present who view you as important to their self-development. How do your two lists compare? Can you explain similarities and differences?

4. Gergen wrote that "fundamental to the feelings we have for others are the feelings we have for ourselves." Think about a day when you felt very low and a day when you felt very pleased with yourself. How did your own feelings affect your actions with the people around you?

5. Consider people with whom you interact daily: family, friends, teachers, workers, employers, etc. Write down at least one way you can demonstrate "unconditional regard" for each person. Be specific about how you will do this.

6. Make a list of the people to whom you are attracted. For each person, describe reasons for this attraction. Compare your reasons with those discussed by Gergen. See if you can categorize your reasons according to the five factors presented by Gergen.

7. Describe your real self and your public selves. How many public selves do you have? How distinct are these from your real self? Have you ever experienced a clash between your real and public selves? Describe the situation and the outcome of that inconsistency.

For Further Reading

BROWN, BARBARA B. *New Mind, New Body; Biofeedback: New Directions for the Mind.* New York: Harper and Row, 1974.

The author defines biofeedback as interaction with the interior self and explores the individual's communication with his or her self through various organs of the body (skin, muscles, heart, etc.).

CANFIELD, JACK, and HAROLD WELLS. *100 Ways to Enhance Self-Concept in the Classroom: A Handbook for Teachers and Parents.* Englewood Cliffs, N.J.: Prentice-Hall, 1976.

The book consists of 100 exercises geared toward students and intended to aid in enhancing some aspect of the self.

ELLIS, ALBERT, and ROBERT A. HARPER. *A Guide to Rational Living.* North Hollywood, Calif.: Wilshire Book Co., 1974.

Based on the premise that "you feel as you think," Ellis and Harper provide numerous examples of therapy for rational thinking. The book is short; the therapy suggested is theory-based, yet practical. The authors describe ten common irrational ideas to work against and conclude with a chapter entitled "Living in an Irrational World."

FITTS, WILLIAM H. *The Self Concept and Self-Actualization.* Nashville, Tenn.: Counselor Recordings and Tests, Dede Wallace Center, 1971.

One of seven monographs on self-concept, this volume discusses theory and research on the development of the self, parental and societal influences on the formation of self-concept, and factors that distort self-perception and self-esteem. This particular monograph discusses the development of the Tennessee Self Concept Scale and some of its major findings. The entire series is excellent for this specific area of research.

GERGEN, KENNETH J. *The Concept of Self.* New York: Holt, 1971.

In less than 100 pages, this book gives a solid review of the study of self, the development of self-concept, the presentation of self, and the self in interpersonal situations. Each section requires a good deal of time, but all are worth it.

JOURARD, SIDNEY M. *The Transparent Self.* 2nd ed. New York: Van Nostrand, 1971.

A modern classic on self-disclosure, its necessary environment, and its relationship to a healthy personality. The relationship of self-disclosure and effective communication is well stated and of considerable value for both intrapersonal and interpersonal communication.

PHILLIPS, GERALD M., and NANCY J. METZGER. *Intimate Communication.* Boston: Allyn and Bacon, 1976.

This book should prove quite interesting (and demanding). It is a study of friendship and the process of friendship development. The authors view interpersonal communication as a form of communication in which people try to influence each other to modify their relationships. Case histories and vignettes about marriages, families, and close friendships are interspersed in the book. The non-scientific approach to interpersonal relations is a welcome and needed one in the field and one with which everyone should become familiar.

STEVENS, JOHN O. *Awareness: Exploring, Experimenting, Experiencing.* Moab, Utah: Real People Press, 1971.

As Stevens indicates in the introduction, his book is designed to "help you to adjust to yourself. . . . It's incredible how much you can realize about your existence by simply paying close attention to it and becoming more deeply aware of your own experiencing." The book provides numerous essays and examples of experiences to increase this awareness. The experiences deal with commnication with self and others, fantasy journeys, pairs and couples, groups, and artistic expression.

PART FIVE

Interpersonal: The Dyad Reacts

To Sherlock Holmes she is always the woman. I have seldom heard him mention her under any other name. In his eyes she eclipses and predominates the whole of her sex. It was not that he felt any emotion akin to love for Irene Adler. All emotions, and that one particularly were abhorrent to his cold, precise, but admirably balanced mind. . . . Grit in a sensitive instrument, or a crack in one of his own highpowered lenses, could not be more disturbing than a strong emotion in a nature such as his. And yet there was but one woman to him, and that woman was the late Irene Adler, of dubious and questionable memory.

A Scandal in Bohemia

As individuals communicate intimate feelings to each other, the most basic nature of interpersonal communication is revealed. Interpersonal communication is in many ways the sharing of the intrapersonal feelings discussed earlier, the interaction among two or more people in direct face-to-face situation. The interpersonal situation relies heavily upon both verbal and nonverbal channels: as Watson suggests, the infrequency of mention may communicate as much as constant discourse. For in interpersonal communication the importance of listening, of actively receiving, as well as sending is most emphasized.

When asked how he became such a success in politics, reticent President Calvin Coolidge is said to have replied: "It was very simple. I just listened my way along." This kind of interpersonal listening and relating underlies any investigation of communication in an interpersonal setting. A great deal has been written about such situations, but it has been muddled in the jargon of psychology, philosophy, history, art, literature, education, and a variety of other fields. Distilling all this conjecture and evidence, some basic conclusions about the nature of interpersonal communication can be drawn.

As so clearly described by William Schutz, three common interpersonal needs provide premises for beginning an investigation. Human interaction is based upon the needs for control, inclusion, and affection; these provide the motivation for all interpersonal action. From this starting point, it is possible to trace the important elements interacting in a setting to meet these basic goals.

The listener is a key element. Watson knows of Holmes's feelings for *the* woman, having listened to a myriad of verbal and nonverbal clues. John Stewart and Gary D'Angelo analyze this listening process, discussing the functions of a receiver: confirmation, understanding, and minimization of defensiveness. A good friend is a good listener, and Watson is clearly a good friend.

The sender, too, is a key element. A variety of sender variables have been described in the literature of communication. Perhaps the most important and best documented is that of credibility, discussed here by Michael Burgoon. Credibility is the link between sender and receiver that reflects the bond between the two. The closer the relationship, the stronger the credibility of the sender and the effectiveness of the interpersonal communication.

In an ideal situation, every listener would be effective and every sender credible. In reality, of course, problems and conflicts occur. In the examination of these conflicts it is possible to detect a great deal about the underlying nature of interpersonal communication. In fact, in describing the intimate interpersonal conflicts that potentially arise between couples, Bach and Wyden provide the key clue in understanding the case of interpersonal communication: "Good communications, in sum, are the lifeline of successful intimacy, and are invariably the result of hard work of dedicated partners working in pairs."

One can't help wondering how *the* woman would describe the detective.

OBJECTIVES

After carefully reading these four articles you should be able to define the following key terms:

listening	(Stewart and D'Angelo)
confirmation	
paraphrasing	
parasupporting	
love	(Bach and Wyden)
pats	
slaps	
kicks	
inclusion	(Schutz)
control	
affection	

credibility   (Burgoon)
competence
composure
sociability
extroversion
initial credibility
transactional credibility
terminal credibility

And:

1. List examples for each of the following: perception checking, paraphrasing, and parasupporting (Stewart and D'Angelo).
2. Distinguish among the three interpersonal needs described by Schutz: inclusion, control, affection (Schutz).
3. Describe characteristic behaviors for each of the following persons: the undersocial, social, oversocial; the abdicat, autocrat, democrat; and the underpersonal, personal, and overpersonal (Schutz).
4. Give an example from personal observation for each of the five attributes of source credibility: competence, character, composure, sociability, and extroversion (Burgoon).
5. Distinguish among initial credibility, transactional credibility, and terminal credibility. Give an example of each type (Burgoon).
6. State three reasons why communication problems often arise between intimates (Bach and Wyden).
7. Provide examples of communication problems between intimates that develop due to (a) the withholding of information, (b) the inability to communicate in a straightforward manner, (c) the camouflaging of true feelings and perceptions, and (d) "bugging" (Bach and Wyden).
8. State at least five of the eight fundamentals of communication noted by Bach and Wyden which can decrease ambiguous messages (Bach and Wyden).
9. Describe the types of conversations that constitute intimate communication and those that do *not* (Bach and Wyden).
10. Distinguish between "pats," "slaps," and "kicks" and the communicative functions of each (Bach and Wyden).

Fourteen

Responsive Listening

John Stewart and Gary D'Angelo

Listening to Confirm

One of the basic things you can do as a listener to encourage interpersonal communication is to *confirm* the person who's talking. Verbal and nonverbal confirming behavior say to the other person, "I'm listening; I might not agree or accept your point of view, but I care about what you're saying, and I'm aware of what's going on." Disconfirmation is the process of communicating as if the other person didn't even exist. People perceive disconfirming behavior to mean that you're not listening—that whether you might agree or disagree, you're ignoring what they are saying and that you're not really interested in taking the time to pay attention to their thoughts and feelings.

It's pretty difficult to continuously confirm the other person. At one time or another, we all lose track of what other people are saying to us. Especially in lengthy conversations, we sometimes daydream or find ourselves thinking about something completely unrelated to what's being discussed. There's nothing abnormal about that; our ability to concentrate for a prolonged period of time is limited. If you want your communication to be interpersonal, however, you should concentrate as much as you can, because it isn't easy to really hear and understand another person. But when you find yourself "tuning out," there's no reason to fake it and pretend that you were listening. In fact, it's much better to let the other person know when you've missed something: "While you were talking just then, my mind was out on a tangent and I missed some things. Would you say that again?" That kind of honesty usually elicits positive reactions from the other person, because it reaffirms your commitment to your communicating and to the other person. And that's confirming, too. In short, communicating confirmation instead of disconfirmation is the first step in listening interpersonally. . . .

. . .

Listening to Understand

Although confirmation is important, paying attention doesn't always lead to genuine understanding of what's being said. It's also important to use listening skills that increase your chances of accurately interpreting the other person.

If people had exactly the same experiences and if they interpreted all words and nonverbal cues in the same way, there would be no need to talk about understanding or misunderstanding. When I used a word, I'd know what it meant to you and you'd know what it meant to me. Unfortunately, that's not the way things are. We interpret the same raw cues differently, and sometimes those differences are extreme. As a result, we need to find ways of reaching each other, of understanding better how we interpret each other's cues.

Genuine understanding doesn't necessarily mean agreement. Understanding involves grasping fully what the other person is trying to say—from her or his point of view—and how he or she feels about it. It comes about when you're able to interpret accurately and empathically the cues the other person makes available.

Accurately understanding the other person's ideas and feelings usually requires you to "listen" with your ears, your eyes, and all of your other sensory equipment. You hear the words being spoken, but you also listen to the tone of voice, pauses and sighs, and you watch for body movements, facial expressions, eye movements, spatial relationships, and so on. In other words, to understand someone, you sometimes have to "hear" both what they're saying and what they're *not* saying in words. People don't always reveal verbally that they're frustrated, afraid, anxious, excited, or depressed. An insightful and understanding listener, though, frequently detects feelings in another person without words being said.

But when the person doesn't express in words certain feelings and ideas, it's not always fair to make inferences from the nonverbal communication. After all, nonverbal cues can mislead. We think that this point is important: you can't develop understanding entirely nonverbally. You probably realize that there are usually many more nonverbal than verbal cues available. But that situation shouldn't lead you, as a listener, to rely exclusively on smiles, gestures, and eye contact, important as these factors are. We believe that when you're listening to understand, it's best to emphasize verbal cues at least as much as nonverbal ones. The best idea is to let the other person know what your interpretation is and to give him or her a chance to respond to your interpretation. The label attached to this process of listening is *perception checking*.

When you're perception checking, you verbalize your interpretation or inferences about what was said—or left unsaid—and you ask the other person to verify or correct your interpretation. Few people use this kind of listening in social conversation. As Larry Brammer says, "We are conditioned to chatter onward socially, even to deliberately confusing the meaning with innuendo, humor, and metaphor. We rarely check with one another about what we are really trying to say."[1] To the extent that what Brammer says is true, very little genuine understanding occurs in most social conversations. But interpersonal communication goes beyond that kind of superficiality, and it does that in part through perception checks.

Paraphrasing

There are at least two dimensions of perception checking you might want to familiarize yourself with. The first is simple paraphrasing. When paraphrasing, *you say in your own words how you've interpreted the other person's ideas and feelings.* Obviously, this kind of response isn't always appropriate. When you hear someone whistling, you don't stop and say, "Pardon me, but do I hear you saying that you're happy?" And if a friend says, "I gotta go; I'm late for class," you don't grab her arm and respond with "Are you saying you have to go because you're late for class?"

Paraphrasing also feels a little mechanical when you first try it. You'll find yourself repeating phrases like "I hear you saying . . ." and "Are you saying that . . .?" At first, it may seem incredibly redundant.

But if your mental attitude as a listener is one of really wanting to understand, you'll find that paraphrasing comes almost naturally. Also, you'll quickly discover that genuine paraphrasing is more than unnecessary redundancy or "word swapping." The two dialogues that follow help illustrate the difference between inadequate and useful paraphrasing:

BOB: My parents are really great!
MARC: You mean you like your parents?
BOB: Yeah, I like my parents.

BOB: My parents are really great!
PHIL: Sounds to me like your parents have either given you something or they've really treated you like a human being recently.
BOB: Well, not exactly that. They've decided to quit pushing my sister about going to college. She wants to stay out of school for a while and get a job so she can put some money away. Three days ago my dad was really upset. Right now, he's helping her look for a job, and he's giving her moral support at the same time. He's really helping her.

In the first dialogue, Marc doesn't give Bob much to respond to, and Marc's words merely repeat what Bob has already said. In the second dialogue, Phil says enough for Bob to know how his statement was interpreted, giving Bob a chance to verify or correct Phil's interpretation. Also note that in neither dialogue does the listener approve or disapprove. Paraphrasing doesn't mean approving or disapproving of what you hear. The goal is simply to give the other person a clear indication of "This is my understanding of what you said and how you feel about it. Are my interpretations accurate?"

Parasupporting

We've labeled the second dimension of perception checking *parasupporting.* In parasupporting, *you not only paraphrase the other person's comments, but also carry his or her ideas further by providing examples or other data that you believe help to illustrate and clarify those ideas.* Here's an example we think will help explain paraphrasing and parasupporting:

A: College is oppressive.
B paraphrases: Are you talking about the fact that students don't get to make very many choices about their education?

A goes into more detail:	Yeah, partly. It's true we're told which courses to take, how many hours, and things like that. But I'm thinking about specific courses and how my profs and T.A.s tell me what I should know, what I should remember, how I should write term papers, what I should write even. I'm just feeling squashed. I can't sit down to study without worrying about what I have to know for a test instead of what I *want* to know.
B parasupports:	There's a course in humanities—201 I think—where they tell you how many times you can miss class and that you have to write three ten-page papers, and they give you topics for the papers and the books you have to use for research. Is that the kind of thing you're talking about?
A verifies B's parasupport:	Yeah, exactly. I'm not taking that course, but I've got some just like it.
B senses A's feeling:	Really, I know what you mean when you say "frustrated." *And* "squashed," too. I think one follows from the other. But sometimes it's the other way around. I've got a couple of courses where we choose our own assignments, and each day in class we decide what we want to talk about. Sometimes, I think that's too much freedom.
A paraphrases:	Sounds like you're not so sure about wanting more freedom in your classes. Like, you wonder whether or not we're able to make decisions if we get the chance to?

Besides the paraphrasing and parasupporting, note two other important characteristics of this dialogue. First, both A and B are motivated by a win/-win attitude. Neither person is trying to "put down" the other's ideas. Neither seems to be concerned about who is right and who is wrong. The win/win atmosphere is evidenced in part by B's parasupporting of A, i.e., a person who wants the other person to lose usually won't parasupport the other's idea. In addition, there are no judgmental responses. Neither directly nor indirectly does B say that A is uninformed, misled, naive, or wrong. Neither does A tell B that. Both persons are concerned about understanding what the other is thinking and feeling.

This leads to a second characteristic of the dialogue: mutuality. Note A's last statement. Up to that point, the primary focus of the conversation was on B trying to understand A. Then, B relates an experience and belief, and in response to that, A tries to understand B. In other words, even though the two persons don't completely agree, *both* are willing to reciprocate listening for understanding.

. . .

Listening to Diminish Defensiveness

There's one more major challenge for the person who wants to listen in ways that promote interpersonal communication. Confirmation and understanding need to be supplemented with listening behavior that keeps other people—so far as you can—from feeling defensive.

After studying group discussion over an eight-year period, Jack Gibb reported that *defensiveness* is one of the major barriers to interpersonal communication. He defined defensive behavior as behavior "which occurs when an individual perceives threat or anticipates threat."[2] He noted that person A's defensiveness usually creates defensiveness in person B, which in turn creates the same thing in person C, and so on to the point where a group's communication can become unproductive and even hostile. Gibb pointed out that one major cause of defensiveness is "speech or other behavior which appears *evaluative*"[3] (italics added). Note that Gibb says *speech* or *other behavior.* Both verbal and nonverbal cues can be evaluative. You may say verbally to someone, "You've gotta be kidding; how can you believe something as stupid as that?" Or, you might accomplish essentially the same thing by covering your face with your hands, taking a deep breath, sighing, and shaking your head negatively. People are sometimes careful about not making evaluative verbal statements, which are relatively easy to control, but at the same time they evoke defensiveness in others through their nonverbal evaluative behavior, which is not so easy to control.

Steve Stephenson (a friend and faculty member in our department) and I (Gary) studied this same phenomenon, and we identified a similar link between evaluation and defensiveness. We found that listeners who were strongly evaluative—who interrupted, disagreed, and continually corrected the other person—evoked significantly more defensiveness than listeners who were less evaluative—who agreed, didn't interrupt, paraphrased, and encouraged the other person.[4] It seems clear, in short, that evaluative listening increases defensiveness and that defensiveness can destroy interpersonal communication.

These conclusions suggest that if you want to communicate interpersonally, you shouldn't be evaluative. But in an important sense that's *impossible;* you *cannot not evaluate* the things—and people—you perceive. Right now, you're probably perceiving the pressure of a chair against your bottom, the fit of shoes around your feet, and the weight of clothes on your shoulders. Yet before you read that sentence, you probably weren't aware of any of those perceptions. You're continuously *selectively* perceiving, and your selection is based on some kind of value judgment: one thing is relevant to you, another is irrelevant; this is important, that's unimportant; this is interesting, that's boring, or whatever.

Your evaluating goes on at different levels of awareness, but it's always there; you cannot not evaluate.

So what do you do? If evaluation creates defensiveness but you can't stop evaluating, what can you do as a listener to help, rather than hinder, interpersonal communication? We think this is a really important question, the answer to which could have a significant effect on the ways in which you listen to other people. We want to respond to that question with six suggestions for listening to diminish defensiveness:

1. Be generally positive
2. Postpone specific evaluations
3. Limit negative evaluations
4. Own your evaluations
5. Keep your evaluations tentative
6. Actively solicit responses

NOTES

1. LAWRENCE BRAMMER. *The Helping Relationship: Process and Skills.* Englewood Cliffs, N.J.: Prentice-Hall, 1973. p. 86.
2. JACK R. GIBB. "Defensive Communication," *Journal of Communication,* XI (September 1961): 141.
3. *Ibid.,* p. 142.
4. STEPHEN J. STEPHENSON and GARY D'ANGELO. "Relationships Among Evaluative Empathic Listening, Self-Esteem, Sex, and Defensiveness in Dyads," unpublished manuscript, University of Washington, 1973.

Fifteen

The Postulate of Interpersonal Needs

William Schutz

Postulate 1. The Postulate of Interpersonal Needs

(a). Every individual has three interpersonal needs: inclusion, control, and affection.

(b). Inclusion, control, and affection constitute a sufficient set of areas of interpersonal behavior for the prediction and explanation of interpersonal phenomena.

Explanation: In studying interpersonal behavior it is important to isolate the relevant variables. "People need people" serves as a good starting point, but, if the frontiers of knowledge are to recede, the next question must be investigated: "*In what ways* do people need people?"

. . .

The Three Interpersonal Needs

The interpersonal need for inclusion is defined behaviorally as the need to establish and maintain a satisfactory relation with people with respect to interaction and association. "Satisfactory relation" includes (1) a psychologically comfortable relation with people somewhere on a dimension ranging from originating or initiating interaction with all people to not initiating interaction with anyone; (2) a psychologically comfortable relation with people with respect to eliciting behavior from them somewhere on a dimension ranging from always initiating interaction with the self to never initiating interaction with the self.

On the level of feelings the need for inclusion is defined as the need to establish and maintain a feeling of mutual interest with other people. This feeling includes (1) being able to take an interest in other people to a satisfactory degree and (2) having other people interested in the self to a satisfactory degree.

With regard to the self-concept, the need for inclusion is the need to feel that the self is significant and worthwhile.

The interpersonal need for control is defined behaviorally as the need to establish and maintain a satisfactory relation with people with respect to control and power. "Satisfactory relation" includes (1) a psychologically comfortable relation with people somewhere on a dimension ranging from controlling all the behavior of other people to not controlling any behavior of others and (2) a psychologically comfortable relation with people with respect to eliciting behavior from them somewhere on a dimension ranging from always being controlled by them to never being controlled by them.

With regard to feelings, the need for control is defined as the need to establish and maintain a feeling of mutual respect for the competence and responsibleness of others. This feeling includes (1) being able to respect others to a satisfactory degree and (2) having others respect the self to a satisfactory degree.

The need for control, defined at the level of perceiving the self, is the need to feel that one is a competent, responsible person.

The interpersonal need for affection is defined behaviorally as the need to establish and maintain a satisfactory relation with others with respect to love and affection. Affection always refers to a two-person (dyadic) relation. "Satisfactory relation" includes (1) a psychologically comfortable relation with others somewhere on a dimension ranging from initiating close, personal relations with everyone to originating close, personal relations with no one; (2) a psychologically comfortable relation with people with respect to eliciting behavior from them on a dimension ranging from always originating close, personal relations toward the self, to never originating close, personal relations toward the self.

At the feeling level the need for affection is defined as the need to establish and maintain a feeling of mutual affection with others. This feeling includes (1) being able to love other people to a satisfactory degree and (2) having others love the self to a satisfactory degree.

The need for affection, defined at the level of the self-concept, is the need to feel that the self is lovable.

This type of formulation stresses the interpersonal nature of these needs. They require that the organism establish a kind of equilibrium, in three different areas, between the self and other people. In order to be anxiety-free, a person must find a comfortable behavioral relation with others with regard to the exchange of interaction, power, and love. The need is not wholly satisfied by having others respond toward the self in a particular way; nor is it wholly satisfied by acting toward others in a particular fashion. A satisfactory balance must be established and maintained.

Inclusion, Control, and Affection Behavior

. . .

In general, *inclusion behavior* refers to association between people. Some terms that connote a relation that is primarily positive inclusion are "associate," "interact," "mingle," "communicate," "belong," "companion," "comrade," "attend to," "member," "togetherness," "join," "extravert." Some terms that connote lack of, or negative, inclusion are "exclusion," "isolate," "outsider," "outcast," "lonely," "detached," "withdrawn," "abandoned," "ignored."

The need to be included manifests itself as wanting to be attended to, to attract attention and interest. The classroom hellion who throws erasers is often objecting mostly to the lack of attention paid him. Even if he is given negative affection he is partially satisfied, because at least someone is paying attention to him.

In groups, people often make themselves prominent by talking a great deal. Frequently they are not interested in power or dominance but simply prominence. The "joker" is an example of a prominence seeker, very much as is the blond actress with the lavender convertible.

In the extreme, what is called "fame" is primarily inclusion. Acquisition of fame does not imply acquisition of power or influence: witness Marilyn Monroe's attempt to swing votes to Adlai Stevenson. Nor does fame imply affection: Al Capone could hardly be considered a widely loved figure. But fame does imply prominence, and signifies interest on the part of others.

From another standpoint, behavior related to belonging and "togetherness" is primarily inclusion. To desire to belong to a fraternal organization by no means necessarily indicates a liking for the members or even a desire for power. It is often sought for its "prestige value," for increase of "status." These terms are also primarily inclusion conceptions, because their primary implication is that people pay attention to the person, know who he is, and can distinguish him from others.

This last point leads to an essential aspect of inclusion, that of identity. An integral part of being recognized and paid attention to is that the individual be identifiable from other people. He must be known as a specific individual; he must have a particular identity. If he is not thus known, he cannot truly be attended to or have interest paid to him. The extreme of this identification is that he be understood. To be understood implies that someone is interested enough in him to find out his particular characteristics. Again, this interest need not mean that others have affection for him, or that they respect him. For example, the interested person may be a confidence man who is exploring his background to find a point of vulnerability.

At the outset of interpersonal relations a common issue is that of commitment, the decision to become involved in a given relation or activity. Usually, in the initial testing of the relation, individuals try to identify themselves to one another to find out which facet of themselves others will be interested in. Frequently a member is silent for a while because he is not sure that people are interested in him. These behaviors, too, are primarily in the inclusion area.

This, then, is the flavor of inclusion. It has to do with interacting with people, with attention, acknowledgement, being known, prominence, recognition, prestige, status, and fame; with identity, individuality, understanding, interest, commitment, and participation. It is unlike affection in that it does not involve strong emotional attachments to individual persons. It is unlike control in that the preoccupation is with prominence, not dominance.

Control behavior refers to the decision-making process between people. Some terms connoting a relation that is primarily positive control are "power," "authority," "dominance," "influence," "control," "ruler," "superior officer," "leader." Some terms that connote primarily a lack of, or negative, control are "rebellion," "resistance," "follower," "anarchy," "submissive," "henpecked," "milquetoast."

The need for control manifests itself as the desire for power, authority, and control over others and therefore over one's future. At the other end is the need to be controlled, to have responsibility taken away. Manifestations of the power drive are very clear. A more subtle form is exemplified by the current magazine advertising campaign featuring the "influential." This is a person who controls others through the power he has to influence their behavior.

The acquisition of money or political power is a direct method of obtaining control over other persons. This type of control often involves coercion rather than more subtle methods of influence like persuasion and example. In group behavior, the struggles to achieve high office or to make suggestions that are adopted are manifestations of control behavior. In an argument in a group we may distinguish the inclusion seeker from the control seeker in this way: the one seeking inclusion or prominence wants very much to be one of the participants in the argument, while the control seeker wants to be the winner or, if not the winner, on the same side as the winner. The prominence seeker would prefer to be the losing participant; the dominance seeker would prefer to be a winning nonparticipant. Both these roles are separate from the affectional desires of the members.

Control behavior takes many subtle forms, especially among more intellectual and polite people. For example, in many discussion groups where blackboards are involved, the power struggle becomes displaced onto the chalk. Walking to the blackboard and taking the chalk from the one holding it, and retaining possession, becomes a mark of competitive success. Often a meeting is marked by a procession of men taking the chalk, writing something, and being supplanted by another man for a further message. In this way propriety is maintained, and still the power struggle may proceed.

In many gatherings, control behavior is exhibited through the group task. Intellectual superiority, for one thing, often leads to control over others so that strong motivation to achieve is often largely control behavior. Such superiority also demonstrates the real capacity of the individual to be relied on for responsible jobs, a central aspect of control. Further, to do one's job properly, or to rebel against the established authority structure by not doing it, is a splendid outlet for control feelings. Doing a poor job is a way of rebelling against the structure and showing that no one will control you, whereas asquiescence earns rewards from those in charge which satisfy the need to be respected for one's accomplishments.

Control is also manifested in behavior toward others controlling the self. Expressions of independence and rebellion exemplify lack of willingness to be controlled, while compliance, submission, and taking orders indicate various degrees of accepting the control of others. There is no necessary relation between an individual's behavior toward controling others and his behavior toward being controlled. The domineering sergeant may accept orders from the lieutenant with pleasure and gratefulness, while the neighborhood bully may also rebel against his parents; two persons who control others differ in the degree to which they allow others to control them.

Thus the flavor of control is transmitted by behavior involving influence, leadership, power, coercion, authority, accomplishment, intellectual superiority, high achievement, and independence, as well as dependency (for decision making), rebellion, resistance, and submission. It differs from inclusion behavior in that it does not require prominence. The concept of the "power behind the throne" is an excellent example of a role that would fill a high control need and a low need for inclusion. The "joker" exemplifies the opposite. Control behavior differs from affection behavior in that it has to do with power relations rather than emotional closeness. The frequent difficulties between those who want to "get down to business" and those who want to get to "know one another" illustrate a situation in which control behavior is more important for some and affection behavior for others.

In general, *affection behavior* refers to close personal emotional feelings between *two* people. Affection is a dyadic relation; it can occur only between pairs of people at any one time, whereas both inclusion and control relations may occur either in dyads or between one person and a group of persons. Some terms that connote an affection relation that is primarily positive are "love," "like," "emotionally close," "positive feelings," "personal," "friendship," "sweetheart." Some terms that connote primarily lack of, or negative, affection are "hate," "dislike," "cool," "emotionally distant."

The need for affection leads to behavior related to becoming emotionally close. An affection relation must be dyadic because it involves strong differentiation between people. Affectional relations can be toward parental figures, peers, or children figures. They are exemplified in friendship relations, dating, and marriage.

To become emotionally close to someone involves, in addition to an emotional attachment, an element of confiding innermost anxieties, wishes, and feelings. A strong positive affectional tie usually is accompanied by a unique relation regarding the degree of sharing of these feelings.

In groups, affection behavior is characterized by overtures of friendship and differentiation between members. One common method for avoiding a close tie with any one member is to be equally friendly to all members. Thus "popularity" may not involve affection at all; it may often be inclusion behavior, whereas "going steady" is usually primarily affection.

A difference between affection behavior, inclusion behavior, and control behavior is illustrated by the different feelings a man has in being turned down by a fraternity, failed in a course by a professor, and rejected by his girl. The fraternity excludes him and tells him, in effect, that they as a group don't have sufficient interest in him. The professor fails him and says, in effect, that he finds him incompetent in his field. His girl rejects him, and tells him, in effect, that she doesn't find him lovable.

Thus the flavor of affection is embodied in situations of love, emotional closeness, personal confidences, intimacy. Negative affection is characterized by hate, hostility, and emotional rejection.

In order to sharpen further the contrast between these three types of behavior, several differences may be mentioned.

With respect to an interpersonal relation, inclusion is concerned primarily with the formation of the relation, whereas control and affection are concerned with relations already formed. Basically, inclusion is always concerned with whether or not a relation exists. Within existent relations, control is the area concerned with who gives orders and make decisions for whom, whereas affection is concerned with how emotionally close or distant the relation becomes. Thus, generally speaking, inclusion is concerned with the problem of *in or out,* control is concerned with *top or bottom,* and affection with *close or far.*

A further differentiation occurs with regard to the number of people involved in the relation. Affection is *always* a one-to-one relation, inclusion is *usually* a one-to-many relation, and control may be either a one-one or a one-many relation. An affectional tie is necessarily between two persons, and involves varying degrees of intimacy, warmth, and emotional involvement which cannot be felt toward a unit greater than one person. Inclusion, on the other hand, typically concerns the behavior and feelings of one person toward a group of people. Problems of belonging and membership, so central to the inclusion area, usually refer to a relatively undifferentiated group with which an individual seeks association. His feelings of wanting to belong to the group are qualitatively different from his personal feelings of warmth toward an individual person. Control may refer to a power struggle between two individuals for control over each other, or it may refer to the struggle for domination over a group, as in political power. There is no particular number of interactional participants implied in the control area.

Control differs from the other two areas with respect to the differentiation between the persons involved in the control situation. For inclusion and affection there is a tendency for participants to act similarly in both the behavior they express and the behavior they want from others; for example, a close, personal individual usually likes others to be close and personal also. This similarity is not so marked in the control area. The person who likes to control may or may not want others to control him. This difference in differentiation among need areas is, however, only a matter of degree. There are many who like to include but do not want to be included, or who are not personal but want others to be that way toward them. But these types are not as frequent as the corresponding types in the control area.

Types of Interpersonal Behavior

For each area of interpersonal behavior three types of behavior will be described: (1) deficient—indicating that the individual is not trying directly to satisfy the need, (2) excessive—indicating that the individual is constantly trying to satisfy the need, (3) ideal—indicating satisfaction of the need, and (4) pathological.

. . .

Inclusion Types

The Undersocial
The interpersonal behavior of the undersocial person tends to be introverted and withdrawn. Characteristically, he avoids associating with others and doesn't like or accept invitations to join others. Consciously he wants to maintain this distance between himself and others, and insists that he doesn't want to get enmeshed with people and lose his privacy. But unconsciously he definitely wants others to pay attention to him. His biggest fears are that people will ignore him, generally have no interest in him, and would just as soon leave him behind.

Unconsciously he feels that no one ever will pay attention to him. His attitude may be summarized by, "No one is interested in me, so I'm not going to risk being ignored. I'll stay away from people and get along by myself." There is a strong drive toward self-sufficiency as a technique for existence without others. Since social abandonment is tantamount to death, he must compensate by directing his energies toward self-preservation; he therefore creates a world of his own in which his existence is more secure. Behind this withdrawal lie anxiety and hostility, and often a slight air of superiority and the private feeling that others don't understand him.

The direct expression of this withdrawal is nonassociation and [non] interaction with people, lack of involvement and commitment. The more subtle form is exemplified by the person who for one reason or another is always late to meetings, or seems to have an inordinate number of conflicting engagements necessitating absence from people, or the type of person who precedes each visit with, "I'm sorry, but I can't stay very long."

His deepest anxiety, that referring to the self-concept, is that he is worthless. He thinks that if no one ever considered him important enough to receive attention, he must be of no value whatever.

Closely allied with this feeling is the lack of motivation to live. Association with people is a necessary condition for a desire to live. This factor may be of much greater importance in everyday interaction than is usually thought. The degree to which an individual is committed to living probably determines to a large extent his general level of enthusiasms, perseverance, involvement, and the like. Perhaps this lack of concern for life is the ultimate in regression: if life holds too few rewards, the prelife condition is preferable. It is likely that this basic fear of abandonment or isolation is the most potent of all interpersonal fears. The simple fear that people are not interested in the self is extremely widespread, but in scientific analyses it, too often, is included as a special type of affectional need. It is extremely useful, however, to make clear the distinction between inclusion and affection.

The Oversocial

The oversocial person tends toward extraversion in his later interpersonal behavior. Characteristically, he seeks people incessantly and wants them to seek him out. He is also afraid they will ignore him. His interpersonal dynamics are the same as those of the withdrawn person, but his overt behavior is the opposite.

His unconscious attitude is summarized by, "Although no one is interested in me, I'll make people pay attention to me in any way I can." His inclination is always to seek companionship. He is the type who "can't stand being alone." All of his activities will be designed to be done "together." An interesting illustration of this attitude occurs in the recent motion picture "The Great Man." José Ferrer, as a newspaper man, is interviewing a woman about her reasons for attending the funeral of a television celebrity.

"Because our club all came together," she replies.
"But," Ferrer persists, "why did you come *here?*"
"I came here because the rest came here."
"Were you fond of the dead man?"
"Not especially," she replies, "but we always do things together."

This scene (the dialogue is from memory) nicely illustrates the importance of being together presumably as an end in itself. The interpersonal behavior of the oversocial type of person will then be designed to focus attention on himself, to make people notice him, to be prominent, to be listened to. There are many techniques for doing this. The direct method is to be an intensive, exhibitionistic participator. By simply forcing himself on the group he forces the group to focus attention on him. The more subtle technique is to try to acquire status through such devices as name dropping, or by asking startling questions. He may also try to acquire power (control) or try to be well liked (affection), but for the primary purpose of gaining attention. Power or friendship, although both may be important (depending on his orientation in the other two interpersonal areas), is not the primary goal.

The Social

To the individual for whom the resolution of inclusion relations was successful in childhood, interaction with people presents no problem. He is comfortable with people and comfortable being alone. He can be a high or low participator in a group, or can equally well take a moderate role, without anxiety. He is capable of strong commitment and involvement to certain groups and also can withhold commitment if he feels it is appropriate.

Unconsciously, he feels that he is a worthwhile, significant person and that life is worth living. He is fully capable of being genuinely interested in others and feels that they will include him in their activities and that they are interested in him.

He also has an "identity" and an "individuality." Childhood feelings of abandonment lead to the absence of an identity; the person feels he is nobody. He has no stable figures with whom to identify. Childhood feelings of enmeshment lead to confusion of identity. When a child is nothing but parts of other people and has not had sufficient opportunity to evaluate the characteristics he observes in himself, he has difficulty knowing who he is. The social person has resolved these difficulties. He has integrated aspects of a large number of individuals into a new configuration which he can identify as himself.

. . .

Control Types

The Abdicrat

The abdicrat is a person who tends toward submission and abdication of power and responsibility in his interpersonal behavior. Characteristically, he gravitates toward the subordinate position where he will not have to take responsibility for making decisions, and where someone else takes charge. Consciously, he wants people to relieve him of his obligations. He does not control others even when he should; for example, he would not take charge even during a fire in a children's schoolhouse in which he is the only adult; and he never makes a decision that he can refer to someone else. He fears that others will not help him when he requires it, and that he will be given more responsibility than he can handle. This kind of person is usually a follower, or at most a loyal lieutenant, but rarely the person who takes the responsibility for making the *final* decision. Unconsciously, too, he has the feeling that he is incapable of responsible adult behavior and that others know it. He never was told what to do and therefore never learned. His most comfortable response is to avoid situations in which he will feel helpless. He feels that he is an incompetent and irresponsible, perhaps stupid, person who does not deserve respect for his abilities.

Behind this feeling are anxiety, hostility, and lack of trust toward those who might withhold assistance. The hostility is usually expressed as passive resistance. Hesitancy to "go along" is a usual technique of resistance, since actual overt rebellion is too threatening.

The Autocrat

The autocrat is a person whose interpersonal behavior often tends toward the dominating. Characteristically, he tries to dominate people and strongly desires a power hierarchy with himself at the top. He is the power seeker, the competer. He is afraid people will not be influenced or controlled by him— that they will, in fact, dominate him.

Commonly, this need to control people is displaced into other areas. Intellectual or athletic superiority allows for considerable control, as does the more direct method of attaining political power. The underlying dynamics are the same as for the abdicrat. Basically the person feels he is not responsible or capable of discharging obligation and that this fact is known to others. He attempts to use every opportunity to disprove this feeling to others and to himself. His unconscious attitude may be summarized as, "No one thinks I can make decisions for myself, but I'll show them. I'm going to make all the decisions for everyone, always." Behind this feeling is a strong distrust that others may make decisions for him and the feeling that they don't trust him. This latter becomes a very sensitive area.

The Democrat

For the individual who has successfully resolved his relations with others in the control area in childhood, power and control present no problem. He feels comfortable giving or not giving orders, and taking or not taking orders, as is appropriate to the situation. Unconsciously, he feels that he is a capable, responsible person and therefore that he does not need to shrink from responsibility or to try constantly to prove how competent he really is. Unlike the abdicrat and autocrat, he is not preoccupied with fears of his own helplessness, stupidity, and incompetence. He feels that other people respect his competence and will be realistic with respect to trusting him with decision making.

. . .

Affection Types

The Underpersonal

The underpersonal type tends to avoid close personal ties with others. He characteristically maintains his dyadic relations on a superficial, distant level and is most comfortable when others do the same to him. Consciously, he wishes to maintain this emotional distance, and frequently expresses a desire not to get "emotionally involved"; unconsciously he seeks a satisfactory affectional relation. His fear is that no one loves him. In a group situation he is afraid he won't be liked. He has great difficulty genuinely liking people. He distrusts their feeling toward him.

His attitude could be summarized by the "formula," "I find the affection area very painful since I have been rejected; therefore I shall avoid close personal relations in the future." The direct technique for maintaining emotional distance is to reject and avoid people to prevent emotional closeness or involvement actively, even to the point of being antagonistic. The subtle technique is to appear superficially friendly to *everyone.* This behavior acts as a safeguard against having to get close to, or become personal with, any *one* person. ("Close" and "personal" refer to emotional closeness and willingness to confide one's most private concerns and feelings. It involves the expression of positive affection and tender feelings.) Here the dyadic relation is a threatening one. To keep everyone at the same distance obviates the requirement for treating any one person with greater warmth and affection.

The deepest anxiety, that regarding the self, is that he is unlovable. He feels that people won't like him because, in fact, he doesn't "deserve" it. If people got to know him well, he believes, they would discover the traits that make him so unlovable. As opposed to the inclusion anxiety that the self is of no value, worthless, and empty, and the control anxiety that the self is stupid and irresponsible, the affection anxiety is that the self is nasty and bad.

The Overpersonal

The overpersonal type attempts to become extremely close to others. He definitely wants others to treat him in a very close, personal way. His response may be summarized by the formula, "My first experiences with affection were painful, but perhaps if I try again they will turn out to be better." He will be striving in his interpersonal relations primarily to be liked. Being liked is extremely important to him in his attempt to relieve his anxiety about being always rejected and unlovable. Again, there are two behavioral techniques, the direct and the subtle. The direct technique is an overt attempt to gain approval, be extremely personal, intimate, and confiding. The subtle technique is more manipulative, to devour friends and subtly punish any attempts by them to establish other friendships, to be possessive.

The underlying dynamics are the same as those for the underpersonal. Both the overpersonal and the underpersonal responses are extreme, both are motivated by a strong need for affection, both are accompanied by strong anxiety about ever being loved, and basically about being unlovable and both have considerable hostility behind them stemming from the anticipation of rejection.

The Personal

For the individual who successfully resolved his affectional relations with others in childhood, close emotional relations with one other person present no problem. He is comfortable in such a personal relation, and he can also relate comfortably in a situation requiring emotional distance. It is important for him to be liked, but if he isn't liked he can accept the fact that the dislike is the result of the relation between himself and one other person—in other words, the dislike does not mean that he is an unlovable person. Unconsciously, he feels that he is a lovable person who is lovable even to people who know him well. He is capable of giving genuine affection.

Sixteen

Credibility as a Source Variable

Michael Burgoon

We are all aware that some people are more effective communicators than others. Many times the reasons for this effectiveness are not readily apparent to the people involved in a communication situation. People who tend to persuade us, or who are naturally likeable, or who are able to enter situations and settle difficulties, are usually held in high esteem by their fellow men. When we cannot explain why these people have the impact they do, we often claim they simply possess "charisma." However, the use of a word like charisma is not very helpful to those of us who wish to obtain more understanding of human communication. Since one is hard pressed to identify those variables which make one person a charismatic leader and another person not, he is also at a loss when asked to help someone else be a more charismatic and thus more effective communicator. Therefore, we must look for specific attributes of a source, including his communication behavior, to understand the real meaning of this ambiguous term.

. . .

The Dimensions of Source Credibility

Contemporary communication scholars have tried systematically to analyze what constitutes a "good" man, or a "credible" speaker, or a "charismatic" leader. It appears that people make decisions about at least five attributes of a source in a communication situation.[1] Earlier writers identified two of these decision points: *competence,* or the source's knowledge of the subject, and *character,* or the apparent trustworthiness of the source. Other source attributes which seem important to a receiver are *composure, sociability and extroversion.*

Each of these dimensions acts independently to influence the source's effectiveness as a communicator. For example, you can decide a person has great expertise on a particular topic but nevertheless believe he is untrustworthy. Similarly, a person can be very likeable and composed but be judged by others as having little competence on a specific subject. In any given situation, one decision may be more important than the others and therefore be a better predictor of communication effectiveness. In a social situation, you may not care whether a person is extremely knowledgeable about Elizabethan drama so long as you enjoy talking with him. However, if you are injured, it may matter little if your doctor is sociable and out-going; you simply want someone who is competent to treat your broken arm.

The Dimension of Competence

It is common in most communication situations for a receiver to judge a source's competence on the subject being discussed. In fact, research indicates that perceptions of competence may contribute most to variance in a receiver's evaluation of a source's credibility.[2] If a speaker is not perceived to be competent or knowledgeable on a topic, it may make little difference how trustworthy, composed, sociable or extroverted he happens to be. People make competence judgments on such variables as level of education, accessibility to current or pertinent information, or direct experience with the subject under discussion. Whether or not the receivers are themselves competent to judge the source's competence seems to make little difference. In short, if the speaker is perceived as competent, he will probably be effective.

There are several things a source may do to increase his perceived competence. In public speaking situations, it is common for a speaker to be introduced to the audience by another person. If the person making the introduction refers to the speaker's title, such as doctor or professor, or even labels him as "a leading expert," this may enhance the audience's perception of the source's competence. The speaker himself may indicate his expertise on the topic by referring to previous experience with the subject or by mentioning other highly competent people with whom he is associated.

If the receivers perceive a source to be low in competence, there is little likelihood that the speaker will be effective, regardless of his actual expertise on the subject being discussed. A good example of this involves a group of students who were invited to hear a lecture on life among the Ashanti. The speaker, a white woman, was given an introduction specifically designed to ensure that she was perceived as competent; the audience was told that the source was born in Africa and raised among the Ashanti. Nevertheless, the predominantly black American audience was extremely unreceptive. The speaker was thoroughly familiar with the African experience of the Ashanti. She could converse easily and at length with the Ashanti people about shared cultural experiences; in fact, the native Africans perceived her to be "one of them" despite her skin color. But the audience of black students had a very different perception of her competence to speak on what they perceived to be the "black experience." Communication was difficult because although the speaker knew what it was like to be an Ashanti, she did not know what it was like to be an American black, and her audience doubted her competence to speak on the announced topic.

Clearly, the woman's skin color was not in her control, but she could have taken steps to change the audience's perceptions. For example, she might have been perceived as more competent if she had directly confronted the situation and admitted to the audience that she did not understand the black American experience but could provide information about Africa that might be of interest. Sometimes an admission of lack of competence in one area is perceived as an indication of other kinds of competence.

Many research studies have demonstrated the importance of perceived competence. In a classic study, a recording of a speech favoring national compulsory health insurance was played to several groups of subjects. When the statement was attributed to the Surgeon-General, it was very effective in persuading people of the need for compulsory insurance; however, when the same recording was attributed to a college student, it had no persuasive impact.[3] In this test, the same voice and message had drastically different effects when the source was perceived differentially on the competence dimension. A number of other studies strongly support the notion that sources perceived as highly competent will be effective, whereas those not perceived as competent will have difficulty in communicating effectively.

In most situations, a source cannot be perceived as "too competent;" an ideal source would be one who is highly competent to discuss the topic under consideration. However, the perception of competence is itself a multidimensional process involving several variables. For example, a nuclear physicist heading a research project may be so brilliant that he cannot effectively express his ideas to his subordinates. In such an instance, his research assistants may perceive him as highly competent on one dimension (mastery of subject matter) but incompetent on another (ability to express himself). Based on this example, one might caution a speaker to carefully determine those variables most important to his audience if he is to be effective.

The Dimension of Character

The popular rejoinder "You're a good man, Charlie Brown" is an estimate of character perceived as goodness, decency or trustworthiness. The dimension of character has a strong influence on the receiver's perception of source credibility. The term "credibility gap," popularized in the early 1960s, refers almost solely to this dimension. The government was saying one thing, and later press accounts indicated it was doing the opposite. Recent scandals in government are said to have reduced the President's credibility. When people believe a communicator to be low in character or trustworthiness, they are less likely even to listen to him, let alone to be influenced by his message. To some extent, we judge competence on the basis of objective qualifications (education, work experience and other credentials), but perceptions of character are highly personal judgments about the nature of a source.

In a recent Gallup poll, CBS newscaster Walter Cronkite was found to be the most trusted man in the United States. One can only speculate as to the reasons for these findings. People obviously feel that he is an honest reporter who does not bias the news with his own feelings and cannot be compromised. Therefore, if Cronkite said one thing and the government said another, the position advocated by Cronkite would probably be believed by the majority of people who heard both messages. Another former network newscaster, Chet Huntley, created some controversy when he appeared in a commercial for an airline. The decision makers at the airline probably did not believe Huntley would be seen as competent to discuss the construction of airplanes; however, they were betting that the American people believed him to be of high character and would therefore be persuaded by the commercials. Other newscasters criticized this arrangement, claiming that Huntley's lack of objectivity on the airline would damage the perceived objectivity of all newsmen.

The question of how one establishes and maintains perceptions of high character is a difficult one. Obviously any past experience that questions a person's integrity reduces perceived character. People who change position over time can be seen as less trustworthy, even if the change itself is a good one. It is doubtful that an ideal source would be anything other than high in character. The best advice to ensure perceptions of high character is to be consistently honest. To the extent a person is perceived to be one of high character, he will be able to facilitate more effective communication. It is certainly a goal worth seeking.

The Dimension of Composure

A person who is composed, especially under conditions of considerable stress, is perceived to be more credible than a person who is not composed. Research indicates that a speaker who is nervous or produces a number of nonfluencies (stammering, "uhs" and "ers") is less credible and less able to persuade others.[4] Many speech students are immediately perceived as more credible in the early part of the course, because they can keep composed during the stress-producing first speeches. Many people we call "good public speakers" are not more competent or of higher character, but more composed.

To increase his perceived composure, the beginning public speaker can practice his delivery to reduce nonfluencies and apparent nervousness. Fidgeting, shuffling of papers and other distracting behavior often reduce a speaker's perceived composure. In American culture, extreme displays of emotion are also perceived as lack of poise. Many political commentators attribute Senator Muskie's defeat in the Presidential primaries of 1972 to a moment when he lost his composure and publicly cried because of newspaper attacks on his wife. However, it is very difficult to predict the effects specific evidence of lack of composure will have. In two different instances, Walter Cronkite lost his composure. During the 1968 Democratic Convention, he became visibly angry when a floor reporter was accosted. When the first man landed on the moon, he was clearly elated and used emotional language unusual for him. Certainly, the Gallup poll indicates that Cronkite did not suffer any loss of credibility because of his behavior on these occasions. However, few of us enjoy the status that Walter Cronkite has in the eyes of the American public. Therefore, the best advice, according to the research available, is for a speaker to retain his composure whenever possible, since evidence of lack of composure may reduce his effectiveness as a communicator.

The Dimension of Sociability

The source that projects likeableness to his receivers is regarded as sociable. People who like each other tend to spend more time communicating with each other and are influenced by each other. Research indicates that our interpersonal communication contacts are very influential in shaping and changing our attitudes on a variety of issues. Peers influence our political behavior, help determine the products we consume, and shape our thinking in numerous ways. The recent trends in advertising try to present advocates of consumer products as likeable people; much of the "image advertising" in politics is also designed to do just this. We tend to like people who give us the feeling that they like and respect us and avoid those who do not. Therefore, we are more likely to attend to and be influenced by those whom we perceive as sociable.

There is more to sociability than just interpersonal liking. Although we may not have a friendship with or a deep liking for a person, if he is cooperative and friendly in task situations, he will be perceived as more sociable. The person who goes about his work in a cheerful, friendly manner is likely to be a preferred co-worker. All of these things combine to make a person appear to be more approachable and communicative. In all likelihood, those we consider unsociable will not be a part of our communication activities and will have little influence on us.

The Dimension of Extroversion

The outgoing personality who engages readily and unselfconsciously in communication situations is considered an extrovert. The person who is talkative and not timid in his communication activities is sometimes said to be a dynamic speaker; he may be a very effective communicator. However, a person who is too extroverted may talk too much and take over conversations. We have all been in situations in which very dynamic, extroverted people so dominated the communication that we felt like an unnecessary part of the conversation. Although the optimum amount of source extroversion varies from receiver to receiver, people generally prefer to communicate with those who possess this attribute in moderation.[5]

Jack Paar, for example, is often criticized for being so extroverted and talkative that his guests are rarely allowed to say anything. These critics probably prefer to watch another talk show host—Dick Cavett or Johnny

Carson—who dominates less and who allows his guests to carry more of the conversation. However, Paar's show has a large audience whose members obviously enjoy his communication behavior. In most social situations, there is a fine line between being "the life of the party" and "a smashing bore." Figure 1 may help to clarify the relationship between extroversion and effective communication.

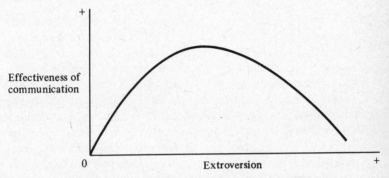

FIGURE 1 *Relationship of extroversion and communicating effectiveness.*

As extroversion increases, people enjoy talking with and listening to a dynamic person. An extroverted person holds their attention and is generally interesting. However, at some point, and this point varies with people and situations, increased extroversion annoys people and makes them either dislike the person or withdraw from the situation.

The Dynamics of Source Credibility

Perceptions of a source's credibility are subject to change. Often a source comes to the communication situation with some degree of credibility already established. The degree of credibility perceived in the source prior to any specific communication event is called *initial credibility*. When we say of a speaker that "his reputation preceded him," we are commenting on his initial credibility. For example, a world-famous Arctic explorer talking before a group of professional geographers could expect to have a high degree of initial credibility with his audience. The speaker with a high degree of initial credibility is likely to use a very different communication strategy than a person who is seeking to establish or enhance his credibility.

During any communication event, the source's credibility may be reevaluated and either heightened or lowered in the receiver's mind. This assessment or modification of initial credibility is called *transactional credibility*. People continually assess a speaker and make evaluative changes during a communication transaction, because they react to many kinds of verbal and nonverbal behavior. For example, if the Arctic explorer told his audience of geographers that he had a poor sense of direction and had to rely on a hired guide, the audience members would probably reduce their initial perceptions of his credibility. A source may also improve his credibility during a transaction by not behaving as expected. Civil behavior on the part of a very militant person may be so unexpected that it catches his audience by surprise and makes him appear to be very "reasonable" or credible and therefore persuasive. What a speaker says and does is continually being processed and evaluated by the people with whom he is communicating. If a source is aware of the criteria by which he is being judged, he can make better decisions about what he must do to ensure continued perceptions of high credibility.

Terminal credibility is the receiver's perception of a source at the completion of a communication event. For example, if the militant person continued to behave in a polite manner throughout his speech, the audience would probably have a higher evaluation of him when he finished than when he began. All of us have, at one time or another, entered a conversation with low regard for someone and ended the communication with a completely altered perception. Terminal credibility is important because it will influence a person's initial credibility if he should communicate again with the same receiver.

People's perceptions of others change between communication events. A receiver might change his attitude or values and therefore be less receptive to a given source the next time they communicate. It is also possible that external variables will cause a receiver to change his evaluation of a source between communication events. We learn about people by receiving new and different information from other sources; this information may, in turn, alter our perceptions. Sometimes this change is positive and allows us to make more valid judgments, but sometimes we allow rumor and innuendo to alter our perceptions. Therefore, it is important to evaluate the sources of information about other people as well as the people with whom we communicate.

Other things may change a receiver's perception of a source's credibility. A person may have high terminal credibility in a previous encounter because the topic of conversation was one which he was competent to discuss. In the next communication transaction, this same source may discuss a subject about which he has little knowledge. This may affect the receiver's perception of his competence in a negative way. However, a source who had high terminal credibility at an earlier time on a completely different topic may be held in high esteem on unrelated topics. This "halo effect" operates in a variety of situations. For example, a student who writes a good first examination paper may have an easier time in the rest of the course because of the early establishment of credibility. Clearly, credibility is ever-changing between and within communication events, topics and people. But even though this variable is subject to change, it deserves serious attention from those wishing to be effective communicators.

NOTES

1. A number of recent studies have delineated these dimensions of source credibility. See James C. McCroskey, Thomas Jensen, and Cynthia Todd, *The Generalizability of Source Credibility Scales for Public Figures,* Paper presented at the Speech Communication Association Con-

vention, Chicago, Ill., 1972 and James C. McCroskey, Thomas Jensen
and Cynthia Valencia, *Measurement of the Credibility of Peers and
Spouses,* Paper presented at the International Communication Association Convention, Montreal, Quebec, 1973.
2. See McCroskey, Jensen, and Todd, 1972 and David K. Berlo, James B.
Lemert, and Robert Mertz, "Dimensions for Evaluating the Acceptability of Message Sources," *Public Opinion Quarterly, 33* (1969), pp. 563–576.
3. FRANKLYN S. HAIMAN, "An Experimental Study of the Effects of Ethos
in Public Speaking," *Speech Monographs, 16* (1949), pp. 190–202.
4. GERALD R. MILLER and MURRAY A. HEWGILL, "The Effects of Variations in Nonfluency on Audience Ratings of Source Credibility," *Quarterly Journal of Speech, 50* (1964), pp. 36–44.
5. For an excellent study providing empirical support for this model see Judee
K. Heston, *Ideal Source Credibility: A Re-examination of the Semantic
Differential,* Paper presented at the International Communication Association Convention, Montreal, Quebec, 1973.

Seventeen

The Language of Love: Communications Fights

George R. Bach and Peter Wyden

It is fashionable nowadays for intimates to complain about their "communications." The very word has acquired a certain cachet as if it were something ultramodern. Husbands and wives accuse each other: "You never talk to me" or "You never listen to me." More honest couples take pride in confiding to each other, "We just can't communicate." Whatever the wording, these grievances are likely to be aired in a tone of acute frustration or resignation, much as if the partners were innocent victims of two electronic circuits that went haywire.

Executives know that communications are the lifeline of business; when the line becomes clogged or breaks down, two things occur; either (1) whatever shouldn't or (2) nothing. Intimates, on the other hand, usually just blame themselves or their mates for communications failures or wallow in lamentations of the "ain't-it-awful" variety. They rarely realize that intimate communication is an art that requires considerable imagination and creativity. They are almost never aware that only a conscious, resolute decision on the part of both partners to work at the problem—continually and for the rest of their lives—can produce good communications. And even if partners are ready to go to work to make their language of love serve them better, they don't know how to go about it.

The job is big because intimate communication involves a lot more than transmitting and receiving signals. Its purpose is to make explicit everything that partners expect of each other—what is most agreeable and least agreeable, what is relevant and irrelevant; to monitor continually what they experience as bonding or alienating; to synchronize interests, habits and "hangups"; and to effect the fusion that achieves the *we* without demolishing the *you* or the *me*.

Intimates usually fail to understand that the language of love does not confine itself to matters of loving and other intimate concerns. It permeates *all* communications between lovers. For example, if one business acquaintance says to another, "I'm hungry," this message almost certainly needn't be weighed for emotional implications. It can be taken at face value and acted upon accordingly. However, if an intimate sends the same message to another intimate, he may be engaging in several activities:

1. Expressing a private sentiment, perhaps "feeling out loud" just to gauge whether the partner's reaction is sympathetic or indifferent;
2. Appealing emotionally to the partner in order to persuade him to do or say something (perhaps, "Come on, let's go to the coffee shop");
3. Transmitting meaningful information (perhaps, "I'm starved, but I can't stop to eat now").

Partner A, then, might well be putting his foot in his mouth if Partner B is saying, "You don't understand how busy I am" and "A" only shrugs and replies, "Why don't you go and have something to eat?" Maybe "B" wants "A" to bring him something to eat from the coffee shop so he can work and eat at the same time. Unfortunately, "A" can't divine this request—which "B" would never expect him to do if he were talking to a business colleague.

Many intimates stubbornly insist that there shouldn't be any communications problems between them. The folklore of romantic love leads lovers to believe that some sort of intuitive click or sensitivity links all intimates; that this should suffice to convey their deep mutual understanding: and that this miracle occurs simply because the partners love one another. So they demand to be divined. In effect, they say, "He ought to know how I feel" or, "You'll decode me correctly if you love me." This permits spouses to think they can afford to be sloppier in their intimate communications than they are in their nonintimate contacts.

Another reason why communications are such a problem is a psychological laziness that has many people in its grip. Encouraged by the romantic fallacy that the language of love falls into place as if by magic, they find it easy to shirk the task and shrug it off.

The third reason is that the popularity of game-playing and the role-taking in today's society has encouraged the suspicion that transparency, even at home, may not be a good idea. This belief is usually grounded in the fear that candor would cause an intimate to reveal something about himself that might cool the partner. It creates still another temptation for partners to try to enjoy a free ride on the vague and often wrong presumption that they understand each other.

The easiest way to create communications problems is to withhold information from one's spouse. When partners don't confide in each other, they are likely to find themselves trying to tap their way through a vaccum, like blind people with white canes. The resulting fights can pop up at any time and place. For Herb and Lonnie Cartwright the place happened to be their kitchen. The time was the evening before they planned to give a big party:

LONNIE: I need another $30 for food for the party.
HERB: That's a lot of money for food.
LONNIE: *(exasperated)*: People have to eat!
HERB: *(reasonable)*: I know that.
LONNIE: *(taking a deep breath before plunging into unaccustomed territory)*: Ever since you bought that new insurance policy we're always strapped for cash.
HERB: *(startled)*: But it's in your name!
LONNIE: *(vehemently)*: I don't want you to die! Let's live a little now!
HERB: *(shaken)*: I resent that! After all, I was trying to do the right thing by you.
LONNIE: *(with finality)*: Then you shouldn't have bought the policy until after you get your next raise. I don't like to come to you like a beggar.

What happened here? These partners had kept each other in such ignorance over the years that they inevitably wound up poles apart on family-financial policy. This wife, like so many others, thought of her husband as a money tree. One reason why she loved him was that he was such a good provider. She believed that, within reason, she could buy anything she wanted. But she carefully avoided a test of her notions by never expressing an interest in the family bank balance. To her, money was to spend, just like a child's pocket money. To her husband, on the other hand, money was the equivalent of security. He had told his wife that he had bought a big new insurance policy, but not how expensive it had been. The lesson of this case is that husbands would do well not to leave wives ignorant about personal finances or other basic realities of their life together.

When intimates refuse to impart strategic information that they possess, or when they refuse to react to information that is offered to them, they are asking for trouble. Sometimes a partner withholds information in the name of tact. This is especially true when it comes to sharing information about sexual preferences. There are times when the state of the union demands that transparency be tempered by tact. But much so-called tact is cowardice or deception —a cover-up to avoid confrontations and feedback from the opponent. The withholding of information only leads to worse explosions later.

Some husbands, for instance, don't tell their wives how broke they are. They "don't want her to worry." Suddenly a man from the loan company appears at home to repossess the wife's car. Not only is this crisis often unnecessary ("Honey, why didn't you tell me? I could have borrowed the money from

Dad!"). Often it leads to irreversible damage because it erodes the wife's trust in her spouse. In true intimacy stress is shared by partners.

There are partners, however, who, without knowing it, *cause* their spouses to withhold information. One such husband tended to get excited and be in the way when things went wrong at home. Then he lectured his wife that she should have managed better. When he went on business trips he called home daily and his wife always reassured him that things were fine. Usually they were, but one day the husband returned from a week's absence and was extremely upset to find that his wife had broken her ankle and hadn't said a word about it on the telephone. In her inner dialogue the wife had said to herself, "He's no help in a crisis." The husband had brought this lack of trust upon himself.

When intimates are frustrated by their inability to communicate clearly and straightforwardly, they tend to confuse matters further by sending messages full of sarcasms, hyperboles, caricatures and exaggerations that befog or over-dramatize. The list of these statics is almost endless, but here are some random examples:

"I'd just as soon talk to a blank wall." "You've got diarrhea of the mouth." "You did *not* say *that;* if you did, I didn't hear it!" "We have nothing to say to each other any more." "You always talk in riddles." "I've learned to keep my mouth shut." "You never say what you mean." "Why do you always interrupt me?" "You just like to hear the sound of your own voice." "You never stand up for yourself." "If I've told you once, I've told you a thousand times. . . ."

When fight trainees are faced with these statics as they try to communicate feelings and wishes to their partners, we sometimes tell them the ancient yarn about the Texas mule who was too stubborn to respond to commands. The owner decided to hire a famous mule trainer to cure the trouble. The trainer took one look at the mule and cracked him over the head with a two-by-four. The owner was appalled.

"That's dreadful," he said, "I thought you were going to train him!"

"Sure," said the trainer. "But first I have to get his attention."

Partners who must deal with statics need to review the techniques for getting a good fight started. The same goes for spouses who find themselves confronted with opponents who blanket out communications with jamming noises, the way the Communists used to jam Western radio broadcasts.

Some intimate jammers can be infuriatingly effective. Suppose a husband knows his wife wants to talk to him about his overspending. But the husband also knows his spouse loves to listen to gossip about his boss's sex life. The husband therefore rattles on interminably about fresh gossip he has just heard on the office grapevine and then dashes to the car to leave for work.

"Hey," shouts his wife. "We've got to talk about those bills!"

"Will do!" shouts the husband—and drives off.

Even partners who seem to appreciate the importance of open, unjammed communications rarely realize just how unambiguous their signals should be and how meticulously a message sender should solicit feedback from the recipient to check out whether his signal was understood as it was intended. Here is what often happens in the three stages of message sending: (1) the intention of the message, (2) the framing of the message, and (3) the interpretation of the message at the other end of the line.

CASE NO. 1: The wife tells the kids not to bother Dad. He is listening.

How Meant	*How Sent*	*How Received*
"I'm protecting you."	"Don't bother him."	"She's fencing me in."

CASE NO. 2: The husband doesn't bring any of his buddies home from his club. She asks him about it.

How Meant	*How Sent*	*How Received*
"It's too much work for you."	"Oh, let's skip it."	"He's ashamed of me."

Husbands and wives who wish to extricate themselves from a jungle of unclear signals find it helpful to fix within their minds the seemingly simple fundamentals of communication:

Obtain the attention of your receiver. Prepare him to receive your message. Send out your message clearly and with a minimum of extraneous static. Make sure your information is beamed toward the receiver's wave length. Stake out your own area of interest and stick to its limits. Keep yourself and your receiver focused on the joint interest area. Stimulate your receiver to respond by acknowledging reception. Obtain feedback to check how your message was received.

These principles are known to anyone who ever placed an important long-distance phone call. Yet intimates, especially while under the emotional stress of conflict and aggression, tend to ignore the basics even though they "know better." Their resistance against forging a clear connection is a sign that they find conflict stressful and don't like to accept the fact that they are involved in one.

This is why noncommunicators lead each other around the mulberry bush with such round-robin jabs as these:

SHE: You never talk to me.
HE: What's on your mind?
SHE: It's not what's on *my* mind; it's that I never know what's on *your* mind.
HE: *(slightly panicky)*: What do you want to know?
SHE: *(jubilantly)*: Everything!
HE: *(thoroughly vexed)*: That's crazy!
SHE: Here we go again.

This game of hide-and-seek may also go like this:

HE: You talk too much!
SHE: About what?
HE: About everything.
SHE: One of us has to talk!
HE: You talk, but you never say anything.

SHE: That's crazy.
HE: You're darned right!
SHE: *(thoughtfully)*: What do you mean?
HE: *(wearily)*: You make a lot of noise, but that makes it impossible for us to have a real talk.
SHE: Here we go again. . . .

Here's what happened after the latter fight, between two unmarried young people:

DR. BACH: *(to the girl)*: What was he really telling you?
GIRL: That he doesn't like me.
DR. B: *(to the boy)*: Is that what you wanted to convey?
BOY: No! I love her!
DR. B: You two are starving for real communication. You're using words like fog to hide your true feelings.

A partner who keeps his own vested interest hidden often enjoys focusing a one-way radar upon his opponent. This kind of spouse-watching may be part of a noble effort to "understand" the partner who is being watched. But it, too, leads only to more frustration, as in the following dialogue:

SHE: You never talk to me.
HE: Why should I? You know all about me.
SHE: What do you mean?
HE: *(heatedly)*: You watch every move I make. You're reading me! And whenever I open my mouth, I'm wrong. You've already figured out what I'm supposed-ly thinking.
SHE: You're just saying that because you don't want to talk to me.

While the marital woods are full of couples who profess "we never talk," the truth is that many intimates—possibly the majority—talk a great deal, even about personal matters. But their virtuosity at camouflaging (and the coy kind of testing that is really inquiring, "Will he get the hint?") is remarkable. Here is a couple driving home after a party:

HE: That was a nice dinner Peggy fixed.
SHE: Yes, those baked potatoes with sour cream were terrific.

When this nebulous exchange was investigated during fight training it turned out that this husband was trying to convey that he thought he and his wife weren't popular and didn't have enough friends. The wife got the message and signaled back: "I know you're critical about our social ineptness, but I don't think Peggy is so much better." The object of this bit of shadowboxing was to reconnoiter a real problem but to avoid facing it openly in constructive talks about possible solutions. Neither spouse was ready to face a showdown about the inadequacies of their social life.

. . .

Even casual conversation . . . can set off incredible confusion if partners don't ask follow-up questions. Suppose the husband asks his wife: "Have you noticed the car brakes are on the blink again?" This could be a straight expression of exasperation at the garage where the brakes were supposedly fixed only the week before. In that event, it is perfectly adequate for the wife to say no more than, "I sure did!"

But this husband's complaint could also mean, "I wish you'd be more careful with our things." Or "I don't want to show her how lonely I get, but I wish she'd come along on more of my dreary business trips." Or "You're spending so much money on yourself that there's never enough left for necessities like car brakes." Among true intimates, therefore, such a complaint about car brakes is at least briefly explored for possible emotional implications.

A failure to expose issues fully, once they have come up, may lead to a depressing communications impasse. This was the situation that lingered at the bottom of the following far from routine early morning household argument:

HE: I don't mind you not making me breakfast, but why do I have to clear away last night's dishes, too?
SHE: I'm sorry, dear. I know it annoys you.
HE: Then why do it?
SHE: I'm just so tired at night.
HE: You're not too tired to look at TV!
SHE: That's relaxing. Dishes aren't.
HE: You just don't give a damn about me.
SHE: You mean to tell me that a little thing like a few dirty dishes and my enjoying TV proves that? That's ridiculous. Why don't you go on to work— you'll be late!

When this couple came into fight training she started doing the dishes at night, but they were no happier. They had to come to grips with their underlying feelings: (1) "He thinks I don't love him any more" and (2) "She thinks I'm unreasonable in my request for love."

They were in a state of withdrawal prior to a new, more realistic fight engagement. They knew neither cared all that much about the dirty dishes. What was wrong?

It developed that he was trying to say, "Sometimes I think you love the idiot box more than me." She was trying to tell him he was being inconsiderate by forgetting to run an occasional errand for her and that she resented his stopping off to have drinks with the fellows from the office on the way home. Only an air-clearing, head-on fight with free-flowing communications finally yielded these answers and a basis for further discussion.

Intimate stalemates can also be caused by attention-seeking signals that are either too strong or too weak to "turn on" the partner in the desired direction. One strategic object of certain fights is to provoke the partner into the right amount and kind of aggressive behavior—the kind that "turns on" without going over the permissible threshold and thereby "turns off" the partner. This subtle, intimate provocation can be calibrated. Very often, however, it isn't.

. . .

A most dangerous time for intimate communications is the moment when the husband comes home from work at night. It is the time when the husband's world, the wife's world, and the family's world are joined for presumably realistic coexistence. Unless the differing expectations are sensitively calibrated, the result is collision, rather than merger.

We advise not to initiate the homecoming ceremonies with the customary "How was your day?" At best this invites the unproductive response, "So-so. How was yours?" More likely, these one-way signals are opening guns for each partner to use the marriage as a garbage can. Sometimes they hit. Sometimes they miss. In any event, it's not an edifying or fruitful exercise and it will not ease the task of merging the partners' necessarily separate daytime roles into an intimate duet.

Homecoming is a favorite time for camouflaging in many households. If the husband groans and says, "I had a terrible day, simply terrible!" he may be telling his spouse, "I think that you think I have a ball at the office, but that's not what I'd like you to think." (If he is a good communicator he sends his message directly: "Sometimes you don't give me enough release for my tensions.")

All too frequently, homecoming time also becomes displacement time. Suppose the husband does manage to tear himself away from his own troubles and asks, "What did the kids do today?" This may be just the opening the wife waited for. Her recital of sad tales begins: "Well, Johnny missed the school bus again. He would have been very late for class if I hadn't borrowed Janie's car and rushed him down there. . . ." Which is the wife's way of telling her husband, "Nobody knows the trouble I've seen. Certainly *you* don't appreciate what it takes to run a house, raise the children, manage things without a second car and . . . and . . . and. . . ."

Curiously enough, most people who become involved in such exchanges are convinced that this type of conversation constitutes intimate communication. This is rarely the case. Intimate communications start after the day's routine business is checked out. In the normal run of daily life, each partner should be able to handle his own usual activities in his own more or less independent way. The real subject of intimate communication is the state of the union; the relationship between the couple; the *us*.

We suggest to our trainees that they start homecoming conversations not with a perfunctory "How are you?" but with a genuinely intimate "How are we doing?" This may sound weird according to conventional etiquette, but it points intimates toward more rewarding directions, helps clear up some communications statics, and prevents the accumulation of secret reservations.

If an exchange of complaints is infected with the here-we-go-again pessimism of chronic, redundant round-robin fights, someone must eventually muster enough common sense to take the needle off the broken record and demand, "Will the real partnership problem please rise?" The weariness signal is often the phrase, "I've told you for the umpteenth time. . . ."

Excessive patience does not serve the cause of realistic intimacy; neither does lack of patience. In fact, the point when to take "no" for an answer is one of the most important things that intimates should learn about each other. Here is the first round of one illustrative case:

HE: Hey, honey, guess what! I got a bonus!
SHE: How much?
HE: Enough for us to spend two weeks at the shore.

And here is Round No. 2 of the same fight:

SHE: You really want to spend all that money going to the beach?
HE: I sure do.
SHE: I don't think we should.
HE: Well, I think we should!

If this merry-go-round were to continue for 10 or 20 or more rounds, the partnership probably would only gain, not lose. The issue is fresh. The controversy is legitimate. Both partners are demonstrating that they care about how to spend their mutual leisure time and their co-owned money. They are also showing that their minds are not closed to each other, or to persuasion. This kind of ritual, uncontaminated by weary pessimism, helps partners to probe how strongly each really feels. It may not sound overly intelligent or "adult," but it is a legitimate method of finding the point where each is convinced that the other "really means it."

Some people can tolerate only one or two "no's" for an answer. The third "no" may provoke them into raising a social gun (the threat of marital exit); or an economic gun (a spiteful money splurge); or possibly even a real gun (murder). Among successful intimates, there will always be enough opportunities to say "no" often enough so each partner can re-evaluate his feelings, weigh the possibility of giving in, or work out a compromise.

Couples who enjoy good communications can signal their partner through a system of "pats," "slaps," and "kicks."

Pats are obviously signals of attraction, approval, affection, or reward. They mean "Yes," "Good," "I dig," "This turns me on," and so forth. No words are necessary. Everybody recognizes the condescending quality of a pat on the head; the more peerlike pat on the back (which may also be a phony "slap on the back"); the amorous, perhaps sex-initiating pat on the rump; or the recognition and reassurance of stroking the partner's hand.

Slaps (meaning "No," "Cut it out," "Let go," "I don't like," etc.) are useful intimate punishments or warnings that can range from the nonverbal "dirty look" to highly verbal, abusive name calling.

Kicks (meaning "Get a move on!" "Get with it!" etc.) serve as reminders, appeals, incentive and aggressive stimulation to get a sluggish or confused partner moving in a desired reaction. They can be administered by a persuasive lecture, a subtle bit of seduction, a pinch in the arm or (hopefully not) a literal kick in the pants.

In the fight for better mutual understanding, as in all fights, it is profitable to give clear cues, to avoid obscurities and, in case of a near miss, to emphasize the nearness rather than the miss. Pats are helpful in these situations.

The following fight all but carried the label "Danger! Bad communications" in neon letters:

HE: You're pretty nervous about your mother coming, aren't you?
SHE: What makes you think so?
HE: Well, you don't usually spend so much time cleaning house.
SHE: Oh, so you think I'm a lousy housekeeper! Boy, you just don't understand me!
HE: *(shrugging)*: Here we go again.

After training, the same fight should go like this:

HE: You're pretty nervous about your mother coming, aren't you?
SHE I'm not nervous about her. I'm nervous about how you're going to get along with her. By the way, what made you think I'm nervous about it?
HE: Because of the way you've been cleaning and cleaning around here.
SHE: You're pretty sharp!

As soon as partners stop putting up with silence, camouflaging, or static and learn to fight for clearer communications, tensions tend to clear up. This represents no "cure." When communications channels become unclogged, couples normally find that they are considerably further apart in their ideas for a livable marriage than they want to be. But at least they are no longer kidding each other about their communications gap. Now they can start going to work on the process of coming as close together as they want to be in order to enjoy a smooth state of swing.

It is worth noting that it is unnecessary to analyze the historical-motivational causes for communications failures in most marriages. Instead of wasting time and money to excavate the causes of behavior, which get them nowhere, couples can learn to appreciate that the function of noncommunication generally is to cover up something that partners are afraid to face openly: hostility of the sadistic variety, perhaps; or exploitative attitudes; or overdependency; or, more frequently, fear of rejection. These factors, too, rarely require detailed analysis. What is important is that the partners catch each other in the use of anticommunications tactics, make an open demand for discontinuance and then practice how to replace them with straightforward types of communication.

Some alienating forms of communication are difficult to recognize for what they really are. The fine art of "bugging" is a good example.

Suppose the wife is in the kitchen cooking a special gourmet dinner. The husband enters, sniffs the delightful aroma that pervades the kitchen and admires the complexity of the culinary operation that his wife has set in motion for their mutual pleasure. He is touched. He may also become aroused. The smelling of delicious food and the fussing over food were sources of his affection for his first love: his mother. Now here is his true love, his own wife, immersed in the act of being lovable. By taking special pains with her cooking, she is showing that she cares about him, about them.

He pinches her playfully. Or he tries to kiss her. Or fondle her lovingly.

She may respond just as lovingly. She may stop cooking, burn the roast, or even let herself be taken to the bedroom to make love. But not if she is like most wives. Most likely, she will be annoyed. If he fails to heed her protests, she will get mad. She is busy. She is busy doing something for him, something he likes! She is involved with her cookbooks and her seasonings. At this moment she does not see herself as a sex object but as a master chef and an efficient executive. She cannot readily desert the scene of her ministrations. Her husband's sexy behavior is incongruent with her definition of the situation and her role in it. It threatens to derail her plans and her personality. It is overloading her tension system. It is bugging her.

Almost everybody has had the disturbing experience of feeling "bugged" during contacts with another person. A relative stranger can do no major bugging because it is unlikely that one cares enough about what he does or how he feels. But if the bugging is being done by an intimate, one does care. Also, the intimate is more likely to know what bugs his partner most. His bugging, therefore, can quickly assume the proportions of a minor torture, especially when it interferes with an offer of love, as in the above example.

If an intimate's bugging is extreme and becomes chronic, it is a technique of dirty fighting and crazy-making. Here we will deal only with the more common and minor forms of bugging between relatively normal intimates who love each other but whose communications are distorted by advanced types of statics.

Complaints about routine bugging are very common indeed. "My husband bugs me," a wife says. "I can't stand being around him." Or "My wife is driving me crazy; anything I say or do seems to annoy her." Or "We can't stay in the same room together." Or "The only way I can stand it is by getting loaded; it immunizes me." Or "We can't put our finger on it, but it's so uncomfortable that we've about given up talking to each other."

Sometimes derailing remarks will do the same job as an act of bugging ("You never . . ."). Frequent reneging on commitments also has a bugging effect (agreeing to make love and then backing out). Or changing ground rules for common activities without previous discussion. Or plain incessant nagging. Children and passively hostile intimates are especially expert at these bugging techniques.

Partner A begins to feel bugged when he senses that Partner B does not really acknowledge "A's" existence unless "A" behaves in a certain way. The desired behavior is probably not clearly defined except that "A" knows it isn't natural to him. When "A" insists on being himself he may be told by "B": "You're mistaken. You're not the way you think you are. I know you: deep inside you are such-and-such."

Prolonged intimate living with such a secretive fighter exacts a heavy emotional price. It is exhausting to accommodate a partner whose ideas of what is lovable are alien to one's ego.

It is tempting to remove bugging by accommodating. It is also uncomfortable. Many an intimate slides into the unpleasant double bind of not knowing whether to be himself and alienate the partner; or accommodate the partner and alienate his own ego.

It is easy to become somebody's psychological patsy. It may do no damage to assume this role in an office by humoring along a boss or someone else with whom one is not emotionally involved. However, in relationships with intimates (especially if, like a dependent child, one cannot get away) accommodation to bugging can be dangerous. It leads not only to alienation but to a threat of the accommodator's emotional well-being; it can distort his natural sense of self and prevent his emotional growth.

Un-bugging an intimate relationship is difficult, but sometimes it may be easier than it seems. Suppose a son wants to borrow a car. If he does his borrowing from Hertz Rent-A-Car and fails to bring it back as promised, he will get "punished" by having to pay an additional charge. But there will be no emotional problems. He can't bug Hertz. If he borrows his father's car, matters will be more complicated:

FATHER: OK, but be sure to have it back by 4 o'clock. I'll need it then.
SON: Sure, Dad.
(Now it's 6 o'clock. The son has just come home.)
FATHER: Where in hell have you been? I *told* you I had to have the car at 4.
SON: But Dad, I had to give Amy a ride home. I couldn't leave her stranded!

Now the father is very bugged indeed. He understands the facts. He likes his son's girl Amy and certainly wouldn't want to see her stranded. But reality must be dealt with: the father was greatly inconvenienced by his son. He must do more than regret that he let the son have the car. His inner dialogue will go somewhat like this: "I feel good as a father for letting my child have a good time. That's love. But I don't want to be exploited. That would shut my love off." This is the root of the conflict aroused by bugging. Intimates who bug other intimates are shutting love off and on, off and on. This is what leads to the charge, "you bug me." It means that love-releasers and love-stoppers are scrambled together.

We usually advise trainees to try one of two techniques for unscrambling the bugging mixup. One way is to throw oneself at the mercy of the bugger and see what happens. ("You *know* this bugs me. When you get your hands on the car keys you have *me* in your hands and I won't tolerate that. I'm a busy man and when I need the car for business I just have to have it.") The other technique is to search for the function of the bugging. What is the son really bugging his father for? Does he understand what he's doing to the father? Or does he understand this *too* well and is he bugging the old man to get sadistic mileage out of it? Or is it simply that he can't ever get the father's attention—or can't influence the father—in any way except by bugging? Once the function of the bugging is determined, it becomes easier to deal with this nagging form of communications stalemate.

Good communications, in sum, are the lifeline of successful intimacy, and are invariably the result of hard work of dedicated partners working in pairs.

Here are some exercises that help:

1. Diagnose how efficient or inefficient your present level of communication is. Is each partner candid and transparent? Does each get a chance to tell the other what's "eating him"? Does each partner really understand what the other is after?

2. Locate some of the causes of poor communication by owning up to yourself and to each other that you occasionally or habitually use one of the statics discussed. . . . Try to catch each other in the use of static and aggressively eliminate its use. Calls of "Static!" or "Foul!" may help.
3. Stop blocking communication by explicitly renouncing the use of static maneuvers.
4. Start making communication flow more freely by deliberately making yourselves accessible, open, and crystal-clear. From time to time, take new readings of the quality of your communications. Has improvement taken place?
5. Respond with full resonance. Be sure you are sharing your private view of yourself and the world with your partner. Expressive communication enhances intimacy; reflective communication is useful but secondary. The more intimate two people are, the more they take turns expressing their views freely.

Part Five

Interpersonal: The Dyad Reacts

Experiences and Discussions

1. Select a situation in which you generally have difficulty listening to another person. During your next five interactions with this person, make a concerted effort to confirm the other person and increase your understanding of what is being said. Assess your success after these interactions and consider ways to continue and improve the relationship.
2. Describe a situation in which either you or another person became defensive. What factors contributed to this defensive atmosphere? How could the situation have been handled to reduce defensive reactions? Provide specific examples of the six suggestions outlined by Stewart and D'Angelo for listening to diminish defensiveness.
3. What public figure would you rate as most credible? Why? Whom would you rate as least credible? Why?
4. You are the campaign manager for a local political hopeful. Select an issue of probable controversy (school busing, tax increases, etc.) and explain how you would present your candidate so that he/she is perceived as the most credible person. Be sure to include each of the five aspects of credibility in your description. Rank these five aspects from most to least important in terms of election victory.
5. Consider the following fictional situation: Frank Pendano was a noted militant leader several years ago. He has decided to "beat the system"

from within and is running for governor. Discuss his probable initial credibility and describe the transactional and terminal credibility necessary for Frank to become governor.

6. Communication breakdowns between intimates often result from jammed messages and ambiguous feedback. Observe a communication breakdown in a marital or close relationship—perhaps one in which you are involved or one between your parents or friends. (Television soap operas also offer a wealth of examples of miscommunication.) Analyze the selected breakdown and determine (a) the intention of the message, (b) the framing of the message, and (c) the interpretation of the message. Try to analyze the breakdown as illustrated in the following example taken from the Bach and Wyden selection:

CASE NO. 1: The wife tells the kids not to bother Dad.

How Meant	*How Sent*	*How Received*
"I'm protecting you."	"Don't bother him."	"She's fencing me in."

7. Carl Rogers has developed a system of interpersonal counseling termed "reflective listening." According to its tenets, the counselor simply repeats statements in slightly different words to let the client know he or she is listening, while allowing the client to work out his or her own solutions. Employ reflective listening in a conversation with a close friend who is describing a minor problem or concern. Is the technique successful? How did your friend feel afterward?

For Further Reading

BACH, GEORGE R., and PETER WYDEN. *The Intimate Enemy: How to Fight Fair in Love and Marriage.* New York: Avon, 1970.
Unlike traditional counselors, the authors propose "constructive aggression" (fair fights) as a means of improving communication between love and marriage partners. What may at first appear controversial should be considered in light of the communication principles studied.

DEVITO, JOSEPH A. *The Interpersonal Communication Book.* New York: Harper and Row, 1976.
In forty-two almost self-instructional units, the author has selected central elements of interpersonal communication, provided information on each, and constructed "experiential vehicles," exercises that help examine the relevance of each element to real-life situations. Topics include the self, verbal and nonverbal behavior, conflict, attraction, love, trust, attitude change, and many more.

GROVE, THEODORE G. (ed.). *Experiences in Interpersonal Communication.* Englewood Cliffs, N.J.: Prentice-Hall, 1976.

The author of this text provides a general introduction to interpersonal communication and goes on to suggest possible explorations in the field. He deals with methods of studying the subject, including games and role playing; approaches for changing communication behavior; and strategies for group problem solving.

KNAPP, MARK L. *Social Intercourse: From Greeting to Goodbye.* Boston: Allyn and Bacon, 1978.

Knapp has empirically derived a theory that can explain and predict stages of interpersonal relationships. Using a set of scales administered over time, it is possible to pinpoint a relationship in either its "growth" or its "decay" stage.

McCROSKEY, JAMES C., and LAWRENCE R. WHEELESS. *Introduction to Human Communication.* Boston: Allyn and Bacon, 1976.

The recent explosion of empirical research in human communication has necessitated some coordination of the findings and the problems involved. McCroskey and Wheeless do a good job at this, and they discuss "the common core of information about human communication to which all beginning students should be exposed." Some of the topics analyzed are human communication and change, communication motivations, personal orientations and personality, developing affinity, information acquisition, and decision making.

SMITH, DENNIS R., and L. KEITH WILLIAMSON. *Interpersonal Communication: Roles, Rules, Strategies and Games.* Dubuque, Iowa: Wm. C. Brown, 1977.

This source covers the traditions, structures, and perspectives of interpersonal communication. The text provides an extended analysis of message systems, considering the contributing roles of language, gestures, and space. A section dealing with intimacy and pseudo-intimacy in human communication is also included.

PART SIX

Groups and Organizations: The Climate Controls

"Well," said he, showing me the advertisement, "you can see for yourself that the League has a vacancy, and there is the address where you should apply for particulars. As far as I can make out the League was founded by an American millionaire, Ezekiah Hopkins, who was very peculiar in his ways. He was himself red-headed, and he had a great sympathy for all red-headed men; so, when he died, it was found that he had left his fortune in the hands of trustees, with instructions to apply the interest to the providing of easy berths to men whose hair is of that colour. From all I hear it is splendid pay, and very little to do."

THE RED-HEADED LEAGUE

Though they are not always so ludicrously conceived, nor with such a sinister hidden purpose as in this most famous of Sherlock Holmes's cases, most of us spend a great deal of time in group and organizational settings. Unless you live as a hermit, there are few situations involving communication that do not in some way relate to groups: classes, families, clubs, dorms, etc. If you made a list of the different groups to which you belong, how long would it be? Potentially every characteristic that defines you could be used to unite other people who share that characteristic: even your hair color could be a commonality around which a group could be formed.

Most groups in which we function do not exist in isolation either. Many groups are affiliated with other groups in more complex systems called "organizations." An organization shares the properties of a group: it is, in fact, a "group of groups."

Several communication features are unique to groups and organizations, serving as defining characteristics of the situations. Had the Red-Headed League ever formally met in conference, for example, we can assume that the members would mold a group personality, establish norms, assume roles, and establish joint goals. Burgoon, Heston, and McCroskey discuss how these features evolve and present the case for the group as a unique communication system.

Once the group has established its norms and goal, it can begin functioning as a unit. Rosenfeld presents the criteria used in evaluating this functioning process, specifically relating to motivation, decision making, and risk taking. To the detective investigating the group-communication situation, these guidelines can be as valuable as fingerprints in identifying "suspect" group-communication problems. The solutions to these problems, presented as techniques of discussion and interaction, are outlined by Baird and Weinberg. Perhaps they can serve an important preventative as well as diagnostic function.

Applying these same principles to organizational situations, Arthur Coon examines the ways in which the tool of brainstorming can be applied in the job market setting. Stewart and Cash add concrete suggestions for another tool of organizational communication: the interview. Their comments add a practical dimension that can reveal even more about the communication process. In looking at interviewing, for example, you can detect the way the basic aspects of inter- and intrapersonal communication apply to this group-organizational situation.

OBJECTIVES

After carefully reading these five articles, you should be able to define the following terms:

small group	(Burgoon)
group personality	
interrelationship	
cohesion	
brainstorming	(Rosenfeld)
risky-shift	
leadership	
efficiency	(Baird and Weinberg)
creativity	
free-wheeling	(Coon)
katharsis (catharsis)	
dyad	(Stewart and Cash)
process	
determination interview	
placement interview	

And:

1. Provide two reasons why it is important to study how groups operate (Burgoon et al.).

2. Discuss at least five factors that distinguish the small group as a unique communication setting. Give an example to illustrate each factor (Burgoon et al.).
3. Describe the three categories of inputs (structural variables) to a small group: individual characteristics, group characteristics, and external factors (Burgoon et al.).
4. Describe the three categories of interaction variables in a small group: task, procedural, and interpersonal factors (Burgoon et al.).
5. Explain five major functions of small groups (Burgoon et al.).
6. Describe three criteria commonly used to assess group functions (Burgoon et al.).
7. Describe at least three ways in which individual behavior is influenced by group members (Rosenfeld).
8. Discuss at least four consistent research findings regarding group decisions (Rosenfeld).
9. List four criteria for determining whether to use an individual or a group in a problem-solving situation (Rosenfeld).
10. Describe five principles for utilizing group discussion (Baird and Weinberg).
11. List and discuss the four criteria for determining maximum efficiency in decision making (Baird and Weinberg).
12. State three results of brainstorming which indicate that it is an effective problem-solving technique (Coon).
13. List the four "Brainstorming Rules" (Coon).
14. Describe the functions of the moderator, recorder, and group members during a brainstorming session (Coon).
15. Explain the two procedures that follow up a brainstorming session: categorization and evaluation (Coon).
16. Describe the seven categories of interviews (Stewart and Cash).

Eighteen

The Small Group as a Unique Communication Situation

Michael Burgoon, Judee K. Heston, and James C. McCroskey

"None of us is as smart as all of us." This notion underlies our faith in the ability of small groups to deal with problems. We generally believe that two heads are better than one, so several heads must be best of all. Not only do we rely on groups to solve problems, groups intrude on every aspect of our existence. We begin life in the most primary and potent of groups—the family. Within the family group our personality is shaped, our intellectual and emotional development is influenced, and our cultural awareness is initiated. When we are first nudged out of the security of the family circle, we are confronted with more groups in the form of schools: nursery schools, church schools, kindergarten. Even our friendships develop in groups, with smaller subgroups developing closer relationships. Beyond the school years, our social and business relationships continue to operate frequently in groups. Just think of all the group memberships the typical college student holds in committees, clubs, dormitory houses or fraternities, classes, work groups, church organizations, political causes, family and friendship networks. Our lives are even governed by groups that we are not members of: decision-making bodies such as the legislature and board of regents, clubs and organizations whose recognition and acceptance we seek, and groups that establish society's norms and values. It is clear that we can never escape the impact of groups on the quality of our day-to-day living. It makes sense, then, for us to study how groups operate and how they affect us so that we can improve those to which we belong and reduce the power of those that we do not want to influence us. By moving our subconscious awareness of groups into consciousness, we can increase control of our own role within the spheres of groups that affect us. Communication provides one key to control. The better we understand our own and others' methods of communication, the better we can maintain our own independence and benefit those with whom we associate in groups.

A Definition of the Small Group

Before analyzing the communication that takes place, we need a common understanding of what constitutes a small group. As the definition is explained, it will become clear why we are confining ourselves to *small* groups. One definition of small groups that combines elements of several other definitions is "the face-to-face interaction of two or more persons in such a way that members are able to recall the characteristics of the other members accurately."

Let us look at this definition in more detail. The first key term is *face-to-face*. This means that people must be in proximity to be considered a small group. Republicans in two separate cities would be members of the same large group but not the same small group. The second key term is *interaction*. To be a small group, the members must communicate with one another. Three people standing face to face waiting for a bus would not be a group; if the same three individuals began complaining to each other about the lateness of the bus, they would have the beginnings of a small group. The stipulation of interaction limits this book to small groups because spontaneous, oral communication is integral to small groups. The third key phrase is *two or more persons,* which indicates simply that two people may constitute a group and that there is supposedly no upper limit. However, as groups become excessively large, interaction is reduced and the group eventually fails to meet the criterion that all members interact. For practical purposes, a small group is generally defined as two to twenty-five people. The final key phrase is that *members are able to recall the characteristics of the other members accurately.* This signifies that the members relate to one another in such a way that they become aware of the existence of a group and their identification with it. If the relationships are significant enough to draw the attention of the members, a group may be said to exist. Take, for example, the people waiting for the bus. If they talk long enough to recall the conversation later and remember the other persons accurately, we could legitimately call them a group. If, on succeeding days, they continue to interact while waiting for the bus, we would have further confirmation of the existence of a group.

There are some additional characteristics of small groups that provide further definition of the concept and serve to distinguish the small group as a unique communication environment.

The Uniqueness of Small Groups

The first characteristic of the small group that makes it a unique communication context is *frequent interaction*. This distinguishes the small group from a public-speaking situation where usually one person is speaking to an audience that has little opportunity to interact. Similarly, it differentiates the small group from a classroom or work group where communication is restricted and infrequent. If a teacher allows her students to talk (or cannot keep them quiet), then a classroom can also be considered a small group. The key factor is whether or not a high degree of interaction occurs.

A second unique characteristic of small groups is the development of a *group personality.* The group takes on an identity of its own. It can be viewed as a singular, separate entity rather than a conglomeration of the various personalities of its members. Just as a person can be extroverted and optimistic, so can a group become outgoing and optimistic in its view. Like the authoritarian person who is highly conventional, dogmatic, and rigid, a group may be traditional, inflexible, and authority-oriented. The point here is that groups develop their own modes of behavior and orientations just as individuals do.

A third characteristic of small groups is the establishment of *group norms.* Groups develop their own value systems and their own normative behavior. An excellent example comes from a description of a typical street gang: "The Cobras" place a high value on toughness and trouble. Members must be skilled in fighting, insulting, storytelling, "rapping," and most of all hustling (conning, selling dope, stealing). Prestige is gained by being in reform school or having connections with pushers or persons with influence on the gang. The norm for members is to spend most of their time "hanging on the set," gambling, flying pigeons, and drinking wine until some kind of "action" presents itself. It is also normative to do poorly in school, since academic success is irrelevant to group status. All of these behaviors and attitudes are defined and maintained by the group. Such group norms, to a large extent, become individual norms. That is, individuals want to be like the group and so behave in that manner.

Intricately related to group norms is a fourth characteristic: *coping behavior.* Groups develop their own patterns for coping with outside threats and maintaining their existence. In the case of street gangs, fighting and carving out actual territories are ways of warding off intrusions by outsiders. A formal structure with a president, vice president, prime minister, and warlord exist to solidify the group and direct its dealings with nonmembers. These behaviors, which are designed to preserve the group and reduce the incursion of outside influences, are examples of coping behavior. Group habits also fit into this category. For instance, a group that is in the habit of meeting for only an hour may be coping with outside demands for the members' time or, in cases of groups in high-stress situations, they may be coping with their psychological and physiological limitations caused by anxiety. In either case, longer meetings might lower attendance or increase conflict, which would threaten the group's cohesion. Another aspect of coping behavior is the development of group language. Groups generally develop their own unique jargon and language patterns. Words like "paradigm," "hypothetical construct," and "teleological system" might be heard from a group of social scientists but would be unlikely at a cocktail party of artists. Similarly, "jive," "dude," "lame," and "bust" would be common vocabulary among a group of young blacks, but not the suburban PTA. Different interaction patterns also characterize different groups. One group may be prone to long, involved comments by its members, while another may tend toward short, concise, businesslike statements. Whatever the pattern, the language that develops evolves out of the unique needs and nature of the group and serves to solidify its identity. It is a partial means of coping with the rest of the world.

A fifth distinguishing characteristic of small groups is *role differentiation.* Within a group, individuals tend to specialize and perform certain roles that are interlocking. These roles include those that are necessary for the completion of a task, such as supplying information, asking for opinions, and giving the group direction, and those that are necessary to maintain a satisfactory social and emotional atmosphere, such as encouraging others, creating harmony, and controlling the flow of communication. Different situations dictate which roles are needed. Usually, each person adopts many roles; in fact, each member could conceivably perform all of them. But generally, different people emphasize different roles or clusters of roles: some people are more concerned with getting the job done, while others are more concerned with personal relationships. Such role differentiations also take the form of a division of labor. By specialization on the part of each member, groups are able to tackle problems more efficiently. This division of responsibilities is a special advantage of groups.

A sixth unique characteristic of the small group is *interdependent goals.* Some members have certain goals that overlap with those of other members. These shared goals become the group's goals and members are expected to subordinate their personal goals to those of the group. For example, suppose you have been assigned to solve a problem in a group in chemistry class. The mutual goals of your group members would be to solve the problem assigned and earn a good grade. To achieve these goals, you might have to suppress your personal desire for separate recognition or superiority over the rest of the group. Because each person's success at achieving the primary goals is dependent on the rest of the group, the goals are interdependent. To cite another example, each member of an encounter group facilitates the common goal of increasing self-awareness. Again, individual achievement of the goal is largely dependent on the rest of the group. Because group members share the same goals, they frequently find themselves in positions of common fate: what is rewarding for one is rewarding for all, and vice versa. This interdependency of individuals influences communication in groups because much of the content centers on these goals or on sustaining satisfactory interpersonal relations to secure them.

The final unique characteristic of small groups is something called the *assembly effect bonus.* This refers to extra productivity that is caused specifically by the nature of groups. A more concise definition of an assembly effect bonus is productivity in excess of the combined product of the same individuals working independently. It is analogous to the extra productivity that results from using an assembly line in a plant rather than having each person do the whole job alone. It is a bonus because the total output of the individual efforts would not equal that of the same people working as a group. The extra productivity results from the division of labor and coordination of effort that takes place in a group. It is also due to the fact that the contribution of one member triggers new ideas and recall of information in the minds of other members. Such ideas and information might not have been spontaneously generated by each person working alone. For example, if a single individual could produce an average of five creative solutions to a problem, a collection of five such individuals working independently would produce an average of twenty-five solutions. By contrast, the same five individuals working in a small group might produce thirty-five solutions. The extra ten solutions produced by the group would be the assembly effect bonus.

The seven characteristics discussed above distinguish the small group from other communication situations. These unique characteristics may serve both as facilitators and inhibitors of communication in the small group.

A Functional Approach to Small Group Communication

Small group communication can be viewed from several perspectives. We have chosen a functional approach. The notion of "function" should be familiar. The function of a typewriter is typing; the functions of a refrigerator are storage and cooling; the functions of a poker game are entertainment, mental stimulation, and, hopefully, financial gain. In the same way, the functions of small groups are the purposes they serve. A functional approach to small groups examines the functions groups serve and how they achieve them. Thus, a group's functions are its desired outcomes. For example, the desired outcome or function of a bridge club is primarily social gratification; the major function of a corporate board of directors is to make decisions. Sometimes a group may have a single function. More often, however, groups are multifunctional. For example, the board of directors may also have the function of persuasion, both persuading its own disagreeing members to conform to the majority position and persuading the rest of the corporation to accept its decision. The board may also function to satisfy social desires or to resolve conflicts. While groups are generally multifunctional, one overriding purpose usually dominates. In fact, some of the functions groups fulfill may be unintended and unnoticed. When the functions of groups are discussed in more detail in later chapters, this should be kept in mind.

Not all of the outcomes of groups are desirable. When the outcome of a group is unproductive or counterproductive, it is commonly labeled as dysfunctional. Thus, if a group produces conflict rather than conflict resolution, conflict is a dysfunction. Whenever small group communication produces negative results, it may be regarded as dysfunctional.

In assessing whether communication is functional one should consider how the elements or people in the small group process are linked or related to one another.

Two basic types of links exist: control links and feedback links. *A control link* exists if one element directly influences the status of another element. A *feedback link* exists if one element transmits information to another about its current state. A good analogy is the thermostat in a house, which both controls and provides feedback to the heating system. Within a small group, control and feedback links operate at several levels. Members control and give feedback to each other through communication within the group. One aspect of the group communication process, such as the interpersonal relationships, affects other aspects, such as the task network. Groups as a whole control and provide feedback to other groups or are controlled and receive feedback themselves. Thus, control and feedback are integral elements of small group communication.

One final consideration in the functional analysis of groups is the focus of analysis. Groups can be analyzed according to how they function to meet society's goals, how they function to satisfy the groups' purposes, or how individuals function within them to meet their own individual goals. While the role of groups in society should not be overlooked, this [discussion] concentrates on group behaviors to satisfy group and individual purposes. We examine the group inputs that create the group's structure, how the group interacts within that structure to achieve its functions, and how well it meets its goals.

Inputs (Structural Variables)

The inputs into a small group determine the structure or framework for group communication. They serve as the foundation or confines of the communication that will occur, much as the concrete foundation and wooden framework of a house dictate the form and functions of the final building. Inputs may be broken down into three main categories of variables: individual characteristics, group characteristics, and external factors. These various elements are called variables because they do not remain a constant quantity. Some elements vary independently of the rest, while others are dependent on another variable or several variables for the direction and amount of their change. Because most of the elements are variables, not constants, we cannot predict or explain the outcomes of the group until we understand the *interrelationship* of the relevant elements.

The first category of variables is *individual characteristics*. Each person in a group has many unique characteristics. These characteristics are individual differences among group members in the way they think and behave. We could probably produce an infinite list of individual characteristics, but let us consider just a few of the more important ones. Personality comes to mind first. A group made up entirely of introverts or pessimists would be expected to behave differently from one comprised entirely of extroverts or optimists. Individual beliefs, attitudes, and values are also important. People differ in their perception of truth, in their negative and positive evaluations of people and events, and in their underlying value systems. The amount and nature of these differences inject variety, interest, and sometimes conflict into groups. A third category of variables might be labeled general abilities: intelligence, aptitude, quickness, and verbal facility. We know that the bright student, the glib politician, and the witty professor all have impact. The initial status of an individual in a group is usually determined by his general abilities plus his competence, achievement, and attractiveness. These qualities will influence the choice of a leader and structure the nature of communication among members. Also, intricately related to these variables is the individual's areas of experience: the events of his past and his previous surroundings, including socioeconomic class, geographic locations, family relations, and education, will to a large extent affect his ability to relate to other group members. In general, the greater the number of similarities the higher the potential for effective communication.

Another group of variables includes individual goals and expectations. Each member has his own private goals and usually develops expectations of how the group will affect attainment of them. Individuals are also likely to have expectations of how rewarding the group will be in comparison to the amount of effort they anticipate expending. A final individual input worth considering is individual personality and tendency to conform. Factors such as age, sex, and several of the inputs mentioned already will determine which members are most susceptible to persuasion or are most likely to conform under group pressure.

The second category of structural variables is *group characteristics*. This category is much smaller. It includes the demographic features of the group upon which predictions can be made prior to any interaction. One such factor is group size. Groups of three people may not function in the same manner as groups of four, which, in turn, may function differently from groups of five or more. A second factor is the type of group. Is the group primarily social, or is it problem-oriented? Are members present voluntarily? Is the group continuous or temporary? Communication can differ according to the type of group. A similar consideration is the implicit and explicit goals of the group. Is the purpose of the group education, self-awareness, problem-solving, action, pleasure or several of these? If the group is task-oriented, the nature of the task is important. The kind of task, its complexity, and any other requirements such as time limitations are all variables that determine the group's structure and influence its outcomes. A final consideration is the frequency and length of interaction. Is the group a several-hours-a-day activity (like a family or class) or more like a monthly business meeting?

The third category of variables is *external factors*. These can be broken down further into externally imposed restrictions and environmental factors. Externally imposed restrictions include any rules or laws governing the group that are determined by a power outside the group. Any time, size, location or content restriction imposed from outside would qualify as an external factor. Designated status or leadership is also an externally applied restriction on the freedom of the group's operations. Environmental factors are elements in the immediate environment of the group which may have impact on its functioning. Temperature, lighting, amount of space, amount of noise and distractions, furnishings, colors, and attractiveness of surroundings all fall into this category.

Recognizing the major individual, group, and external characteristics that serve as inputs is important to understanding why a group behaves as it does. These variables not only identify for us the initial state of the group (i.e., its starting point) but they allow us to make certain predictions about the functioning of the group before it has begun operation. Once the group begins processing these inputs, a second set of factors comes into play: interaction variables.

Group Interaction

Inputs establish the group's communication predispositions, that is, the communication patterns and content most likely to occur. When interaction actually commences, three new classes of variables begin to act upon the initial inputs. They are task, procedural, and interpersonal factors; these three sets of variables affect each other and the communication that results.

Task variables include all factors that are relevant to the completion of the group's task (whether it be solving a complex task or just satisfying a need for conversation). Considerations such as the nature of the task, the method of information exchange, the task roles members assume, and the amount of conflict over ideas affect the channels of communication used, the networks that are established, and the messages that are created. The communication that occurs can, in turn, facilitate or create obstacles to task completion.

The second category is *procedural variables.* They concern the manner in which tasks are handled rather than the exact nature of the tasks. All organizational issues, including patterns of problem solving and decision making are procedural issues. A beginner can glimpse the effect of these factors by observing groups that strictly adhere to *Robert's Rules of Order* and comparing them with those that have no procedures for maintaining order. (The former may become hopelessly bogged down while the latter may be chaotic.) Even in social groups, we frequently decide the timing and order of activities.

A third classification is *interpersonal variables.* This category includes all factors that are relevant to the establishment of interpersonal relations in the group. They concern the way in which group members relate to one another and how they communicate, regardless of their specific tasks. Some key variables that have an impact on the interpersonal relationships are members' credibility, personal attraction, power or status, degree of similarity, conformity pressures, degree of trust among members, level of competition, language usage, and communication strategies. All these variables determine the socioemotional atmosphere of the group.

The interaction of these three sets of task, procedural and interpersonal variables significantly affects the communication that occurs in the group. The effectiveness or ineffectiveness of the communication, in turn, influences how successfully the group achieves its desired outcomes. These outcomes may be regarded as the major functions of groups.

Small Group Functions

The five most significant functions or outcomes of small group communication are persuasion, therapy, conflict resolution, social relationships, decision making, and problem solving.

The group outcomes can be evaluated by comparing them to the goals established by the group. Three common criteria used to assess group outcomes are productivity, group cohesion, and member satisfaction. Quantity, quality, and efficiency are all aspects of productivity. If a group's goal is to exchange a great deal of information or produce a decision in a short period of time, the quantity and efficiency aspects of productivity are relevant criteria. Group cohesion signifies how solidified the group is at the conclusion of an interaction period and how attractive the group remains to its members. This criterion is especially relevant to social and therapeutic groups. The final criterion is member satisfaction, or how well the group satisfies each individual's needs, goals, and expectations. The success of a persuasive campaign or the resolution of a conflict, or both, may provide high member satisfaction. Groups that fail to meet these criteria may be regarded as dysfunctional.

The ability of the group to satisfactorily fulfill its functions is dependent on its adaptability to the constraints of its individual, group, and external characteristics, and the balance of feedback and control in the communication that occurs during group interaction. Too little or too much feedback or control among members may result in unsatisfactory task, procedural, or interpersonal relationships within the group, leading to dysfunctional outcomes.

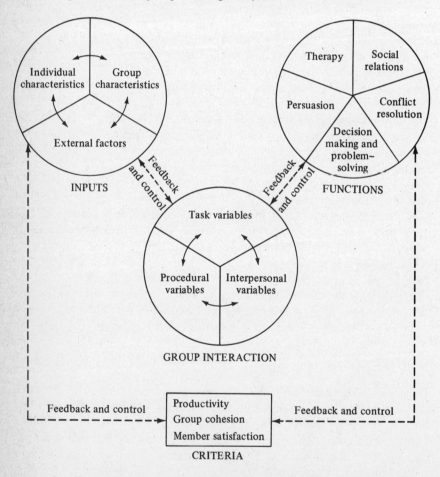

FIGURE 1   *Small group communication: a functional approach.*

Nineteen

The Group and the Individual

Lawrence B. Rosenfeld

Our discussion of norms and conformity indicated that groups influence their members to behave in certain ways, ways which help the group define itself. A Jet is a Jet Because ... and a Kiwanian is a Kiwanian because ... and a Boy Scout is a Boy Scout because. ... Fill in the blanks, and you'll have a notion of the norms which separate these groups.

Let's focus now on the specific areas in which individual behavior is influenced by others in a group. Research is available concerning motivation, branstorming, decision making, speed, and risk-taking behavior.

In general group interaction tends to *stimulate* the performance of group members. The first experiments to test this date back to the late 1800s when Triplett[1] observed bicycle racers alone and unpaced, alone and paced, and in competition. The fastest time was recorded in the competition situation, next fastest was when racers were paced, and the slowest was when they were unpaced. Triplett explained these results by arguing that the presence of others released "latent energy" normally unavailable to individuals working alone.

Experiments conducted since Triplett's early study provide mixed results: although the presence of others is always motivating, this motivation may not always facilitate performance. Triplett's bicycle racers were facilitated by the presence of others, but what about tasks which are less concerned with motor ability and more concerned with cognitive ability? The results differ. Shaw found that a task requiring mental concentration, such as solving math problems, was not facilitated by the presence of others.[2] Although we may conclude that an individual working with others is subject to a great many pressures not evoked when working alone, these pressures either have no effect on performance, especially when the task is cognitive in nature, or have a facilitative effect.

Working on the assumption that group participation motivates individuals to create new and often radical ideas, Osborn[3] investigated a group participation method named named *brainstorming*. The technique for generating ideas uses the following guidelines: (1) ideas, no matter how wild, are expressed without evaluation or critical analysis; (2) the emphasis is on quantity, not quality; (3) ideas are used to generate new ideas, i.e., ideas build on each other ("hitchhike"); and (4) the group's focus is on a single issue or problem.

Compared with the number of ideas generated by individuals working alone, brainstorming groups produce more. This might be a result of the many beneficial effects brainstorming has on the group: it increases participation and involvement, reduces the threat of having to find *the* solution to a problem, makes interaction fun and exciting, and virtually eliminates competition.

Brainstorming is used to help a group begin its *decision-making* task: it allows a group to generate ideas quickly and easily. But once a group is formed to make a decision, to come to some agreement about which solution should be implemented, other aspects of group influence come under consideration. What are the effects of group interaction on individual judgments? When is it best to use a group and when is it best to use an individual to perform some task or solve some problem?

We live in an age when groups are used for almost every type of problem solving, and this is because, in general, groups produce superior products. An early summary of research on group discussion written by Dickens and Heffernan offered conclusions which, almost thirty years later, are still supported:

1. Group judgments tend to be *less extreme* than individual judgments (although, as we shall see, group decisions tend to be riskier than the average group member's decision).
2. Group judgments tend to be *superior* to individual judgments.
3. *Majority opinion exerts a great deal of influence* in the decision-making process.
4. *Correct answers are given more support* in a group than incorrect ones.
5. *The greater the range of responses* permitted by a given problem, *the greater the superiority of the group method* over the individual method.[4]

Working in a group has a great many advantages over working alone, advantages which account for the general superiority of group problem solving.[5] A group, first of all, contains several people, allowing for a division of labor and the assignment of overlapping tasks. The former puts more information at the group's disposal, perhaps increasing alternative solutions and the probability of selecting the best one. The latter gives the group the opportunity to establish an informal series of checks.

If one individual can produce so many ideas, then two people should produce twice as many. And once you get into five and six person groups, the number of ideas available is tremendous, especially since discussing ideas seems to generate more of them. Logically, the greater number of alternatives a group has to consider, the greater the chance of choosing the best one.

Related to this point are two others. (1) If more ideas about possible solutions are available, then so are ideas about what the best solution should contain. Sorting through suggested solutions, a group is more likely than an individual to see all the relevant aspects. (2) A group accepts ideas when they are well supported, logically sound, and appear consistent with past experiences. The end result of these two factors should be a superior product.

If groups are better vehicles for problem solving, why are individuals used at all? The reason is simple: groups aren't *always* superior. Certain tasks lend themselves to group work, and others do not. It is necessary to analyze the relevant aspects of a given problem so that the best decision, whether to organize a group or go with an individual, can be made.

Research on the relationship between task characteristics and small group interaction helps in the development of criteria for choosing a group or individual problem-solving procedure. Because groups allow for a division of labor, tasks which *require many steps,* or *have many parts,* are best handled by a group. An individual may be incapable of handling a multifaceted problem requiring several related subtasks to be performed.

Large and complex problems normally require *a great deal of information,* and it is unlikely that any single individual will possess all of it. So, for such tasks, a group may be more efficient than someone working alone.

Groups motivate individual members and stimulate the generation of a great many more ideas than may have originally existed prior to interaction. This means that tasks which require *many solutions* are best handled by a group. Likewise, if *diverse solutions* are required, a group may be the best bet. Groups contain unique individuals, no two of whom are likely to see the same task or the same solution in precisely the same way. Diverse solutions are the natural product of member differences.

How *difficult* is the task? If it is very easy, an individual may suffice. If it is very difficult, a group may become frustrated. When group members spend more time and effort trying to convince each other that the task is beyond the group's capability than they do trying to complete the task, the interaction is dysfunction. It diverts the group from its central activity and, if the vocal members are successful in convincing others that the task is, indeed, too difficult to handle, the group's attractiveness decreases. As attractiveness decreases, so does cohesiveness, and the final outcome may be the disbanding of the group.

If easy tasks are best handled by someone working alone, and very hard tasks may destroy a group's cohesiveness, it seems that the best task for a group is one which is of *moderate difficulty.* Such tasks allow the group to be successful, and success, in turn, increases cohesiveness.

Related to task difficulty is *solution verification* or *evaluation.* Solutions which are easy to verify do not need a group to waste time with them. Each member of a group, for example, may be as capable of verifying the solution to a simple math problem as any other. To give a group the task of verifying the solution is unnecessary.

As a solution becomes more *difficult to verify,* it becomes more reasonable to use a group. Solutions difficult to verify normally require that diverse attitudes, opinions, beliefs, and sources of knowledge be considered, all of which are available in almost any group.

However, if a solution is extremely difficult to verify, either because it requires special knowledge not available in the group, or because it raises complex issues, a group may become bogged down in the verification process. The longer this stage in the group's task performance continues, the higher the probability that the group will either disband or move on to another task without completing the first one.

Another consideration which we may make of a task to help us determine whether a group or individual problem-solving procedure should be used, is the degree to which it is likely to be perceived as *impersonal.* The more impersonal the task, the greater the probability that it will stimulate task-oriented behaviors, in which case a group may be better than someone working alone. If, however, a task is highly personal, a group may get sidetracked in conflicts over matters unrelated to the task. Of course, a problem which is impersonal for one group may be perceived as highly personal for another. For example, consider the following task: develop a method for evaluating a teacher's performance in a class, a method which will be used for helping with promotion decisions. Because the problem demands a good deal of information, is too large and complex for any one individual, and will end with a method which is hard to verify, our first response is to use a group. So far so good. Now, we have to consider whether the groups we have available are suitable. We may use teachers in groups, but they're likely to get sidetracked with personal concerns, especially if any of the group members happen to be up for promotion in the near future. We may use students in groups, but they may not have enough information and might get sidetracked with personal concerns, especially if any who have been hurt by poor teachers are out for revenge. Finally, we may use administrators in groups, but they're also likely to get sidetracked with personal concerns, especially if they feel that too many (or too few?) teachers are being promoted.

In the end, we may have to give up trying to assign a group to the task, and look for the most qualified individual.

A final consideration to be made to determine the suitability of a task for a group or individual problem-solving procedure concerns *available time*. If only a short time is available, a group may prove unsatisfactory because it consumes a great deal of time while developing: members must orient themselves to each other and the task, whereas an individual is only concerned with the task; members must interact in order to determine areas of agreement and disagreement, which may mean dealing with matters tangentially related to the task, whereas an individual is able to focus directly on the task; group members engage in conflict an individual is unlikely to be burdened with; and, finally, when the task is completed, group members have to spend time congratulating themselves on the wonderful job, whereas an individual may settle for a quick, quiet beer.

Time is money. Even if a great deal of time is available to handle a particular task, it may be wiser to use an individual and consume fewer *man-hours*. For example, ten people working ten hours consume one hundred man-hours (which might mean $500.00 in salaries); someone working alone on the same task, even if it takes 20 hours, has only consumed 20 man-hours (which might mean only $100.00).

So, task time involves the consideration of two criteria: (1) how much "real" time is available, i.e., clock hours; and (2) how many man-hours are available. If either (1) or (2) is short, an individual is the only alternative; if both are long, a group is a feasible alternative.

It was noted earlier that the presence of other people ("social facilitation") has an effect on the motivation of group members, as well as on the number and quality of decisions a group generates. Another effect of the presence of other people concerns risk-taking behavior. Comparing how much risk a group is willing to assume as opposed to how much risk individuals, alone, are willing to assume, it has been demonstrated that groups are likely to make either riskier or more cautious decisions. This phenomenon, first systematically observed and experimented with only a decade ago,[6] is called the *risky-shift phenomenon.*

In a typical risky-shift experiment, subjects are presented with a problem such as the following:[7]

> Read the following situation and decide what probability for success you must have in order to accept the alternative. Situation: You may stay in the boring communication class which you preregistered for and, given the teacher's past performance, be assured a grade of B, or you may switch to an exciting communication class with a teacher whose past grading record indicates no assurance of any particular grade. What probability for success (an A or B in the exciting class) is necessary for you to make the switch? You might, for example, say to yourself: "I'll accept the attractive alternative (the exciting class) if the chances are 9 out of 10 that the results turn out to my advantage (an A or a B)." You might say, "I'll accept the attractive alternative if the chances are 2 out of 10 that the results turn out to my advantage." You may select odds of 1, 2, 3, 4, 5, 6, 7, 8, 9, or 10 out of 10. Of course, selecting 10 is the same as refusing to accept the alternative because you are demanding a 100% guarantee of success.

Individuals indicate their choices without discussion, and then are formed into groups and instructed to arrive at a group choice. The results are consistent: groups determine that they need a lower probability of success in order to make the switch to the exciting class; i.e., groups take more risks than individuals. On problems dealing with matters which generate conservative choices, such as "You may put your money in blue-chip, low return, high security stocks, or speculative, high return, low security stocks," groups show a conservative shift. This is especially apparent during times of recession and depression.

Why does the risky-shift occur?[8] Four major theoretical explanations for the phenomenon have been advanced: (1) risk as a result of a diffusion of responsibility; (2) risk as a derivative of leadership; (3) risk as a consequence of familiarization; and (4) risk as a social value.

One of the first plausible explanations for the risky-shift phenomenon, offered by Wallach, Kogan and Bem,[9] relates risk taking to a *diffusion of responsibility.* Simply stated, the explanation goes like this: whereas an individual must assume *all* the responsibility for his or her own decision, in a group the group members *share* the responsibility; therefore, the responsibility is diffused throughout the group.[10]

Think back to the last movie you saw in which an angry mob tries to attack the jailhouse, get the prisoner (who we learn at the end is innocent), and string him up. What happens? First, one person in the saloon says, "Let's get him." Note that he does not say, "Watch *me* get him." No, he's looking for support for his risky behavior. After his line and another belt of red-eye, a second voice is heard: "Yeah, let's get him!" The cry rings forth: "Get him! String him up! The lousy———(fill in your own dirty deed)." And, as a *group* they march to the sheriff's office, thinking individually, "It's not my responsibility, at least not altogether. I'm just part of the mob. Anyway, the sheriff can't lock *all* of us up."

As individual responsibility decreases, risk-taking behavior increases.

The second explanation[11] argues that risk taking is a function of the kind of *leadership* a group has. According to this explanation, high risk takers are more persuasive in those situations which produce a risky-shift. Similarly, low risk takers (cautious individuals) are more persuasive in those situations which produce a cautious shift.[12]

This view of risk takers as highly persuasive is supported by some recent research which Tim Plax and I conducted.[13] We had people respond to a variety of decision-making situations similar to the choice of classes decision, and also complete a battery of psychological examinations. We found that individuals exhibiting riskiness in decision making were characterized as effective communicators, persistent, confident, outgoing, clever and imaginative, aggressive, and independent, which all seem to sum to the following: dynamic, task-oriented leaders.[14]

Another aspect of this explanation which supports the probability of high risk takers being successful leaders considers the nature of our language. Persuasive arguments advocating risky behavior are inherently more interesting than those advocating caution. Consider the difference between "[shouting] Let's get over to the jailhouse and string up the son-of-a-gun! What are we, MEN or mice?" and "[calmly] Let's be careful about taking any action which might be dangerous." Clearly, the first speaker has the advantage.

The third major theoretical explanation argues that risk-taking behavior is a natural consequence of increased *familiarization* with a situation. This explanation differs from the others in that while risk diffusion and dynamic leadership may only be explained in terms of *group interaction,* the act of becoming familiar with a given situation may be explained in terms of *individual* processes.

According to this explanation, when an individual is confronted with a novel situation, the first response is marked by uncertainty and cautiousness. Increased exposure and study reduce this uncertainty, and the individual feels free to make a riskier decision. Also, increased exposure causes serious reconsideration of the initial cautious position, a reconsideration which often leads to a riskier final position.[15]

Consider the following group situation—as common as the jailhouse scene —in which a gang is planning a robbery, and the following dialogue is spoken:

"We can take this bank easy," the first person says, ungrammatically.
"I don't like it," Johnny Cautious responds.
"Yeah, waz the matta?"
"Too risky."
"Yeah?"
"Yeah."

Then the semiliterate leader explains the plan, noting all the right details such as the time the bank opens and closes, where the exits are, what time the guard falls asleep, and so on. After what seems like the longest scene in television history, Johnny finally becomes familiar with the operation. Then he says what we know has to be said:

"I like the plan."
"Not too risky for ya?"
"Nah."

And on to the last explanation: riskiness is exhibited by groups because it is *highly valued behavior.*[16] According to this explanation, cultural norms cause people to label problems as warranting either a risky or cautious approach. Because of individual differences, group members take different amounts of risk: some initially take more risk than others. The risky-shift, occurring only with problems that generate a value of risk, is due to an exchange of information about initial positions. During discussion, group members discover that others have taken as much or more risk than they have, and this stimulates thinking about whether they are actually in line with the value of risk they initially adopted. Comparisons with others suggest that they were taking only an average amount of risk, or even less. Consequently, they become riskier to conform to their new interpretation of risk.

The following internal monologue may help clarify what's going on: "I'll tell the others that if the probability is 50% of getting an A or B in the more exciting class, the switch should be made. Boy, am I risky!"

Then group members share their initial responses, and our hero/heroine finds that others selected 40% and 30%, so they are riskier.

"Hey! How can I think that I'm risky when everyone else is riskier than I am? I'll have to change the percentage I think is necessary to make the switch, and let the others know this as we discuss the problem."

Then the group discusses the problem, and our hero/heroine, to maintain the value of risk first decided upon, tells the others 20%, and smiles broadly.

Another aspect of this fourth explanation considers the social value of risk in American society. Levinger and Schneider[17] found that students, when asked what they would choose, what others would choose, and what the best choice would be in several risk-taking problems, see themselves as riskier than others, and that they admire even greater risk takers. Taking risks is valued, and, therefore, we try to look riskier than the other members of our group. And we raise our status by doing so!

Current research indicates that regardless of the intuitive appeal of the diffusion of responsibility explanation, and the logical reasoning of the leadership and familiarization arguments, the risk-as-value theory appears to be the most thoroughly substantiated explanation.[18] The evidence, however, is not conclusive, and it may well be that one or another explanation is best for a particular situation, or that combinations of these explanations may, in the final analysis, offer the best reasoning.

NOTES

1. N. TRIPLETT, "The Dynamogenic Factors in Pacemaking and Competition," *American Journal of Psychology* 9 (1897): 507–33.
2. M. E. SHAW, "Some Effects of Irrelevant Information Upon Problem-Solving by Small Groups." *Journal of Social Psychology* 47 (1958): 33–37.
3. A. F. OSBORN, *Applied Imagination,* 3rd. rev. ed. (New York: Scribner's, 1963).
4. M. DICKENS and M. HEFFERNAN, "Experimental Research in Group Discussion," *Quarterly Journal of Speech* 35 (1949): 23–29.
5. BARRY COLLINS and HAROLD GUETZKOW, *A Social Psychology of Group Processes for Decision Making* (New York: Wiley, 1964), pp. 54–55.
6. M. A. WALLACE, N. KOGAN, and D. J. BEM, "Group Influence on Individual Risk Taking," *Journal of Abnormal and Social Psychology* 65 (1962): 75–86.
7. For a detailed outline of the procedure, see Lawrence Rosenfeld, Gerald Goldhaber and Val Smith, *Experiments in Human Communication: A Laboratory Manual and Workbook* (New York: Holt, Rinehart and Winston, 1975), pp. 134–43.
8. D. CARTWRIGHT, "Determinants of Scientific Progress: The Case of Research on the Risky Shift," *American Psychologist* 28 (1973); 222–31; and K. L. Dion, R. S. Baron, and N. Miller, "Why Do Groups Make Riskier Decisions Than Individuals?" in *Advances in Experimental Social Psychology,* ed. L. Berkowitz (New York: Academic Press, 1970), pp. 306–72.
9. WALLACH, KOGAN, and BEM, "Group Influence on Individual Risk Taking."
10. Cf. M. A. WALLACH, N. KOGAN, and D. J. BEM, "Diffusion of Responsibility and the Level of Risk-Taking in Groups," *Journal of Abnormal and Social Psychology* 68 (1964): 263–74.
11. J. RABOW, "The Role of Social Norms and Leadership in Risk-Taking," *Sociometry* 29 (1966): 16–27.
12. Cf. G. C. HOYT and J. A. STONER, "Leadership and Group Decisions Involving Risk," *Journal of Experimental Social Psychology* 4 (1968): 275–84; and Y. Rim, "Machiavellianism and Decisions Involving Risk," *British Journal of Social and Clinical Psychology* 5 (1966): 30–36.
13. Cf. TIMOTHY PLAX and LAWRENCE ROSENFELD, "Dogmatism and Decisions Involving Risk," *Southern Speech Communication Journal,* in press.
14. N. BATESON, "Familiarization, Group Discussion, and Risk-Taking," *Journal of Experimental Psychology* 12 (1966): 119–29; J. P. Flanders and D. L. Thistlethwaite, "Effects of Familiarization and Group Discussion upon Risk-Taking," *Journal of Personality and Social Psychology* 5 (1967): 91–97; and N. Miller and K. Dion, "An Analysis of the Familiarization Explanation of the Risky-Shift," *Proceedings of the*

Annual Convention of the American Psychological Association 5 (1970): 337–38.

15. ROGER BROWN, *Social Psychology* (New York: Free Press, 1965); Roger Brown, "Further Comment on the Risky Shift," *American Psychologist* 29 (1974): 468–70; D. Korger and I. Briedlis, "Effects of Risk and Cautious Norms on Group Decision Making," *Human Relations* 23 (1970): 181–90; R. St. Jean, "Reformulation of the Value Hypothesis in Group Risk-Taking," *Proceedings of the Annual Convention of the American Psychological Association* 5 (1970): 339–40.

16. G. LEVINGER and D. J. SCHNEIDER, "A Test of the Risk as a Value' Hypothesis," *Journal of Personality and Social Psychology* 11 (1969): 165–69.

17. D. G. PRUITT, "Conclusions: Toward an Understanding of Choice Shifts in Group Discussion," *Journal of Personality and Social Psychology* 20 (1971): 495–510.

Twenty

Leadership

John E. Baird and Sanford E. Weinberg

The Dilemmas of Discussion

. . .

In our view, discussion too often is seen as a panacea for problems in decision making, so that whenever some body has difficulty making a decision (for example, the United States Congress), they habitually refer the problem to a committee. In fact, this habitual use of groups overlooks some of the many problems inherent in the group setting. In this last section, then, we will consider two "dilemmas of discussion" which suggest that group discussion is an appropriate tool in some, but not all, decision-making situations.

Efficiency

The first dilemma is one of *efficiency*—a measure of the energy required to arrive at a group decision. Strange as it seems, the group situation simultaneously encourages and inhibits the efficiency with which individuals work. The presence of others usually stimulates us to greater performance outputs. Our innate desire to impress the other group members causes us to determine which behaviors are valued by the groups and then to perform those behaviors as best we can. Thus we tend to produce more in groups than when alone.

Efficiency also is increased when the group task allows a division of labor. That is, if the job can be split among the members so that each of them can independently complete one phase, the job will be completed much more quickly than if one person tried to complete all phases alone. The business, social, governmental, and service organizations which dominate our society are built upon this principle.

While efficiency is increased through social stimulation and division of labor, other factors, however, cause efficiency to be lost. First, groups tend to be wasteful of talent. The most able of the group's members rarely can work at his own fast pace; he must help the slower members of the group. Much of his time and effort are therefore wasted, so that the group performance is worse on some tasks than would have been the performance by the best individual.

Second, groups waste time. An individual can make decisions quickly—groups usually have to deliberate, fight, resolve their fights, maintain social stability, and so on, before a decision can be reached. Indeed, situations in which some members are inalterably opposed to one another may actually make a decision impossible.

Given this dilemma of efficiency, what can we conclude about the appropriate uses of discussion? Generally, these suggestions seem in order:

1. If stimulation is needed, group discussion is desirable. Groups generate interest, even excitement, among their members and through this stimulation cause members to be more productive.
2. If a division of labor is possible, use a group. While some time will be wasted in coordinating the members' efforts, considerably more time will be saved by having them perform separate operations simultaneously.
3. If division of labor is impossible and a particularly capable individual is available and willing, use him (or her) alone. The other members of a group would only slow him down.
4. If time is of the essence, do not use a group. They probably would still be discussing long after the deadline has passed.

Creativity

A second dilemma of discussion concerns *creativity*. The group situation again produces a trade-off: some aspects of creativity are enhanced by the group setting, while others are hampered.

Groups are often more creative than individuals. Whether the stimulation provided by the presence of others, the diversity of experience represented by the group membership, or some other set of factors accounts for this phenomenon, we are not sure; nevertheless, groups generally seem more able to produce ideas that are individuals. This creativity in turn leads to another advantage for the group situation: when time is unlimited, groups usually produce a better decision. Again, these performance levels may not equal those of extremely capable individuals, but they usually exceed the levels of average and below average group members.

On the other hand, other aspects of creativity may be hampered by the group setting. Occasionally, ideas or beliefs may be suppressed by the group. Rather than risk appearing foolish, disagreeable, obnoxious, or socially unacceptable, we may choose to say nothing rather than voice some disagreement we may have with the other members. Or if we do voice our opinions and someone responds with "Wow, is that dumb!" we probably will simply drop the subject rather than demand that our ideas be explored. Group pressure in these situations inhibits creativity since ideas are suppressed before they are expressed or squelched when they are given voice.

Another disadvantage related to creativity is the tendency for groups to substitute talk for action. While group members become excited in the group situation and generate a remarkable number of ideas, carrying out those ideas may be something else. Often, the members spend all of their energies finding a solution, so that none are left to implement it. Our own observations of the tenants' meetings of a large apartment complex illustrate the point. The tenants would arrive at the meeting prepared to tear the complex down. They would read long lists of grievances, scream for the landlord's hide to be nailed on the clubhouse wall, and plot courses of action. Then they would all go home. The emotional release provided by the meeting apparently was enough, for no action ever was taken. Perhaps the landlord had taken a course in group discussion: apparently recognizing this characteristic of groups, he published notices announcing the meetings himself!

Landlords aside, we again can suggest some principles concerning the appropriate uses of group discussion:

1. *When many diverse ideas are needed, use a group.* The group setting probably will produce ideas which never would have occurred to any of the members working alone.
2. *When a decision must be made and when time is virtually unlimited, use a group.* The diversity and stimulation the group offers increase the likelihood of a good decision being formulated.
3. *When individual opinions are of greatest importance, avoid the group situation.* Such opinions could be better obtained on an individual basis where group pressure is not present to inhibit their expression.
4. *When action is needed, see to it that someone has responsibility to carry it out.* If no responsibility is assigned, no action is likely to occur. If, however, action is a specified part of the group's agenda, or if certain group members are charged with implementing the group's decisions, then the tendency for groups to substitute talk for action will be subverted.

Our aim is to promote effective group decision making. While we will devote our discussion primarily to the development of group synergy through effective communication techniques so that groups may operate well, the principle we have been considering should be kept in mind: effective group decision making is facilitated if the situation is conductive to group discussion and hampered if the situation is inappropriate to group discussion.

Twenty-One

Brainstorming—A Creative Problem-Solving Technique

Arthur M. Coon

Simply put, brainstorming is a technique for stimulating the generation of ideas and facilitating their expression. To define further: brainstorming is an application of methods suggested by Alex F. Osborn for explicit stimulation of the imagination in the production of ideas. It usually involves cooperative thinking by groups and is usually directed to the solution of specific problems.

The technique has been so bandied about by Babbitts, so juggled by journalists, so pawned and promoted and perverted by proselytes that the above definition may come as a surprise to many. Such distortions are to be expected when some new process or attitude catches the fancy of the public. First the press celebrates it with awe, and its disciples and converts cannot say enough in its praise. Then a new crop of journalists have to write new stories. Since praise has been exhausted, they go to the other extreme (ironically using a device of brainstroming itself!) and condemn. Meanwhile rival "innovators" spring up to claim the new process is not so novel as theirs, or that it is not new at all, or that their model is a vast improvement over the original.

If the process or attitude has real merit, it will survive these superficial gusts and squalls. The almost universal testimony of those who have tried brainstorming, according to the suggestions of its inventor, is that it does have real merit. It stands the pragmatic test. It works.

Not that it is a cure-all, nor the only way to do creative thinking. But the results so far indicate that through its employment individuals produce more ideas than they would otherwise; in some cases two or three times as many as when they do their cerebrating solo. Further, they tend to retain this greater fluency of ideation. They also experience side- or after-effects which perhaps are even more important. (These will be referred to later.) Therefore, brainstorming—with whatever refinements and improvements are suggested by research and experiment—will probably be around for some time.

I should like to conclude these prefatory remarks with the reminder that brainstorming is by no means all there is to Osborn's theory of creative thinking. It is simply one of a number of advocated techniques which happens to have caught the public fancy. As a result it has been ballyhooed out of all proportion in the public press. Those wishing to understand its relative and full significance are referred to Osborn's books which I shall shortly mention. . . .

In the course of his work [as a successful advertising man] Osborn found himself constantly confronted with the necessity of producing, or creating, new ideas that would help sell the products of his clients. In other words, he was in the business of using his imagination. He also found it incumbent upon him —to a small degree at first, more and more later—to supervise the similar creation of ideas in his assistants, and teach them, too, to be more creative.

At this point, for some reason difficult to explain, Osborn began to become interested in the processes of imagination: perhaps because he was more analytical than others, perhaps just because it was a way of getting a job done better. At any rate, he found that some things helped him think up ideas, and that others hindered or inhibited the process. He began to experiment—to try to find more things that helped, and things that helped more; at the same time trying to identify and avoid things that were inhibitive: times, places, attitudes, what-not. . . .

As usually practiced, brainstorming is engaged in by a group. The group may range from as many as several hundred to as few as three or four. But the optimum number averages ten or twelve. The group does not meet to *settle* a problem, but to get ideas on how to settle it, or at the very least (if the problem is intricate, or highly difficult or technical) to evolve fresh approaches to the problem. But here again Osborn frequently points out that a specific problem is not absolutely essential.

Therefore, it is not strictly correct to call brainstorming either a group technique or a problem-solving technique, although in practice it is usually both. Neither, though it involves discussion, is it exactly a discussion technique. It is best to think and speak of it simply as a device for stimulating the production of ideas.

With the above matters clarified, we come to the four "Brainstorming Rules" with which practitioners of the Osborn technique always preface their sessions, and which they constantly emphasize. These are of great importance, as they are the heart of the method:

1. Adverse criticism is taboo.
2. "Free-wheeling" is welcomed.
3. Quantity of ideas is desired.
4. Combination and improvement of ideas are sought.

It is difficult to say that one of these rules is more important than another. But if one had to be so designated, it would be the first. It is probably also the most misunderstood. Osborn observed that nothing had so inhibiting an effect on his production of ideas as concurrent criticism.

What causes some people to underrate the magnitude of Osborn's contribution to creative thinking is that most of us have observed the same thing. We have all been excited over some new idea, and are full of further thoughts upon it, only to have someone nip our enthusiasm in the bud by saying, "That won't work," or "It's too expensive," or "We tried that in 1943 and it was no good." The result was that we never expressed the further ideas.

But Osborn had the originality to do something about the fact that he and others had observed. He suggested that adverse criticism be held back for the time being. Therefore, at all Osbornian brainstorms there is a wielder of a bell, empowered and instructed to sound it at any manifestation of adverse judgment of ideas—even a derisive laugh.

Almost everyone is surprised at how freely ideas flow forth, once the critical attitude is suspended. Please note the word "suspended"—not "abandoned." This point is one that results in a good deal of misunderstanding, and it is often mistakenly said that Osborn underrates the importance of criticism. This is not the case. He only advocates postponing operations of the critical faculty until the creative faculty has had a chance to function. "Don't try to drive with your brakes on," is how he puts it. "Evaluation is important, essential, but it can and should come later."[1]

By "free-wheeling is welcomed" Osborn means to encourage the wild, implausible, even impossible flights of fancy without which the wings of imagination cannot be fledged. No one knows how the imagination works, but it certainly cannot soar if "cabined, cribb'd, confined."

A third objective in brainstorm sessions is to get as many ideas as possible, the theory being that if the number is great, the laws of probability will work in favor of the proportion of good ideas being larger than otherwise.

Finally, Osborn advocates building and improving upon ideas already expressed. This, indeed, is a key point, since everyone's experience is different, and that of one person in a group may well reinforce and supplement that of another. In practice, Osbornian Brainstormers use here what is called the "hitch-hike" technique. A person who thinks of an addition to an idea already expressed snaps his fingers to get attention. The moderator or leader of the session then recognizes him ahead of the person with the completely new idea.

Some observations may be offered here as to various other mechanical aspects of brainstorming. The moderator just referred to has the duty of recognizing participants with ideas. He announces the subject or problem, and gives necessary background information upon it, answering questions if necessary. He may offer a few suggestive ideas or solutions, as pump-primers, at the beginning. He should also keep the ideation moving, with an occasional priming suggestion if needed, such as, "Who else could help?" "How could color be used?" or "Can this be combined with that in some way?" It is important that he recognize speakers only when they raise their hands. Otherwise the less self-assured are left out, or some ideas lost.

To another person will also usually be assigned the function of writing the ideas down, reportorially. Such a person should be quick-witted to catch them all rapidly, and it is best that he write the ideas where all can see them, as on a large flip-chart or blackboard. In practice with actual problems, it has been found productive of best results to announce the subject to participants some little time in advance—several days, perhaps—so they can be thinking about it.

The statement of the problem also demands considerable thought. Time spent on getting it exact, specific, and clear is usually rewarded by a more productive brainstorm. A good beginning for a Brainstorm question is, "How many ways can we think of to . . .?"

A relaxed yet alert attitude in participants produces the best results, and Osborn employs various techniques to secure this attitude. Brainstorm sessions in Batten, Barton, Durstine, and Osborn usually take place after a luncheon. Often it is found best to break large questions into smaller ones so that about half an hour can be spent on each.

Sometimes the best ideas emerge after the participants have been going for some time, and are even slightly weary. Osborn theorizes that at the beginning they are skimming the familiar and superficial ideas off the surfaces of their minds, and that only after these are gone do the brains really get busy and begin to think creatively.

At least two operations follow the actual brainstorm session. These are of great importance.

One is the evaluation of ideas. Here the critical faculty, suspended before, comes into its own. The evaluation is usually done by others than the brainstormers, though the moderator often participates, if only to interpret some of the ideas.

Before the ideas can be evaluated, they often have to be categorized. Here the discovery of a new or missing category often leads to further ideas.

Still further ideas may also occur to one or more of the participants after the brainstorm session. These ideas are often as good as or better than the original ones. For this reason Osborn places great emphasis on this part of the "follow-up." Sometimes, also, a new brainstorm session may be held after the follow-up, categorization, and evaluation.

It will be observed that each of these rules embodies the "horse sense" of which Osborn speaks, no doubt because each is the result of trial and error, selection, elimination, and all that this implies—in other words, is based upon successful pragmatic experience.

Many other aspects of Osborn's techniques deserve comment. For instance, one realizes after some experience with brainstorming that many of the reasons ideas are never born, or—once born—quickly stifled, have nothing to do with the value of the ideas themselves. A cartoon which showed a conference leader addressing his group well illustrated an aspect of this. The leader says "Those opposed will signify by clearing out their desks, putting on their hats, and saying: 'I resign.' "

Osborn observed in the advertising business what is equally true elsewhere, that fear, jealousy, pride, timidity, and other emotions and attitudes discourage the conception of ideas.

One result of this understanding is that the person with the problem is almost never invited to sit in on its brainstorming. He already knows too many ways in which the thing cannot be done, and is likely to inhibit the ideas of others by word, gesture, or even silence, and at best to contribute little to the discussion. In Osborn's method, the person closest to the problem presents it as clearly and specifically as he can to the brainstorm group: then leaves the room before brainstorming actually starts.

Connected is the fact that many of us spend most of our entire days critically evaluating ideas and saying "no." Such ingrained habits and attitudes are very difficult to shake off, and are apt to carry over into brainstorming. For this reason executives and others whose critical judgment is their stock in trade may have the most difficulty using the Brainstorm technique, and sometimes succeed only imperfectly even after training and practice.

It will be observed also that Osborn's technique sets up what the psychiatrists call a "permissive situation." In psychiatry, the patient is encouraged to feel that he need fear no punishment—of which critical and especially adverse judgment is of course a type—no matter what he says.

In this way he is encouraged to discharge all his troubles, just as by similar means the brainstormer is encouraged to pour out all his ideas—good, bad, or indifferent. I believe that this element of what Aristotle would call *katharsis* is an important aspect of the satisfaction people find in brainstorming, and in its consequent success.

One may also observe a parallel with education, in which many a successful teacher finds—by experience or through instruction—that the best way to encourage success and happiness in students is to create in the classroom this permissive situation. Probably it is not necessary here again to refer to the derivation of the word "education."

In fact, many feel that the importance of brainstorming for business, where it originated, or for any problem-solving situation, will be less than its importance for education generally. Some who have tried it in business, perhaps with a good deal of skepticism, report, "There are many worthwhile by-products of brainstorming beyond new solutions arrived at. We were amazed at the new attitudes encouraged among our employees. Many of them have gained self-confidence at having their ideas listened to with respect for the first time. They are more willing to advance new ideas. And those to whom the new ideas are advanced seem to have a more receptive and tolerant attitude not only toward the ideas, but toward those who submit them."

I submit that if by practice with this technique educators can stimulate in students more creative and original thought along with a greater sympathy and tolerance for the ideas of others, they will have achieved something of major importance—whether or not the students reach any final conclusive solutions in their Brainstorm sessions.

NOTE

1. Cf. the similar doctrine of Wordsworth and Coleridge that colored the whole romantic movement in English literature: "the willing suspension of disbelief."

Twenty-Two

An Introduction to Interviewing

Charles J. Stewart and William B. Cash

The Interview Defined

We define interviewing as *a process of dyadic communication with a predetermined and serious purpose designed to interchange behavior and involving the asking and answering of questions.* The word *process* denotes a dynamic, ever-changing interaction with many variables operating with and acting upon one another, and a degree of structure or system without being fixed. An interview, regardless of its intent, does not occur in isolation. Once a relationship begins, impressions that are inputs into our mental programming are not reversible and may affect our perceptions of the other party, regardless of the length or depth of the relationship. When an individual or party comes into our perceptual field and into a relationship with us, he cannot ignore or avoid the ongoing dynamic potential of the relationship.

The word *dyad* denotes that the interview is a person-to-person interaction between two parties or units. Thus, more than two people may be involved in an interview (*e.g.,* two members of a company interviewing a job applicant, a journalist interviewing three members of a championship team), but never more than two parties—an interviewer party and an interviewee party.

Predetermined and serious purpose means that at least one of the two parties comes to the interview with a purpose or goal in mind—other than mere enjoyment of the interchange—and has planned and organized the interview to focus on some specific subject matter. The predetermined and serious purpose distinguishes the interview from social conversation and from most intimate interactions and fights. This does not mean that polite conversation, chitchat, or reasonable and necessary digressions are not parts of many interviews.

Each participant in the interviewing process has some critical content that he hopes to transact and a purpose, either consciously thought out in advance or developed within the context of the interview. The degree to which the purpose is achieved is a crude measure of the degree of satisfaction achieved in the interview, a way of measuring the success of the interview process. The extent to which we are able to accomplish our objectives, to deal with critical content, and to provide the same opportunity for the other party is a measure of the satisfaction which we can achieve in a fully productive interview.

Interchanging behavior connotes a sharing of relevant programmings and expectations or, if you will, getting it together *together*—a sharing of facts, times, names, places, and feelings. The interrogation, debate, and fight, unlike the interview, typically do not involve a mutual sharing of each other, with each other. The interchange of behavior may encourage us to express our total humanness in verbal expressions of joy, fear, loneliness, anxiety, and in nonverbal touches, hugs, punches on the arm, handshakes, winks, and quick looks of concern or knowledge. The free expression of our humanness involves various levels of risk that can be minimized but never eliminated. If one or both parties elect to "play it safe," the interchange and the quality of the interview will suffer.

The asking and answering of questions is crucial to the interviewing process. It is the primary means of interviewer/interviewee interaction and allows both parties to get at crucial subject matter and to achieve their purposes and goals. The mere mouthing of questions and responses, or questions asked solely for the purpose of politeness, or ones that do not facilitate the progression of the interview toward its goal are wasted questions and time. The use of purposeful questions, thought out in advance and used at the appropriate time during the interview, is vitally important to the interview.

. . .

There are a wide variety of interviewing dyads, and Redding has developed a "situational schema" or classification into which interviews fit according to the functions they perform. Figure 1.1. is an elaboration of Redding's classification to include virtually all types of interviews.

The first category, information-giving, includes interviews designed to orient new employees or new members to their organizations or to train, instruct, or coach individuals in particular behaviors. Examples include explaining benefits of an insurance program to an employee, clarifying rules or procedures for meetings, training individuals to fill out application forms, and coaching a door-to-door sales representative on how not to get the door slammed in his face. Job-related instructions (orders) also fit under this first category. For example, head nurses in hospitals give reports to shifts of nurses coming on duty. They must give special information or instructions about the conditions, medications, and behaviors of patients. Foremen in factories often give orders to work crews prior to shift changes.

The second category, information-gathering, includes interviews designed to gain information from the interviewee, and includes surveys, polls, some exit interviews, the journalistic interview, the research interview, and the investigation interview. This category encompasses surveys designed to assess the feelings, attitudes, or trends of belief of a particular audience or market. Exit interviews are often not intended to discover the reasons for an employee leaving, but are used as public relations gimmicks to salve the conscience of the employer, "I did the best I could to find out why Irving left us. Heaven knows I tried." An exit interview should ascertain the true reasons why an employee is leaving, with the underlying assumption that no organization can afford to lose a good employee. If the employee's reasons can be discovered and remedied, other employees may not leave for the same reasons. Where it is used to improve the work climate, the exit interview has been a success. The research interview is used primarily to delve deeply into a subject of interest such as product usage, community planning, or recreation facilities. The investigation interview is employed by police, governmental agencies, and other investigatory bodies and is designed to get information from an interviewee

1. Information-giving
   a. Orientation
   b. Training, instruction, coaching
   c. Job-related instructions

2. Information-gathering
   a. Surveys and polls
   b. Exit interviews
   c. Research interviews
   d. Investigations: insurance, police, etc.
   e. Medical: psychological, psychiatric, caseworker
   f. Journalistic

3. Selection
   a. Screening and hiring
   b. Determination
   c. Placement (internal)

4. Problems of interviewee's behavior
   a. Appraisal, evaluative, review
   b. Separation, firing
   c. Correction, discipline, reprimand
   d. Counseling

5. Problems of interviewer's behavior
   a. Receiving complaints
   b. Grievances
   c. Receiving suggestions or answering specialized questions

6. Problem-solving
   a. Objective (mutually shared problems)
   b. Receiving suggestions for solutions
      (especially to problems covering a large group of people)

7. Persuasion
   a. Selling of products
   b. Selling of services
   c. Quasi-commercial selling

FIGURE 1.1   *Types of interviews.*

about an incident in which the individual was involved or witnessed, or to get information about an event, person, place, or thing. For instance, the investigative interview occurs at the scene of an accident or when a claims investigator seeks information for an insurance company.

The third category, selection, includes a broad spectrum of interviews used for screening, hiring, or placement of employees, students, etc. The *initial screening interview* is designed to weed out applicants who do not meet the special qualifications of a particular organization. The screening interview is the most common interview in business, government, and many colleges and universities. The *determination interview,* often referred to as the plant or office interview, usually follows the screening interview. Its basic purpose is decision-making; the decision being whether an individual should remain in a formal relationship (hired immediately, tested, given a further interview) with this organization or whether this formal relationship should be terminated. The party with hiring authority may hire a highly qualified individual even though an opening is not available at the moment. Employees are shifted from department to department to provide them with a degree of cross-training. Once a position becomes available within the organization, a third interview, called the *placement or transfer interview,* may take place. This interview is designed to place the most qualified person in the most desirable position for the benefit of the organization. Sometimes corporation manpower development departments keep replacement charts (a chart used to plot and plan visually what people might replace others within the organization) and the transfer interview is used as an internal method of selecting the most desirable replacement.

The fourth category, problems of interviewee behavior, includes appraisal, evaluation or performance reviews, and counseling interviews dealing with perceived problems related directly to an interviewee's behavior. This type of interview poses difficult and special problems for both interviewer and interviewee, and is one of the "big three" interviews in organizations: employment, performance appraisal, and counseling. Besides formally evaluating employees within the framework of appraisal interviews, many organizations conduct disciplinary, corrective, or what are sometimes called reprimand interviews. These interviews are conducted at the insistence of the interviewer and are mostly directive in nature. The counseling interview is a common interview, especially in education and business. Counseling interviews are partially nondirective (controlled by the interviewee) because the interviewee usually initiates and controls the communication in such situations. An important consideration in counseling interviews is the extent to which the problem is perceived by the interviewer and interviewee. A problem tends to be unimportant until it is *our* problem.

The fifth category, problems of interviewer's behavior, deals with perceived problems directly related to the interviewer's behavior or the behavior of the organization the interviewer represents. These interviews involve the receiving of complaints or the accepting or discussing of grievances. These include formal union grievance procedures and other formalized processes in nonunion organizations, and informal grievances such as employee complaints and gripes, customer complaints about faulty merchandise or service, and customers returning unwanted merchandise.

The sixth category, problem-solving, deals not with problems related to the personal behavior of interviewer or interviewee but with genuinely shared problems of mutual concern. The interview should result in some form of decision-making. We are not talking about pseudo problem-solving approaches manifested in the phony, "Now Johnson, what is our problem (meaning your problem) today?" We can best characterize problem-solving interviews as "true" when both parties in the dyad share in the problem and the development of a viable solution.

The seventh category, persuasion, is one of the most frequently used and least understood types of interviews. The term "persuasion" connotes different things to different people. Some time ago, one of the authors was discussing interviewing with a professor of marketing and, when the subject of sales came up, the author said, "Oh, you mean a persuasive interview." The marketing professor shot back indignantly, "I do not deal with that arm-twisting business called persuasion." When we say "persuasion" we simply mean an effort to change behavior (way of thinking, feeling, or acting) of the interviewee without compulsion or duress. The persuadee maintains the freedom of choice in selecting (perceiving) a message as well as the freedom to act or not to act as a result of the message. The persuader may deal with ideas, events, policy, or with commercial or quasi-commercial matters. Persuasive interviews include sales situations that involve institutional selling or the personalized selling of a product or service.

PART SIX
Groups and Organizations: The Climate Controls

Experiences and Discussions

1. Make a list of all the groups to which you belong. Use the following chart to determine the uniqueness of each situation in terms of a small group.

	Frequency of Interaction	Group Personality	Group Norms	Coping Behavior	Role Differentiation	Interdependent Goals	Assembly Effect Bonus
Situations							

2. Review the small groups in which you interact. Choose one group that is important to you and make the following analysis:
   a. What is the function of this group?
   b. How do the control links operate in this group?
   c. How do the feedback links operate in this group?
   d. How do individual characteristics affect this group?
   e. How do group characteristics affect this group?
   f. How do external factors affect this group?

    g. How does this group handle task concerns?

    h. How does this group handle procedural matters?

    i. How does this group handle interpersonal relationships?

    j. How would you describe the success of this group in terms of productivity and solidification?

    k. Are group members satisfied with this group?

    Based on this analysis, what recommendations would you make for improving any operations in this group?

3. You are the supervisor of an advertising firm and must decide about the renewal of a client's contract. Describe the situation in which you are involved and use the criteria presented by Rosenfeld to determine if the decision should be made by an individual or a group.

4. Recall a situation in which a decision had to be made that involved some risk (changing a relationship, making a large financial investment, moving to an unfamiliar area, etc.). Was this decision made by an individual or by a group? According to explanations of the risky-shift phenomenon (diffusion of responsibility, leadership, familiarization, social values), what predictions can you make about decisions made by an individual and by a group?

5. If you are working with a group on a class project and are having difficulty in getting started or in determining how to approach a decided-upon topic, suggest that the group participate in a brainstorming session. Follow Coon's guidelines and follow-up procedures. Find out the group's reactions to the brainstorming procedure.

6. Teaming with another student, role play a job interview situation. How will you structure the environment? What are the goals of each "player"? What tactics and strategies will you each employ?

7. You are about to appear for an interview before a board of faculty and peers. These individuals have the authority to overturn a course grade you are appealing on grounds of prejudice. How will you prepare yourself? What tactics will you employ? How would you act if you were sitting on the board?

8. Imagine you are leader in a group where you have a great deal of power—much more than the other members—but the others seem to resent your power. What would you do to overcome those feelings?

9. Studies of leadership have shown that at the beginning of a discussion virtually all group members, when asked, express a desire to be group leader. Taking into account social norms and individual motivation, explain why people express this desire in the first place and why some people who express it then fail to participate in the subsequent discussion.

For Further Reading

BRILHART, JOHN K. *Effective Group Discussion.* 3rd ed. Dubuque, Iowa: Wm. C. Brown, 1978.

    After an introduction to group processes, Brilhart provides information on various types of group discussions and on observing and evaluating the discussions. The brief yet complete text is supplemented with field-tested exercises and objectives to guide the reader. Topics emphasized include learning discussions, encounter processes, direct confrontation, interpersonal feedback in small groups, and organizing of group problem solving.

BURGOON, MICHAEL, JUDEE K. HESTON, and JAMES C. McCROSKEY. *Small Group Communication: A Functional Approach.* New York: Holt, 1974.

The strength of this text is its coverage of small group communication in an extremely well-organized and easy-to-follow format. The functional approach to this area of study is welcomed. Topics covered in this text include use of small groups to persuade and resolve conflict, small groups in social relationships and therapy situations, and effective participation in small groups.

CATHCART, ROBERT S., and LARRY A. SAMOVAR. *Small Group Communication: A Reader.* 3rd ed. Dubuque, Iowa: Wm. C. Brown, 1979.

This newly revised collection of readings has retained the foundation essays and theoretical essays dealing with small group communication and added discussions of contemporary techniques for participation in and study of small groups. The areas covered are definitions and models, group patterns and processes, and communication theory and practice.

GOLDBERG, ALVIN A., and CARL E. LARSON. *Group Communication: Discussion, Processes and Applications.* Englewood Cliffs, N.J.: Prentice-Hall, 1975.

Material centers around the nature of group communication, research, theory, and traditions. Specific focus is on observation of group communications, leadership, and problem solving.

GULLEY, HALBERT E., and DALE G. LEATHERS. *Communication and Group Process: Techniques for Improving the Quality of Small-Group Communication.* 3rd ed. New York: Holt, 1977.

A conceptual perspective that concerns itself with the nature of small group communication, preparation for interaction, communicative interaction, quality of group outcomes, and leadership.

HUSEMAN, RICHARD C., JAMES M. LAHIFF, and JOHN D. HATFIELD. *Interpersonal Communication in Organizations.* Boston: Holbrook, 1976.

This text deals primarily with the process of perception and its applications to communicator effectiveness. The book explicates the problems caused by conflict in organizations and suggests possible solutions. The book is illustrated with various realistic examples of the concepts and situations it deals with.

OFSHE, RICHARD J. (ed.). *Interpersonal Behavior in Small Groups.* Englewood Cliffs, N.J.: Prentice-Hall, 1973.

A challenge to any student, this work combines readings in both the classic experiments and the more recent empirical investigations. Some topics presented in this encyclopedic work are attraction and consensus, group membership, status, organizational processes, power relationships, aggression and deviance, crisis situations, and games. Recommended for advanced students.

ROSENFELD, LAWRENCE B. *Now That We're All Here ... Relations in Small Groups.* Columbus, Ohio: Merrill, 1976.

This is an easy-to-read, concise review that puts together issues in small group interaction. The text is supplemented with illustrations and exercises/questionnaires that are extremely helpful for self- and group analysis. Some topics covered are self-concept and roles in small groups, interpersonal influence, conflict, power and leadership, and problem solving and group discussion.

SCHEIDEL, THOMAS M., and LAURA CROWELL. *Discussing and Deciding: A Desk Book for Group Leaders and Members.* New York: Macmillan, 1979.

The book focuses on discussion procedures generally and the leadership of discussion groups primarily. The source presents what the authors call "a rich variety of possible procedures as alternatives from which an individual leader or team member can draw ideas for ways to meet particular situations and purposes appropriately."

PART SEVEN

Public Communication: Audience Interaction

" 'It is rather an absurd business, this ritual of ours,' he answered. 'But it has at least the saving grace of antiquity to excuse it. I have a copy of the questions and answers here if you care to run your eyes over them.'

"He handed me the very paper which I have here, Watson, and this is the strange catechism to which each Musgrave had to submit when he came to man's estate. I will read you the questions and answers as they stand."

" 'Whose was it?'

" 'His who is gone.'

" 'Who shall have it?'

" 'He who will come.'

" 'Where was the sun?'

" 'Over the oak.' "

THE MUSGRAVE RITUAL

So began the famous speech entitled the "Musgrave Ritual," containing a hidden message designed for a secret audience—a message that would reveal the location of a fabulous treasure.

Not all public communications yield such fine prizes, of course. Nevertheless, public speaking is a well-developed method of exchanging information with an audience and a significant part of the overall communication picture.

Like the Musgrave Ritual, it has the "saving grace of antiquity" about it. The earliest investigations of communication were centered upon the public situation. Quite possibly the very first such serious study, and still one of the most thorough, was conducted during the Golden Age of Greece (circa 400 B.C.) by Aristotle. The selection here from his *Rhetoric* provides a classical framework for the studies that follow it.

How many ways could you deliver the Musgrave Ritual? Its hidden meaning was further obscured by the rote catechism of its delivery. A sensitive speaker might have revealed much behind the stark words, just as any public speaker can add depth and power to his or her speech. Byker and

Anderson apply the principle of identification between speaker and audience as a means of suggesting devices for the development of a public message. Their suggestions include a catalog of steps any Musgrave might use to hold and enthrall an audience.

A real understanding of the ritual, though, depends upon more than the speaker: the audience must actively respond. Listening is the key to interpretation. The speaker may help structure the listener's attention, just as the author of the Musgrave speech focuses us upon some nebulous "it" that serves as the solution to the puzzle. This act of shaping and encouraging listening is called "feedforward" and is carefully described by Bill Colburn in an article revealing some of the hidden facts about effective public address.

Of course, if your purpose is to persuade or inform or enlighten or entertain your audience the structure of your speech is a prime consideration. The Musgrave Ritual is frustratingly obscure; John Keltner presents advice to any speaker who wants to structure a presentation in a clear, interesting manner to avoid frustrating his other audience.

Whatever your goal, though, audience adaptation is a major theme in speech preparation and a theme running throughout these selections. Whether you are speaking to a brood of Watsons or a gaggle of Holmeses, your presentation must be adapted to those who will be responding. Perhaps that message is the most important clue to be discovered in any investigation of public communication.

OBJECTIVES

After carefully reading these three articles you should be able to define the following key terms:

rhetoric	(Aristotle)
credibility	
induction	
enthymeme	
syllogism	
invention	(Byker and Anderson)
organization	
style	
memory	
delivery	
identification	(Colburn and Weinberg)
perceived norms	

group demographics
feedback
feedforward

introduction   (Keltner)
closing
interaction core

And:

1. Describe the three modes of persuasion presented by Aristotle (Aristotle).
2. Describe the role of example in persuasion. Relate the use of examples to syllogisms (Aristotle).
3. List the qualities that make a statement credible. Relate these qualities to the three modes of persuasion (Aristotle).
4. List and define the five rhetorical canons (Byker and Anderson).
5. Analyze "Joe's" communication attempt using the five canons (Byker and Anderson).
6. How do speakers "define their audiences"? Furthermore, how can they "define likely listener responses"? How can an audience member develop strategies to improve his or her listening abilities? (Colburn and Weinberg).
7. Describe the cycle reaction of feedforward and feedback (Colburn and Weinberg).
8. Describe the three parts of speech and the role of each part (Keltner).
9. Relate the interaction core to the concept of persuasion presented by Aristotle (Keltner).
10. Describe the advantages of an outline in planning a public address (Keltner).

Twenty-Three

Rhetoric

Aristotle

Rhetoric may be defined as the faculty of observing in any given case the available means of persuasion. This is not a function of any other art. Every other art can instruct or persuade about its own particular subject-matter; for instance, medicine about what is healthy and unhealthy, geometry about the properties of magnitudes, arithmetic about numbers, and the same is true of the other arts and sciences. But rhetoric we look upon as the power of observing the means of persuasion on almost any subject presented to us; and that is why we say that, in its technical character, it is not concerned with any special or definite class of subjects.

Of the modes of persuasion some belong strictly to the art of rhetoric and some do not. By the latter I mean such things as are not supplied by the speaker but are there at the outset—witnesses, evidence given under torture, written contracts, and so on. By the former I mean such as we can ourselves construct by means of the principles of rhetoric. The one kind has merely to be used, the other has to be invented.

Of the modes of persuasion furnished by the spoken word there are three kinds. The first kind depends on the personal character of the speaker; the second on putting the audience into a certain frame of mind; the third on the proof, or apparent proof, provided by the words of the speech itself. Persuasion is achieved by the speaker's personal character when the speech is so spoken as to make us think him credible. We believe good men more fully and more readily than others: this is true generally whatever the question is, and absolutely true where exact certainty is impossible and opinions are divided. This kind of persuasion, like the others, should be achieved by what the speaker says, not by what people think of this character before he begins to speak. It is not true, as some writers assume in their treatises on rhetoric, that the personal goodness revealed by the speaker contributes nothing to his power of persuasion; on the contrary, his character may almost be called the most effective means of persuasion he possesses. Secondly, persuasion may come through the hearers, when the speech stirs their emotions. Our judgements when we are pleased and friendly are not the same as when we are pained and hostile. It is towards producing these effects, as we maintain, that present-day writers on rhetoric direct the whole of their efforts. This subject shall be treated in detail when we come to speak of the emotions. Thirdly, persuasion is effected through the speech itself when we haved proved a truth or an apparent truth by means of the persuasive arguments suitable to the case in question.

There are, then, these three means of effecting persuasion. The man who is to be in command of them must, it is clear, be able (1) to reason logically, (2) to understand human character and goodness in their various forms, and (3) to understand the emotions—that is, to name them and describe them, to know their causes and the way in which they are excited. It thus appears that rhetoric is an offshoot of dialectic and also of ethical studies. Ethical studies may fairly be called political; and for this reason rhetoric masquerades as political science, and the professors of it as political experts—sometimes from want of education, sometimes from ostentation, sometimes owing to other human failings. As a matter of fact, it is a branch of dialectic and similar to it, as we said at the outset. Neither rhetoric nor dialectic is the scientific study of any one separate subject: both are faculties for providing arguments. This is perhaps a sufficient account of their scope and of how they are related to each other.

With regard to the persuasion achieved by proof or apparent proof: just as in dialectic there is induction on the one hand and syllogism or apparent syllogism on the other, so it is in rhetoric. The example is an induction, the enthymeme is a syllogism, and the apparent enthymeme is an apparent syllogism. I call the enthymeme a rhetorical syllogism, and the example a rhetorical induction. Everyone who effects persuasion through proof does in fact use either enthymemes or examples: there is no other way. And since everyone who proves anything at all is bound to use either syllogisms or inductions (and this is clear to us from the *Analytics*), it must follow that enthymemes are syllogisms and examples are inductions. The difference between example and enthymeme is made plain by the passages in the *Topics* where induction and syllogism have already been discussed. When we base the proof of a proposition on a number of similar cases, this is induction in dialectic, example in rhetoric; when it is shown that, certain propositions being true, a further and quite distinct proposition must also be true in consequence, whether invariably or usually, this is called syllogism in dialectic, enthymeme in rhetoric. It is plain also that each of these types of oratory has its advantages. Types of oratory, I say: for what has been said in the *Methodics* applies equally well here; in some oratorical styles examples prevail, in others enthymemes; and in like manner, some orators are better at the former and some at the latter. Speeches that rely on examples are as persuasive as the other kind, but those which rely on enthymemes excite the louder applause. The sources of examples and enthymemes, and their proper uses, we will discuss later. Our next step is to define the processes themselves more clearly.

A statement is persuasive and credible either because it is directly self-evident or because it appears to be proved from other statements that are so. In either case it is persuasive because there is somebody whom it persuades. But none of the arts theorize about individual cases. Medicine, for instance, does not theorize about what will help to cure Socrates or Callias, but only about what will help to cure any or all of a given class of patients: this alone is its business: individual cases are so infinitely various that no systematic knowledge of them is possible. In the same way the theory of rhetoric is concerned not with what seems probable to a given individual like Socrates or Hippias, but with what seems probable to men of a given type; and this is true of dialectic also. Dialectic does not construct its syllogisms out of any haphazard materials, such as the fancies of crazy people, but out of materials that call for discussion; and rhetoric, too, draws upon the regular subjects of debate. The duty of rhetoric is to deal with such matters as we deliberate upon without arts or systems to guide us, in the hearing of persons who cannot take in at a glance a complicated argument, or follow a long chain of reasoning. The subjects of our deliberation are such as seem to present us with alternative possibilities: about things that could not have been, and cannot now or in the future be, other than they are, nobody who takes them to be of this nature wastes his time in deliberation.

Twenty-Four

The Classical Bases for Improving Communication

Donald Byker and Loren J. Anderson

For centuries, human beings, especially certain scholars who studied the area, have sought to avoid communication failures by improving communication skills. Underlying this study has been the conviction that communication is not a natural, uncomplicated activity; instead, it is a complex, coactive process. Communicators must choose the correct means to achieve the desired identifications, and to choose intelligently requires careful study and practice.

As the Greeks and Romans developed instruction in effective communication, they set out five major areas for consideration. These areas came to be known as the five rhetorical canons: (1) *invention*—finding ideas to communicate and choosing among them; (2) *organization*—arranging the ideas chosen; (3) *style*—encoding ideas into symbols; (4) *memory*—maintaining control over the ideas, the organization, perhaps even over the exact signs and signals that have been selected;[1] (5) *delivery*—presenting orally or otherwise the product of the previous canons. Each canon can be viewed as a relatively distinct area for communicators to master in the search for better and better means to achieve identifications.

Breaking down communication into these components is a useful step in learning; one must keep in mind, however, that in any communication all the parts are intertwined, thus delivery elements cannot be separated completely from the symbolization, and so on throughout the canons. For example, Vince's ideas (invention) cannot be separated completely from the verbal (style) and nonverbal (delivery) encoding of them. Organization within and

---

[1] The fourth canon, memory, is frequently dropped from consideration.

among Vince's sentences is complexly interrelated with aspects that would usually be placed in other canons.

We shall use a familiar example to illustrate the rhetorical canons. Picture a college student, Joe, with too much term left at the end of his money. Joe would like aid from his father back home. The thesis of Joe's communication with Dad will be: "Dad, you should send me more money!" Joe's appeal for further funding could take many forms. He has a lot of information readily apparent to him: among his deprivations he notes his diminished love life, his curtailed eating choices, his immobile wheels, and his depleted wardrobe; Joe thinks wearily of creditors, fondly of the generally assumed obligation of fathers to offspring, and remorsefully of the shoddy stewardship accorded the last dole from the family pocketbook. Many other items of information might be considered, but the foregoing serve to indicate that Joe is working to bring forth potential bases for his communication with Dad. Joe now must choose among the available pieces of information; he knows he would not do well to discuss last week's poker losses. Joe selects the starkness of his present existence as a useful means of touching on parental sympathies. He decides to underscore, not too boldly of course, the father-son relationship, thus intimating a father-son obligation. He also believes that a direct mention of his bankruptcy is needed; in a more oblique appeal, Dad might miss this crucial issue (or feel too comfortable in appearing to miss it). In trying to find information and choose which items to use in seeking the wanted identification, Joe has labored in the province of invention.

Extending the example to the second rhetorical canon, organization, Joe now thinks of the placement or arrangement of his three points. Should the order be: sonship, stark existence, bankrupt state? This is possible, as are a number of other arrangements. Joe decides that bankruptcy, bleakness, sonship is the best organization to use.

Now the action moves to canon three, style. Joe has decided to send a telegram (primarily a delivery matter that must be considered later in the canon scheme). The telegram medium limits the number of words to be used.[2] Such limitations are often undesired, but on certain occasions, they can be grasped as advantages. Joe's past indiscretions, he hopes, can be hidden judiciously in the shorthand summary that directly tells his financial plight: "No mon." Joe's yearnings for better vibrations, not all of which would reflect well under parental scrutiny, are captured discreetly in "No fun." And the gentle prod to parental obligation is administered neatly by signing off: "Your Son." Joe's little poem

> No Mon,
> No fun,
> Your Son.

is, of course, a familiar lament. Joe is probably right in expecting that his father

---

[2] The choice of the telegraph medium is an encoding in its own right. It connotes urgency and has other factors that are consonant with Joe's appeal.

will be well aware of the thesis implied: "Dad, you should send me more money!"

The last canon, delivery, often plays a most important role in communication; this role will tend to be less significant in a delivery mode like the telegram than in the face-to-face oral mode; nevertheless, some elements Joe might have considered are worth remarking here. Delivering his message by telegram is quick; hence urgency is suggested by the channel chosen, and Joe hopes his father will recognize the need for a rapid response. The telephone probably would be faster and more intimate, but on this subject Joe prefers the distance. An open line would allow for, even require, amplification, and Joe is uncomfortable with the details he would have to add. Since the telegram may get results with minimum revelation and risk, Joe figures he should try to get by with this delivery device.

As you probably know, the old story we have been embellishing to illustrate the rhetorical canons has an apparently unhappy outcome. Joe's father wires back:

> Too bad,
> So sad,
> Your Dad.

Foiled, Joe tries to figure out where he went wrong. Should he have sent an airmail letter with his poem etched in white on a black background? Perhaps the telegram was too novel and the intended urgency was grasped instead as flippancy, and the identification created by him and his dad became light-hearted rather than serious, as Joe had hoped. After weighing this and assessing still other channels, Joe decides that the telegram was probably all right as a delivery choice.

Now the post mortem can move to the next canon, style. Joe wonders whether the cuteness of his iambic monometer triplet is a flaw. Dad just did not take the little ditty seriously; instead, Dad saw it as a tossing of the gauntlet and gleefully sharpened his pencil to reply in kind. The mimicking of Joe's form gives some weight to this possibility. Joe decides that he will do well in future appeals not to fudge over a point by being flippant and cryptic.

Organization seems to have been sufficiently clear. Dad had no trouble following it to launch a point-by-point rejoinder. Perhaps the organization is *too* clear, suggesting cool, manufactured crafting rather than the agonized utterance of a son in distress. Joe judges that the possible flaws he could find in placement are inconsequential. The undesired identification cannot be blamed on arrangement.

Invention heads the canons. Joe looks ruefully at the relatively rapid and insensitive choices he made. He should have thought more about how well his father knew the justifiable expenses and the sufficiency of the allowance given. He certainly should have been more sensitive to his father's wish for a prudent son. Joe surmises that any future appeal for funds must rely less heavily on his own credibility in the area of supply and demand; he has spent much of his credit on the subject of finances by coming yet again to ask for more. Joe sees that he will have to take a much harder course, now, by confessing past errors and giving a strict account of planned allocations for the new gift. Perhaps through Dad's forgiveness and Joe's improved performance, a good relationship can be rebuilt.

As we leave our extended illustration, we pause to stress a final point. While attempting to improve communication, one often tinkers with delivery when adjustment of style would bring the desired end more efficiently. Long, difficult sentences usually are easier to improve in style than to master in delivery. Virtuosity in vocal and visual elements can hardly cover weakness in wording. Similarly, some quick repairs in organization will save much grief over tortuous transitions and other forms of aimless verbiage in the style. A sure sense of where one is going and what are the right paths will make selecting the appropriate style a far easier task. And, more importantly, strong foundation work in the canon of invention will give the other canons easier, more worthwhile roles. In the finding and choosing of appeals, when one shows sufficient sensitivity to self, others, and the subject, this strength is likely to infuse the efforts made in the other canons. Putting primary effort into invention, then, yields a significant multiplier effect throughout the canons. This does not mean that effects cannot arise from delivery to influence the other canons. Surely this does occur; but the major currents of influence usually flow the other way, from invention to delivery. This indicates that one should parcel out energy accordingly.

Twenty-Five

Audience Analysis and Listening Behavior

William Colburn and Sanford B. Weinberg

Assume for a moment that you are a member of any one of the many potential audiences available to you. You might select your church congregation, a particular class at school, a service club, a work group, or a social group that you are part of and in which you spend time listening. Assume further that someone comes to you and asks you to describe in detail one of the audiences in which you are a regular member. If you attempt to answer the inquiry, you would probably find that you know much more about your listening group than you had realized. Most audience members, even audience members drawn together for the first time, can make meaningful observations about those with whom they share the situation. The fact that people can make meaningful comments about others in their groups is related to the concept of *identification*.

Human motivation is such that observation of those around us constitutes an important element in our ability to function within a rapidly changing society. Several examples outside the speech-communication situation may aid in understanding the concept. Most of us have had occasion to step into an unknown restaurant and, after a brief survey of the clientele and surroundings, make a decision as to whether to stay or to go elsewhere. There have been occasions when we have encountered a group, made several assessments about its members, and then determined whether or not the group would be to our liking. The process of identifying a situation or a group is one that we use regularly. Identification forms the basis of the ultimate evaluation that we render of people, ideas, groups, and institutions.

The concept of identification is very important in our consideration of the question of how and why an audience affects its members' listening ability. It is important because of the the relationship that exists between the process of identifying and efficient listening. It is our perception of the composition of the audience that determines the degree to which their collective response will affect our response. If an audience is identified favorably along dimensions that a listener holds to be important, social facilitation is of immediate consequence and has great and lasting impact upon the listener and upon his identifying with the audience.

There are three separate questions that contribute to a final determination of audience identification. These questions are

1. What are the demographic characteristics of the listening group?
2. What are the perceived norms that characterize the listening group?
3. How important are the perceived norms to those within the listening group?

In the first question, a consideration of *group demographics* means that observable and factual information about any given audience must be tabulated in a formal or informal manner as a first step in the identification process. Demographic elements such as age, sex, occupation, income level, education, political party preference, religious affiliation, race, and avocational interests are assessed in aggregate fashion, thus partially defining the audience. People use demographic analysis to assess groups in many everyday situations, whether they realize it or not. As a matter of fact, through trial and error, most people become quite expert in drawing meaningful conclusions about groups of people based upon the demographic characteristics of those groups. These conclusions about a group enable an individual to develop a mental set that prepares him or her to react in a prescribed way. Here too, then, the audience has a definite impact upon the individual member. The demographic characteristics of the composite listening group will contribute to the individual listener's willingness or unwillingness to listen to available inputs.

The second question that must be reviewed in order to identify an audience concerns assessing *perceived norms* that seem to characterize the groups. Traditionally, there has been talk of the country club set, the businessmen's luncheon group, the street freaks, the letterman's club, or the thespian society as special groups with special defining characteristics. These groups have characteristics that are best described in terms of goals, ideas, or values important to the membership. The goals, ideas, or values of a group form the *norms* of the group. Group norms in many respects transcend the demographic elements. That is to say, norms of a group are more important to know and to understand than the statistics (demographics) of the group if one wishes to become a member or simply wishes to participate in their deliberations. If the goals, ideas, or values of the listening group are perceived to coincide with those held by a prospective participant, that participant's desire to join the group and to become involved in the group will be greater than if group norms do not align with those held by the prospective participant. And as we have established, involvement contributes to effective listening.

The third question essential in identifying a group is really an extension of the second question: How *important* are the perceived norms to those within the listening group? Not much discussion is needed on this point because it logically follows that the importance a group places upon its norms dictates the degree to which *all* group members are expected to follow the norms. In addition, the stronger the listening group feels about their shared values, ideas, and goals, the more overt their expression of support becomes which, in turn, creates greater social facilitation.

The desire to listen, because it is under the manipulative control of each individual, becomes a volatile element as that individual moves from audience to audience. Identifying each audience in terms of its demographic characteristics, its norms, and the importance placed upon those norms is an essential process for people who wish to predict the likelihood of individual audience members listening to what transpires in a given speaker-audience situation. . . .

By definition, an audience must have the element of polarization. This means quite simply that audiences are audiences only when there is a designated speaker and a clearly defined group of listeners. There must be an established speaker-listener relationship in an audience situation. This observation may seem somewhat sterile, yet examination of the concepts of feedback and feedforward may provide some interesting insights into the dynamics of speaker-audience situations.

There exists an interplay between the polarized roles of participants that is clearly linked to a whole set of possible behavioral responses; responses available to the speaker and responses available to those who listen. Discussion of the complex interplay between a speaker and his or her audience is made somewhat clearer by the definitions of feedback and feedforward offered by Clevenger and Matthews in their book *The Speech Communication Process.* These authors define the terms in this way:

Feedback [a term taken from the field of cybernetics] . . . is the process whereby a system modifies its operation so as to adjust to the known consequences of those operations. In the case of human communication, this refers to the process of adjusting one's communication behavior so as to take account of the observed influence of that behavior on the listener.

Like feedback, feedforward is a term that originated in cybernetic theory. In the same sense that the operation of a thermostat is the simplest example of feedback, setting the thermostat is the simplest example of feedforward. By setting the thermostat to a desired temperature range, the operator may be said to "feed forward" the maximum and/or minimum temperature to the point in the heat cycle where these temperature values will be needed.

Feedback is a process whereby the speaker makes adjustments in the message based upon the reactions of his or her listeners. It is a process that is situational-responsive; that is to say, feedback calls for *immediate* adjustments as dictated by the respondents within the situation. The speaker's decision to adjust is not a matter of premeditation or advance planning, it is a decision made during the actual presentation of ideas and expressions of feeling. As you can see, a speaker committed to a totally prepared text (manuscript) cannot use feedback to change the message content.

Feedforward is a process in which the speaker, in advance of the actual speech or presentation, establishes a course of action. Just as a person sets his thermostat at 72 degrees because that setting will meet his temperature needs, a speaker develops an approach or strategy that will make it possible to gain consensus on his or her point of view. I.A. Richards comments on the process in a 1968 *Saturday Review* article entitled "The Secret of Feedforward." He views feedforward in this way:

> Whatever we may be doing, some sort of preparation for some design, arrangement for one sort of outcome rather than another is part of our activity. This may be conscious, as an expectancy—or unconscious, as a mere assumption. If we are walking downstairs, a readiness in the advanced leg (but indeed in our whole body) to meet something solid under its toe is needed if we are to continue. Usually, on the stairs, this feedforward is fulfilled. There is confirmatory feedback at the end of each step cycle—the foot finds the expected, the presupposed footing. Compare pitch dark and broad daylight as to the degree of awareness we may have of our feedforward. If the feedback does not come, if it is falsifying and not verifying, we have to do something else and rather quickly. The point is that feedforward is a needed presciption or plan for a feedback, to which the actual feedback may or may not conform.

Feedforward, then, is establishing objectives and setting plans for a scheduled communication effort. It may also include the development of alternative strategies *in advance* of the communication situation that can be used to meet various listener responses. Alternative strategies in a practical sense can be seen in statements such as "If she says this, I am going to say . . .," or "I will ask for a grade change if he seems to be in a good mood," or "If Mom says 'maybe,' I will ask Dad, if she says 'yes' I'll just tell Dad I am going."

The reality of feedforward becomes important because speakers come to the communication situation with messages in mind that do, in fact, *define their audiences.* A second feedforward reality is that prepared messages not only define audiences but also *define likely listener responses.* If you consider carefully what you have just read, you will find that several important ideas are implicit in the process of feedforward. First, a person does not have to rely solely upon his judgments to identify an audience, its characteristics, its norms, and the importance the audience places in its norms. The speaker will assist a person attempting to analyze his fellow listeners by sharing his analysis of the audience, which comes through in the message he or she delivers. This analysis becomes especially important in situations where a listener is isolated from fellow listeners, as in a mass communication situation. A person may get a feel for others watching a television program based upon the message that program carries. Therefore, an understanding of the audience of which one is a part can be gained by careful assessment of the communicator's message. A second idea brought to bear by feedforward is that a listener can improve his or her listening efficiency by noting the strategy employed by the speaker. If, for example, the speaker makes his or her intentions known early in the speech, it becomes much easier to listen to the development of the speech. If you are able to figure out what it is that the speaker is after, appeals made by the speaker carry fuller meaning. The will-to-listen might well be enhanced or dampened by a determination on the part of the listener of what it is that the speaker has in mind.

Feedforward is real. It has meaning and has implications for the student of speech communication. Understanding feedforward, as a concept, is vital to understanding the dynamic process of communication.

Twenty-Six

Private Speaking to Public Speaking

John W. Keltner

Structure of the Speech

Obviously, the ideas that we select to use in any given speech will have within them certain structure. We consider the problem of organizing an array of ideas into an argument, into a description, a narration, or some other form of spoken discourse. What principle should we use in determining the nature of the order?

Erwin P. Bettinghaus reviewed the studies of structure and argument and concluded that *"no consistent set of relationships has been found between speech or arguments organized in various ways and audience response to those speeches or arguments.*"[1]

Current research indicates that the use of a rigid and preset structure does not accomplish the target purpose any more effectively than other means and that *the order of a speech should be a function of the interaction of the audience and the speaker in relation to the particular ideas being presented.* Obviously, if an audience is likely to expect and to respond to an organization that has formal logical structure of proposition plus support type, then such an approach should be used. However, the evidence suggests that the usual audiences are not aware of the structure of a speech; yet, there is always some kind of structure present. The effective speaker uses the kind which is most effective for a particular purpose and a particular audience even though the audience may be unaware of the form. Structure should be determined by the nature of the audience in relation to the speaker and his target and ideas. I also suggest that it is impossible for you to provide a static structure principle or form that will fit all situations and all types of ideas.

So, where do we go? I suggest that six criteria be used in developing the structure of public speaking: (1) Organize your speech to fit the type of structure from which the particular audience is most likely to get the most of your target ideas. (2) Avoid setting up a precise and standard form for all speeches. (3) Select several basic models to use selectively as they fit the situation. (4) Develop your own system of models from your own analysis of the audiences, your purpose, your needs for order, and the possibilities of success. (5) Try to provide your audience with orderly ideas that will fit its ability to deal with order. (6) Maintain a central concentration upon your main theme and target regardless of the type of system of arrangement you may use.

Opening the Speech

The opening statements of a speech are of particular importance, since in them several things must be accomplished at once. (1) We must get the attention of the audience. (2) We must get it to accept us so that it will accept what we are going to say. (3) We must arouse interest in what we are going to say. (4) We must give the audience some idea of what is to come. These things can be done separately or all of them can be done with a single phrase.

Getting the attention of the audience performs several very significant functions. We want to polarize an audience, that is, give it a central focus of attention. An audience, when it finds its attention directed toward a common center, performs more as a unit than if attention is dispersed in many different directions. Attention is the process of selecting the event or phenomenon on which to focus the perception; thus, as a speaker, you want to bring the

[1]Erwin P. Bettinghaus, "Structure and Argument," in Gerald R. Miller and Thomas R. Nilsen, eds., *Perspectives on Argumentation* (Chicago: Scott, Foresman and Co., 1966), p. 132.

audience to focus upon you and your ideas. Good speakers use many different systems to focus attention, a few of which are given here:

Plunge immediately into the most dramatic or significant part of the speech.
Use an anecdote, story, or joke that is related to the occasion or to the people in the situation or to the subject.
Use some startling or sudden movement or noise.
Begin with intense directness and earnestness (this is perhaps the most used of all the physical devices for getting attention).
Use a series of questions, unanswered, that result in a focus of curiosity toward the main topic or idea.
Stand and look at the audience for an extra long time, keeping firm eye contact and an intentness that communicates, through the nonverbal channels, the seriousness, concern, and desire to speak to that audience.
Get the audience to perform some physical act such as standing together, singing together, or raising hands.

The beginning of a speech can make a great deal of difference in the total effect.

The person who introduces the speaker may do a great deal to get an audience polarized and ready to listen to the speaker. On the other hand, an introduction can be highly disruptive also. On some unfortunate occasions, the introduction is more of a speech than the speech itself. Some people take so much time to introduce a speaker that, when he finally gets the floor, the audience is exhausted and pretty well polarized on getting away from the situation. An effective introduction establishes the right of the speaker to speak on the particular subject, enhances the credibility of the speaker, reveals the nature of the topic (unless specifically not desired by the speaker), polarizes the audience so that there is an expectancy and readiness for the speaker, and delivers to the speaker an audience unit that has a warm and friendly feeling and is ready to respond. A good introducer is rare; and when one is not available, the above functions must be performed by the speaker himself.

Getting an audience to accept the speaker involves relating the speaker's experience, background, interests, and the like to those of the audience. When a person rises to speak on a subject of some significance he must establish with his audience a relationship that will permit it to accept him as an authority or one in a position to speak of the matters he brings to its attention. Here, the effective speaker knows what kinds of information will convince an audience that he has sufficient prestige to speak with authority.

The audience needs also to have its interest whetted for what is to come. In most instances, the subject of the speech is known to the audience. However, the particular slant or development that the speaker intends to bring to the event should be shown to have some particular interest for the audience. Since people are usually interested in things that aid them in satisfying their needs or wishes, the successful opening usually establishes an anticipation in the audience that something it wants or needs will be provided.

Some speakers prefer to keep their audiences in the dark about what is to be revealed or developed in a speech. This development generally is used for the type of speech that leads the audience through various bits of information until the key idea is suddenly apparent. As a general rule, speakers who use this device effectively are quite skilled and know their audiences quite well. Most good speakers give the audience some idea of what is to come. The Greek orators probably knew versions of a classic story often told today. A very successful politician was asked the basis of his success on the platform. He answered: "First I reveal to the audience what I am about to say. Then I say it. And finally, I reveal to them again what I have said."

Closing the Speech

The closing of a speech is likewise important because, having developed an idea, we must use the concluding remarks to accomplish at least two objectives: (1) summarize or recapitulate the things we want the audience to recall or do and (2) stimulate the audience to recall and to do.

The manner in which the speech is ended depends a great deal on the condition of the audience when the speaker comes to his final remarks. If the audience has come to the purpose for which the speaker addressed it, the conclusion by summary generally is all that is needed. If, however, the speaker feels that the audience needs an additional punch in order to fully accomplish his purpose, he may then add some form of stimulation. Several methods have been identified:

Some speakers start with an anecdote, then bring it to an end as the close of the speech; or they refer back to the opening remarks or comments in some manner.

Some speakers tell a new and fresh anecdote or give a particularly vivid and exciting example of their intent or purpose.

Other speakers end with a quotation from poetry or prose or drama that has special relevance to their topic, purpose, and their audience.

A few speakers end by having the audience do something together in the same vein as at the opening.

One of the more common types of closing is what might be called "the dawn of a new day" conclusion: The speaker portrays in vivid style what great things are in store for the audience if it does as he prescribes.

An opposite approach is used by the speaker who predicts dire and fateful consequences unless his advice is followed.

The Interaction Core

Throughout the process of speaking, the most significant principle of organization is that which provides for the interaction with the audience. As we speak, we should observe the behavior of the audience. If we perceive that the audience is missing some aspect of the speech, we should adjust immediately to provide for sufficiently more material than we will use so that we are free to select what to use in terms of the manner in which the audience reacts to what we are saying.

It is helpful, in planning and organizing a speech, to state the main purpose, the reasons, and the action in a single paragraph. We should start our preparation with this paragraph, which will aid us in maintaining a unity to our presentation and will be available to us when it becomes necessary to adjust to the audience and the situation.

The in-depth outline form for a speech provides for maximum adaptation and still gives us something in the way of an organization for reference. With this form, the speech is plotted in terms of the listeners' probable and desired reactions, the planned message, and the changing needs of the speaker in relation to the message he wishes to produce and to the listener reaction.

The advantage of this type of preparation is that it causes us to think in terms of the listener reactions to what we plan to say and the necessary adjustments we may have to make in order to handle the audience variations in response. Such a method of preparation makes it much easier to change and alter our plans when the situation does not come out just they way we expect.

PART SEVEN

Public Communication: Audience Interaction

Experiences and Discussions

1. Prepare a short speech for extemporaneous presentation. How will you select a topic? What will you need to know about your audience? What style, delivery, organization will you use?
2. Read another section of Aristotle's *Rhetoric.* Are most of the generalities about types of people true? What corrections or updating would you suggest?
3. Listen to a speech on campus or on television. Analyze what you hear according to the techniques of Byker and Anderson. How did the address fare? What improvements can you suggest?
4. Find a copy of an address in a textbook, newspaper, or magazine. Outline the text. Does it include all the steps described by Keltner? What stages or portions are missing?
5. Is public speaking a topic for modern consideration? What opportunities will you have to give a public address? What kinds of skills do you need to develop?
6. Stand up in front of an audience of peers and give a three-minute impromptu (unprepared) address. Did you include the canons?

Did you follow Aristotle's suggestions for making your speech persuasive?

7. As a member of an audience, analyze the adaptations made to you by a good public speaker. Do your instructors modify their lectures according to the audience? Would a presentation to other professors at a convention use the same style? Vocabulary? Organization?

8. Find a classic speech in the library. Rewrite the same address for a very different type of audience; for example, what should John Kennedy have said in his inaugural speech if he were addressing a high school class instead of the American people?

For Further Reading

BARKER, LARRY L., and ROBERT K. KIBLER (eds.). *Speech Communication Behavior: Perspective and Principles.* Englewood Cliffs, N.J.: Prentice-Hall, 1971.

This book is composed of original essays and selected readings by noted scholars on seven aspects of communication behavior. Each section contains objectives and discussion questions to help you analyze such topics as persuasion and attitude change, the acquisition of communication behaviors, physiological principles, and transracial communication.

COLBURN, WILLIAM C., and SANFORD B. WEINBERG. *An Orientation to Listening and Audience Analysis.* Palo Alto, Calif.: Science Research Associates, 1976.

This module considers in detail how listening influences the public speaking process. By understanding your audience through the techniques suggested, you can better understand what the audience will listen for and how to enhance the listening process.

CONNOR, W. ROBERT. *Greek Orations.* Ann Arbor: University of Michigan Press, 1966.

Connor introduces and edits a collection of the finest speeches of Lysis, Isocrates, Demosthenes, Aeschines, Hyperides, and Philip. The selections serve as examples of rhetoric as well as a history of the early development of rhetorical principles.

DEVITO, JOSEPH A. (ed.). *Communication.* Rev. ed. Englewood Cliffs, N.J.: Prentice-Hall, 1976.

A well-chosen collection of twenty-eight readings offering a variety of articles on communication processes, messages, sources, and receivers. The combination of classic and contemporary writings provides a foundation for both the theoretical and the practical aspects of communication. This new edition includes readings on self-perception and interpersonal dimensions.

FISHBEIN, MARTIN, and ICEK AJZEN. *Belief, Attitude, Intention and Behavior: An Introduction to Theory and Research.* Reading, Mass.: Addison-Wesley, 1975.

This text lays the groundwork for basic theories about attitude, intention, and behavior and goes on to suggest various applications in the area of persuasion.

KING, STEPHEN W. *Communication and Social Influence.* Reading, Mass.: Addison-Wesley, 1975.

King examines the process of social persuasion, posing a model ideally suited for analyzing an audience and public-speaking situation. His strategic suggestions are of particular interest, transcending rhetorical settings.

LEE, IRVING, and LAURA LEE. *Handling Barriers in Communication.* New York: Harper and Row, 1957.

Two manuals in one—a workbook that contains both a discussion section and a readings section. The cases illustrate communication barriers involved in jumping to conclusions, giving and getting information, making corrections, and being closed-minded. The analysis of everyday thinking, speaking, and behaving should stimulate your investigation of your own encounters.

McCROSKEY, JAMES C., and LAWRENCE R. WHEELESS. *Introduction to Human Communication.* Boston: Allyn and Bacon, 1976.

This book provides research on communication behaviors often neglected in introductory texts. Discussion topics include human communication and change, the motivation to communicate. communication apprehension, personality variables and communication, interaction versus transaction, interpersonal confirmation, and information processing.

MINNICK, WAYNE C. *The Art of Persuasion.* 2nd ed. Boston: Houghton Mifflin, 1969.

In addition to offering a comprehensive analysis of the components of persuasion, the author also considers the ethical dimensions of influencing attitudes and behaviors.

PERELMAN, C., and L. OLBRECHTS-TYTECA. *The New Rhetoric.* Notre Dame, Ind.: University of Notre Dame Press, 1971.

This originally French work is a modern classic updating Aristotle and expanding the philosophic meaning of rhetoric. Though a bit difficult to follow at times, its consideration of quasi-logical devices is well worth the effort.

WINDES, RUSSELL R., and ARTHUR HASTINGS. *Argumentation and Advocacy.* New York: Random House, 1965.

Though dated, this book clearly and concisely presents the process of proving a statement for public address. It discusses structure and content of argument, refutation, reasoning, and persuasion.

PART EIGHT

Mass Communication

"Give me a pencil, and that slip of paper. Now, then: 'Found at the corner of Goodge Street, a goose and a black felt hat. Mr. Henry Baker can have the same by applying at 6:30 this evening at 221 B Baker Street.' That is clear and concise."

"Very. But will he see it?"

"Well, he is sure to keep an eye on the papers, since, to a poor man, the loss was a heavy one. He was clearly so scared by his mischance in breaking the window, and by the approach of Peterson, that he thought of nothing but flight; but since then he must have bitterly regretted the impulse which caused him to drop his bird. Then, again, the introduction of his name will cause him to see it, for everyone who knows him will direct his attention to it. Here you are, Peterson, run down to the advertising agency, and have this put in the evening papers."

THE BLUE CARBUNCLE

And so, having evolved the principles of selective attention and of gate-keeping influence, Sherlock Holmes effectively employs the mass media of his day. The effect of the media on various aspects of society is certainly not a new concern, but seems more important in our era of electronic mass media. In an introductory essay, Robert Avery outlines the unique qualities of mass communication that separate it from the interpersonal and group settings presented earlier. He explains the five functions of the media, including those used here by Holmes to concentrate attention, present information, and guarantee wide dissemination.

Looking to the future, Melvin DeFleur discusses the impact of the media and analyzes the progression of mass communication theories. If we are to investigate the principles of communication in this rapidly expanding setting, DeFleur's suggestions on integrating theory may well provide the necessary keys to understanding what is happening. Gumpert goes a step further in the same direction, presenting his mini-comm theory as the solution to a mysterious problem: how to integrate large audiences with restricted interests into the mass media audience the setting demands.

In the story that introduced this section, Holmes receives a single reply to his ads and hence solves the case he is investigating. But could his advertisements have added more confusion? Could he have, in effect, created more suspects by encouraging readers to pretend to be the Henry Baker solicited for the reward of a free goose? Nicholas Johnson, former commissioner of the Federal Communications Commission (FCC), warns that today that possibility of the media creating more problems than it solves is a practical reality. He suggests that television may be hazardous to your health and raises important questions about the role of TV in "preaching" materialistic lifestyles and minimizing the importance of personal growth. Certainly the danger is worth considering; one wonders whether or not Holmes had carefully thought it through . . .

OBJECTIVES

After carefully reading the four articles in this section you should be able to define the following terms:

watchdog   (Avery)
correlation
gatekeeper
dysfunctions
selective attention, perception, retention

conditioning   (DeFleur)
social categories
social differentiation

hot-cool   (Gumpert)
mini-comm
CATV

FCC   (Johnson)
humanness

And:

1. Explain what is included and what is *not* included in defining "mass communication" (Avery, Gumpert).
2. Describe six ways in which interpersonal and mass communication can be distinguished (Avery).
3. Explain the five media functions as described by Lasswell (surveil-

lance, correlation, social transmission), Mendelsohn (entertainment), and Schramm (advertising) (Avery).

4. Define the positions of each of the following regarding the impact of the media on individuals and groups: (a) social organizational theory, (b) Innis's technological determinism, (c) McLuhan's "medium is the message," (d) individual differences perspective, (e) social categories perspective, and (f) social relations perspective (DeFleur).
5. Explain the "two-step flow of communication" in the dissemination of information and the usual direction characteristic of the flow of opinion leadership. Use an original or observed example to illustrate this process (DeFleur).
6. In your own words, explain Nicholas Johnson's concerns about how television preaches styles of living (Johnson).
7. List at least five alternatives to "Big Television" (Johnson).
8. Distinguish between mass communication and mini-comm and give the assumptions made by each approach (Gumpert).
9. List at least five basic characteristics of mass communication (Gumpert).
10. Describe the following theories of mass communication: Stephenson's Play Theory, Loevinger's Reflective-Projective Theory of Broadcasting and Mass Communication, and Innis's Technological Theory (Gumpert).
11. Provide a minimum of four examples from the media that indicate the mini-comm approach (Gumpert).

Twenty-Seven

Communication and the Media

Robert K. Avery

It is difficult for the college student of the 1970's to imagine living in a world without communication media. We are the product of a society that depends upon a continuous stream of messages that are transmitted via radio, television, motion pictures, newspapers, magazines, and books. In fact, the media are so much a part of our daily lives that we often take their presence for granted. Similarly, we grant them almost unlimited power in determining what current events will be brought to our attention each day. Even though we are well aware of the frequent attacks on the media by such outspoken critics as Spiro Agnew and Nicholas Johnson, we have a tendency to forget the seriousness of their accusations and return to our evening newspaper or favorite television newscast to discover what is taking place in the world "out there." Living in a decade that has been labeled as the "age of communication" and characterized by the doubling of all human knowledge every five years, we share a common responsibility to develop an understanding of the characteristics, functions, and potential impact of the mass media in our modern society.

Human communication is the process of transmitting meaning between individuals. It is a process that is both fundamental to man's nature and vital to his existence. Since the birth of primitive cultures, man has been heavily involved in expanding his capacity to express his feelings, desires, concerns, and experiences to those around him. At first, man seemed satisfied to transmit meaning to others in close proximity to himself, but as man developed his intellect, he found it desirable (perhaps imperative to his very existence) to enlarge the parameters of his communicative transmissions. Thus, man extended the boundaries of human communication through the use of smoke signals, jungle drums, flashes of light, and crude trumpets. Later, with the invention of the alphabet, man transmitted his knowledge through written communication, first using pen and ink, and later carved wooden blocks. But it was not until the fifteenth century and the invention of movable metal type that man developed an efficient means of providing written communication to a mass audience in a relatively short period of time. Then, in the early 1840's, Samuel F. B. Morse, using his knowledge of electricity, developed a device for transmitting a code of dots and dashes over a wire that made possible the instantaneous telegraphic transmissions of our alphabet over long distances. Within five decades, Guglielmo Marconi had discovered the secret of transmitting Morse's code by wireless (radio). With the turn of the century came Lee DeForest's invention of the vacuum tube amplifier that made voice transmission possible, thereby opening the realm of modern broadcasting. The list of inventions and technological innovations that have contributed to the extension of human communication from those early tribal drums and smoke signals to today's satellite transmission seems endless. Yet it is important to note that each new development has contributed to increasing the complexity of our modern systems of mass communication.

Students frequently respond to the question, "What is mass communication?" with such answers as "radio," "television," "newspapers," or "motion pictures." Although such responses are certainly true in part, we must remember that the images generally evoked by these descriptors are only the instruments or tools that make the *process* of mass communication possible. To illustrate this important distinction, let us devise a hypothetical situation. You are probably enrolled in a college or university that operates a closed-circuit television system or videotaping facility of some kind. Now, let us assume that you are given the opportunity to stand before the television camera, record a speech, and then sit down in front of the television monitor to watch yourself on the screen. You have just utilized many of the technical instruments of the television medium to transmit a personal message, but has mass communication taken place? The answer is obviously, "no." However, if you carry the videotaped speech to a local television station and have it broadcast to the entire community, mass communication has taken place. In other words, it is not just the "hardware" of radio, television, and newspapers that distinguishes them as systems of modern mass communication but rather it is the special characteristics of the total mass communication process.

. . .

All forms of mass communication can be distinguished from . . . levels of interpersonal communication by the fact that they interject an electronic or print medium into the interpersonal communication paradigm. The radio receiver, television set, newspaper, magazine, and book all serve to remove the communicator from direct contact with his audience. In other words, the instruments of the mass media eliminate the opportunity for face-to-face interaction and the changing of "speaker" and "listener" roles. With the opportunity for information sharing lost, the relationship between communicator and audience becomes much more impersonal. This is due not only to the interjection of mass media's complex technology but also to the requirements of the speaker's role as a public communicator. It is the nature of the public communicator, the nature of the audience and the communication experience itself that further distinguishes the various forms of mass communication.

Behind the warm, personal delivery of the evening television newscaster or the fast-paced chatter of your favorite disc jockey is a formal and highly complex media organization. The establishment and regular operation of a television or radio station, for example, involves large capital investment and consequently places decision-making authority in the hands of the financial backers. The internal personnel structure of a broadcast facility is built upon certain basic policy guidelines, established by the station's owners and implemented by station management. Decision-making that determines what you see and hear does not take place in a vacuum. Pressures from federal regulatory agencies (Federal Communications Commission, Federal Trade Commission), professional organizations (National Association of Broadcasters, Radio Television News Directors Association), trade associations (American Federation of Television and Radio Artists, Screen Actors' Guild), citizens' groups (Action for Children's Television, National Citizens' Committee for Broadcasting), and local community organizations force the media organizations to respond to normative controls and standards. In some instances, these controls impose requirements on the mass media that are far more restrictive than the usual social conventions and standards that are typical of informal, unstructured, interpersonal communication.

For anyone who has felt frustration over the cancellation of a favorite television program or dissatisfaction with the musical format of a radio station, it will come as no surprise that another distinguishing characteristic of mass communication is that the flow of information (messages) is primarily one-way. Various verbal and nonverbal feedback mechanisms do exist—letters to the editor, telephone calls to the broadcast station, correspondence with citizens' groups and regulatory agencies, circulation figures, box office receipts, and audience ratings—but the ratio of mass media output to audience input is very large. Then, too, the kinds of feedback channels that are available to members of the audience are often subject to a substantial time lag.

An excellent example is the letter to the newspaper editor or the radio and television station manager. Sometimes action in response to these letters is immediate, but more frequently it is delayed. The recent upsurge of radio's sex talk shows, "topless radio," illustrates this point very well. Many listeners who were disturbed by the open discussion of sexual issues over radio wrote letters to both the radio stations involved and the Federal Communications Commission demanding that the programs be taken off the air. The FCC responded to the outcries by conducting a closed-door inquiry to investigate the situation. At the conclusion of the inquiry, the FCC outlined definite limits for the broadcasting of sexually oriented discussions, and fined an Oak Park, Illinois, radio station $2,000 for violating a criminal statute barring the broadcast of obscene or indecent material. Between the initial letters of complaint and the commission's final action, many weeks had passed and a significant number of programs continued to be aired (in direct response to high audience ratings). Admittedly, there were some stations that discontinued their sex talk shows well in advance of the FCC decision. One such radio station in Salt Lake City, Utah, created a unique situation to elicit face-to-face audience response. This station simply encouraged listeners to drive by the downtown studios and give their reaction to the program by showing a "thumbs up" or "thumbs down" signal. When the "thumbs down" votes won by a striking margin, the program was immediately taken off the air. Thus, we have a special instance of how a newly created feedback channel greatly increased the number of audience responses and brought prompt results.

It should be obvious from this discussion that another characteristic of mass communication is that the messages of a relatively small number of communicators are widely disseminated to large audiences. Even when we combine the number of "communicators" associated with all the individual radio and television stations and the national broadcasting networks in the United

States, the total is dismally small when compared with a population of approximately 205 million people. But since not everyone is a member of a given radio, television, motion picture, or newspaper audience at any one time, the natural question is, "How large must an audience be in order to qualify as a mass audience?" Certainly, an audience of 50 million television viewers watching the annual Super Bowl game would be large enough to qualify as a mass audience. But what about the thousands of fans who have packed into the football stadium to see the game in person? At this point it must become a matter of definition, and not all students of mass communication agree on what that definition should be. One well-respected scholar, Charles R. Wright, has proposed the following specification for a mass audience: "A tentative definition would consider as 'large' any audience exposed during a short period of time and of such a size that the communicator could not interact with its members on a face-to-face basis."[1] Thus, the point at which an audience is large enough to be considered "mass" is a purely arbitrary one. Perhaps more important than the matter of size are questions concerning mass audience composition.

As we consider the nature of the mass audience, we should remember that the mass media's messages are open to the public. When the technologies of printing, radio, television, or film are used for private consumption, as in the case of the private showing of our videotaped speech discussed previously, it cannot be regarded as mass communication. Obviously, unlimited open access to the message is an ideal that is seldom, if ever, achieved. Numerous technical, sociological, cultural, and economic factors influence the degree to which the mass media are available to their potential audiences. In underdeveloped countries, problems associated with multiple languages, illiteracy, and severe poverty frequently create additional barriers [to] media consumption.

Taking for granted that at least some of these factors will contribute to the composition of any given audience, the fact that the mass audience consists of a sampling of the general public assures that the audience for the mass media will be heterogeneous in nature. That is, it will be composed of an aggregation of individuals living under widely different conditions and occupying a variety of positions within society. There will be persons of many ages with different interests, standards of living, and levels of influence. There will be representation from both sexes, widely varying cultural and religious heritages, different races, levels of education, and so on. Yet, this gross description can be somewhat misleading. Scholars have totally rejected the notion of a single mass audience, since common sense tells us that the viewers of a television program or the readers of a newspaper are constantly changing, making it highly unlikely that the exact same mass audience will ever be assembled more than once. This fluid, dynamic characteristic prompts these scholars to talk in terms of mass *audiences* rather than audience. One suggested method of classification begins with a hypothetical *general* mass audience representing the *potential* public that is capable of being reached by the media. The general mass audience, by definition, is the largest most scattered, anonymous, and heterogeneous collectivity possible. Under this major heading is an extensive list of *specialized audiences,* each one being heterogeneous in many ways. However, these specialized audiences are composed of individuals who share some common interest or orientation, thus making a particular message appealing to all members of any one specialized audience. For example, viewers of "Hee Haw" enjoy country music, readers of *Playboy* are interested in a liberal discussion of sexual issues, listeners of Saturday's Metropolitan Opera broadcast share a taste for opera, and fans of the Monday night football telecast typically enjoy sports. Hence, with reference to the specific interest or concern that causes members of each audience to attend to the mass communicator's message (product) we can say that the audience members are homogeneous. In other words, although each specialized audience is heterogeneous in the sense that it may represent a cross section of ages, educational levels, and socioeconomic strata, there is at least one area in which there is evidence of homogeneity. Whether the existence of limited homogeneity in this respect is more or less significant than the variety of individual circumstances and backgrounds of the audience members remains a question for communication researchers.

It is important to consider that the mass media are not only capable of communicating messages to a large number of people who are located at long distances from both the communicator and other members of the audience but they are also capable of communicating these messages *simultaneously.* Naturally, the electronic media are more successful in achieving this result than are the print media, since the messages transmitted over electronic channels are transitory and therefore force all audience members to attend to the message at the same time. Newspapers, magazines, and books, on the other hand, are read at different times at the convenience of the reader. Therefore, it can be argued that the electronic media are superior in providing information instantaneously and simultaneously to a vast, widely separated audience, whereas the print media are superior in affording messages that are both permanent and capable of being received at the discretion of the consumer. Although it is true that audio and videotape playback equipment have contributed to the permanence and convenience of receiving electronic transmissions, audience usage of such equipment for in-home recording of regularly scheduled broadcasts is still quite limited.

To summarize, we have considered six major characteristics of the mass media that distinguish them from the different forms of interpersonal communication: (1) The mass communicator does not have an opportunity for face-to-face interaction with his audience, since the communication channel is either an electronic or print medium. (2) Mass communication systems are much more complicated than interpersonal communication and require formal, complex organizations to maintain their operation. (3) The organization of the mass media permits the flow of messages in primarily one direction, with the opportunity for feedback being much more limited than in the interpersonal setting. (4) The messages of a relatively small number of mass communicators are widely disseminated to large audiences in much the same way that enormous quantities of mass-produced goods are turned out by modern manufacturers. (5) In addition to being large, the mass-media audiences are heterogeneous, anonymous, fluid, and widely scattered, although members of any particular mass audience generally share one or more interests, concerns, or orientations. (6) The mass media are capable of communicating messages to many people in different parts of the world both instantaneously and simultaneously.

With some possible exceptions, all of these characteristics should be present in varying degrees in any mass-communication situation. Taken individually, these characteristics can be viewed as either advantageous or disadvantageous when compared with the circumstances surrounding interpersonal communication. Actually, the mass media cannot be studied in isolation from interpersonal channels if one is to fully understand the total mass communication process. However, before examining the important relationship between mass and interpersonal communication, it is necessary to understand the functions served by the mass media in our modern society.

Critics and supporters of the mass media have been engaged in heated debate over the virtues and evils of the media for many years.[2] Seldom has there been complete agreement on appropriate criteria for measuring their worth, let alone consensus on the major issues being debated. The most frequently agreed upon criteria evolve from the work of social scientists who have endeavored to specify the various functions normally performed by systems of mass communication. Undoubtedly, the most well-known contributor to this area of study is Harold D. Lasswell, a leading pioneer in mass communication research. Dr. Lasswell's classic paper on the structure and function of communication in modern society outlined three basic media functions: "(1) The surveillance of the environment; (2) the correlation of the parts of society in responding to the environment; (3) the transmission of the social heritage from one generation to the next."[3] Lasswell never intended to suggest that the performance of these functions was suddenly initiated with the advent of modern mass media of communication. Man has always been concerned with monitoring developments in his environment, circulating facts and opinions that would contribute to intelligent decision-making, and passing on the lore and experiences of one generation to the next. Rather, Lasswell focused our attention on the fact that the mass media had acquired these basic functions and, subsequently, caused us to ponder the possible consequences of leaving surveillance, correlation, and social transmission in the hands of the media practitioners.

Using more familiar language, the *surveillance* function refers to the collection and distribution of information about the environment or what is generally regarded as news. Other students of mass communication have labeled this the "reporting" or "watchdog" function of the electronic and printed press. Through a constant flow of information concerning events occurring around the world (and beyond), the mass media serve as a sentinel, warning us of floods, earthquakes, hurricanes, military attack, disease epidemics, and political rioting. Such everyday information as traffic reports, local weather forecasts, announcements of meetings and other institutional activities are examples of less dramatic occurrences.

Our dependence upon these daily services is not realized until we suddenly find ourselves without them. This was graphically illustrated by a research study conducted by Bernard Berelson and his associates during a New York City newspaper strike in 1945. Area residents complained of being disoriented, confused, and at a loss without their daily newspapers. Listener and viewer requests during more recent newspaper strikes in New York, Pittsburgh, and San Francisco resulted in the local broadcast media serving a much greater surveillance function until the strikes were over.

For some newsmen, the term *watchdog* has special significance with reference to monitoring our systems of government. There is probably no better example of the mass media's vital role in keeping watch over our country's political affairs than the disclosure of the Watergate coverup. As observed by prominent columnist Max Lerner, following the Senate Watergate Hearings, "The media are so crucial to everything that happens in our time that they have in effect become a fourth branch of the governing process." Two young *Washington Post* reporters, Robert Woodward and Carl Bernstein, were credited with tracking down most of the startling details from the time the Watergate burglars were apprehended. For months, Woodward and Bernstein interviewed potential news sources on the street, in people's homes, in deserted parking lots, in private offices, and over the telephone until the fragmented pieces started to fall into place. When the Senate Committee began its formal inquiry, it was again through the media, especially television, that the American people became aware of Watergate's significance.

Lasswell's second media function, *correlation,* refers to the selection, evaluation, and interpretation of the news. In effect, the mass media determine what are the most important events in our environment and, hence, what will be presented to us as "news." Kurt Lewin, another outstanding social scientist, was the first to apply the term *gatekeeper* to decision-making positions such as those held by news editors in television, radio, and the printed press. The numerous research studies growing out of this line of inquiry revealed that the editorial function of the media embodies an extremely complex process. Equally important were the findings that we are not only highly dependent upon the media for the evaluation and interpretation of the news but frequently accept, unchallenged, the media's prescription of how we should respond to it. The radio and television commentaries of Eric Sevareid, Howard K. Smith, Harry Reasoner, John Chancellor, Paul Harvey, Edward P. Morgan, and David Brinkley and the syndicated columns of Jack Anderson, Smith Hempstone, Joseph Alsop, William F. Buckley, and James Reston are familiar examples of the media's correlation function. There can be no question that by leaving the task of evaluation and interpretation to a few qualified individuals, the majority of society frees itself from a difficult and time-consuming chore. Despite the criticism of former Vice President Agnew, it is through the "instant analysis" of television newscasters following a State of the Union message that many Americans gain their only understanding of what the President's goals and legislative objectives might mean to the country. Left to their own initiative, relatively few citizens would make the necessary effort to place important events into their proper historical and social context.

As indicated previously, the *transmission of social heritage* refers to the passing on of cultural norms, values, mores, customs, and traditions to all members of a society and from generation to generation. This is frequently described as the "socialization" or "education" function of the media. As conveyors of a society's heritage, the mass media serve as a mirror to the society itself. For example, visitors to other developed countries can often tell much about the values and priorities of the people simply by spending several days in front of a television set. Similarly, researchers have utilized the content and structure of mass-media systems in their investigation of the norms and ideologies of modern societies.

Building upon the work of Harold Lasswell, other students of mass communication have identified additonal media functions. Charles Wright has suggested that *entertainment* is another primary function of the mass media. He explains that there are many "communicative acts primarily intended for amusement irrespective of any instrumental effects they might have."[4] Even a brief glance at the motion-picture listings or radio and television schedules for any given day not only offers support for Wright's contention but suggests that entertainment is probably the biggest service provided by the American mass media. The comprehensive studies of television viewing habits by Gary A. Steiner in 1960 and Robert T. Bower in 1970 clearly indicate that the primary factor influencing program selection for the vast majority of television viewers is entertainment value.[5] Although it is certainly true that television ranks as the number one entertainment medium in the United States, motion pictures, radio, magazines, and newspapers are important entertainment media as well. The impact of television on the movie industry has been deeply felt since the late 1940's, but the record-breaking box office receipts from *The Godfather* are a fair indication that many people still depend upon motion-picture films as a major source of entertainment. Harold Mendelsohn's investigations of today's radio audience indicate that radio provides listeners with a constant "companion" that helps to fill the personal voids created by routine tasks and feelings of loneliness.[6] Radio is entertaining in the sense that it soothes and satisfies, and affords the listener a desired psychological climate. Newspapers are generally considered the principal communicators of hard news, but readership studies have shown that some readers not only turn first to the comics section but select their newspapers on the basis of the comic strips they print. Such regular features as "Dear Abby" and "Ann Landers" must also be considered primarily as entertainment.

In his book, *Mass Entertainment,* Harold Mendelsohn links the entertainment function of the media with the socialization process. He points out that people in all social strata seek mass entertainment because some social functions are served by sharing a common entertainment experience. For instance, teen-agers identify with a particular segment of mass entertainment, which gives them the basis for rapport and group identity with other teen-agers.

Comedy and humor also serve significant sociological functions in that they reinforce social norms by ridiculing deviant behavior and allow us to consciously consider socially sensitive issues without involving guilt feelings. A typical example of mass entertainment that serves this function is the popular television program "Maude." Following its first year of weekly episodes that touched upon such taboo subjects as abortion, "Maude" began its second season with a socially relevant script centering on the problems of alcoholism. Using Maude's television husband, Walter Findlay, for their character study, the show's writers struggled through ten revisions of the dialogue before they were satisfied that their message would come through: "Wake up America! We're drinking too much and it is getting out of control."

Concurring that entertainment is a basic function of mass communication, Wilbur Schramm adds a fifth function; "to sell goods for us."[7] He explains that *advertising* through the mass media contributes to a free and healthy economy in the United States. Advertising offers both opportunities and challenges to the buyers and sellers of goods and services. With the exception of public broadcasting, radio and television in America are strictly commercial operations. Without advertising as a base of support, there would be very few mass media of any kind. This is not to suggest that a nonprofit system of mass communication could not exist. Many foreign countries enjoy such systems; the most familiar being England's British Broadcasting Corporation (BBC), which is financed by license fees on radio and television receivers. But if we are to believe the opinion polls, the American public would rather endure media advertising than make a special payment for the services they presently receive free of charge.[8] Figures released in May, 1973, by The Roper Organization, Inc., indicate that only 24 per cent of the 1,982 people surveyed expressed any interest in a subscription television service (Pay TV).

Adding the suggested functions of Wright and Schramm to those identified by Lasswell results in a total of five: (1) surveillance, (2) correlation, (3) social transmission, (4) entertainment, and (5) advertising. Another contributor to the study of mass communication functions, Robert K. Merton, was the first writer to warn us that any or all of these functions could have negative as well as positive effects. He called these negative consequences *dysfunctions* and proposed that there was always the possibility that they might accompany the positive effects of any single act.[9] By reviewing the five media functions, it is relatively easy to recall instances when mass communication performed a disservice rather than a service to society.

Perhaps one of the most frequently cited instances of a mass medium serving a dysfunction is Orson Welles' radio broadcast of the play "War of the Worlds" in 1938. Using a dramatic format patterned after actual news reports of the period, Welles' Halloween prank resulted in a nationwide panic. At a press conference following the broadcast, Welles claimed that he had no idea the radio audience would take the play seriously. Although the Martian invasion scare is one of the most dramatic media dysfunctions in history, it is far from being the most damaging. Just minutes after the assassination of Martin Luther King, the nation was alerted to the event by radio and television news bulletins. Within hours there were riots and demonstrations in over one hundred American cities, catching police and other law enforcement agencies completely unprepared. As a result of this and similar occurrences, the news media became the target for repeated attacks, accusing them of "fanning the flames of social unrest."[10] In response to this criticism, broadcasters and newspapers agreed to cooperate with local authorities by either delaying or avoiding news coverage of outbreaks of civil disorder.

Since the release of the Pentagon Papers and the unveiling of the Watergate conspiracy, the American public has accepted as commonplace the leaking of confidential information to the media. Yet we should be reminded that the printing and broadcast of confidential documents is a service to society only so long as it is in the public's interest to know the information and there is a high degree of certainty that no citizen's individual rights will be jeopardized by the disclosure. Being in a position to make decisions concerning the withholding and releasing of such information, the media gatekeepers share both an enormous responsibility and far-reaching power. When Woodward and Bernstein were preparing their articles for release in the *Washington Post,* the newspaper's editors subjected each story to intensive cross-examination prior to publication. The result was a Pulitzer prize for superior investigative reporting and an eventual apology from President Nixon. However, not all gatekeepers have been quite so thorough. Columnist Jack Anderson published verbatim excerpts of testimony before the Watergate grand jury, thus possibly endangering the rights of the accused to a fair trial. In another case concerning an investigation of alleged kickbacks to Maryland officials, *Time* magazine reported that unnamed sources in the Justice Department believed the indictment of former Vice President Agnew was "inevitable" at a time when the former Vice President had not been legally accused of any crime. Unfortunate disclosures such as these are undoubtedly a product of the fierce competition existing among media organizations. We can only hope that in a large majority of situations calling for a mature, intelligent, professional judgment, the media gatekeepers will respond to the best interests of everyone.

There are numerous other instances that critics cite as examples of possible media dysfunctions. For example, instant reports of national election results and victory predictions on the East Coast may prompt West Coast citizens to stay away from the polls, feeling that their votes no longer matter. Television's persistent display of products and services within the financial reach of white middle-class America implies measures of normalcy and standards of living that can create frustration and unrest among the disadvantaged segments of our population. The frequent portrayal of racial minorities in the conflicting roles of menial laborers or heroic superstars may leave viewers with a distorted image of the normal distribution of roles that exist in our society. Finally, the perpetual complaint of popular critics is that the mass media are responsible for lowering public tastes to the lowest common denominator. In defense of the available entertainment fare, media practitioners retort, "Look at the circulation figures and audience ratings. What you read, watch, and listen to is what you'll get!"

In the limited space available here, it is impossible to adequately deal with the controversial topic of mass media effects that has been argued for many years. Claims of intemperate critics have included charges that the different media are responsible for destroying the moral fiber of the country, increasing juvenile delinquency and crime, suppressing creativity, and killing the art of conversation. Other attacks have centered around concerns that the media have fantastic persuasive powers that might make us shift our political ideologies, purchase worthless products, abandon our cultural heritage, and alter "normal" patterns of behavior in ways that would prove detrimental to a healthy family and social life. With claims of such magnitude and serious implication, it is little wonder that, long ago, critics and media practitioners alike turned to the communication researcher for help. The critic went in hopes of receiving empirical evidence that would support his charges, and the practitioner went for just the reverse. So encompassing were the questions concerning the media effects that they completely dominated the field of mass-communication research for decades.

Early research explorations coincided with the emergence of an image of society as a mass of isolated individuals who lacked any unifying purpose. It was a view that depicted the masses at the mercy of a communicator who could influence them at his will. Melvin DeFleur has described this orientation as the "mechanistic S-R theory."[11] Other writers have more commonly referred to it as the "hypodermic needle theory" because the relationship between the media and general public was seen as direct and simple: " . . . the omnipotent media, on the one hand, sending forth the message, and the atomized masses, on the other, waiting to receive it—and nothing in between."[12] That is, messages would reach every member of the audience uniformly, would be perceived in the same manner, and would result in eliciting the same response from all.

During the 1930's, scholars in various branches of the social and behavioral sciences began to turn away from mere speculation about media effects from which concepts and propositions could be inductively formulated. The developments were the result of a new stress upon objective experiments within the field of psychology as an aid in the formulation and testing of learning theories. Along with this intellectual movement came increasing recognition of individual motivation and learning differences of human perception. Hence, it became clear to students of mass communication that the audience of a given medium was not a "monolithic collectivity." DeFleur dubs this new awareness of the 1930's the "individual differences theory of mass communication" and suggests that the theory predicts that "media messages contain particular stimulus attributes that have differential interaction with personality characteristics of members of the audience . . . [and therefore] there will be variations in effect which correspond to such individual differences."[13]

Out of the behavioral research generated by the individual differences theory came new concepts that soon became familiar to every student of mass communication. The terms *selective attention, selective perception,* and *selective retention* were quickly incorporated into his working vocabulary. The principle of *selective attention* states that individuals will typically expose themselves to communications that they find pleasing and in agreement with their personal frame of reference. For example, people who enjoy listening exclusively to rock music will have little motivation to tune in radio stations that feature classical or country and western formats. Once exposed to the communication, *selective perception* will determine how the message will be interpreted by the individual. Experimental studies of human perception have revealed that an individual's predispositions, past experiences, attitudes, beliefs, values, and needs will largely determine how he selects and interprets information about the events around him. In simple terms, the principle of *selective retention* states that an individual will remember only what he wants to remember. That is, people tend to remember better messages that are compatible with their attitudes and forget messages that are not. These concepts revolutionized our thinking about the mass audience and created an awareness that such variations in the communication process as changing the communicator, the medium, the message, or the audiences's environment could have a significant influence on the effectiveness achieved by mass communication. Thus, fears of unlimited persuasive powers in the hands of the media practitioners were somewhat dispelled. Researchers reported that mass communication generally served to reinforce existing attitudes, tastes, predispositions, and behavioral tendencies, but seldom, if ever, were the media responsible for changing one type of person into another.

It has been demonstrated that the media are most influential in situations where individuals have no pre-established disposition on a given subject. This was vividly illustrated by the experiences of media experts during the nonpresidential campaign year of 1970. With the amazing success of Richard M. Nixon's extensive television campaign of 1968 planted firmly in their minds, campaign strategists mapped out cleverly contrived and slickly polished promotional schemes for their political candidates. To their sad surprise, they learned that the success of Nixon's 1968 political campaign was probably the result of the mobilization of voters who were either leaning toward or already committed to the Republican ticket. The image-maker who suffered most was Harry Treleaven, a major contributor to Nixon's 1968 TV image. His record included four losses and only one win (Senator-elect William Brock of Tennessee). The conclusion reached by Treleaven and others with not so disappointing score cards was that in future campaigns, television's major image-making role would come during the primaries, when the candidate is still pretty much an unknown. Once the public meets the candidate and creates an impression of him in their own minds, television alone cannot be expected to greatly alter that image. In the words of campaign strategist Robert Goodman, shortly after the election, "What was proved last week is that image-making can't run counter to strong national currents. TV can't overwhelm. It can only amplify."

Another major turning point in our understanding of the mass communication process, especially for students of interpersonal communication, resulted from a classic study of the 1940 presidential campaign. As you might expect from our previous discussion, researchers discovered that very few people changed their voting intentions during the campaign. However, those who did were influenced far more by family, friends, and co-workers than by direct exposure to the media. It was further realized that within every social context there were individuals who were considered "influentials" or "opinion leaders" by their peers. These opinion leaders could be identified at all socioeconomic levels and in every walk of life. Not too surprisingly, they were also found to exceed noninfluentials in exposure to relevant campaign messages transmitted via the mass media. These findings led to the formulation of the "two-step communication flow" hypothesis, which proposed that influence moves from the media to opinion leaders, and from these influentials to their immediate associates. Later studies refined the original hypothesis to suggest that a complex "multi-step flow" was a more accurate depiction of the important role played by interpersonal relationships.

Since those early exploratory studies of the 1920's, the volume of research in the field of mass communication has been almost overwhelming. Unfortunately, concrete answers to many of the important questions that were posed by critics decades ago have not yet been found. The three-year, $1.5 million Surgeon General's Report that was to resolve once and for all whether the portrayal of violence and crime on television was in some way dangerous to the mental health of our nation failed to do so. One of the most conclusive statements that can be gleaned from the five-volume report issued in January, 1972 reads, "We have noted in the studies at hand a modest association between viewing of violence and aggression among at least some children, and we have noted some data which are consonant with the interpretation that violence viewing produces the aggression. This evidence is not conclusive, however, and some of the data are also consonant with other interpretations."[14] Several years earlier, a noted communication researcher who contributed to the Surgeon General's Report stated, "It is surely no wonder that a bewildered public should regard with cynicism a research tradition which supplies, instead of definitive answers, a plethora of relevant but inconclusive and at times seemingly contradictory findings."[15]

At this point it might be beneficial to summarize much of what has been said so far by way of a simple illustration. Figure 1 provides a visual representation of some of the various elements that contribute to the mass-communication process. This illustration is not intended as a communication model in the usual sense, as it does not attempt to incorporate all of the factors and characteristics that typify the mass-communication patterns of modern society. Rather, it serves to remind us of a number of important concepts: Man is being bombarded regularly by enormous quantities of messages via mass media systems. The unique characteristics of each medium influence the structure of the message and contribute to the way it will be perceived and interpreted by the listener, viewer, or reader. These communications will be received not only through direct contact with the products of the media but through second- and third-hand messages from family, friends, and other influentials as well. Our past experiences, attitudes, values, and beliefs, coupled with the interpretations and commentary of those around us, determine how each of us selects, per-

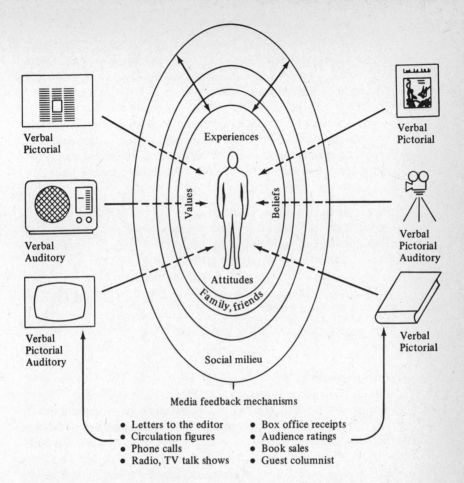

Verbal
Pictorial

Verbal
Auditory

Verbal
Pictorial
Auditory

Experiences

Values

Beliefs

Attitudes

Family, friends

Social milieu

Verbal
Pictorial

Verbal
Pictorial
Auditory

Verbal
Pictorial

Media feedback mechanisms

- Letters to the editor
- Circulation figures
- Phone calls
- Radio, TV talk shows

- Box office receipts
- Audience ratings
- Book sales
- Guest columnist

FIGURE 1

ceives, and recalls the messages. Although the ratio of media output to audience input is terribly biased in favor of the media, we are constantly communicating something about ourselves to them by our choice of newspapers, television programs, or motion-picture shows. The media organizations, eager to satisfy our expression of tastes, will respond to these quantitative indicators in providing more programs, news features, or movies that appear to meet with our approval. When we wish to respond verbally to media institutions to express approval, file a complaint, or make a request, other feedback channels are available to us, although desired results are frequently slow in coming.

There can be no question that we are living in a mediated environment that is largely the product of the mass media of communication. Every indication points to the somewhat frightening prediction that in the years ahead, man will come to rely more and more on the instruments of modern technology and less and less on first-hand, personal experience. Whether the nightmares of a "1984" will eventually engulf our society will be determined by how modern man responds to the communication challenges of the next two decades. The warnings of such contemporary prophets as H. A. Innis, Marshall McLuhan, Gene Youngblood, and Alvin Toffler rest heavy on the minds of media critics who share a common concern that the media are molding us in ways that cannot be detected by the crude research instruments of the social scientists. The media have influenced either directly or indirectly too many tangible events to deny the possibility that they might also be shaping our world through invisible means. Yet, logic and reason should tell us that all social influences must be examined within a suitable context. Rivers, Peterson, and Jensen have advanced an interesting analogy that seems to make this point very well:

> we must consider the power of the mass media not as a tidal wave but as a great river. It feeds the ground it touches, following the lines of existing contours but preparing the way for change over a long period. Sometimes it finds a spot where the ground is soft and ready, and there it cuts a new channel. Sometimes it carries material that helps to alter its banks. And occasionally, in time of flood, it washes away a piece of ground and gives the channel a new look.[16]

NOTES

1. CHARLES R. WRIGHT, *Mass Communication: A Sociological Perspective* (New York: Random House, Inc., 1959), p. 13.
2. The number of volumes devoted to the subject of media criticism is growing at a steady pace. Two editions that have become "standards" for dissatisfied television viewers are Harry J. Skornia, *Television and Society* (New York: McGraw-Hill Book Company, 1965), and Nicholas Johnson, *How to Talk Back to Your Television Set* (New York: Bantam Books, Inc., 1970).
3. HAROLD D. LASSWELL, "The Structure and Function of Communication in Society," L. Bryson, ed., *The Communication of Ideas* (New York: Harper & Row, Publishers, Inc., 1948), p. 38.
4. WRIGHT, p. 16.
5. The results of these studies appear in two published works: Gary A. Steiner, *The People Look at Television* (New York: Alfred A. Knopf, Inc., 1963), and Robert T. Bower, *Television and the Public* (New York: Holt, Rinehart and Winston, Inc., 1973).
6. HAROLD MENDELSOHN, "The Roles of Radio," A. Kirschner and L. Kirschner, eds., *Radio and Television: Readings in the Mass Media* (New York: The Odyssey Press, 1971).
7. WILBUR SCHRAMM, *Responsibility in Mass Communications* (New York: Harper & Row, Publishers, Inc., 1975), p. 34.
8. To imply that the costs of advertising are not passed on to the public would be in error. However, few consumers stop to consider what percentage of a product's retail price goes for advertising.

9. ROBERT K. MERTON, *Social Theory and Social Structure*, rev. ed. (New York: The Free Press, 1957). See Chapter I, Manifest and Latent Functions.

10. For an interesting account of the media's role in the riots and demonstrations of 1967, read the *Report of the National Advisory Commission on Civil Disorder* (New York: Bantam Books, Inc., 1968).

11. MELVIN L. DeFLEUR, *Theories of Mass Communication*, 2nd ed. (New York: David McKay Co., Inc., 1970), p. 115.

12. ELIHU KATZ and PAUL LAZARSFELD, *Personal Influence* (New York: The Free Press, 1954), p. 20.

13. DeFLEUR, p. 122.

14. *Television and Growing Up: The Impact of Televised Violence*, Chapter I. A very readable analysis of this highly publicized document can be found in a three-part article in *TV Guide* beginning November 11, 1972. A more scholarly review by Dr. James A. Anderson is printed in the Spring, 1972, issue of *Journal of Broadcasting*, pp. 224–227. *Television and Your Child: The Surgeon General's Inquiry*, an extensive evaluation, Aspen Program on Communications and Society, Palo Alto, California, 1974.

15. JOSEPH KLAPPER, "The Effects of Mass Communication," B. Berelson and M. Janowitz, eds., *Reader in Public Opinion and Communication* (New York: The Free Press, 1966), p. 474.

16. WILLIAM L. RIVERS, THEODORE PETERSON, and JAY W. JENSEN, *The Mass Media and Modern Society* (New York: Holt, Rinehart and Winston, Inc., 1971), p. 35.

Twenty-Eight

Encountering the Media

Melvin L. DeFleur

This chapter presents an overview of how thinking concerning the impact of the media on individuals and groups has undergone progressive change. Some mass society theorists attributed to the mass media the power to manipulate the minds and actions of the masses. Discovery of psychological and sociological mechanisms which limit the impact of media messages moved social science thinking away from this mass society perspective. At the center of this change in theoretical perspective was a fundamental redefinition of the nature of the encounter between media and individuals. The idea that people encounter the media as a mass of unconnected individuals was rejected. In its place emerged a conception of the media audience as a set of individuals who encounter the media as social beings connected to their social environments.

This change of perspective is somewhat analogous to the growth of understanding about the organizational and structural intricacies of mass media systems. Developments in social science theory and research led to an increased understanding of the sometimes subtle ways in which audiences are structured and organized. As media structure and organization affects its approach to their audiences, the informal social organizational ties of audience members affect how they approach the media. As we shall see, the perspective which emerged and prevails today is that individual audience members encounter media messages as members of groups and that they do so with a constructed social reality which reflects their past and present social experiences.

Another perspective that posited enormous power to the mass media and that was subsequently rejected by most social scientists was Innis's technological determinism. Innis contended that the nature of the media technology prevailing in a society at a given point in time greatly influenced how the members of that society think and behave.[1] Books and other print media, for example, are said to promote cause-effect thinking in societies where print media dominate, because the technology of print forces a linear form of presentation either across or up or down a page. McLuhan, the contemporary reformulator of Innis's thesis, characterizes television as a "cool" medium because its capacity for rich configurations of audiovisual stimuli elicits high but passive audience presentation.[2] From the technological determinist's perspective, the most important characteristic of the audience-media encounter is the technological properties of the medium. Thus, McLuhan asserts that "the medium is the message."[3] While we saw in the previous chapter that some social scientists are attempting to understand the potential impact of the nature of new media technologies on audiences and society, few would accept the proposition that technology *alone* determines how people encounter and respond to the mass media. Most, for example, would reject McLuhan's claim that the *content* of media messages has no impact on audiences. Essentially, mass media theorists reject the extreme form of technological determinism put forth by McLuhan for two reasons. Social scientists generally reject the idea that any single factor (be it technology, the economy, or chromosomes) can be the single cause of social behavior. This distrust of single-factor theories was buttressed by theory and research developments that demonstrate the influence of both psychological and social factors on the individual's or group's encounter with the mass media. This is not to say that Innis's thesis was rejected out of hand; most media theorists would accept the proposition that the technological characteristics of a mass medium may be one of many factors that should be taken into account.[4]

We turn now to an examination of the three most important prevailing perspectives on how people encounter the media—the *individual differences* perspective, the *social categories* perspective, and the *social relations* perspective. We will attempt to show the progression of theory and research that led to each perspective's assumptions about the psychological and social variables which intervene in the audience's encounter with the mass media.

The Individual Differences Perspective

When psychological theorists seeking basic understanding of human conduct turned away from explanations of complex behavior based primarily on inherited mechanisms, they sought new explanations built upon very different principles. If nature failed to endow human beings with the automatic ability to guide their behavior, then they surely had to *acquire* it from their environment. Great interest was to develop among psychologists in the process of human learning. By the end of World War I, academic psychology was intellectually prepared for new directions. One new direction was provided by the concept of *conditioning*.

From English empiricism, psychologists had inherited a persistent interest in "association" and "habit" as important aspects of learning. As early as 1890, William James had suggested that habits formed through association may have a physiological basis.[5] John Watson introduced a further significant element to modern psychology with his emphasis on behaviorism.[6] But more than anything else, it was the classical conditioning experiments that fired the imagination of the psychologists of the late 1920s and the early 1930s.[7] Thus, there was a renewed interest in habit formation through learning, a new stress upon objective experiments as an aid in the development of theories of learning, and a broad new concept that promised to link the learning process to physiology. The result of these intellectual trends was a great expansion of interest in learning processes and a host of experiments with animal and human subjects. A number of competing theories of learning were formulated.

Along with this intellectual movement came an associated interest in "motivation." The study of incentives in laboratory experiments convinced psychologists that some motivational urges can be acquired through learning and that not all individuals can be motivated by precisely the same incentives. Adding to this trend in the increasing recognition of individual motivation and learning *differences* were the findings of students of human personality. Variations in personality traits became increasingly recognized, and the mental testers began to construct sophisticated devices to quantify those differences.[8]

New concepts were also formulated in social psychology to replace the idea of instinct. In particular, the term "attitude" grew in importance as a means of explaining differing directions of human preference and action. Introduced as a systematic concept in the writings of Thomas and Znaniecki at the end of World War I, this concept became the most basic and central theoretical tool of social psychology.[9] The invention of several rather elaborate and mathematically sophisticated techniques for attitude measurement added to its importance as a research tool and gave additional emphasis to the study of individual differences and their correlates.[10]

As these basic ideas concerning the psychological organization of the human individual were successively clarified, certain fundamental postulates became rather widely held. It was said that human beings *varied* greatly in their personal-psychological organization. These variations in part began with differential biological endowment, but they were due in greater measure to differential learning. Human beings raised under widely differing circumstances were exposed to widely differing points of view. From these learning environments they acquired a set of attitudes, values, and beliefs that constituted their personal-psychological makeup and set each person somewhat apart from others. Even twins of almost identical biological makeup became rather different in personality structure when raised in different social environments.

Added to this increasing recognition of human psychological modifiability and differentiation was the recognition that personality variables acquired from the social milieu provided a basis for individual differences in *perception*. The experimental study of human perception had revealed that values, needs, beliefs, and attitudes played an influential role in determining how stimuli are selected from the environment, and how meaning is attributed to those stimuli. Thus, one important product of human learning was the acquisition of stable predispositions or habits concerning the perception of events. Perception differed systematically from one person to another according to the nature of individual personality structure.

With these new theories in the background, students of mass communication had to alter their thinking about the media. It became clear that the audience of a given medium was not a monolithic collectivity whose members attended uniformly to whatever content was directed toward them. The *principle of selective attention and perception* was formulated as a fundamental proposition regarding the way ordinary persons confronted the content of the mass media. General psychological theory had established the concept of selective perception based upon individual differences in cognitive characteristics. It was not difficult to show that different types of people in an audience selected and interpreted mass communication content in widely varying ways.[11]

Although never specifically formulated as a theory, it can be suggested that selective attention and perception had become intervening psychological mechanisms that entered into the S–R schema of mass communication theory. From a multiplicity of available content, individual members of the audience selectively attended to messages, particularly if they were related to their interests, consistent with their attitudes, congruent with their beliefs, and supportive of their values. Finally, response to such messages was also modified by psychological makeup. This general idea may be called the *individual differences perspective on the mass communication process.* Rather than being *uniform* among the mass audience, the manner in which audience members are exposed to media content could now be seen as *varying* from person to person because of individual differences in psychological structure. This in turn was said to lead to varying effects.

When communication "effects" are a focus of research attention, the assumption that the media are in some way "causes" of those effects is a natural one. Even if it is granted that intervening processes of some sort can modify this relationship, the underlying cause-effect conceptualization is not different, only more complicated. The individual differences perspective implies that media messages contain particular stimulus attributes that have differential interaction with personality characteristics of audience members. Since there are individual differences in personality characteristics among such members, it is natural to assume that there will be variations in effect which correspond to these individual differences. Thus, the logical structure of the individual differences theory is a "cause (intervening processes)-effect" structure, just as was the instinctual S–R theory before it. However, the intervening processes are the result of learning rather than inheritance.

The Social Categories Perspective

Sometimes overlapping the individual differences approach, but stemming from completely different disciplinary sources, is the *social categories perspective.* The latter assumes that there are broad collectivities, aggregates, or social categories, particularly in urban-industrial societies, whose behavior in the face of a given set of stimuli is more or less uniform. Such characteristics as age, sex, income level, educational attainment, rural-urban residence, or religious affiliation provide examples. In fact, knowledge of several simple variables— age, sex, and educational attainment—provides a reasonably accurate guide to the type of communication content a given individual will or will not select from available media. Comic books are read primarily by the young and less educated; *Ms., Playgirl,* and *The Ladies Home Journal* are read primarily by females; the readers of *Playboy, Field and Stream,* and *Mechanics Illustrated* are predominantly male.

An early research trend in mass media studies made such category membership a central focus. It sought to establish the ways in which such behaviors as newspaper reading, the selection of books, radio listening, and motion-picture attendance were related to a variety of simple characteristics by which people could be grouped into aggregates.[12]

The basic assumption of the social categories perspective is a sociological one, namely, that in spite of the heterogeneity of modern society, people with a similar location in the social structure will have similar folkways. These similar modes of orientation and behavior will relate them to such phenomena as the mass media in a fairly uniform manner. The members of a particular category will select more or less the same communication content and will respond to it in roughly equal ways. The social categories approach is a descriptive formula that can serve as a basis for rough prediction and as a guide for research.

Actually, it has a more complex theoretical basis than is apparent on the surface. It will be recalled that the sociological theorists of the nineteenth century stressed the increasing degree of *social differentiation* that was taking place in the developing industrial society. In the society with a rudimentary division of labor, Durkheim had suggested, people would be very much alike. But in a society with a complex division of labor, there would be much greater development of what he called "personality" (e.g., "individual differences"). However, people located at similar positions in this social structure would be similar in personality because of similarity of their immediate social environment. Thus, they would be attracted to one another and form categories that were somewhat homogeneous. Earlier, Comte had suggested that people who formed groupings on the basis of similar characteristics would become a "multitude of unconnected corporations, which almost seem not to belong to the same species"[13] (in modern terminology we would refer to "subcultures").

While the individual differences perspective presented a view of the communication process more consistent with findings in general psychology, the social categories perspective was consistent with, and seemingly derived from, general sociological theories of the nature of the urban-industrial society. Taken altogether, they brought contemporary mass communication theory to a point where both the social differentiation of the early sociological theorists and the individual differences of the personality theorists were taken into account. Both approaches represent modifications of the original instinctual S–R theory, substituting on the one hand latent psychological processes and on the other uniformities within social categories as intervening variables between communication stimuli and responses. In 1948 Lasswell summed up precisely these two theoretical orientations, and the situational variables related to them, when he stated:

> A convenient way to describe an act of communication is to answer the following questions:
>
> *Who*
> *Says What*
> *In Which Channel*
> *To Whom*
> *With What Effect?*[14]

While these two perspectives on mass communication remain useful and contemporary, there have been further additions to the set of variables intervening between media stimuli and audience response. One additional elaboration of the S–R formula represents a somewhat belated recognition of the importance of patterns of interaction *between* audience members.

The Social Relations Perspective

Like many other significant discoveries in science, the role of group relationships in the mass communication process seems to have been discovered almost by accident. Also like many other important ideas, it appears to have been independently discovered at about the same time by more than one researcher. From the standpoint of mass communication research on how people encounter and respond to the media, one study stands out as the context within which the importance of group ties, as a complex of intervening variables between media and audience influence, was discovered. Early in 1940, before the adoption of television as a mass medium, Lazarsfeld, Berelson, and Gaudet developed an elaborate research design to study the impact upon voters of that year's mass-communicated presidential election campaign. At first, they were interested in how the members of given social categories selected material related to the election from the media, and how this material played a part in influencing their voting intentions.[15]

Erie County, Ohio, the site of the research, was a rather typical American area which had voted as the nation voted in every prior presidential election. Media campaign materials presented during the contest between Wendell Willkie and Franklin D. Roosevelt constituted the stimulus material. Several representative samples of residents of the area were the subjects. The study used an imaginative procedure that permitted repeated interviewing of a 600-member panel with suitable controls to check for possible effects of the seven independent monthly visits of the interviewers.

Some of the effects under study were: participating in the campaign (seeking information about the candidates and the issues), formulating voting decisions, and actually going to the polls. As it turned out, still other kinds of effects could be attributed to the campaign. Some respondents were *activated* by the mass-communicated material; that is, they had latent predispositions to vote in a given direction, but these predispositions needed to be crystallized to the point where they would become manifest. Others among the electorate had pretty much made up their minds early in the campaign and these decisions were *reinforced* by a continuous and partisan selection of additional material from the media. Early vote intentions were reversed in only a small portion of cases. Thus, the campaign had only limited success in converting individuals from one party to another.

The influence of the social categories perspective as a guide to this research was clear. Age, sex, residence, economic status, and education were the key variables. These social category memberships determined "interest" and led to an early or late decision. Acting in concert, this complex of variables influenced not only people's degree and direction of exposure to the mass-communicated campaign material, but also the kinds of effects that such material would have upon them.

As suggested, designing the study around a search for the important intervening social categories was perfectly consistent with the mass society concepts that communication researchers had inherited from European sociological theorists. Little attention was given to the possible role of informal social relationships and such factors as primary group ties because these were presumed to be declining in the emerging *Gesellschaft* society. Elihu Katz has stated this argument cogently in the following terms:

Until very recently, the image of society in the minds of most students of communication was of atomized individuals, connected with the mass media, but not with one another. Society—the "audience"—was conceived of as aggregates of age, sex, social class, and the like, but little thought was given to the relationships implied thereby to more informal relationships. The point is not that the student of mass communication was unaware that members of the audience have families and friends but that he did not believe that they might affect the outcome of a campaign; informal interpersonal relations, thus, were considered irrelevant to the institutions of modern society.[18]

But when the interviewers talked with the people of Erie County, they kept getting somewhat unanticipated answers to one of their major lines of questioning:

Whenever the respondents were asked to report on their recent exposures to campaign communications of all kinds, *political discussions* [italics added] were mentioned more frequently than exposure to radio or print.[17]

As a matter of fact, on the average day during the election campaign period, about 10 percent more people engaged in some sort of informal exchange of ideas with *other persons* than were exposed to campaign material directly from the mass media. About midway through the series of interviews, the researchers began to probe systematically into this kind of personal influence in an attempt to unravel the role of informal contacts with other people as an important set of variables in determining the effects of the media.

The end result of this somewhat unanticipated turn of events was the recognition that *informal social relationships* play a significant part in modifying the manner in which given individuals will act upon a message that comes to their attention via the mass media. In fact, it was discovered that there were many persons whose firsthand exposure to the media was quite limited. Such people obtained most of their information about the election campaign from other people who *had* gotten it firsthand. Thus, the research began to suggest a kind of movement of information through two basic stages. First, information moved from the media to relatively well informed individuals who frequently attended to mass communications. Second, it moved from those persons through interpersonal channels to individuals who had less direct exposure to the media and who depended upon others for their information. This kind of communication process was termed the "two-step flow of communication."[18]

Those individuals who were more in contact with the media were called "opinion leaders" because it was soon discovered that they were playing an important role in helping to shape the voting intentions of those to whom they were passing on information. They were not only passing on information, of course, but they were also passing on their *interpretations* of communication content. This kind of "personal influence" became immediately recognized as an important intervening mechanism which operated between the mass communication message and the kind of responses made to that message.

Subsequent studies were aimed more directly at studying the mechanisms of interpersonal influence and the part played by social relationships in mediating the movement of information from the media to the masses. In fact, a rich literature has accumulated indicating that informal social relationships operate as important intervening variables between the stimulus and the response in the mass communication process.

It was suggested earlier that the role of informal social relationships in the communication process was independently discovered by more than one researcher at about the same time. Students of rural sociology had long recognized that informal social relationships among farmers played an important part in determining their propensity to adopt a given agricultural innovation. The rural society is one in which the farm family normally has strong social ties with its neighbors. When new ideas come from the outside, the interpretations made by neighbors in such a setting can be of critical importance in determining the likelihood of adoption. The adoption of new farm technology is a process closely related to the mass communication process. New ideas are first presented to farm operators via communication media of one kind or another. These may be mass communication media, or they may be other formal channels of communication such as county agents or agricultural experiment station bulletins. The question is whether or not the individual farmer will respond to these communications in ways advocated by the communicators, namely, by adopting the recommended practice. Thus, conceptually speaking, a considerable similarity exists between the case of a farmer being advised to adopt a new form of weed spray via a radio program devoted to farm problems and the case of a person being advised to adopt a new household detergent via a radio commercial designed to sell soap. Both may adopt the innovation in accordance with the communicated suggestion, or they may resist it. The mechanisms that operate to mediate the decision to adopt or not to adopt may be quite similar in each case.[19]

The recognition of the convergence of theory between the students of mass communication and students of rural sociology who were studying the diffusion of farm technology stimulated a surge of interest in the diffusion and adoption process insofar as it was linked to mass communication. Intensive studies were undertaken concerning the nature of opinion leadership, the way it functioned in various contexts, and the part played by interpersonal relationships. In general it has been found that opinion leaders who are influential in the adoption process are in some respects very much like those whom they influence. They tend to conform closely to the norms of their groups, and they tend to be leaders in one area but not necessarily in others.[20] Opinion leadership does not seem to travel down the social structure, but is more likely to be horizontal. It appears to take place primarily between persons of somewhat similar status, although this is not always true. Katz and Lazarsfeld found that position in the "life cycle" was a key variable in determining who would influence whom in areas such as marketing, fashions, and public issues.[21] Young working women, in closer contact with fashion magazines and other media information about such issues, were sought by the less informed for advice about hairstyles, clothing, and the like. Married women with large families, who were well informed from appropriate media sources about household products, were sought as advisers on marketing, trying out new products, and so on. Thus, the age, marital status, and number of children (social categories) of traditional women predisposed them to acquire information about issues related to their traditional roles. These in turn were the criteria used by those needing advice on particular subjects when they turned to an opinion leader (social relationships) for information and influence.

DeFleur has suggested a number of conditions of social structure and of social functioning that will lead to the emergence and functioning of an opinion leader.[22] Further study is required, however, to identify the exact conditions under which a given person emerges as an opinion leader (individual differences). Moreover, the conditions that lead to the institutionalization—relatively permanent establishment—of an opinion leader also need additional research.[23]

The Future of Mass Communication Theory

One of the most pressing problems in the interdisciplinary study of mass communication is the strengthening of its theoretical base. There has been an unfortunate tendency among students of the media to equate the idea of "theory" with relatively unsophisticated matters such as classification schemes, the preparation of abstract diagrams that purport to symbolize the communication process, or the mere listing of factors that somehow will "make a difference" in the way some communication effect takes place. Criteria of what constitutes a theory in more sophisticated fields are considerably more demanding. In a very real way, the three perspectives on mass communication that have been discussed in the present chapter reflect these limitations. By any formal criteria, they are certainly not theories. They are conceptual perspectives that have been given easy-to-remember names for purposes of convenience. In reality, these conceptualizations did not emerge full-blown from research in precisely the way they have been discussed. They have been pulled together for the purposes of the present chapter and given these names, although they have been implicit or explicit in debates, writing, and research for years.

To some extent the lack of continued dedication to fundamental theoretical problems related to the media may be a product of the history of mass communication as a field of research and study. Until recently, it has been little more than a kind of intellectual way station—a kind of unclaimed territory where people from all kinds of disciplinary backgrounds have come in, picked up research problems, worked through them for a while, and then dropped them in favor of more pressing interests or pursued their implications back into the mainstream of their own discipline. Perhaps as communication continues to develop as a discipline in its own right, with its own research training, formal degree programs, increasing specialization, and a growing conceptual apparatus, it will be able to concentrate more fully on the systematic accumulation of theories of mass communication.

The three perspectives on the mass communication process discussed above need to be completely revamped and rewritten as systematic sets of propositions that show in straightforward terms just what is supposed to be related to what in terms of *independent* and *dependent* variables. To do this, some difficult definitional work will have to be undertaken so that the exact phenomena to which the concepts in the theories refer can be specified. Relationships between concepts within given propositions will have to be identified by means of some logical *calculus*—some set of recognized rules for reasoning—so that orders of dependency between propositions can be established. If this is done, such theories will yield *derived propositions* that can be tested empirically. Only then can their validity be adequately assessed.

This does not mean that all mass communication theory must be reduced to algebraic equations. The steps suggested above are possible without resorting to mathematics. Nevertheless, it is one thing to state propositions like this: "Ideas often flow from the media to opinion leaders and from them to less active populations." It is quite another thing to specify precisely what quantitative relationships are meant by such terms as "often" and "less," and to note exact empirical referents for other terms in such a statement, such as "ideas," "flow," "leaders," etc. In other words, we must specify more rigorously the conditions under which these events will occur, in what quantity or with what probability, and with what step-by-step theoretical implications for related media behavior.

This call for raising scientific standards in media theory construction indicates that students of mass communication have a great deal of homework to do before they can increase the sophistication of their theoretical formulations to the level of other disciplines. There is a serious gap between what we *think* we know about how people encounter and respond to the mass media and a rigorous set of theoretical formulations that specify how these events *actually* take place. In other words, there is a need to establish increased confidence that these basic perspectives are true (or else replace them) and thereby increase the degree to which we can discuss cause-effect sequences in mass communication in precise terms. Until the formulations identified in this chapter have been studied, restudied, reformulated, and restudied again, they will remain forever as "pre-theories"—interesting and seemingly plausible speculations that appear to be more or less consistent with our limited amount of media research but about which we really are not sure.

One obvious approach would be to *combine* the three perspectives discussed in this chapter. Such an *integrated* perspective would recognize that the effects of a given mass-communicated message sent over a given channel will depend upon a large number of psychological characteristics and social category similarities which audience members bring to their encounters with the media and will, moreover, depend upon the kind of social groups within which these people are acting and the relationships that they have with specific types of persons within them. Perhaps when it is possible to pin down some of these variables in specific detail, we can truly develop theories of mass communication.

NOTES

1. HAROLD A. INNIS, *Empire and Communication* (London: Clarendon Press, 1950).
2. MARSHALL McLUHAN, *Understanding Media* (New York: McGraw-Hill, 1964).
3. Ibid.
4. Couch has criticized sociologists for ignoring the form of audience-media relations that derives, in large part, from the nature of media technology. See Carl Couch, "Theoretical Notes of the Form and Consequences of Mass Communication" (Paper presented at the annual meeting of the American Sociological Association, August 1972).
5. WILLIAM JAMES, *Principles of Psychology* (New York: Henry Holt, 1890); see p. 566.
6. JOHN B. WATSON, *Behavior: An Introduction to Comparative Psychology* (New York: Henry Holt, 1914).
7. Although the basic idea of conditioning was understood before the turn of the century, physiologists such as Ivan Pavlov and Vladimir Bekhterev made it popular among American psychologists. An excellent discussion of this historical development is that of Ernest Hilgard and Donald Marquis, *Conditioning and Learning* (New York: Appleton-Century-Crofts, 1940), esp. pp. 1–50.
8. For an outstanding overview of development during this period of thought concerning human personality, see Gordon W. Allport, *Personality: A Psychological Interpretation.* (New York: Henry Holt, 1937).
9. W. I. THOMAS and FLORIAN ZNANIECKI, *The Polish Peasant in Europe and America,* 5 vols. (Chicago: University of Chicago Press, 1918–21).
10. For a discussion of the history and present status of attitude and its measurement, see Melvin L. DeFleur and Frank R. Westie, "Attitude as a Scientific Concept," *Social Forces* 42 (October 1963): 17–31.
11. A major section in one of the first textbooks in mass communication consists of a series of reprinted research reports dealing with audience selectivity and its basis. See Wilbur Schramm, ed., *Mass Communications* (Urbana: University of Illinois Press, 1949), pp. 387–429.
12. The following are representative examples of research reports guided by the social categories theory: Paul F. Lazarsfeld, "Communications Research," *Current Trends in Social Psychology* (Pittsburgh: University of Pittsburgh Press, 1949), pp. 233–48; Wilbur Schramm and David White, "Age, Education, and Economic Status as Factors in Newspaper Reading," in Schramm, *Mass Communications,* pp. 402–12; and H. M. Beville, Jr., "The ABCD's of Radio Audiences," in Schramm, *Mass Communications,* pp. 413–23.

13. AUGUSTE COMTE, *The Positive Philosophy*, trans. Harriet Martineau (London: George Bell and Sons, 1915), vol. 2.

14. HAROLD D. LASSWELL, "The Structure and Function of Communication in Society," in *The Communication of Ideas*, ed. Lyman Bryson (New York: Harper & Brothers, 1948), pp. 37–51.

15. PAUL F. LAZARSFELD, BERNARD BERELSON, and HELEN GAUDET, *The People's Choice* (New York: Duell, Sloan & Pearce, 1944).

16. ELIHU KATZ, "Communication Research and the Image of Society: Convergence of Two Research Traditions," *American Journal of Sociology* 65, no. 5 (1960): 436.

17. LAZARSFELD, BERELSON, and GAUDET, *People's Choice*, p. 150.

18. An excellent summary of this process is contained in Elihu Katz, "The Two-Step Flow of Communication: An Up-to-Date Report on an Hypothesis," *Public Opinion Quarterly* 21, no. 1 (Spring 1957): 61–78.

19. For an excellent summary of research on farm adoption, see C. Paul Marsh and A. Lee Coleman, "Group Influences and Agricultural Innovations: Some Tentative Findings and Hypotheses," *American Journal of Sociology* 61, no. 6 (May 1956): 388–94. See also C. M. Coughenour, "The Functioning of Farmers' Characteristics in Relation to Contacts with Media and Practice Adoption," *Rural Sociology* 25 (September 1960): 263–97.

20. For a review of literature on such issues, see Everett M. Rogers, *Diffusion of Innovations* (New York: Free Press of Glencoe, 1962), esp. pp. 208–47.

21. ELIHU KATZ and PAUL F. LAZARSFELD, *Personal Influence* (Glencoe, Ill.: Free Press, 1954).

22. MELVIN L. DEFLEUR, "The Emergence and Functioning of Opinion Leadership: Some Conditions of Informal Influence Transmission," in *Decisions, Values and Groups*, ed. Norman Washburne (New York: Macmillan, 1962), 2:257–78.

23. For a recent review of relevant research, see Walter Weiss, "Effects of the Mass Media of Communication," in *Handbook of Social Psychology*, ed. Gardner Lindzey and Elliot Aronson (2nd ed., Reading, Mass.: Addison-Wesley, 1969), 5:77–195. Also see chaps. 3–11 in Ithiel de Sola Pool et al., eds., *Handbook of Communication* (Chicago: Rand McNally, 1973).

Twenty-Nine

The Rise of Mini-Comm

Gary Gumpert

To point out that contemporary society is in the midst of a communication explosion is to state the obvious. Certainly man is bombarded, caressed, fondled, soothed, harangued, influenced, swayed, narcotized, entertained, and taught via the mass media. But the image of the mass communication phenomenon is not quite accurate. The phrase "media of mass communication" does not adequately describe the present media process. The purpose of this discussion is to amend the presently held concept of "mass-comm." In order to achieve this goal it will be necessary to provide a common ground by describing those characteristics which currently define the area of mass communication. Then the concept of "mass-comm" will be related to some of the grand theories of McLuhan, Stephenson, and Loevinger. It is the author's contention that these theories provide only a partial and incomplete explanation of media process and impact. Finally, a modification will be suggested of our current view of mass communication.

The term "mass communication" is a generic one. It is a shortened form of the phrase "media of mass communication." According to Joseph Klapper, "the term connotes all mass media of communication in which a mechanism of impersonal reproduction intervenes between the speaker and the audience."[1] Therefore, a number of forms can be excluded: theatre, personal conversation, and public address. The following basic characteristics define the mass communication event:

1. *Mass communication is public communication.* It is not private communication involving carrier pigeon, secret code, or semaphore signals. The content of mass communication is open to public inspection and is available to that public.

2. *The dissemination of mass communication content is rapid.* Rapidity refers to speed in transmission and speed in production. Some media operate with a sense of simultaneity. That is, events will be perceived by a large mass of people at the same time the event is occurring. This generally includes the electronic media. The print media, however, are based upon speed of production rather than simultaneous transmission. The ultimate expression of speed in production is exemplified by the "Instant Book" born with the publication of the *Report of the Warren Commission.* The Instant Book is one based on the coverage of an important government or legal report and is published in a matter of days on a crash schedule. The two main publishers in this area are Bantam and New American Library. Bantam had prepared two covers, ahead of time, for the trial of James Earl Ray—one for guilty and one for innocent. Within about ten days after the conclusion of the trial, *The Strange Case of James Earl Ray* hit the newsstands.

3. *The content of mass media is transient.* For the most part, the content

or product is meant for consumption on a short-term basis. The products are not meant to endure—unless you are an academic saver of all things. The content is manufactured rather than created. Not all mass communication content can be described as "kitch." There are exceptions, of course, since the techniques of mass communication can be used for the dissemination of enduring ideas and content. We can distinguish between the formula-based paperbacks such as *The Violent Erotics, Sex Secrets of the Mod Wife, Girls Together, Innocent in Chicago,* and *Romance of Lust* and Henry Miller's *The Tropic of Cancer.* The philosophical intent of the communicator must be considered. Generally, however, when the mass audience is sought, content becomes standardized. The typical television situation comedy represents standardized content based upon a formula.

4. *The direct cost to the public of mass communication content is minimal.* The indirect costs are very high—the supermarket costs. The mass media are available to most people because of low direct costs. Over 95% of American households own television sets (57 million U.S. households).[2] As of March 20, 1969, there were 6,593 radio stations on the air in this nation.[3]

5. *The mass communication audience is large, heterogeneous, and anonymous.* The audience consists of a great number of isolated individuals who are not known to each other or by the communicator. A large audience is "any audience exposed for a short time and of such a size that the communicator could not interact with its members on a face-to-face basis."[3A] There is, therefore, an obvious lack of immediate feedback which characterizes the mass-comm situation.

6. *The nature of the mass communication institution is complex.* The mass communicator, broadly defined, is a corporate organization embodying an extensive division of labor and a high degree of expense. For example, the ABC-20th Century Fox contract for 23 motion pictures involved 20 million dollars. The average half-hour show on CBS costs 94 thousand dollars to produce. The production expenses emphasize the commonplace, since the advertiser deals with a concept or standard of cost per thousand. He seeks the greatest return for his money. At the same time, the production expenses decrease the access to the media for people who wish to use them.

Mass-comm is represented by the world of the conglomerate corporation. It is manifested by national sameness. It is often described by the minority as the establishment. It is a one-dimensional view of national culture. In order to exist as the mass media, sameness or oneness is perpetuated in the search for the largest possible audience. The broadcasting rating game is a trap from which there is no escape—if the mass media are to retain their present status. What we have, or more accurately, had, is a monopoly of gatekeepers. There is little difference between a *Life* magazine or a *Look* magazine. Nor is there a significant difference between CBS and NBC or between the Hollywood films produced by Columbia and those produced by Paramount. In fact, the relationship between Hollywood and the television networks represents another dimension of actual or contractual conglomerate corporations and the monopoly of ideas.

It is this milieu of mass-comm that is dealt with by the grand theorists.

William Stephenson's "Play Theory of Mass Communication" might also be called the "Sham Theory of Mass Communication." The crux of Stephenson's theory is that people consume most mass communication because they derive pleasure and subjective fulfillment from it. He dismisses the common cry of media manipulation of the masses, and he claims that because the individual has an extremely broad choice of programming (or reading material, etc.), selecting that which best suits his needs, the individual is subjectively manipulating the mass media. Stephenson calls this subjective free choice, "convergent selectivity," and claims it is a new development in history, a by-product of the mass media which permits a "heightened self-awareness."[4] This individuality of choice is quite desirable for it permits us "to exist for ourselves, to please ourselves, free to a degree from social control."[5] But the "communication pleasure" of which Stephenson speaks is an illusion through which an individual is kept busy via the provision of the daily "fill" by the media of mass communication. Stephenson presents an elitist theory and thereby provides a rationale for the existence of mass-comm. It is ironic that he preaches the selectivity of sham, because the reality of selectivity is evident in the newer developments of mini-comm.

Lee Loevinger's "Reflective-Projective Theory of Broadcasting and Mass Communication" . . . "postulating that mass communications are best understood as mirrors of society that reflect an ambiguous image in which each observer projects or sees his own vision of himself and society,"[6] is an apology in the guise of an explanation for the nature of American broadcasting. The most provocative aspect of Loevinger's theory is his belief that in the field of communications, media technology reverses psychology in order of development. Loevinger provides a challenge to the McLuhan "Hot-Cool" media syndrome.

> Television is a medium which . . . conveys the most information in the most literal form by giving us oral language combined with visual perceptions and requiring the least effort to interpret the abstractions. Thus television is a multichannel communication which is more elemental and therefore has greater immediacy and impact than other media.[7]

The Reflective-Projective theory deals with an explanation of the mass impact of the mass media of communication—of media which seem to reach the greatest possible share of an available audience. But what about WEVD in New York City, which at one time was advertising for a Chinese disc jockey? "Applicants must be acquainted with Poon Sow Keng (the hottest rock 'n' roll singer today in Hong Kong), be able to report the time, news and temperature in easy going Cantonese, and quote Confucius in the original."[8] What about the *National Turkey News, The New York Review of Books,* underground films, or television for stockbrokers? Where do they belong?

It is difficult to evaluate the theory of Marshall McLuhan, if there is one theory. During some correspondence McLuhan clarified his point of view.

> My theme is quite simple, in this respect at least; that I see the entire Gutenberg 500 years as a repetition in all levels of life and culture of the

basic matrix of the Gutenberg press itself. The Greeko-Roman world, from the phonetic alphabet forward, was in the same way a repetition of the technology of that alphabet as applied to papyrus and to-day our world shows the beginnings of a repetition in all human transactions of the basic electric circuit. I mention this because if we can consider the 500 years of Gutenberg dominance as located between two other technologies it should help to define our problems.[9]

There have been few effective critics of McLuhan. Most of them capitulate by attacking his style. McLuhan should be considered a Happening—a most effective Happening, since his message appears to equally effect and explain the nature of media. Man began in the tribal village. The media have accelerated the process of returning him to a tribal existence—the tribal world.

> Through radio, TV, and the computer, we are already entering a global theatre in which the entire world is a Happening ... a simultaneous "all-at-once" world in which everything resonates with everything else as in a total electrical field ... [10]

We have all experienced a taste of this global village. For some people the tribal world is rather disturbing and threatening. McLuhan speaks of the United States "as a nation which is doomed, in any case, to break up into a series of regional and racial mini-states."[11] Obviously, man can communicate with any part of the world if world politics allows him the freedom of his capability. Media do not have to heed the warning of national boundaries. But what happens to the needs of primary groups, subgroups, and specific communities or cultures in that global village? It seems that Marshall McLuhan does not provide a satisfactory answer to that question. He speaks of "the electronically induced technological extensions of our central nervous system,"[12] but he does not account for the communication vacuums induced by global interrelationships and a situation in which communication channels are monopolized by the few.

It is Harold A. Innis in *The Bias of Communication* who provides an explanation of the process which has created the need for a shift or modification of our current thinking in regard to mass communication. In his scholarly fashion, he shows that a monopoly of knowledge creates new media in the way that the "monopoly of knowledge centering around stone and hieroglyphics was exposed to competition from papyrus as a new and more efficient medium."[13] He suggests that "a stable society is dependent on an appreciation of a proper balance between the concepts of space and time."[14] The key word is balance. Although stability of a civilization is rarely achieved, it can occur only when competitive balance and a non-monopolistic climate prevail. Innis can be interpreted to say that when monopoly of knowledge prevails, this very situation stimulates the need and invention of countering media. And this is what is happening today and will continue to happen.

The "traditional" concept of mass communications no longer describes "the way it really is." There is a psycho-sociological want for media which are addressed to us, our own group—as we see ourselves as members of a society.

As isolated entities in a mass society individuals wish to be heard, to be linked with others like themselves. This coupling is manifested in geographical or avocational binding. At times, the focus is on the immediate community. At other times, the focus is upon a belief system which transcends geographical lines. This focusing is accomplished through media of communication which reach specific select audiences, and yet these audiences consist of enough people to fit the criteria of a mass audience. They are, however, a small mass audience. In addition, this audience is motivated to non-standardized content. The author refers to this development as the rise of "mini-comm." Mass-comm still exists and serves important functions, but it is a coexistence and not sole-existence.

A cursory examination of several media will indicate the trend toward mini-comm.

1. Magazines

For many people the death of the *Saturday Evening Post* suggested the final demise of the magazine field. The opposite is true. In 1968, ninety-four new magazines were started, nine others merged or were sold, and only twelve went out of business. According to John Tebbel, writing in the *Saturday Review,*

> In a country of two hundred million people, producing successful mass magazines has become increasingly more difficult, while those reaching smaller audiences within the mass have been increasingly successful. Thirty years ago a magazine with a circulation of 500,000 to 3,000,000 was considered large, or even mass, and most specialized publications were limping along with circulations ranging roughly from 50,000 to 150,000. Today a magazine has to have more than 6,000,000 to play with the big boys.[15]

The magazine world is adopting new methods and is carefully analyzing its markets. Some publications are based upon controlled circulation methods— they are sent free to more or less carefully selected audiences. *Charlie* is a magazine for coeds under twenty-five and is mailed to department store customers. Started in 1968, *Charlie* is expected to have a circulation between 150,000 and 200,000. *Go* is a free circulation tabloid distributed through record stores in thirty-five cities with a 750,000 circulation. Magazines are published in the name of cities and states—*New York Magazine, Florida, The New Californian,* and *Arizona Highways.* There is a publication for everyone. Among the limitless list can be found *Afternoon TV, Censorship Today, Modern Bride's Guide to Decorating Your First Home, Yellow Submarine, Government Photography, Musical Electronics, Weight Watchers,* and the *Southern Hog Producer.* The left and right of the political spectrum, and shades in between, have publications which link the believers. Part of a more serious list includes *Ramparts, Saturday Review, America, Atlantic Monthly, Harpers,* and the *Reporter.* These are publications which probably affect the decision-making process in our society. Are they examples of mass communication?

2. Radio

The FM spectrum is now fractionalized, and the AM spectrum is becoming fractionalized. In New York, and that city is unique only in terms of numbers, there is a left-of-center, a high-brow good music, a low-brow good music, and a number of folk-rock stations. The all-news, all-music, and all-ethnic stations have been around for some time. The manager of one noncommercial FM station, WRVR, stated that a recent survey revealed 32% of that station's audience had some postgraduate education. In New York, suburban radio consists of twenty-nine AM and fifteen FM stations. You listen to suburban radio to find out whether the schools are open, which ice ponds are safe, the score of the local basketball game, and the scandal of the week. WNBC and WCBS serve the New York megalopolis. But do they serve the unique pockets of community that exist both within and outside large urban areas? "Henry S. Hovland, general manager of WGCH in Greenwich, thinks the success of his and other suburban stations is not service or even snobbery, but 'seeking an identity in megalopolis, not for the stations, for the people; they resent being swallowed up.' "[16] Mini-comm provides a partial answer to an individual's quest for identity and the individual has the added advantage of changing that identity with the mini-comm he chooses.

3. Television

In the near future it will be possible for each home to have thirty channels available. The rise of UHF, Public Television, and, most important, CATV tends to support the contention that the medium will become fractionalized. In addition, satellite communication has the potential of altering the present configuration of television transmission. The days of the network might be doomed.

4. Newspapers

The daily newspaper is on the decline, but the weekly is rising in importance and number. *The New York Times* does not adequately serve the typical suburban community. The ordinary traffic accident involving one or two deaths is often not reported in *The New York Times.* A local paper is required for that piece of information. In fact, a number of papers and media is necessary in order for the individual to understand the operation and nature of his environment. Jack Lyle in *The News in Megalopolis* makes the point that:

While the specialty press may not be able (or even wish) to vie with the daily press in performing the general function of maintaining a general surveillance of the environment, they do compete with the daily press in attempting to correlate society's interpretation of, and reaction to, the major events of the period.[17]

In this way, mini-comm supplements mass-comm.

In addition to community papers, the underground papers (not really a satisfactory label) continue to grow in circulation and importance. When the *Village Voice* veered from its avant-garde position, a number of other papers filled the void: *Other Scenes, Rolling Stone, The New York Review of Sex, Rat, Fun, Screw, Jive Comics,* and *The East Village Other.* Such papers are not limited to New York. Sold on the newsstand and by subscription, their existence cannot be dismissed. What are the functions of *The Berkeley Barb, The Los Angeles Free Press,* and *The Black Panther?* The papers continue to proliferate and some are united through the service of an underground news service.

The same trends can be found in the motion picture area, the recording industry, and the comic book field. The causal relationships of mini-comm and mass-comm are demonstrated by the developments in each medium. While mini-comm fills needs not served by mass-comm, both tend to define each other and influence each other.

The Hollywood film helped to create the independent producer who, in turn, influenced the birth of the art film. The underground film is also a response and has influenced the total film industry. The "new" film has had a fantastic impact. Part of this impact is described by Anthony Schillaci when he discussed "Film as Environment" in the *Saturday Review:*

> The new multisensory involvement with film as total environment has been primary in destroying literary values in film . . . it means the emergence of a new identity for film.[18]

The recording field is an exciting kingdom of creativity which caters to a stratified audience. The Jefferson Airplane's "White Rabbit" is aimed at an acid sympathetic subgroup. Tim Buckley's "No Man Can Find the War" is an anti-Vietnam statement. There is a grammar of "rock" which the older generation refuses to learn.

The comic book is another example of splendid splinters. How do you generalize about "Young Romance," "Superman," and "The Silver Surfer" (a comic book you must read in order to believe)? "Feiffer," "B.C.," "Pogo," "Peanuts," "Dick Tracy," "Lil Abner," and "Little Orphan Annie" are comic strips which accurately reflect the problems and philosophies of our society. They appeal to sections of the mass, not necessarily to the entire mass.

The rise of mini-comm is going to require some adjustments on the part of the academic community. There is a need for research which examines mini-comm. Since mini-communication alters the functions of mass-comm, a new functional analysis of media is in order. It is time to re-examine the "Two Step

Flow of Communication"—in light of newer configurations of primary groups and subgroups. Content analysis would also be highly revealing.

In addition to research, it is most important that man learn to cope with a multiplicity of sounds and images. He may think that he is bombarded now, but the barrage is going to increase. And the increase will bring with it the diversity and differences of mini-comm. The search for truth will rest with the individual and his wisdom. It will take wisdom and perception to tolerate and perhaps understand the alien, the strange, and the opposition. Diversity brings with it the multiple point of view and the proclivity to condemn the opposition and the ideology of commitment. To condemn the right of man to express himself is to censor in the name of a creed in vogue. The result is merely to drive ideas underground, for ideas can never be destroyed. Mini-comm will play a critical role in the future, if it is allowed to thrive.

NOTES

1. GEORGE GERBNER. "Mass Media and Human Communication Theory." In *Human Communication Theory.* (edited by Frank E. X. Dance.) New York: Holt, Rinehart and Winston, 1967, p. 44.
2. *Nielsen Television 1969.* Chicago: A. C. Nielsen, 1969, p. 5.
3. "Summary of Broadcasting." *Broadcasting* 76: 168, March 24, 1969.
3A. CHARLES R. WRIGHT. *Mass Communication: A Sociological Perspective.* New York: Random House, 1964, p. 13.
4. WILLIAM STEPHENSON. *The Play Theory of Mass Communication.* Chicago: University of Chicago Press, 1967, p. 35.
5. *Ibid.,* p. 2.
6. LEE LOEVINGER. "The Ambiguous Mirror: The Reflective-Projective Theory of Broadcasting and Mass Communication." *Journal of Broadcasting* 12: 108, Spring 1968.
7. *Ibid.,* p. 110.
8. WILLIAM H. HONAN. "The New Sound of Radio." *The New York Times Magazine,* December 3, 1967, p. 56.
9. Letter from Marshall McLuhan, May 5, 1960.
10. "Playboy Interview: Marshall McLuhan." *Playboy,* March 1969, p. 70.
11. *Ibid.*
12. *Ibid.,* p. 62.
13. HAROLD A. INNIS. *The Bias of Communication.* Toronto: University of Toronto Press, 1951, p. 35.
14. *Ibid.,* p. 64.
15. JOHN TEBBEL. "Magazines New, Changing, Growing." *Saturday Review,* February 8, 1969, p. 55.
16. ROBERT WINDELER. "Radio and Suburbs Discover Each Other." *New York Times,* December 30, 1968, p. 24.
17. JACK LYLE. *The News in Megalopolis.* San Francisco: Chandler, 1967, pp. 36–37.

18. Anthony Schillaci. "The New Movie: 1. Film as Environment." *Saturday Review,* December 28, 1968, p. 9.

Thirty

The Careening of America

Caution: Television Watching May Be Hazardous to Your Mental Health

Nicholas Johnson

The general semanticist Alfred Korzybski described three categories of mental health: sane, insane, and unsane. His point was that most of us, while not *insane,* are *un*sane. That is, we are not living up to our potential as human beings; we are not fully functioning. The so-called "human potential movement," including the late Abraham Maslow, argues that even the *healthy* human beings among us function at perhaps 5 per cent of their potential.

Reflect: How many people do *you* know whom you think of as "fully functioning personalities"? How many are there in whose daily lives there is a measure of beauty, contact with nature, artistic creativity, some philosophical contemplation or religion, love, self-fulfilling productivity of some kind, participation in life-support activities, physical well-being, a spirit of joy, and individual growth? That's what the world's great theologians, psychiatrists, poets, and philosophers have been telling us human life is all about. But few of us have come close to realizing that potential.

As an FCC commissioner, I think I have a responsibility to examine the possibility that this potentiality gap may be related in some way to the operation of radio and television.

It is, of course, preposterous to suggest—or even suspect—that television is responsible for everything wrong with America, or that it is the sole cause of any individual problem. We had social problems before we had television, and since its coming we have made some progress of which we can be proud. But it would be equally shortsighted to ignore the findings of the many task-force reports and academic studies that link television, in greater or lesser degree, to virtually every national crisis.

Television programming is not, of course, the only influence on a child; but the fact remains that it is a large one. The average child will have received more hours of "instruction" from television by the time he enters first grade than he will later spend in college classrooms earning a B.A. degree. By the time he is a teenager he will have spent 15–20 thousand hours with the television set and will have been exposed to 250–500 thousand commercials. It would seem simple common sense to assume that this exposure has its influence; in any event, since "hard-headed businessmen" are willing to bet three billion dollars a year in advertising budgets on the proposition that it is having an effect, they at least are effectively estopped from arguing the contrary.

We are all vaguely aware that Big Television is allied with Big Business. But you may not be aware of the full reach of that alliance. The most influential broadcast properties—talent, programs, studios, network contracts, and stations—are actually owned by big business, lock, stock, and barrel. Each of the three networks is a major industrial-conglomerate corporation. The time on the stations is purchased by big business—virtually all the available programming and advertising time on 7,500 radio and television stations. The entire enterprise, programs as well as commercials, revolves around the consumer merchandisers who find the medium the most effective way to sell their wares. The top talent (let alone the executives) are paid salaries that place them well up in the ranks of America's wealthiest businessmen.

Very little is programmed anytime during the broadcast day that is in dissidence with this overall domination by big business. Procter and Gamble's editorial policy provides that "There will be no material that may give offense, either directly or by inference, to any . . . commercial organization of any sort." The only exceptions are tokenism: an occasional news item (carefully kept out of prime time; network news is programmed as early as 5 P.M. in many sections of the country), or an even rarer documentary. Even these programs are larded with commercial messages sold for as much as the networks can extract. History—the moon walk, election returns—is also "brought to you by" some commercial sponsor. Whatever the benefits of news, documentaries, and live coverage, for those millions of American families whose television watching is limited to prime-time series shows, or soap operas during the day, Procter and Gamble's policy reigns supreme.

You may think, "Of course big business dominates television—so what? It may be separating a few fools from their money in exchange for products of questionable worth—a hazard of any foray into the marketplace. There are occasional fraudulent or misleading ads, but that's the Federal Trade Commission's problem. What other cause for concern is there?"

In the process of trying to answer that question, I have become more and more aware of the extent to which television not only distributes programs and sells products, but also preaches a general philosophy of life. Television tells us, hour after gruesome hour, that the primary measure of an individual's worth is his consumption of products, his measuring up to ideals that are found in packages mass produced and distributed by corporate America. Many products (and even programs), but especially the drug commercials, sell the gospel that there are instant solutions to life's most pressing personal problems. You don't need to think about your own emotional maturity and development of individuality, your discipline, training, and education, your perception of the world, your willingness to cooperate and compromise and work with other people; you don't need to think about developing deep and meaningful human relationships and trying to keep them in repair. "Better living through chemistry" is not just DuPont's slogan—it's one of the commandments of consumerism. Not only do the programs and commercials explicitly preach materialism, conspicuous consumption, status consciousness, sexploitation, and fantasy worlds of quick shallow solutions, but even the settings and subliminal messages are commercials for the consumption style of life.

The headache-remedy commercials are among the most revealing. A headache is often the body's way of telling us something's wrong. What is wrong may have to do with the bad vibes one picks up working in big corporations' office buildings, or shopping in their stores. The best answer may be to stay out of such places. Obviously, such a solution would be as bad for the corporate state generally as for the headache-remedy business in particular. So the message is clear: Corporate jobs and shopping trips are as American as chemical additives in apple pie. You just keep driving yourself through both; and when those mysterious headache devils appear for no reason at all, you swallow the magic chemicals.

But what's true of the magic-chemical ads is true of commercials and programs generally. Look at the settings. Auto ads push clothes fashion and vacations. Furniture-wax ads push wall-to-wall carpeting and draperies. Breakfast-cereal ads push new stoves and refrigerators. Not surprisingly, the programs do the same—after all, they're paid for by the same guys who pay for the commercials.

In fact, there's a rather intricate "corporate interlock" of jobs, products, and life-style. Once you come into the circle at any point you take on nearly all of it, and once you're in it's very difficult to get a little bit out. The choices you are left are relatively meaningless—like which color and extras you want with your Chevrolet, scotch or bourbon, how "mod" your ties will be, and which toothpaste you'll use. It all fits: corporate white-collar jobs, suburban home, commuting by automobile, eating in restaurants, and the clothes. There is the canned "entertainment" of radio and television for boredom, bottled alcohol and aspirin for pain, and aerosol cans of deodorant and "room freshener" to maintain the antiseptic cleanliness of it all. You wear your office, your home, and your car as much as your clothes and deodorant. And from the corporate layers of externals comes your very identity—and the smothering of your soul.

I would be the first to acknowledge that we are, of course, talking about matters of personal taste. People should be free to choose the life they want. Certainly it ought not to be the business of government to choose life-styles for its citizens. But two facts remain. First, the wholly disproportionate—if not exclusive—emphasis of television is pushing only one point of view. The choice you'll never know is the choice you'll never make. Many Americans are not sufficiently informed of the alternatives to make an intelligent choice of the life they most want. Second, independent students of our society—wholly apart from their own personal preferences—believe there is a correlation between the philosophy preached by television and many of our social problems.

The gospel of television simultaneously seems to create tremendous anxiety and alienation in the poor and emptiness and neuroses in the affluent. As we are sold the products we are given the belief that our worth as individuals turns on our capacity to consume. We are given a shot of anxiety for free, told to buy more to make it go away, and find the feeling only gets worse.

But apart from the content, the mere act of television-watching is a passive activity. When we turn it on we turn ourselves off. If it is true that passivity and a sense of powerlessness are among the most dangerous epidemics in our society today, the television set is suspect at the outset regardless of what's programmed on it. The only exceptions would be programs like Jack La-Lanne's exercises, or Public Broadcasting's offerings of Laura Weber's guitar lessons and Julia Child's cooking programs. Television could urge us to get up, turn off the set, and go live a little. It could help us to lead more interesting, more informed, more fulfilling lives. With rare exceptions, it doesn't.

Humanness as an Alternative

I think television could—and should—help us understand the alternatives to the conspicuous consumption, chemical, corporate life-style. Not because I'm "right," but because there *are* alternatives; people are entitled to know about them, and experience them if they choose. And today's televised theology seems to be contributing very little to life, or liberty, or the pursuit of happiness —which somebody once thought *was* the business of government.

Suppose you don't want to drop out or camp out. Maybe you want to step in, try to make things a little better, or just earn a living. What then? How can we make life *in* a corporate state more livable and more human? It became obvious to me that if I were going to criticize television for not offering alternative life-styles, I would have to be able to find the answer to that question. So I set about it.

Camping in the West Virginia mountains for two weeks reaffirmed my latent but basic commitment to the psychic values of simplicity. You not only "get along with" substantially fewer "things" when camping in the woods, you actually enjoy life more because it is not so cluttered with objects. The experience gave me a way of thinking about simplicity, objects, and natural living that I had not had before. And it impressed upon me, for perhaps the first time, a sense of the interrelated totality of "life-support activities."

By life-support activities I mean the provision of those things that are necessary to sustain physical life for ourselves: food, clothing, shelter, transportation, and so forth. These are the kinds of activities that I became most fully aware of in the woods, because I had to, and because they can be most easily comprehended when reduced to their basics. And yet I used to give almost no attention to these kinds of activities. Food simply appeared on my dinner table ready to eat. The house I lived in was purchased; it was warmed or cooled by some equipment in the basement that I knew very little about, and was attended to by repairmen when necessary. Clothing was something I found in closets and dresser drawers; it was cleaned and mended by my wife, the maid, or a cleaning establishment. Transportation was provided by the municipal bus system for commuting, and by FCC drivers during the day. At my office I was not only surrounded by machinery—copying machines, electric typewriters, dictating machines, and so forth—but also by people paid to operate them for me, answer my telephone, and bring me coffee.

I had, in short, taken very nearly all my life-support activities—"my life" —and cut them up into bits and pieces which I parceled out to individuals, corporations, and machines around me. The upshot was that there was very little of it left for me to live. This was extraordinarily "efficient" in one sense. That is, I was working at perhaps 98 per cent of the ultimate level of professional production of which I am capable. But what I concluded was that it was bad for life. For I was *living* only a small percentage of my ultimate capacity to live.

In an industrialized urban environment it is easy to forget that human life still is, as it was originally, sustained by certain basic functions. I think *some* participation in the support of your life is essential to a sense of fulfillment. I do not, however, think that you need to do everything for yourself. For one thing, you cannot trace everything back to first elements. You can build your own furniture. But are you going to saw your own boards from your own trees? Are you going to insist upon having planted the trees? Are you going to insist on making your own nails from your own iron ore? Even the most deeply committed do-it-yourselfers reach some accommodation with civilization.

In the second place, you simply don't have time to do it all. To raise and can all your own fruits and vegetables, for example, would take substantially more time per year than most people are prepared to give to it—especially if you are also personally constructing your own home, weaving your own material and making your own clothes, and walking everywhere.

In the third place, many conveniences of urbanized life are there anyway and you might as well use them. They can save you time you might spend in other, more satisfying ways. There's no point to cooking in your fireplace every night —or on your corporate-cookout charcoal grill—if you have a gas or electric range sitting in your kitchen.

So my conclusion is that you ought to try to do a *little bit* of all your life-support activities, and a substantial amount of whichever one or two of them appeal to you the most and make the most practical sense for you. I have taken to buying and preparing my own simple foods, doing some modest mending of clothes, preparing some logs I intend to make into furniture, and providing my own transportation by bicycle. Undoubtedly other activities will fit better with your own life pattern.

If you start looking around for simplification, ways to make you less possession-bound and give you more chance to participate in your life, the opportunities are endless. Start by searching your house or apartment for things you can throw away. Ask yourself, "If I were living in the woods, would I spend a day going to town to buy this aerosol can?" Look for simple substitutes. Bicarbonate of soda, for example, can substitute for the following products: toothpaste, gargle and mouthwash, burn ointment, stomach settlers, room freshener, icebox cleaner, children's clay, baking powder, and so forth. And it only costs 12 cents a box! Get the idea?

Look for unnecessary electrical and other machinery and appliances. Bread can be toasted in the broiler of the stove. Carving knives and toothbrushes really need not be electrically powered. Put fruit and vegetable waste in a compost heap instead of down an electric disposal. I took up shaving with a blade, brush, and shaving soap instead of an electric razor. It's kind of bloody, but it's more fun. On the same principle, you can easily ignore most of the products in your supermarket and do a little more food preparation from basic ingredients.

Personally, I'm not interested in giving cooking or any other of these activities a lot of time. I'll walk up to a mile in dense urban areas because I can move faster that way than in a car—as well as get exercise, not pollute, help fight the automotive life-style, save money, and do a "life thing" (transportation) myself. But I'm not going to walk 20 miles into the suburbs—at least not often. I can make cornbread with baking soda in 20 minutes, about the time it takes to go to the store, or put supper on the table. But I won't often take the time to make yeast bread, unless there's somebody there to visit with, or something else to do at the same time. I make my own muesli (rolled oats, wheat germ, raisins, and so on) in less time than it takes to open a box of Captain Crunch, but I don't often take the time to crack and pick walnuts to add to it.

It is often possible to find activities that serve more than one function at the same time. Bicycle riding is perhaps my best example.

As you may have observed, my own reasons for adopting (and sharing and urging) the kind of approach to life I have been describing could be described as almost hedonistic. I ride a bicycle because I enjoy it more than driving a car. It makes me *feel* better. It gets my lungs to breathing and my heart to pumping. Dr. Paul Dudley White and others have long advised it as a means of warding off heart attacks. If you can use a bicycle to get to and from work, you can have the added satisfaction of knowing that you are providing one of your own life-support activities: transportation. In my case, I bicycle along the C & O Canal tow path, so that it also provides my daily time in a natural setting with canal, river, trees, birds, changing seasons, and sky. I find this time especially good for doing some of my best thinking (something I found very difficult to do during an earlier phase when I was jogging). So it also serves as a time when I compose little poems and songs, get ideas for opinions and speeches, and think about matters philosophical.

Bicycling has many peripheral benefits. It is cheap; you can buy an entire bicycle, brand new, for the cost of operating an automobile for a couple of weeks. The costs of operation are negligible, perhaps a penny or two a day. During rush hours, it is a significantly faster means of transportation than automobiles or buses, as "races" in numerous cities have demonstrated.

It happens that bicycle riding has some significant social advantages over the automobile, too. Compared to the car, the bicycle is a model citizen. It does not kill or maim; it does not pollute; it does not deplete natural resources, it makes no noise; and it takes up a great deal less space.

Why do I bicycle? Who knows? In one sense it makes no difference why people think they are doing what they are doing. If others' activities are consistent with what you think is constructive and delightful you can take some satisfaction from their joining with you. Most people don't think very precisely about their motivations, or the philosophies underlying their actions. It is probably just as well. It makes life more spontaneous and lighthearted. Besides which, if the truth were known, we often do things for other than the reasons we think we do; or for a complicated interrelationship of reasons that are sometimes consistent, sometimes inconsistent, and often constantly changing. Nevertheless, whatever the peripheral benefits may be, it seems to *me* that bicycling is just one example of a more satisfying, fulfilling, and joyful way to live *in* the corporate state.

Whether the truths I am dealing with are biological or metaphysical, my own experience supports the lessons of the world's great teachers. If man is to develop the rich individuality and full potential of which he is capable, he needs more than the hollow values and products of consumerism. He needs not only productive "work," but also love, beauty, creativity, contemplation, contact with nature, and participation in the support of his own life. When we live our lives in ways that take us too far from those basic truths, we begin to find ourselves in all kinds of troubles that ultimately show up in social statistics. And the evidence seems to suggest that as we return to a richer and more natural life, our problems subside. Whether or not that is enough for you, it is enough for me.

Central to all that I suggest is the necessity that you work it out for yourself. You need to discover who you are; what feels right and best for you. You not only need to walk to the sound of a different drummer, you need to be that different drummer. You need to write your own music. You need to look inside yourself and see what is there. I think some time in the woods is useful for this purpose; but camping may not be right for you, for a variety of quite sensible reasons. The purpose of self-discovery is not to stop copying Howard Johnson and start copying Nick Johnson, or anybody else. The point is to find your own soul and kick it and poke it with a stick, see if it's still alive, and then watch which way it moves.

I see evidence all around us that people are in fact rejecting materialism and looking for more meaningful lives for themselves. Without the internal or external direction of an ideology or an operating manual, ordinary people by the thousands are, in a violent spasm of reaction, simply casting off the chains of corporate control of their lives. The point is not that I find this encouraging —although I do. The point is not even that I think the system may be capable of righting itself—although it may. The point is is that the actions of all these people are simply additional evidence that the corporate life is, like war, unhealthy for children and other living things.

Nevertheless, I do not foresee a meaningful revolution without—at least— a good old-fashioned political battle. My principal disagreement with the Greening of the Third Reich concerns the prediction that new attitudes are going to bring the downfall of the corporate state, and that they constitute a new and powerful political movement. I think not. I think we are talking about 10 to 30 per cent of the population at best, and that while it will have a substantial impact, meaningful reforms are still going to require more conventional political action and legislation. There will continue to be a majority of people who, for a variety of reasons, can't or won't break out of the corporate trap. They would rather continue to tell themselves that they really want to drive that car, and smoke those cigarettes, and use that hair spray. Under it all may be the fear that if they went out in search of themselves they might come back empty-handed. Almost any alternative is preferable to that nightmare.

Creative Lives and Commercialized Television

Earlier I mentioned the opportunity for creativity as one aspect of a full human life. Because it is a quality that is especially related to television, it deserves a little fuller discussion.

Creativity is an essential quality of humanness in two respects. If a person is to have his own individuality, his own unique self, it will be expressed in creative and artistic ways most honestly and fully. If you do not give him the opportunity to be creative, you are in a very meaningful sense depriving him of the opportunity to be human. Second, and equally important, is the concept of Ezra Pound and Rollo May that the artist is the "antenna of the race." Throughout history some of the most perceptive analysis and forecasting has been done not by public officials or social scientists, but by the artists.

If you accept this thesis that creativity is central to humanness and society's well-being, I believe that you should be extremely concerned about the impact of commercial television. When a nation takes its most powerful soap box-theater-lecture hall and turns it over exclusively to the sale of snake oil, it is not only depriving its citizens of the opportunity to grow and develop as people, it is also cutting off their vision of their future.

The tendencies toward lack of diversity, reality, and controversy are only reinforced by the oligopolistic uniformity inherent in the current patterns of ownership. In the nation's 11 largest cities there is not a single network-affiliated VHF television station that is independently and locally owned. All are owned by the networks, multiple station owners, or major local newspapers —and many of these owners are large conglomerate corporations as well. Compounding this problem, most national news comes from the two wire services, AP and UPI, each serving approximately 1,200 newspapers and three thousand radio and television stations. Newspaper cross-ownership figures are also depressing. Of the 1,500 communities with daily newspapers, for example, 96 per cent are served by single-owner monopolies, and approximately 28 per cent of all television stations are owned by newspapers. In 1945 there were 177 cities with separately owned dailies; by 1966 there were only 43—one-third as many.

Equally important is the already dominant network monopolization over the production and purchase of television programming. For all practical purposes, any writer, director, or producer of television programming has only three buyers for his product: ABC, CBS, and NBC. The networks customarily purchase both the first-run and the syndication rights—the entire package of ownership and control. The networks are involved in every aspect of programming production: the choice of a theme, the designation of the writer, the rewriting of the script, the choice of actors, director, and producer, and the day-to-day shooting and censorship of the series. It is no accident that the three networks and their 15 wholly owned and operated television stations earn more than 50 per cent of all television revenues (in an industry of 642 television stations), and more than one-third of all profits.

The inhibitions on creative television programming inherent in the industry's present structure are only part of the problem. Equally important are the inhibitions on individual expression that are built into our present system. Individuals need to express themselves—to communicate to others, to share thoughts and ideas, to build a sense of community, to overcome the alienation caused by a highly urbanized, industrialized, mechanized life. Yet speech depends on access to a medium of communication. A soap box in the town square is no longer sufficient. Ideas must be communicated to society as a whole, and they cannot be unless the structure of television permits and encourages the participation by individuals with something to say.

Communications in the Creative Society

Given the extraordinary political and economic power of Big Broadcasting, radical restructuring of the commerical television networks and stations will come slowly, if ever. For the foreseeable future, commercial television will continue to exert perhaps the most influential impact on our nation of any single industry. Unless we continue to try to reform commercial broadcasting, we cannot have much of an impact. But the fact that the impact will be minimal does not detract from the necessity of making the effort. Broadcasting reform groups in Washington and throughout the United States are mushrooming, and chalking up an impressive record of accomplishments.

Let me itemize a few of our present rules and decisions. There are at least *some* limits on television station ownership—no one can own more than seven stations, of which no more than five can be VHF (channels 2 through 13). The FCC has announced that it intends to forbid future acquisitions of television-radio combinations in the same community. Commonly owned AM and FM radio stations in communities of over 100 thousand people cannot duplicate programming simultaneously for more than 50 per cent of the time. Cable-television system owners must permit the origination of programming. The Commission has provided that networks can no longer control more than three hours of prime-time programming each evening, a policy that opens up the market a crack for independent suppliers. And, of course, the advent of new technology has significantly increased the number of broadcast voices in the country—AM radio was first augmented by FM radio; then came VHF television, the UHF television (channels 14 through 83), and now cable television, with a potential for an unlimited number of channels.

The Public Broadcasting Corporation constitutes a somewhat more significant institutional restructuring. Although it necessarily has the rigidities of any large institution, and the local public television stations tend to have as directors and corporate contributors the same kind of men who control commercial broadcasting, it is nevertheless directly dependent neither on commercial sponsorship nor on attracting the largest possible mass audience.

Pay, or subscription, television could offer another significant change. The only meaningful use of the marketplace mechanism in audience control of programming today is in the listener-supported community radio stations run by organizations like Pacifica. Those stations are dependent upon the financial contributions of the listeners—who obviously are free to listen to the station without contributing, should they choose. They are also free to stop their contributions on the merest whim. How many commercial stations in this country would continue in operation if they had to rely upon voluntary contributions from the audience for all their operating costs? Pay television would offer an even more precise marketplace mechanism. If one million people are willing to pay one dollar apiece to watch a show that can be produced and distributed at a profit with gross revenues of one million dollars, they would have at least some chance of watching the program. Under the present system, they do not. A combination of pay television with cable television, with its potential for a larger number of fragmented audiences, makes such an approach even more viable.

One reform holds out perhaps the greatest potential for meaningful impact: The Justice Department, or the Federal Communications Commission, could order the abolition of network ownership of stations and the present restrictive affiliate contracts. There is a very striking analogy in the motion-picture business. During the 1930's and 1940's the motion-picture industry had the kind of control of theaters that the networks now have of their owned and affiliated stations. The large studios owned the talent, the books, the studio lots, the films, the distribution facilities, and the theaters. They produced movies according to formulae, and then pointed to the number of people who came to see the films as evidence that the companies knew what the public wanted.

In the Paramount divestiture case [*United States* v. *Paramount Pictures,* 344 U.S. 131 (1948)] the Department of Justice successfully argued in court the proposition that major motion-picture studios should not own theaters. Of course, the coming of television at about the same time also had a great impact upon the motion-picture business; but nevertheless, once the theaters were sold and the distribution channels opened up, there was a burgeoning of independent filmmakers. Not only did the motion-picture industry discover that the cost of producing films could be significantly reduced (*Easy Rider,* which will gross about 30 million dollars, was produced for about 300 thousand dollars), it also discovered a new flowering of creativity, diversity, and effervescence the like of which the industry had not seen for decades.

The parallel to the present network television is striking enough that the Justice Department finally, in 1972, filed against the networks an action comparable to the Paramount divestiture case.

Nevertheless, no such reforms are adequate to create the kind of flowering of creativity we seek, nor do they affect the fact that television programming is created to sell products and maximize profits. Big Business controls Big Television, which in turn influences the Congress and the Federal Communications Commission. And even if they did not, no matter how effective the FCC might be, the regulation of large corporations by a large governmental agency can do very little to humanize the product of radio and television programming.

What we seek are two goals. First, we want the opportunity for every American citizen who cares to do so to be able to express himself creatively in the television medium. Second, we want every American citizen at least to have the *opportunity* to see on television the product of the very best creative individuals (as distinguished from corporate committees). Fortunately, there is a potential answer. Even more fortunately, it is one that may be economically, politically, and socially viable.

Creative expression requires some new and cheaper television equipment—which is already on the market—and a vast increase in the number of training programs for its use. In 1967, Sony introduced on the American market a do-it-yourself television kit—including television camera, video tape-recording equipment, and television set—for scarcely more than the first color television receiving sets had cost (about one thousand dollars). Since that time an alternate-television movement has sprung up across the country—principally centered in New York and San Francisco.

With a whole generation of filmmakers coming along that would like to work in the television medium, there is reason to believe that this movement may be in for a boom. Audio tape recorders are widespread today; videotapes and discs are about to come on the market. (Even for the home-movie buff, videotaping has a number of advantages over film.) And the prices on the equipment will probably continue to decline as demand increases. Hopefully, institutions such as city recreation departments, community colleges, universities, and high schools will begin acquiring this equipment and providing training programs for those who would like to use it.

But how do we take the best of their output—and that of the more professional creative people in television—and make it available to all the American people? That is where cable television comes in—or at least cable television with a twist. Up to now, cable television has been largely conceived and utilized as an alternative means of distributing over-the-air commercial television signals. As such it is merely a part of the problem. What cable television also offers—in terms of greater profits to the cable operators as well as greater service to the customers—is an alternative approach to program distribution.

Cable-television operators could be treated like the telephone company, and required to make channels available on their systems to anyone who wants to use them for the distribution of television programs. The telephone company cannot tell you that they are temporarily out of telephones when you ask to have one installed, nor can they refuse to install one because they don't like what you talk about. The same principles, tariff agreements, and traditions could apply to the cable-television industry. The cable-television operator could post prices (of course, charging more for 8 P.M. than for 4 A.M.), and anyone who could pay the rates could get a channel. As a result, he would make money not only from the monthly fees paid by subscribers, but from the leasing charges paid by those who used his channels. Because the cost of adding additional channels to a system is minimal (a 40-channel system costs only about 10 per cent more than a 20-channel system), there is no reason why channels could not be made available free to those unable to pay for them. Some channels could be allocated free to community purposes on a permanent basis—to the local school system, the city council, police and fire training, and so forth. In fact, something like these proposals have now been adopted by the FCC.

There then would be a large number of alternative ways of funding programming. (1) There still would be programming from the networks and commercial stations. (2) There would be the programming of the Public Broadcasting System and the local public television stations. (3) Advertiser-funded programming could be provided by independent producers. (4) There could be subscription television (for which the viewer would pay an additional fee); this would be funded directly by the audience. (5) Foundations might wish to lease channels on a permanent or spot basis for projects of their own, including the showing of programs produced with their grants. (6) There would be the channels set aside for community purposes. (7) Finally, some channels would be available at no charge to citizens who were engaged in nonremunerative efforts or otherwise unable to pay for them.

This blend of new technologies—cheap videotaping equipment and unlimited-channel cable distribution systems—holds the promise for a practical flowering of the creative society. Whether it comes about will depend upon individual citizens and community-action groups seeking unlimited-channel provisions in the franchises granted by city councils to local cable-television systems, and upon regulations ultimately promulgated by the FCC and acts of Congress.

Summary and Conclusion

Television is involved, in one way or another, in virtually everything that is right and wrong with America. It has decidedly more influence on our information, politics, education, moral values, aesthetic taste, and mental health than any other institution in the history of our country. Because of its influence, and the Federal Communications Commission's responsibility to regulate broadcasting "in the public interest," it is necessary for me, an FCC Commissioner, to keep a constant watch on the possible implications of television in new developments in our society.

There is presently a considerable body of evidence—as well as personal experience—that a great many Americans are experiencing stresses and strains formerly unknown. As we examine the programming and commercials of television, we see that they are encouraging a particular life-style—one in which conspicuous consumption of mass-produced goods, rather than the growth of individuality, is held out as central to one's worth as a human being. Alternatives to that life-style get little time and attention on television— principally because they run counter to the profit motive of those who control the system. There is considerable evidence that a great many Americans are beginning to cast those standards aside, and trying to bring more humanness and creativity into their lives. Commercial television, as now structured, is the keystone of the corporate system, which makes such efforts very nearly impossible. The combination of the new, cheaper videotaping equipment and the possibility of cable-television systems that would make available as many channels as demand warranted, offers a potential solution to this problem.

There are many researchers and writers in this country who know far more psychiatry and political science than I do, and they report that we are in serious danger as a people. They predicted the social disintegration we are now experiencing some 10 or 20 years before it happened: the nervous breakdowns and mental illness, the alcoholism and drug addiction, the unwanted illegitimacy and divorce rates, the crime and the violence. They told us that these symptoms would occur because human beings have to be able to grow and develop as individuals; that they need whole lives in which love, productivity, dignity, and creativity can play a daily role. They say if people do not lead full and whole lives they will not only suffer as individuals, but will make a society that is bad for everyone else. In other words, the "quality of life" does not just mean getting the smoke out of the air. That's necessary for us as animals; pollution is as bad for cows and citrus trees as it is for people. But the "quality of life" for human beings has to do with the smog inside our minds. The same people who are putting the garbage in the air are putting the garbage in our heads.

I have hope we may have begun to evolve the tactics for talking back to our corporate state. I welcome your interest and support, for we are talking about nothing less precious than your life and mine.

PART EIGHT

Mass Communication

Experiences and Discussions

1. The five functions of mass communication listed in Avery's article can be performed by family, peers, and teachers as well as by the media. For each of these functions, determine whether mass media are the

sources of influence you rely on most frequently. What other sources of influence exist for you?

2. Assume you are a speech writer for the President of the United States. Based on your understanding of the characteristics of mass communication, outline a five-minute speech for a national broadcast. In your outline, note how the nature of the audience, of the communication experience, and of the communicator will influence the development of the speech.

3. Relate Avery's discussion of specialized audiences to Gumpert's notion of mini-comm. For each of the following media forms, list several specialized audiences and the preferred media presentations for each audience.

	Specialized Audiences	Media Preferences
Magazines	1. Body- and weight-conscious persons. 2.	*The Wrestler, Weight Watchers, Glamour*
Films	1. 2.	
Radio Programs	1. 2.	
TV Programs	1. 2.	
Newspapers	1. 2.	
Records	1. 2.	

4. There has been much controversy in the 1970s about the media's role in surveillance of and criticizing government affairs, most notably the Watergate cover-up and CIA operations. Describe the advantages and disadvantages (problems) of the media's handling of these matters. Develop a list of guidelines to facilitate unbiased, professional reporting.

5. Work with a group of your classmates to prepare arguments (pro and con) for the following media operations:
   a. reports to the public of leaked, confidential information
   b. predictions of election victories and defeats prior to determination of final results
   c. stereotyped portrayals of various ethnic and minority groups
   d. television programs for "adult and mature audiences," commonly concerned with issues of sex, violence, and drugs

6. In a discussion of perspectives on the media's impact, DeFleur writes that "the perspective which emerged and prevails today is that individ-

ual audience members encounter media messages as members of groups and that they do so with a constructed social reality which reflects their past and present social experiences.'' Compare De-Fleur's statement with Gumpert's discussion of mini-comm. In what ways do they differ? In your opinion, which of the two positions is the more accurate?

7. Use the following chart to compare the three prevailing theories of mass communication as described by DeFleur.

	Basic Premise	Attention/Perception of Message	Response to Media Messages	Specific Example
Individual differences				
Social categories				
Social relations				

8. Select a situation that requires a decision to be made. Keep a written account of the flow of ideas. Specify as accurately as possible (1) the conditions under which the decision-making process occurs, (2) the quantity of ideas presented, (3) the quality of the ideas, and (4) the role of the media and specific individuals during this process. Compare your findings with those described by DeFleur.

9. Watch television for an hour or two. As you watch, list as many examples as you can of the philosophy of life and the social mores that are evident in the programs and commercials. How would you categorize the list you have developed? Compare your impressions with those of Johnson.

10. As might be expected, Johnson's article on Big Broadcasting–Big Business–Big Television elicits cries of support and rebuttal. Identify one specific group of people and prepare a survey questionnaire. Explain Johnson's viewpoint and the alternatives he proposes. Question your sample of people as to their own opinions and preferred alternative(s). Summarize your results. How do your results compare with Johnson's suggestions? What new information have you obtained as a result of this survey?

11. How does the form of mini-comm differ from the form of mass communication? Are the two interrelated or are they distinct entities?

12. In your opinion, is mini-comm a salient concept? What function(s) does mini-comm serve? Are there indications of mini-comm in your exposure to and selection of media? Are these indications only for particular media or are they evident for all media?

13. Make three predictions about the effect of the rise of mini-comm on the individual and on society as a whole.

For Further Reading

ALTHEIDE, DAVID L. *Creating Reality: How T.V. News Distorts Events.* Beverly Hills, Calif.: Sage, 1976.
The author argues that "the organizational, practical and other mundane features of newswork promote a way of looking at events which fundamentally distorts them." The book considers TV news in general; discusses news bias, commercialism, and the roles of ratings and audiences; and uses Watergate, the Eagleton affair, and news coverage of the 1972 political conventions as concrete examples.

ATWAN, ROBERT, BARRY ORTON, and WILLIAM VESTERMAN (eds.). *American Mass Media Industries and Issues.* New York: Random House, 1978.
This anthology is the most comprehensive and up-to-date collection of readings in mass media. Each section focuses on a single communications medium (print, sound, visual) and discusses the issues— economic, political, social, and legal—that influence and are influenced by the different media. The editors incorporate scholarly, trade, and popular selections by writers such as William Rivers, Wilbur Schramm, Tom Wicker, John Dessauer, William Blankenberg, Michael Arlen, Edward J. Epstein, and Robert Sklar.

DEFLEUR, MELVIN L., and SANDRA BALL-ROCKEACH. *Theories of Mass Communication.* 3rd ed. New York: McKay, 1975.
One of the best discussions of both the theoretical and the practical issues confronting the media and affecting society. The authors discuss the media as social systems and present an overall integration of the theories of mass communication at their present stage of development. Other topics include the media and persuasion, the media and violence, mass press, motion pictures, and broadcasting.

GLESSING, ROBERT J., and WILLIAM P. WHITE (eds.). *Mass Media: The Invisible Environment Revisited,* rev. ed. Chicago: Science Research Associates, 1976.
Here is an attractive introduction to the mass media that looks at media forms (electronics, print, film, music, comics, and graffiti), media content (news, advertising, children and education, sports, and sexism), and media environments (politics, persuasion, economics, drugs, and the counterculture). The illustrations and discussion questions make this a most worthwhile book.

KATZEN, MAY. *Mass Communication: Teaching and Studies at Universities.* Paris: UNESCO Press, 1975.
Professional training and teaching in mass communication and systematic appreciation and criticism of media output are considered here. Also dealt with are a number of developments and trends in 64 countries.

KLAPPER, JOSEPH T. *The Effects of Mass Communication.* Glencoe, Ill.: Free Press, 1960.

Klapper's classic work remains on the "must" list for students of mass communication. His study focuses on two areas: (1) mass communication as an agent of persuasion, reinforcement, and change; and (2) the social effects of specific kinds of media (crime and violence, escapist media, and adult television). Each chapter also includes a discussion of theoretical considerations related to the issue.

McLUHAN, MARSHALL. *Understanding Media: The Extensions of Man.* New York: McGraw-Hill, 1964.

Although this book may take some time to assimilate, your efforts will be well rewarded. Proclaimed as "the most influential book by the most debated man of the decade," McLuhan's work discusses hot and cool media, the notion that the medium is the message, and the idea of a global village. His provocative statements about print, television, and the electronic media may be disagreed with but cannot be ignored.

RISSOVER, FREDERIC, and DAVID C. BIRCH. *Mass Media and the Popular Arts.* 2nd ed. New York: McGraw-Hill, 1977.

This collection of readings covers a number of topics of controversial interest: social protest, sexual identity, stereotypes and social images, and news slanting. The authors look at these issues as they appear in the different media: advertising, journalism, cartoons, radio, television, photography, film, and popular literature. Recommended as a good jumping-off point for your own concerns.

SCHRAMM, WILBUR, and DONALD F. ROBERTS (eds.). *The Process and Effects of Mass Communication.* Rev. ed. Urbana, Ill.: University of Illinois, 1971.

These readings provide in-depth coverage of research in mass media. Some of the topics presented are the function of media in society, the social and political effects of the media, education of children through media, and attitudes and innovations. An excellent and comprehensive collection of essential readings for students of mass communication.

WRIGHT, CHARLES R. *Mass Communication: A Sociological Perspective.* 2nd ed. New York: Random House, 1975.

If you are interested in a concise overview of mass communication, this brief paperback will provide a good starting point. In addition to the nature and functions of mass communication, Wright discusses four national systems of mass communication as well as the nature of the mass audience and the cultural content of American mass communications.

Intercultural Communication: The Cross-Setting Setting

"What a woman—oh, what a woman" cried the King of Bohemia, when we had all three read this epistle. "Did I not tell you how quick and resolute she was? Would she not have made an admirable queen? Is it not a pity she was not on my level?"

"From what I have seen of the lady, she seems, indeed, to be on a very different level to Your Majesty," said Holmes, coldly.

A Scandal in Bohemia

Cultures apart, worlds apart! How are we to communicate across such barriers? The languages, the nonverbal codes, the assumptions and goals can differ so dramatically from culture to culture that it is a mystery that persons of differing backgrounds ever manage to interact at all. Samovar and Porter outline the problems as they discuss *Communicating Interculturally,* suggesting that attitudes, thought processes, roles, languages, and behaviors all provide difficult barriers that inhibit information exchange across cultures.

But, of course, each kind of culture presents different kinds of problems. In the Holmes story quoted above, status and nationality spelled the difference between two persons. Barna examines these problems in more detail in the setting of contemporary America. Andrea Rich pursues the same questions through the nonverbal channel, following the tangled clues provided to determine whether or not any consistent nonverbal messages transcend cultural barriers.

Cultural differences involve more than nations and classes; race, ethnic background, education, and even sex have an influence upon the problems and procedures of cross-cultural communication. Cheris Kramer examines the linguistic characteristics of sex roles and the implications of so-called feminine speech. Her article utilizes a technique known as "folk-linguistics," with interesting implications for other areas of intercultural research.

It is in the area of intercultural communication that the most detective work remains to be completed, and the clues are spaced and confused. Truly, though, the pursuit is worth the price, for it can help to answer key questions about the fundamental nature of other cultures and, ultimately, about the nature of our own culture.

OBJECTIVES

After carefully reading the four articles in this section, you should be able to define the following key terms:

intercultural communication   (Samovar and Porter)
encoding
decoding
culture
ethnocentrism
cognitive
experiental

preconceptions   (Barna)
stereotypes

proximity   (Rich)
gesture

folk-linguistics   (Kramer)
mommy talk
stereotype

And:

1. Explain how each of the following affects social perceptions and inter-cultural communication: (a) attitudes, (b) social organization, (c) patterns of thought, (d) roles and role prescriptions, (e) language, (f) use of space, (g) time conceptualization, and (h) nonverbal expressions (Samovar and Porter).
2. Provide examples for each of the following: ethnocentrism, world view, and absolute values (Samovar and Porter).
3. Using examples, distinguish between stereotypes and prejudices (Samovar and Porter).
4. Using examples, distinguish between connotative and denotative meanings in intercultural settings (Samovar and Porter).
5. Describe five major stumbling blocks in intercultural communication (Barna).
6. Explain the effects of these stumbling blocks on an individual's self-perception (Barna).

7. Explain the importance of nonverbal communication in interracial situations (Rich).
8. Explain the implications of each of the following nonverbal factors or behaviors for interracial communication: (a) environment, (b) personal space, (c) territoriality, (d) clothing, (e) physical characteristics, (f) posture, (g) gestures, (h) eye contact, and (i) facial expressions (Rich).
9. Distinguish between folklore and fact in the context of "Wishy-Washy" (Kramer).
10. Describe the experimental methodologies used by Kramer to test her hypotheses (Kramer).

Thirty-One

Communicating Interculturally

Larry A. Samovar and Richard E. Porter

Two seemingly unrelated occurrences took place during the late 1960s and early 1970s. Events transpired that had profound effects on the field of communication. On one front the world, in a figurative sense, had begun to shrink; the global village prophecy was upon us. For a variety of reasons, we had improved our mobility until distances no longer mattered. A jet airplane could place us anywhere within hours. This new-found mobility was not exclusively ours; people around the world were on the move. International tradesmen, foreign students, diplomats, and especially tourists were moving in and out of an assortment of cultures—cultures that often appeared unfamiliar, alien, and at times mysterious. Close cultural contact was further underscored as the United States inaugurated communication satellites that could provide education as well as entertainment. As many as 400 million people could be taught to read at the same time. People in remote areas of countries like India could now be reached by television.

While this global phenomenon was taking place, there also was a kind of cultural revolution within our own boundaries. Domestic events forced all of us to focus our attention upon new, and often demanding, cultures and subcultures. Blacks, Chicanos, women, homosexuals, the poor, "hippies," and countless other groups became highly visible and vocal—and they disturbed many of us. Frequently, their communicative behaviors seemed strange or even bizarre and failed to meet our normal expectations.

The focus of attention on minority cultures just described made us realize not only that intercultural contact was inevitable but that it was often unsuccessful. We found, in short, that intercultural communication was difficult. Even when we overcame natural barriers of language, we could still fail to understand and be understood. These failures in both the international arena and the domestic scene gave rise to the marriage of culture and communication and to the recognition of intercultural communication as a field of study. Inherent in this fusion of academic disciplines was the idea that the study of intercultural communication entails the investigation of culture and the difficulties of communicating across cultural boundaries.

Intercultural communication occurs whenever a message producer is a member of one culture and a message receiver is a member of another. Therefore, in this essay we shall discuss intercultural communication and point out the relationships among communication, culture, and intercultural communication.

Communication

As we have already indicated, intercultural interaction occurs through the process of communication. By definition, and in practice, communication and intercultural communication are inseparable. It is impossible to talk about one without the other. It is even more obvious that we cannot share ideas and feelings cross-culturally if we do not communicate. Culture A can contact Culture B only by sending messages. In short, intercultural interaction means communication between individuals of different cultures.

Because human communication is such a vital part of intercultural interaction, we believe that an understanding of the workings of communication is paramount if one is to understand intercultural interaction. Therefore, let us define what communication is and explain how it operates.

Definitions and descriptions of communication are legendary and numerous. They run from the very general "Communication is the discriminatory response of an organism to a stimulus" (Stevens, 1950, p. 698) to the specific "Communication has as its central interest those behavioral situations in which a source transmits a message to a receiver(s) with conscious intent to affect the latter's behavior" (Miller, 1966, p. 92). There are even definitions that speak only of the verbal elements—"Communication is the verbal interchange of thought or idea" (Hoben, 1954, p. 77). It is easy to see that the term communication is indeed an enigma. Communication is an activity in which we all engage, yet it is very difficult to specify its parameters. However, for our purposes we would suggest that *communication is a dynamic process whereby human behavior, both verbal and nonverbal, is perceived and responded to.* A closer examination of this definition will enable us to see most of the specific components and ingredients of communication.

1. *Communication is a dynamic process.* It is ongoing and active, rather than static and passive. In this sense, communication has no beginning or end. There are, instead, a series of behaviors—actions, activities, and responses— taking place during an encounter. Most of these patterns are in operation before people make contact. So communication seems to be a flowing together of many interdependent functions. We are capable of seeing, hearing, thinking, talking, moving, and countless other activities all at the same time. In short, it is foolish to try to visualize communication as a "still-life" picture.

2. *Communication is symbolic behavior.* All communication entails the use of symbols of some kind. They are used to express our ideas and feelings. We cannot transfer internal notions or states directly; they must be symbolized in a code that stands for and represents our internal states. The process of producing a symbolic code is called *encoding* and is a form of human behavior. Any behavior, consciously or unconsciously produced, has the potential to function as a symbol. In fact, a symbol may be thought of as any human behavior, verbal or nonverbal, to which meaning may be attached. Simply, "one cannot not communicate" (Watzlawick, 1967, p. 48) as long as he or she

is capable of behavior and there is someone to attribute meaning to the behavior. Linguistic or verbal symbols are, of course, the most manifest coding system we employ. However, we also use nonverbal symbols to share experiences and feelings. Our clothes, actions, facial expressions, and use of time and space are just a few of the nonverbal symbolic codes we use. Whether we call on word symbols or nonverbal symbols, we are creating and using behaviors as a code to represent thought.

3. *Communication elicits a response.* Whenever we become aware of another person's verbal or nonverbal behaviors we must transform them into meaningful experience. By this we mean that the behaviors only have meaning for us in the context of our past experiences, and it is from these experiences that we derive the meaning we attach to the observed behaviors. This process of deriving meaning for symbols is called *decoding,* and it is an internal activity. Attaching meaning to someone else's symbolic behavior carries with it a corresponding effect on the behavior of the perceiver. If you see a Japanese woman and she smiles at you, you interpret her symbolic behavior (smile) as communicating something to you. Obviously, communication is taking place. But there is also communication when this same woman puts on her ceremonial tea-serving costume and you attach meaning to her attire. In both cases you perceived her behavior and responded to it by attributing meaning to her smile and to her dress. In addition, your behavior of attributing meaning may have led to additional behavior on your part—you may have returned her smile or commented on the beauty of her costume.

4. *Communication is a receiver phenomenon.* Weaving its way throughout our discussion is the idea that Person A produces a message that travels via a channel to Person B. Person B then attaches meaning to the message. No communication occurs unless we have Person B—the receiver—someone to interpret and give meaning to symbolic behavior. If someone waves a hand as if to symbolize the concept "good-bye," but you fail to see it, communication has not taken place. If, however, you see the arm movement and decide someone is leaving, communication has occurred. It matters little if the arm action was produced to swat at a bee, for it is the *receiver* who must eventually determine what the behavior symbolizes.

5. *Communication is complex.* One fact is evident from our brief analysis—human communication is not a simple matter. It is a process that calls for the simultaneous production of a number of highly intricate and interdependent activities. If communication were a linear phenomenon, with one action producing one response, the issue of complexity would not be so prevalent. Furthermore, communication is complex because it contains so many variables. Among these variables are the many aspects of human personality that each person brings to the encounter, the diverse forms that messages can take, the various channels the message can use, and the influence of the context and environment on communication.

Having briefly sketched the essential characteristics of communication, we are now ready to talk about culture and its relationship to communication.

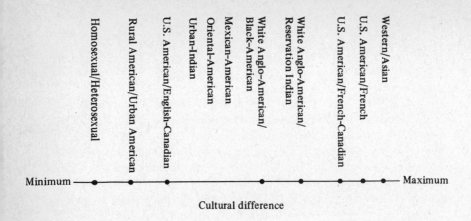

FIGURE 1 *Arrangement of compared cultures along a scale of minimum to maximum cultural difference.*

we also find the least commonality. Physical appearance, religion, philosophy, social attitudes, language, heritage, and basic conceptualizations of self and the universe are among the cultural factors that differ sharply.

An example nearer the center of the scale is the difference between American culture and French culture. Less variation is found; physical characteristics are similar, and the English language is in part derived from French and its ancestor languages. The roots of both French and American philosophy lie in ancient Greece, and most Americans and French share the Christian religion.

Examples near the minimal end of the scale are characterized in two ways. First are the variations found between members of separate but similar cultures —for instance, between U.S. Americans and Canadians. The difference is less than that found between American and French cultures but greater than that generally found within a single culture. Even in this case we are not totally accurate, because we must distinguish between English-Canadian and French-Canadian cultures (note the differences on the scale). Second, minimal differences may be seen in the variance between subgroups of the same general culture—for instance, Anglo-Americans, and Mexican-Americans residing in separate parts of the same city. Similarly, socio-cultural differences can be found between members of the John Birch Society and the Americans for Democratic Action, between mainstream middle class Americans and the urban poor or the "drug culture," and between heterosexuals and homosexuals.

In both categorizations, members of each cultural group share much more in common than in the prior examples. They probably speak the same language, share the same general religion, attend the same schools, and inhabit the same geographical area. Yet, these groups of people are culturally different; they do not share the same experiences nor do they share the same perceptions.

Culture is a communication problem because it is not constant; it is a variab
And, as cultural variance increases, so do the problems of communicatic

Culture, Communication, and Social Perception

The concept of culture presents some difficulties in the discussion of interc
tural communication. In the classic anthropological sense, culture refers to t
cumulative deposit of knowledge, experience, meanings, beliefs, values, at
tudes, religions, concepts of self, the universe, and self-universe relationshi]
hierarchies of status, role expectations, spatial relations, and time concej
acquired by a large group of people in the course of generations throu
individual and group striving. Culture manifests itself both in patterns
language and thought and in forms of activity and behavior. These patter
become models for common adaptive acts and styles of expressive behavi
which enable people to live in a society within a given geographical envirc
ment at a given state of technical development.

This definition is extremely useful when considering intercultural commu
cation as an international event, where people come from widely dive;
geographic areas separated and isolated from one another. But what about c
domestic events? We earlier pointed out that domestic events during the 196
and 1970s were partly responsible for the development of intercultural co
munication as a field of study. Obviously if there are ethnic or racial groupir.
our definition is still applicable. But how does an emerging minority such
the drug culture or the gay liberation movement meet our definition, wh
calls for the acquisition of a cumulative deposit of knowledge and other aspe
of culture over generations? Obviously it doesn't. However, there are sigr
cant minority groups within our society—within any society—whose memt
ships transcend racial and ethnic lines that nevertheless are unique enougl
be viewed as cultures, at least for the purposes of intercultural communicati
This may be stretching the tradition concept of culture a bit, but we beli
that the communication problems we must deal with can best be conside
as deriving at least in part from cultural differences, even if these differei
developed during a single generation.

Culture is extremely complex, varying along many dimensions. Any atte
to factor out the dimensions and to provide a scale for their measuremer
far beyond our purposes in this article. But, if we think of cultural differe
varying along a minimal-maximal dimension (see Figure 1), the amour
difference between two cultural groups depends on the social uniqueness o
two groups. Although this is a crude scale, it does permit us to examin
intercultural communication act and to understand the effect of cultural d
ence. To illustrate how the dimension helps us, let us look at the exampl
cultural difference positioned along the scale.

The first example is maximal—differences between Asian and Westerr
tures. Here we find the greatest number of cultural factors subject to varia

They see the world differently. Their life styles are vastly different, and their beliefs, values, and attitudes are far from being the same.

Social perception, which is the process by which we attach meaning to the social objects and events we encounter in our environment, is an extremely important aspect of any communication act. It is the means by which we assign meanings to the messages we receive. Social perception becomes even more important when we consider intercultural communication, because culture conditions and structures our perceptual processes in such a way that we develop culturally determined perceptual sets. These sets not only influence which stimuli reach our awareness, but more importantly they have a great influence on the judgmental aspect of perception—the attachment of meaning to these stimuli. It is our contention that *intercultural communication can best be understood as cultural variance in the perception of social objects and events. The barriers to communication caused by this perceptual variance can best be lowered by a knowledge and understanding of cultural factors that are subject to variance, coupled with an honest and sincere desire to communicate success-fully across cultural boundaries.*

The ultimate aim of social perception is to give us an accurate account of the social aspects of our environment. Unfortunately, this often is *not* the result, because various cultural elements prejudice the meanings we attach to social stimuli. A social object or event perceived simultaneously by members of different cultures may be and often is interpreted quite differently by each member. For example, Bagby (1957), in a study of cross-cultural perceptual predominance in binocular rivalry, found that culture influenced the outcome of the perceptual process. Matching twelve Mexican children with twelve U.S. American children, Bagby flashed a series of stereograms in which one eye was exposed to a scene of a bullfight and the other eye exposed to a scene of a baseball game. Under these conditions, Bagby found the viewers predominantly reported the scene appropriate to their culture: Mexican children tended to see the bullfight and American children tended to see the baseball game, although they were simultaneously exposed to both scenes. Even physical objects are subject to different interpretations in different cultures. For instance, the star constellation we refer to as the "Big Dipper" is often called the "Big Bear" or the "Big Plow" in parts of Northern Europe.

There are many variables in the communication process whose values are determined, at least in part, by culture. These variables have the ability to influence our perceptions and to affect the meaning we assign to communicative acts. In the following sections, we will discuss eight such variables: (1) attitudes, (2) social organization, (3) patterns of thought, (4) roles and the role prescriptions, (5) language, (6) use and organization of space, (7) time conceptualization, and (8) nonverbal expression. The isolation of these variables is somewhat arbitrary and artificial because they overlap and interact with one another. For instance, a person's concept of the universe is in part derived from his culturally influenced thinking and reasoning habits and patterns; it is also a function of his attitudes. Yet, because of the interactive effect, attitudes are a function of a person's views of the universe as well as his beliefs, values, perceptions, stereotypes, and thought patterns. Thus, although we will use the eight categories as a convenient means of division, do not assume these factors exist or exert influence in isolation. In reality, they all work with and against one another in affecting our intercultural communicative behaviors.

Attitudes

Attitudes are psychological states that predispose us to act in certain ways when we encounter various social events or objects in our environment. Not only do attitudes influence our overt behaviors, they also cause us to distort our perceptions—that is, to interpret events so they are in accord with our predispositions. We often tend, therefore, to see things as we *want* them to be rather than as they *are*. Attitudes that affect intercultural communication the most can be categorized as ethnocentrism, world view, absolute values, stereotypes, and prejudices.

Ethnocentrism

A major source of cultural variance in attitudes is *ethnocentrism,* which is a tendency to view people unconsciously by using our own group and our own customs as the standard for all judgments. We place ourselves, our racial, ethnic, or social group, at the center of the universe and rate all others accordingly. The greater their similarity to us, the nearer to us we place them; the greater the dissimilarity, the farther away they are. We place one group above another, one segment of society above another, one nation-state above another. We tend to see our own groups, our own country, our own culture as the best, as the most moral. This view also demands our first loyalty and produces a frame of reference that denies the existence of any other frame of reference. It is an absolute position that prohibits any other position from being appropriate for another culture.

Political and nationalistic ethnocentric attitudes are a chief barrier to intercultural communication. When we identify with specific political units—cities, counties, states, nations—we restrict our area of moral obligation. Our ability to accept cultural differences is affected by this restriction. When a boundary, even a state or local line, is present, our allegiance to one group restricts our ability to accept another or to view them favorably. This boundary may be something as definite as a political division or as arbitrary as a railroad track or river.

Another and sometimes more potent source of ethnocentristic attitudes is religion. Many religious denominations emphasize the rightness of their way as distinguished from that of others. Some of us even become dogmatic in our views and see anyone else as an "infidel." This type of religious fervor has led sociologist Talcott Parsons to observe:

> Ethnocentrism is accentuated by this religious dogmatism because it interferes with the understanding of other cultural groups. . . . So far as one

cultural group differs from another, it tends to be held as suspect. This dogmatism often extends beyond matters of religion to include extreme hostility to other aspects of culture (1964, p. 500).

Our problem lies in the fact that we have a carryover from religion to other aspects of culture. Not only do we sometimes feel hostility toward another culture's religion, but that hostility also affects our perception of customs, modes of dress, food, art, traditions, and racial characteristics. To give an extreme case, how can two people interact successfully if one believes the other to be guilty of deicide? Or, in a less extreme case, how can we successfully communicate interculturally if we perceive another's cultural customs as foolish if not utterly ridiculous?

Ethnocentrism has also manifested itself as a colonial attitude toward racial minorities in the United States. We have generally viewed racial minorities as less than equal; they have been viewed as second class members of society—not quite as good as the white majority—and treated as such. Historically the development of this attitude is easy to see. Blacks came to America as slaves; the Indians and Mexicans were defeated by the white man's guns; and the Orientals, although not technically slaves, were brought here to live in wretched conditions and perform menial labor. This attitude has prevailed throughout our history and has been epitomized in such slogans as "The only good Indian is a dead Indian." Today the laws have changed to some degree, but the attitudes remain. Blacks, Mexican-Americans, Indians, and Orientals are still subject to prejudice and discrimination and treated in many respects as colonized subjects.

This treatment of racial minorities is different from that accorded to emigrant ethnic minorities who were white. True, many ethnic minorities were the object of prejudice and discrimination upon their arrival. But they were able to assimilate into the general population and lose their visibility as someone different. The melting pot concept we idealize in the United States has worked for many who came to this country—as long as they were white enough and Anglo enough to be assimilated. Today many of these ethnic minorities are idealized in our folklore and, instead of being the butt of ridicule, they are looked upon with pride. How many Americans without a trace of Irish ancestry wear green on St. Patrick's day?

Yet, all ethnic minorities are not fully assimilated—especially those who attempt to maintain their ethnic identity. Especially for Jews, prejudice and discrimination still result from our ethnocentristic views. We welcome those who will become like us, but we reject those who wish to retain their own cultural heritage.

When we allow ethnocentrism to interfere with our social perception, the effectiveness of intercultural communication is reduced because we are unable to view aspects of another culture that differ from our own in an objective manner. The degree to which these attitudes reduce our communication effectiveness cannot be predicted because of the variety of circumstances under which they can be present. However, we do know that ethnocentrism is strongest in moral and religious contexts, where emotionalism may overshadow rationality and cause so much hostility that communication ceases. And, finally, at the extreme, ethnocentrism robs us of the willingness and desire to communicate interculturally.

World View

The way we view our world is a function of our culture, and it affects our social perception. As Americans, we tend to have a human-centered view. The world is a vast space in which we may carry out our desires. We build what we wish, we control nature as we can, and when we are displeased we tear it all down and start again.

In other cultures the relationship between the person and the cosmos is viewed differently. An Oriental world view is apt to be one of balanced relationships in which humans share a place with heaven and earth. Each thing that a person does has some effect on the balance of that relationship. Consequently, he must act carefully so as not to upset the balance because it is the nature of the cosmos to tend toward harmony.

Our world view gives us a perspective from which we shape and form our attitudes. As we encounter people with differing world views, our communicative behavior is hampered because we view events differently; we use frames of reference that may seem vague or obscure to others, just as theirs may seem to us. Our perceptions become clouded and our attitudes interfere with our ability to share perceptions with others.

Absolute Values

Closely related to and often derived from ethnocentrism and world view are absolute values. Or perhaps systems of absolute values lead to ethnocentrism and world view. The antecedent-consequent relationship is not really clear. Anyway, absolute values are culturally derived notions we have of right and wrong, good and bad, beautiful and ugly, true and false, positive and negative, and so on. They influence our social perception by providing us with a set of basic precepts from which we judge the behavior and beliefs of others. We take these notions to be absolute—to be "truth"—and do not or cannot realize that these "absolutes" are subject to cultural variation. An absolute value or a concept of right and wrong that is "truth" should be meaningful to us only in the relative sense of what is accepted or believed within a given culture.

In our social perception, we find that absolute value systems lead us to inaccurate judgments about social reality. What we regard as "truth," as an absolute, may be seen as sheer folly by someone from another culture. For example, in the American culture it is generally held that one can attain salvation only through the acceptance of Christ. But to a Jew, Moslem, Shintoist, Hindu, Taoist, or Buddhist, this notion may seem foolish. Because of absolute values, we can find ourselves in situations where we oppose someone else because of our conviction that he sees reality in a completely mistaken way. If we hold to the absoluteness of our position, we find ourselves where compromise is impossible; we *know* the "truth" and to yield would be a confession that we really do not. Admitting that we do not know is probably the most difficult confession for us to make. Because of the religious and moral context found in most absolute values, we can be emotionally involved to such a degree that our behavior becomes totally irrational, reducing our communicative capacities.

Stereotypes and Prejudices

Stereotypes are attitudinal sets in which we assign attributes to another person solely on the basis of the class or category to which that person belongs. Stereotyping might lead us to believe, for example, that all Irish are quick-tempered and red-headed; that all Japanese are short, buck-toothed, and sly; that all Jews are shrewd and grasping; or that all Blacks are superstitious and lazy. Although these generalizations are commonly held stereotypes, they are untrue! Prejudices, on the other hand, are attitudinal sets that predispose us to behave in certain ways toward people solely on the basis of their membership in some group. For example, because a person is an Oriental, a Jew, or a Black, he may be denied membership in a country club, be forced to live in a ghetto or barrio, or be restricted to low-paying jobs and the performance of menial tasks. Stereotypes and prejudices are closely related.

An example of the effect stereotypes and prejudices can have on perceptual judgments was reported by Lambert (1960). Lambert and his associates had five bilinguals speak to English-Canadian test subjects in both French and English. When asked to judge personality traits of ten speakers (the five bilinguals) heard over a telephone, test subjects judged the English speakers more favorably than the French. In a parallel study, Lambert and his associates (1966) found, on the basis of speech patterns, language, and dialect, that English-Canadians rated French-Canadians unfavorably in a number of personality traits including ambition, self-confidence, religiousness, intelligence, dependability, likeability, and character. In these examples, English-Canadians held stereotypes of French-Canadians that led them to behave in a prejudicial manner toward stimuli identified as being French-Canadian. What this tells us is that we are likely to make social judgments about others based not on their true attributes but on stereotype attributes we assign to them on the basis of such insufficient evidence as the sound of their voice.

Prejudice and stereotype effects on social perceptions are further illustrated by Secord and Backman:

> A prejudiced person perceives selectively certain aspects of the behavior of the Negro: those that fit in with his preconceived ideas concerning the Negro. Thus he observes and notes behavior incidents that demonstrate stupidity, laziness, irresponsibility, or superstition; he overlooks other incidents that might contradict his prevailing ideas. The behavior of the Negro as he observes it thus supports his prejudicial beliefs (1964, p. 15).

Stereotypes and prejudices work in various ways to affect our communication. By predisposing us to behave in specific ways when confronted by a particular stimulus and by causing us to attach generalized attributes to people whom we encounter, we allow stereotypes and prejudices to interfere with our communicative experiences and to limit their effectiveness. We spend our time looking for whatever reinforces our prejudices and stereotypes and ignore what is contradictory.

Social Organization

The societal composition of cultures can also affect our perception. Flack (1966) has described two societal compositions related to the perception and communication processes. The first is based on *geographic* societies and is composed of members of a nation, nationality, tribe, cast, or religious sect. The second, based on *role* societies, acts within or transcends geographic cultures; it is composed of members of a profession, elite or ideological, racial, or religious confraternity.

This concept is especially useful in relating to such diverse cultural groups as Russian wheat farmers or gay liberationists. In the first instance, the Russian farmer is a member of a geographic society. The gay liberationist, however, belongs to a role society and may be found in many geographic locales —even perhaps among Russian wheat farmers. Most international intercultural communication is based upon cultural differences in geographic societies while domestic intercultural communication is usually more a matter of cultural differences in role societies. This is especially true when we consider such culturally diverse groups as the gay community, the drug culture, youth, the urban poor, women's rights advocates, and pimps. Domestically, there also exists what we might call a hybrid form that relies on both geographic and role differences. Racial and ethnic minorities who are limited in geographic location by ghetto, barrio, or reservation may in part reflect a cultural difference resulting from geographic separation. They also are partly influenced by role differences.

These cultures have different effects on their members. In the geographic culture, people tend to live and feel a "common way of life" and to perceive relatively similar contexts, meanings, and motives. In the role culture, people share common definitions of situations and perceive intra- and intersocietal functions, codes of procedure, and specialized contexts, meanings, and motives in relatively similar terms.

Based on these two types of cultures, Flack (1966) has divided communication into two types: *cognitive* and *experiential.* Cognitive communication deals with things we know about; and it is possible between members of both geographic and role cultures. In contrast, experiential communication, which occurs when knowledge inheres in feeling, occurs only between members of geographic cultures. Basically, intercultural communication is dependent upon the ability to share social perceptions. As perceptions vary culturally, the experiential level of communication diminishes. For example, what are the circumstances when both a Mexican and a North American view the film *Viva Zapata?* If both are members of the same role culture, such as professional motion picture producer, they could communicate intraculturally about the technical and artistic aspects of producing the film. But, were the subject to leave the cognitive level and focus on the character of Zapata the man, the differences in experience could make communication difficult. To many North Americans, Zapata is remembered as a ruthless bandit, but to many Mexicans he is a national hero. These experiential differences place our communicators in different experiential cultures, and now we have a form of intercultural communication.

Hayakawa (1958) has divided the development of human cooperation and communication into three organizational stages: societies organized around physical symbols, around "master" verbal symbols, or around shared perceptions. The first is typified by the pyramids of Egypt and Mexico, Indian burial mounds, and various shrines, churches, and temples. The second is represented by master symbols held in respect by groups—for example, the secret world of a fraternity or a greeting such as "Allah is Great." In societies built around master symbols, agreement reached at the highest levels of abstraction— "God," "Divine Right of Monarchs," and so on—provides the basis for agreement at lower levels of abstraction. The third level of organization transcends local or regional loyalties. In these societies, the agreement process is opposite to that of the second stage; here agreement is first reached at the lowest levels of abstraction and then the sharing of perceptions proceeds step-by-step to higher levels. Unfortunately, religious notions do not lend themselves to being shared perceptions at low levels of abstraction. "Allah is Great" or "Christ is my Savior" are perceptions shared by millions, but they are such high-level abstractions that they function as master symbols. Hayakawa's (1958) notion of shared perceptions at low levels of abstraction proceeding step-by-step to higher levels of abstraction is best illustrated mathematically: $1 + 1 = 2$, $2(a + b) = 2a + 2b$, $ax^2 + bx + c = 0$,

$$x = \frac{-b \pm \sqrt{b^2 + 4ac}}{2a}$$

and so on. Each mathematical step is agreed upon and serves as the basis for the next, which is more complex and abstract.

Hayakawa (1958) suggests that when there is too much social organization around master symbols, the sharing of perceptions cross-culturally is difficult if not impossible. For instance, the history and current events of the Near East reflect what happens when the master symbol "Allah is Great" is answered by the master symbol "Christ is my Savior."

Another effect of cultural variance in social organization is seen in the ways by which legal systems are administered. Hall (1959, pp. 81–82) has cited an example of this cultural difference as it existed in a small Western U.S. town. The town was predominantly Mexican-American in population and government with the Latin culture prevailing. A 15-mph speed limit was rigidly enforced by a Mexican-American motorcycle policeman. Acting on the letter of the law, he would arrest people for driving 16 mph. Mexican-Americans brought before the court usually had a cousin or an uncle sitting on the bench and were quickly acquitted. Anglos were rarely that lucky and usually had to pay a fine. Unhappy with their treatment, the Anglos led the policeman out of town at a high rate of speed and ran him off the road. His legs were severely broken, and he could no longer ride a motorcyle as a result of his injuries.

At the heart of the matter was the different view each culture took of law, government, and family. Law in Mexico and Latin America tends to be enforced technically, or by the book, but it is mediated by the family. U.S. law tends to be enforced in accordance with the formal systems of the culture. North American law is not expected to be stricter than the rest of the culture. When the North American considers a law unjust, he is more likely to violate it than when he considers it to be realistic and sensible.

These approaches to law enforcement are differences in the way both cultures organize themselves for the enforcement and administration of their legal systems. Although it might be argued that the foregoing incident was merely one group of people disliking their treatment at the hands of another and seeking revenge, it also seems obvious that no successful intercultural communication was achieved. Both groups looked at the situation and perceived it in accordance with their culturally derived perceptual sets. The Anglos could see it as strange and unfair. The Latins perceived it as normal and quite possibly could not understand the Anglos' dislike of the procedure. Because there was an almost total lack of shared perceptions, however, these groups had little or no understanding of one another.

Patterns of Thought

The form of reasoning prevalent in a society is another aspect of culture that influences social perception. Pribram has suggested:

> Mutual understanding and peaceful relations among the peoples of the earth have been impeded not only by the multiplicity of languages but to an even greater degree by differences in patterns of thought—that is, by differences in the methods adopted for defining the sources of knowledge, and for organizing coherent thinking. . . . the most striking differences among philosophical doctrines are attributable to deepseated divergencies in the methods of forming fundamental concepts and of defining the functions of Reason—that is, the cognitive power of the human mind and the extent and validity of that power (1949, p. 1).

In analyzing Western thought, Pribram found the Western mind to be capable of arriving directly at insight into the order of the universe. But, as he points out, societies have arrived at vastly different concepts of the order of the universe and of the methods to be employed in comprehending the laws underlying that order.

Oliver (1962, pp. 77–78) has suggested that a major difficulty in intercultural communication is the differences between Aristotelian modes of reasoning prevalent in Western cultures and the non-Aristotelian systems of the Orient.

The Aristotelian system was developed by men presumed to be free and having the right to cast ballots; it views man as a rational being available to factual and sound reasoning.

But Western assumptions are not universal. There are many modes of thinking, many standards of value, many ways in which people conceive of their relationship to the universe. In the Taoist view, humans are not rational beings, nor is truth to be conceived in terms of reason and logic. Taoist philosophy states that human life is conditioned and unfree and only when a person recognizes this limitation and makes himself dependent upon the harmonious and beneficent forces of the cosmos does he achieve success. Tao holds that truth is most likely to emerge when we wait for it, when we accept it as it comes rather than setting forth along a preconceived path in a predetermined manner to define a preconceived truth.

The extent of variance that may be found among cultural patterns of reasoning may be found by contrasting Western Aristotelian and Oriental Taoist modes of reasoning. Tao teaches the wisdom of being foolish, the success of failure, the strength of weakness, and the futility of contending for power—all of which might be seen as irrational by the traditional Western mind. The Taoist, whose basic philosophy is based upon the need to achieve harmony with the cosmos, observes nature in order to achieve this relationship. Instead of perceiving the concept of strength-in-weakness as an irrational attempt to be both A and not-A simultaneously, the Taoist sees a rational relationship because he has observed such in nature. A tree limb that is strong and does not bend eventually breaks under the increasing weight of winter snow, but the weak limb—the one that is limber and bends—gives way to the weight of the snow and lets it fall to the ground before enough can accumulate to break the limb. Weakness is perceived as strength; strength is seen as weakness. In Tao, this is rational.

To improve our intercultural communication abilities, we must determine what effect differences in reasoning patterns have on communicative behavior. If, for example, a Taoist does not actively search for truth but is content to wait for it to appear, his passiveness could present a difficult problem to those of us who have been influenced by Western tradition to seek the truth. To search for truth when it must be waited for most certainly could be perceived as foolish or improper behavior by a Taoist, and to quietly wait for truth when it must actively be sought would quite probably exasperate the Western mind.

Roles and Role Prescriptions

Roles are important in intercultural communication because role expectations or prescriptions vary culturally. If we encounter members of other cultures and their behavior seems strange to us, it could very well be a matter of different role prescriptions. And, although we might want to argue the value of such prescriptions, we must realize—if we are to succeed in our task of communication—that, for members of the culture with which we are in contact, their behaviors are completely natural, normal, and *moral.*

A good example of cultural difference in role prescriptions and the effect it had on intercultural communication comes from England during World War II. British women saw American servicemen stationed in England as immoral and lustful. Simultaneously, American servicemen found English girls to be wanton and without morals. Yet neither of these was the general case. Cultural differences in the role of moderating sex behavior caused social misperceptions. In America, this responsibility is prescribed for the female role; in England, the responsibility was a male role behavior. Thus, American servicemen, used to being told "no" by American women, suddenly found themselves dating English women who had not learned to say "no." And English women, used to men not making advances unless they were seriously intended, found themselves dating Americans who were used to making sexual advances until told to stop.

Another example of how the values associated with roles vary and lead to conflict and lack of successful communication may be seen domestically in the case of so-called victimless crime. One segment of society fulfills the role of society protector and has a value system that *holds* such things as nude sunbathing, homosexual acts, getting stoned, buying sex, or viewing "pornographic" matter as absolutely evil and not to be permitted under any circumstance. On the other hand, those who fulfill the roles of nude sunbather, homosexual, pot smoker, pimp or prostitute, and explicit sex film producer or viewer hold a vastly different set of values. Their values allow these acts and hold that they are not evil but are the exercise of free choice by mature people in a free society. The values held by these various role groups often conflict and may lead to ineffective communication or even violent interaction. At the very least, one value system will be attempting to prevent the other from existing or at least being visible.

These examples have shown how cultural variance in role prescriptions can cause confusion and misunderstanding. When we assume that the rest of the world should and does share the same role behaviors as we, our ability to communicate will be reduced sharply. Again, although we might want to argue the value of a particular role prescription, we must remember that what seems strange and perhaps wrong to us is completely natural and normal for others. And, our customs and behaviors probably seem just as strange to others.

Language

We obviously are aware that there are language differences between cultural groups. But many of us naively believe that a competent interpreter is all that is necessary for people of different cultures to communicate. This notion fails to acknowledge the relationship between culture and language. To a very great extent our language is a product of our culture. At the same time, our culture is very much a product of our language. Culture and language are inseparably intertwined. What we think about and how we think about it are direct functions of our language; and what we think about and how we think about it in part determine the nature of our culture.

A major problem found in language differences is the part words play in the perception process. Since judgment and attachment of meaning are a part of perception, the ultimate meaning associated with a word is culturally determined. Even within our "American culture," there are groups that share perceptions not shared by others. For instance, if we ask a Christian Scientist, a pharmacist, and an addict what the word "drug" means, we would expect and most likely receive quite different responses. These different responses result from the dissimilar perceptions each person has of drugs. A Christian Scientist, a pharmacist, and an addict each have a unique set of experiences with drugs. These experiences influence their perception and thus affect the meaning they attach to the word "drug." The background of experience provides the connotative meanings for the symbol "drug."

When we communicate interculturally, we are likely to encounter problems where cultural differences in word *connotations* affect our ability to communicate. And many times these difficulties are likely to turn up when least expected. Let's take, for instance, the word "ancestor," a word that seems neutral enough not to cause meaning problems. Yet, look at these cultural differences: North Americans tend to perceive ancestors as distant relatives of foreign origin; Colombians tend to see them in terms of national and family history; and Koreans look upon ancestors as mythical persons of supernatural character with nearly divine status.

Another language problem is cultural differences in *denotative meanings.* In America, we think of all cars as automobiles, whereas in certain parts of the Arab world only the Cadillac is considered an automobile. This fact might not seem too important, but consider the ramifications of offering someone from that culture the use of your automobile. If you owned a Cadillac, there would be no problem; if your "automobile" turned out to be a psychedelically painted van, some obvious problems might arise.

Language also provides us with another important problem. Because the meanings we assign to words are in part the result of our cultural experiences, we often lack applicable experiences in encountering foreign words. This is why some words and phrases do not lend themselves to direct translation; or if directly translated, we fail to experience them as we do the same words in our own language. The term "My God" evokes much more of an emotional response from us than the comparable Spanish *¡Dios Mios!*

Use and Organization of Space

The way people use and organize space is another cultural variable we must consider. Cultures often attach different meanings to the same or similar interpersonal distances. We unconsciously structure space as a function of our culture, and it often serves as a nonverbal means of communication. Hall has observed:

> Space communicates in very much the same ways as the tone of voice. It can be, like language, formal or informal, warm or cold, public or private, masculine or feminine, and indicative of high or low stature (1960, p. 41–42).

The manner in which a culture views space is manifest throughout its society. For instance, in the United States we live in close relationships with one another; we borrow things, share rides to work, provide social activities, and serve as sources of help in emergencies. Other cultures are often different. The Latin American culture tends to build houses around patios, which are hidden from outsiders behind walls. About this Hall has commented:

> It is not easy to describe the degree to which small architectural differences such as this affect the outsiders. American Point Four technicians living in Latin America used to complain that they felt "left out" of things, that they were "shut off." Others kept wondering what was going on "behind those walls" (1959, p. 99).

The effect of space on communication, both intra- and interculturally, is only beginning to become known. Sommer (1962) has found that North Americans seated in a large room find the most comfortable conversation distance to be about five and one-half feet and that they show a preference to be seated face-to-face rather than side-by-side. He has also hypothesized that the distance for comfortable conversation varies as an inverse function of the size of the room. As the room becomes larger, the distance for comfortable conversation becomes smaller. Hall (1966, pp. 144–153) has described how interpersonal distances vary culturally, with vast differences existing for the Arab and Latin American compared to the North American. In the United States, we tend to keep a greater distance between ourselves when engaged in face-to-face interpersonal communication; Arabs and Latins tend to stand closer. In our culture physical contact tends to be reserved for intimate events, whereas other cultures do not make this reservation.

Cultures develop appropriate distances for people engaged in conversation, depending on the purpose and nature of the message. A culturally influenced zone of personal space surrounds each individual. People are allowed to enter this space only for the most intimate forms of interaction. When personal space is violated, we usually experience feelings of intrusion, overbearing, and dominance, often with negative sexual connotations. Depending on the social relationships involved, the intruder may be perceived as pushy, overbearing, disrespectful, sexually aggressive, homosexual, or even a boor. Though the result of ignorance, such intrusions can disrupt interaction.

Time Conceptualization

An American agriculturalist, recently arrived on assignment in a Latin American country, had this experience:

> After what seemed to him a suitable period he let it be known that he would like to call on the minister who was his counterpart. For various reasons, the suggested time was not suitable; all sorts of cues came back to the effect that the time was not yet ripe to visit the minister. Our friend, however, persisted and forced an appointment which was reluctantly

granted. Arriving a little before the hour (the American respect pattern), he waited . . . five minutes—ten minutes—fifteen minutes . . . forty-five minutes (the insult period)! He jumped up and told the secretary that he had been "cooling his heels"in an outer office for forty-five minutes and he was "damned sick and tired" of this type of treatment. The message was relayed to the minister, who said, in effect, "Let him cool his heels." The attaché's stay in the country was not a happy one (Hall, 1959, p. 18).

The difficulty between the attaché and the minister resulted from differences in the way the North American and the Latin cultures conceive of time. Not only were there misperceptions about the appropriate "time" to call on the minister, but there were gross misperceptions about waiting patterns. The North American's concept caused him to perceive the 45-minute delay as an insult; in the Latin concept, 45 minutes, instead of being at the end of the waiting scale, was just barely at the beginning. The minister's manner of handling time caused him to perceive the visitor's protestation to be as absurd as if the visitor had raised a storm about cooling his heels after five minutes of North American time.

The manner in which time is conceptualized is another cultural variable. Western cultures tend to conceptualize time in *lineal-spatial* terms, meaning that we are aware of a past, a present, and a future. Time is something we can manipulate, something we can save, waste, make up, or spend. We place a strong emphasis on time as an aspect of history rather than as an aspect of immediate experience. We treat the present as a way-station, an intermediate point between past and future, and an immersion in the present is considered by some of us to be paganistic.

Unlike us, others are more concerned with immediacy or what is called *felt time*. Japanese Zen treats time like a limitless pool in which events occur, cause ripples, and then subside. There is no past, no present, no future—only the event in the absolute present. The Navajo concept of time assigns reality only to the immediate; thoughts of the future are not worth much consideration. The Sioux Indian presents an even greater problem; that language does not contain words for time, late, or waiting.

As time conceptualizations vary culturally, so will the norms concerning time sequences in communication. Moore states:

> Communication effectiveness may be influenced or affected by the speed of response. The fast talker may be regarded as foolish or with suspicion. The response that comes "too fast" may cause doubt about the consideration given to the stimulus, and the response that is "too slow" may raise doubt about the quality of the reception or the receiver's interest in the message (1963, pp. 49–50).

The problem for us is to know what the appropriate speed of response is in intercultural communication situations. Culture determines when a response is too fast or too slow, when a person talks too fast or too slowly. As the complexity of these cultural norms increases, our perceptual problems increase, and errors or failure may occur in the interpretation we make of messages we receive from persons in other cultures.

Nonverbal Expression

It is a common experience among people who travel to find that it is difficult to interpret the facial expressions of peoples of cultures other than their own. This difficulty has frequently been voiced with reference to Oriental people whose modes of expression are found to differ from those of Caucasians (Vinacke, 1949, p. 407).

Another cultural variable that affects the social perception process is nonverbal expression. Culture determines the form nonverbal messages take as well as the circumstances calling for their expression and the amount of expression permitted. Klineberg has pointed out:

We find that cultures differ widely from one another in the amount of emotional expression which is permitted. We speak, for example, of the imperturbability of the American Indian, the inscrutability of the Oriental, the reserve of the Englishman, and at the other extreme of the expressiveness of the Negro or the Sicilian. Although there is always some exaggeration in such clichés, it is probable that they do correspond to an accepted cultural pattern, at least to some degree (1954, p. 174).

The Japanese smile is a law of etiquette that has been elaborated and culturated from early times; and it is not necessarily a spontaneous expression of amusement. This smile is a silent language that is often inexplicable to Westerners. The Japanese child is taught to smile as a social duty so that he will always show an appearance of happiness and avoid inflicting sorrow upon his friends.

The problem as it affects social perception can be seen in the following anecdote. A Japanese woman servant smilingly asked her Western mistress if she might go to her husband's funeral. Later she returned with his ashes in a vase, and actually laughing said, "Here is my husband." Her mistress regarded her as a cynical creature, although her smile and laughter may have been reflecting pure heroism.

The amount of emotional expression permitted by a culture also varies according to the emotion involved.

The Chinese, who feel that a display of anger is never warranted and that affection should be shown only in privacy, insist upon a public manifestation of grief or sorrow. . . . Not only is grief expressed, but there is an elaborate set of rules and regulations which ensure that it will be properly expressed. One of the Chinese classics is the *Book of Rites,* a considerable portion of which is devoted to the technique of the mourning ceremonial, with elaborate instructions as to just what procedure should be followed in order that the expression of the grief may be socially acceptable. The Plains Indians, in spite of their deserved reputation for imperturbability, expected a man literally to wail and howl for hours at a stretch at the death of his wife or child. . . . It is clear that the repressive influence of a culture with regard to emotional behavior is not applied equally in all directions. It is perhaps unnecessary to add that the absence of the manifestation of an emotion does not prove that it is not experienced. It merely prevents our direct knowledge of its existence (Klineberg, 1954, pp. 177–178).

Even in what may be considered a more basic form of expression—the nonverbal expression of what we call verbal expressions, there are cultural variations. In our culture, the verbal statement "no" is often expressed nonverbally by moving the head from side to side. Yet an Abyssinian is apt to express "no" by jerking the head to the right shoulder; a Dyand of Borneo may express it by contracting the eyebrows slightly; and Sicilians express "no" by raising the head and chin. Among the Ainu of northern Japan our particular head noddings are unknown; "no" is expressed by a movement of the right hand and affirmation by a simultaneous movement of both hands.

The importance of the nonverbal aspect of communication cannot be overlooked. We rely on nonverbal cues to help interpret verbal cues. When we detect incongruencies between the verbal and nonverbal, we tend to assign greater credibility to the nonverbal. This may be all right within a culture where perhaps we know what the cues mean. But when we encounter new or different cues, we are unable to interpret them correctly. In fact, we may assign totally wrong meanings to nonverbal cues and react to them as if they implied what we take them to mean. Remember the Japanese woman who "laughingly" displayed her dead husband's ashes. The *judgment* of "laughingly" is purely from our culture. To another Japanese, the smile and appearance of "joy" might have been perceived as a sign of bravery under trying emotional circumstances and probably would have evoked an interpretation of respect and admiration as well as sympathy.

There is much for us to learn about how people from other cultures use nonverbal cues to express themselves. Until we gain this knowledge we are going to encounter trouble whenever we interact with people from other cultures. Nonverbal aspects of intercultural communication are probably among the most difficult because of the reliance we place on the interpretation of nonverbal cues in decoding verbal cues.

Summary

Here we have suggested that the chief problem associated with intercultural communication is error in social perception brought about by cultural variations that affect the perceptual process. The attribution of meaning to messages is in many respects influenced by the culture of the message decoder. When the message being interpreted was encoded in another culture, the cultural influences and experiences that produced that message may be entirely different from the cultural influences and experiences that are being drawn upon to decode the message. Consequently, grave errors in meaning may arise that are not intended nor really the fault of the communicators. They are the result of entirely different backgrounds being unable to accurately understand one another.

The approach we have taken is also based upon a fundamental assumption: The parties to intercultural communication must have an honest and sincere desire to communicate and seek mutual understanding. This assumption, therefore, requires favorable attitudes on the part of intercultural communicators and an elimination of superior-inferior relationships based upon membership in particular cultures. Unless this basic assumption has been satisfied, our theory of cultural variance in social perception will not produce improvement in intercultural communication.

We have discussed eight cultural variables that are major sources of communication difficulty: attitudes, social organization, patterns of thought, roles and role expectations, language, space, time, and nonverbal expression. Although they were discussed in isolation, we cannot allow ourselves to conclude they are unrelated. They are all related in a matrix of cultural complexities.

For there to be successful intercultural communication, we must be aware of the cultural factors affecting communication in both our own culture and the culture of the other party. We need to understand not only cultural differences but also cultural similarities. While understanding differences will help us know where problems lie, understanding similarities may help us be closer.

This discussion is only an introduction to the arena of intercultural communication. The variables discussed here have merely been highlighted, and not all of the relevant variables have been mentioned. One reason is the obvious lack of space. Another is that our knowledge of the effect of culture on communication is woefully inadequate.

REFERENCES

BAGBY, J.W., "A Cross-Cultural Study of Perceptual Predominance in Binocular Rivalry," *Journal of Abnormal and Social Psychology,* 54 (1957), 331–334.

FLACK, M. J., "Communicable and Uncommunicable Aspects in Personal International Relations," *Journal of Communication,* 16 (1966), 283–290.

HALL, E. T., *The Silent Language,* Greenwich, Conn., 1959.

HALL, E. T., "Language of Space," *Landscape,* 10 (1960), 41–42.

HALL, E. T., *The Hidden Dimension,* Garden City, N.Y., 1966.

HAYAKAWA, S. I., "Communication and the Human Community," *ETC.,* 60 (1958), 5–11.

HOBEN, J. B., "English Communication at Colgate Re-Examined," *Journal of Communication,* 4 (1954), 77.

KLINEBERG, O., *Social Psychology,* rev. ed., New York, 1954.

LAMBERT, W. E., et al., "Evaluation Reactions to Spoken Languages," *Journal of Abnormal and Social Psychology,* 60 (1960), 44–51.

LAMBERT, W. E., et al., "Judging Personality Traits through Speech: A French-Canadian Example," *Journal of Communication,* 16 (1966), 305–321.

MILLER, G. A., "On Defining Communication: Another Stab," *Journal of Communication,* 16 (1966), 92.

MOORE, W. E., *Man, Time, and Society,* New York, 1963.

OLIVER, R. T., *Culture and Communication,* Springfield, Ill., 1962.

PARSONS, T., "Intercultural Understanding and Academic Social Science," in *Approaches to Group Understanding,* ed. L. Bryson, L. Finkelstein, and R. M. MacIver, New York, 1964.

PRIBRAM, K., *Conflicting Patterns of Thought,* Washington, D.C., 1949.

SECORD, P. F., and C. W. BACKMAN, *Social Psychology,* New York, 1964.

SOMMER, R., "The Distance for Comfortable Conversation," *Sociometry,* 25 (1962), 111–116.

STEVENS, S. S., "A Definition of Communication," *Journal of the Acoustical Society of America,* 22 (1950), 698.

VINACKE, E. W., "The Judgment of Facial Expressions by Three National-Racial Groups in Hawaii: I, Caucasian Faces," *Journal of Personality,* 17 (1949), 407–429.

WATZLAWICK, P., J. BEAVIN, and D. JACKSON, *The Pragmatics of Human Communication,* New York, 1967.

Thirty-Two

Intercultural Communication Stumbling Blocks

LaRay M. Barna

There are many viewpoints regarding the practice of intercultural communication but a familiar one is that "people are people," basically pretty much alike; therefore increased interaction through travel, student exchange programs, and other such ventures should result in more understanding and friendship between nations. Others take a quite different view, particularly those who have done research in the field of speech communication and are fully aware of the complexities of interpersonal interaction, even *within* cultural groups. They do not equate contact with communication, do not believe that the simple experience of talking with someone insures a successful transfer of meanings and feelings. Even the basic commonalities of birth, hunger, family, death are perceived and treated in vastly different ways by persons with different backgrounds.[1] If there *is* a universal, it might be that each has been so subconsciously influenced by his own cultural upbringing that he assumes that the needs, desires, and basic assumptions of others are identical to his own.[2]

It takes a long time of noninsulated living in a new culture before a foreigner can relax into new perceptions and nonevaluative thinking so that he can adjust his reactions and interpretations to fit what's happening around him. The few who achieve complete insight and acceptance are outstanding by their rarity. After nine years of monitoring dyads and small group discussions between U.S. and international students, this author, for one, is inclined to agree with Charles Frankel, who says: "tensions exist within nations and between nations that never would have existed were these nations not in such intense cultural communication with one another."[3] The following typical reactions of three foreign students to one nonverbal behavior that most Americans expect to bridge gaps—the smile—may serve as an illustration:

> Japanese student: On my way to and from school I have received a smile by nonacquaintance American girls several times. I have learned they have no interest for me; it means only a kind of greeting to a foreigner. But if someone smiles at a stranger in Japan, especially a girl, she can assume he is either a sexual maniac or an impolite person.

> Korean student: An American visited me in my country for one week. His inference was that people in Korea are not very friendly because they didn't smile or want to talk with foreign people. That's true because most Korean people take time to get to be friendly with people. We never talk or smile at strangers.

> Vietnamese student: The reason why certain foreigners may think that Americans are superficial—and they are, some Americans even recognize this—is that they talk and smile too much. For people who come from placid cultures where nonverbal language is more used, and where a silence, a smile, a glance have their own meaning, it is true that Americans speak a lot. The superficiality of Americans can also be detected in their relations with others. Their friendships are, most of the time, so ephemeral compared to the friendships we have at home. Americans make friends very easily and leave their friends almost as quickly, while in my country it takes a long time to find out a possible friend and then she becomes your friend—with a very strong sense of the term. Most Americans are materialistic and once they are provided with necessities, they don't feel the need to have a friend. Purposes of their friendships are too clear, and you can hardly find a friendship for friendship's sake.

An American girl in the same class gives her view:

> In general it seems to me that foreign people are not necessarily snobs but are very unfriendly. Some class members have told me that you shouldn't smile at others while passing them by on the street. To me I can't stop

smiling. It's just natural to be smiling and friendly. I can see now why so many foreign people stick together. They are impossible to get to know. It's like the Americans are big bad wolves. How do Americans break this barrier? I want friends from all over the world but how do you start to be friends without offending them or scaring them off—like sheep?[4]

One reason for the long delay in tackling the widespread failure to achieve understanding across cultures might be that it is not readily apparent when there has been miscommunication at the interpersonal level. Unless there is overt reporting of assumptions such as in the examples above, which seldom happens in normal settings, there is no chance for comparing impressions. The foreign visitor to the United States nods, smiles, and gives affirmative comments, which the straightforward, friendly American confidently translates as meaning that he has informed, helped, and pleased the newcomer. It is likely, however, that the foreigner actually understood very little of the verbal and nonverbal content and was merely indicating polite interest or trying not to embarrass himself or his host with verbalized questions. The conversation may even have confirmed his stereotype that Americans are insensitive and ethnocentric.

In a university classroom U.S. students often complain that the international members of a discussion or project seem uncooperative or uninterested. The following is a typical statement from the international's point of view:

I had difficulty with the opinion in the class where peoples in group dicuss about subject. I was surrounded by Americans with whom I couldn't follow their tempo of discussion half of the time. I have difficulty to listen and speak, but also with the way they handle the group. I felt uncomfortable because sometimes they believe their opinion strongly. I had been very serious about the whole subject but I was afraid I would say something wrong. I had the idea but not the words.[5]

Typically, the method used to improve chances for successful intercultural communication is to gather information about the customs of the other country and a smattering of the language. The behaviors and attitudes are sometimes researched, but almost always from a secondhand source. The information is seldom sufficient and may or may not be helpful. Knowing "what to expect" too often blinds the observer to all but what is confirmatory to his image or preconception. Any contradictory evidence that does filter through is likely to be treated as an exception.[6]

A better approach is to study the history, political structure, art, literature, and language of the country if time permits. But more important, one should develop an investigative nonjudgmental attitude and high tolerance for ambiguity—which means lowered defenses. Margaret Mead suggests sensitizing persons to the kinds of things that need to be taken into account instead of developing behavior and attitude stereotypes, mainly because of the individual differences in each encounter and the rapid changes that occur in a culture pattern.[7] Edward Stewart concurs with this view.[8]

One way to reach an improved state of awareness and sensitivity to what might go wrong is to examine five variables in the communication process that seem to be major stumbling blocks when the dyad or small group is cross-cultural. The first is so obvious it hardly needs mentioning—*language*. Vocabulary, syntax, idioms, slang, dialects, and so on all cause difficulty, but the person struggling with a different language is at least aware when he's in this kind of trouble. A worse language problem is the tenacity with which someone will cling to "the" meaning of a word or phrase in the new language once he has grasped one, regardless of connotation or context. The infinite variations, especially of English, are so impossible to cope with that they are waved aside. The reason the problem is "worse" is because each thinks he understands. The nationwide misinterpretation of Khruschev's sentence "We'll bury you" is a classic example. Even "yes" and "no" cause trouble. When a Japanese hears, "Won't you have some tea?" he listens to the literal meaning of the sentence and answers, "No," meaning that he wants some. "Yes, I won't" would be a better reply because this tips off the hostess that there may be a misunderstanding. In some cultures, also, it is polite to refuse the first or second offer of refreshment. Many foreign guests have gone hungry because their U.S. hostess never presented the third offer.

Learning the language, which most foreign visitors consider their *only* barrier to understanding, is actually only the beginning. As Frankel says, "To enter into a culture is to be able to hear, in Lionel Trilling's phrase, its special 'hum and buzz of implication.' "[9] This brings in *nonverbal areas* and the second stumbling block. People from different cultures inhabit different nonverbal sensory worlds. Each sees, hears, feels, and smells only that which has some meaning or importance for him. He abstracts whatever fits into his personal world of recognitions and then interprets it through the frame of reference of his own culture.

An Oregon girl in an intercultural communication class asked a young man from Saudi Arabia how he would signal nonverbally that he like her. His response was to smooth back his hair which, to her, was just a common nervous gesture signifying nothing. She repeated her question three times. He smoothed his hair three times and, finally realizing that she was not recognizing this movement as his reply to her question, automatically ducked his head and stuck out his tongue slightly in embarrassment. This behavior *was* noticed by the girl, and she interpreted it as the way he would express his liking for her.

The lack of comprehension of obvious nonverbal signs and symbols such as gestures, postures, and vocalizations is a definite communication barrier, but it is possible to learn the meaning of these messages (once they are perceived) in much the same way a verbal language is learned. It is more difficult to correctly note the unspoken codes of the other culture that are further from awareness, such as the handling of time and spatial relationships, subtle signs of respect or formality, and many others.

The third stumbling block is the presence of *preconceptions* and *stereotypes*. If the *label* "inscrutable" has preceded the Japanese guest, it is thus we explain his constant and inappropriate smile. The stereotype that Arabs are "inflammable" causes U.S. students to keep their distance when an animated and noisy group from Libya is enjoying lunch in the cafeteria. A professor who "knows" of the bargaining habits of natives of certain countries may unfairly interpret a hesitation by one of his foreign students as a move to "squirm out" of a commitment. Stereotypes help do what Ernest Becker[10] says the anxiety-prone human race *must* do, and that is to reduce the threat of the unknown by making the world predictable. Indeed, this is one of the basic functions of culture: to lay out a predictable world in which the individual is firmly oriented. Stereotypes are overgeneralized beliefs that provide conceptual bases from which to "make sense" out of what goes on around us. In a foreign land they increase our feeling of security and are psychologically necessary to the degree that we cannot tolerate ambiguity or the sense of helplessness resulting from inability to understand and deal with people and situations beyond our comprehension.

Stereotypes are stumbling blocks for communicators because they interfere with objective viewing of stimuli. Unfortunately, they are not easy to overcome in others or in ourselves by demonstrations of the "truth," hoping to teach a lesson of tolerance or cultural relativity. They persist because they sometimes rationalize prejudices or are firmly established as myths or truisms by one's own national culture. They are also sustained and fed by the tendency to perceive selectively only those pieces of new information that correspond to the image. The Asian or African visitor who is accustomed to privation and the values of denial and self-help cannot fail to experience American culture as materialistic and wasteful. The stereotype for him turns into a concrete reality.

Another deterrent to an understanding between persons of differing cultures or ethnic groups is the *tendency to evaluate,* to approve or disapprove, the statements and actions of the other person or group rather than to try to completely comprehend the thoughts and feelings expressed. Each person's culture, his own way of life, always seems right, proper, and natural. This bias prevents the open-minded attention needed to look at the attitudes and behavior patterns from the other's point of view. A midday siesta changes from a "lazy habit" to a "pretty good idea" when someone listens long enough to realize the midday temperature in the country is 115° Fahrenheit.

The author, fresh from a conference in Tokyo where Japanese professors had emphasized the preference of the people of Japan for simple natural settings of rocks, moss, and water, of muted greens and misty ethereal landscapes, visited the Katsura Imperial Gardens in Kyoto. At the appointed time of the tour, a young Japanese guide approached the group of twenty waiting American strangers and remarked how fortunate it was that the day was cloudy. This brought hesitant smiles to the group who were less than pleased at the prospect of a light shower. The guide's next few sentences included mention that the timing of the midsummer visit was particularly appropriate in that the azalea and rhododendron blossoms were gone and the trees had not yet turned to their brilliant fall colors. The group laughed loudly, now convinced that the young man had a fine sense of humor. I winced at his bewildered expression realizing that, had I come before attending the conference, I would have shared the group's inference that he was not serious.

The communication cut-off caused by immediate evaluation is heightened when feelings and emotions are deeply involved; yet this is just the time when listening with understanding is most needed. It takes both awareness of the tendency to close our minds and courage to risk change in our own values and perceptions to dare to comprehend why someone thinks and acts differently from us. As stated by Sherif, Sherif and Nebergall, "A person's commitment to his religion, politics, values of his family, and his stand on the virtue of his way of life are ingredients in his self-picture—intimately felt and cherished."[11] It is very easy to dismiss strange or different behaviors as "wrong," listen through a thick screen of value judgments, and therefore fail miserably to receive a fair understanding. The impatience of the American public over the choice of the shape of the conference table at the Paris peace talks and their judgment of a "poor reception" for the President of the United States because there were no bands or flag-waving throngs waiting for Nixon as he was driven through towns in North China on his historic visit are two examples.

The following paragraph written by an international student from Korea illustrates how a clash in values can lead to poor communication and result in misunderstanding and hurt feelings:

> When I call on my American friend, he had been studying his lesson. Then I said, "May I come in?" He said through window, "I am sorry. I have no time because of my study." Then he shut the window. I thought it over and over. I couldn't understand through my cultural background. In our country, if someone visits other's house, house owner should have welcome visitor whether he likes or not and whether he is busy or not. The next, if the owner is busy, he asks to visitor, "Would you wait for me?" Also the owner never speaks without opening his door.[12]

This example also illustrates how difficult it is to bring one's own cultural norm into awareness. It is unlikely the "American friend" ever knew that he insulted the young Korean.

The fifth stumbling block is *high anxiety,* separately mentioned for the purpose of emphasis. Unlike the other four (language, illusive nonverbal cues, preconceptions and stereotypes, and the practice of immediate evaluation), the stumbling block of anxiety is not distinct but underlies and compounds the others. The presence of high anxiety/tension is very common in cross-cultural experiences because of the uncertainties present. An international student says it well:

> During these several months after my arrival in the U.S.A., every day I came back from school exhausted so that I had to take a rest for a while, stretching myself on the bed. For, all the time, I strained every nerve in order to understand what the people were saying and make myself understood in my broken English. When I don't understand what American

people are talking about and why they are laughing, I sometimes have to pretend to understand by smiling, even though I feel alienated, uneasy and tense.

In addition to this, the difference in culture or customs, the way of thinking between two countries, produces more tension because we don't know how we should react to totally foreign customs or attitudes, and sometimes we can't guess how the people from another country react to my saying or behavior. We always have a fear somewhere in the bottom of our hearts that there are much more chances of breakdown in intercultural communication than in communication with our own fellow countrymen.[13]

The native of the country is uncomfortable when talking with a foreigner because he cannot maintain the normal flow of verbal and nonverbal interaction to sustain the conversation. He is also threatened by the unknown other's knowledge, experience, and evaluation—the visitor's potential for scrutiny and rejection of himself and his country. The inevitable question, "How do you like it here?" which the foreigner abhors, is the host's quest for reassurance, or at least the "feeler" that reduces the unknown and gives him ground for defense if that seems necessary.

The foreign member of the dyad is under the same threat, with the added tension of having to cope with the differing pace, climate, and culture. The first few months he feels helpless in coping with messages that swamp him and to which his reactions may be inappropriate. His self-esteem is often intolerably undermined unless he employs such defenses as withdrawal into his own reference group or into himself, screening out or misperceiving stimuli, rationalizing, overcompensating, even hostility—none of which leads to effective communication.

Since all of the communication barriers mentioned are hard to remove, the only simple solution seems to be to tell everybody to stay home. This advice obviously is unacceptable, so it is fortunate that a few paths are being laid around the obstacles. Communication theorists are continuing to offer new insights and are focusing on problem areas of this complex process.[14] Educators and linguists are improving methods of learning a second language. The nonverbal area, made familiar by Edward T. Hall in his famous books, *The Silent Language* and *The Hidden Dimension,* is getting a singular amount of attention.[15] The ray of hope offered by Hall and others is that nonverbal cues, culturally controlled and largely out-of-awareness, can be discovered and even understood when the communicator knows enough to look for them, is alert to the varying interpretations possible, and is free enough from tension and psychological defenses to notice them.

In addition, textbooks are appearing and communication specialists are improving means for increasing sensitivity to the messages coming from others in an intercultural setting.[16] Professional associations are giving increased amounts of attention to intercultural communication, and new societies such as the Society for Intercultural Education, Training and Research are being developed. The *International and Intercultural Communication Annual*[17] has a complete listing of these.

What the interpersonal intercultural communicator must seek to achieve can be summarized by two quotations. The first is by Roger Harrison, who says:

> ... the communicator cannot stop at knowing that the people he is working with have different customs, goals, and thought patterns from his own. He must be able to feel his way into intimate contact with these alien values, attitudes, and feelings. He must be able to work with them and within them, neither losing his own values in the confrontation nor protecting himself behind a wall of intellectual detachment.[18]

Robert T. Oliver phrases it thus: "If we would communicate across cultural barriers, we must learn what to say and how to say it in terms of the expectations and predispositions of those we want to listen."[19]

NOTES

1. MARSHALL R. SINGER, "Culture: A Perceptual Approach," in *Readings in Intercultural Communication,* Vol. I (Regional Council for International Education, University of Pittsburgh), and Edward T. Hall, *The Hidden Dimension* (New York: Doubleday and Company, Inc., 1966), p. 2.

2. EDWARD T. HALL, *The Silent Language* (Greenwich, Conn.: Fawcett Publications, Inc., 1959).

3. CHARLES FRANKEL, *The Neglected Aspect of Foreign Affairs* (Washington, D.C.: Brookings Institution, 1965), p. 1.

4.&5. Taken from student papers in a course in intercultural communication taught by the author.

6. For one discussion of this concept, see Daryl J. Bem, *Beliefs, Attitudes, and Human Affairs* (Belmont, Calif.: Brooks/Cole Publishing Co., 1970), p. 9.

7. MARGARET MEAD, "The Cultural Perspective," in *Communication or Conflict,* ed. Mary Capes (Association Press, 1960).

8. EDWARD C. STEWART, *American Cultural Patterns: A Cross-Cultural Perspective* (Pittsburgh, Pa.: Regional Council for International Education, University of Pittsburgh, April 1971), p. 14.

9. FRANKEL, *The Neglected Aspect of Foreign Affairs,* p. 103.

10. ERNEST BECKER, *The Birth and Death of Meaning* (New York: Free Press, 1962), pp. 84–89.

11. CAROLYN W. SHERIF, MUSAFER SHERIF and ROGER E. NEBERGALL, *Attitude and Attitude Change* (Philadelphia: W.B. Saunders Co., 1965), p. vi.

12.&13. Taken from a student's paper in a course in intercultural communication taught by the author.

14. An early book, now in its second edition, which adapted the language of information theory to communication and stressed the influence of culture, remains one of the best sources: *Communication: The Social Matrix of Psychiatry* by Jurgen Ruesch and Gregory Bateson (New York: W. W. Norton & Co., 1968).

15. See for example: *Silent Messages* by Albert Mehrabian (Belmont, Calif.: Wadsworth Publishing Co., 1971).

16. Sources include: Edward D. Stewart, "The Simulation of Cultural Differences," *The Journal of Communication,* Vol. 16, December 1966; Alfred J. Kraemer, *The Development of Cultural Self-Awareness: Design of a Program of Instruction* (George Washington University, Human Resources Research Office, Professional Paper 27–69, August 1969); David Hoopes, ed., *Readings in Intercultural Communication,* Vols. I–IV (Regional Council for International Education, University of Pittsburgh).

17. *International and Intercultural Communication Annual,* Vol. 1, December 1974, published by Speech Communication Association, Statler Hilton Hotel, New York.

18. ROGER HARRISON, "The Design of Cross-Cultural Training: An Alternative to the University Model," in *Explorations in Human Relations Training and Research* (Bethesda, Md.: National Training Laboratories, 1966), NEA No. 2, p. 4.

19. ROBERT T. OLIVER, *Culture and Communication: The Problem of Penetrating National and Cultural Boundaries* (Springfield, Ill.: Charles C Thomas, 1962), p. 154.

Thirty-Three

Interracial Implications of Nonverbal Communication

Andrea L. Rich

Much communication that takes place between members of different racial and ethnic groups is nonverbal. The importance of nonverbal communication in interracial settings is even more evident than in racially homogeneous settings because in the United States basic geographical and psychological separation of the races has made it difficult for them to get close enough together to communicate verbally. Because of this segregation much interracial communication has occurred with communicators sending nonverbal messages. Nonverbal communication is significant in interracial settings not only because of this physical separation of the races but also because the lack of trust among the races has caused interracial communicators to reject the face values of verbal communication and to search for nonverbal cues as indicators of real meaning and response in interracial communication situations.

Dimensions of Nonverbal Communication

Nonverbal communication is very important in interracial situations, for even when verbal communication breaks down or ceases, nonverbal communication continues. Nonverbal communication refers to all forms of expression that are not linguistically based. We shall include the following variables as components of nonverbal communication and examine the manner in which these variables facilitate and/or disrupt interracial interaction.

1. *Environment.* This dimension includes those external factors that affect interaction, especially interracial interaction. The major divisions of this aspect of nonverbal communication are: (1) general ambience, which includes climate, population density, and aesthetic surroundings, and (2) proxemics, which can be viewed as the use of "social and personal space and Man's perception of it."[1]
2. *Communicator appearance.* This dimension includes considerations of both the communicator's personal style of attire and his unique physical characteristics.
3. *Nonverbal behavior.* Included in this dimension are all nonlinguistically based acts that serve as communication stimuli. Specifically this dimension includes: (1) kinesics, which encompasses the study of body movement, posture, and facial expression, and (2) paralanguage, which refers to non-language sounds, vocal qualities, pronunciation, and inflection patterns.

. . .

Implications of Environment for Interracial Communication

The environment in which communication occurs, including factors of climate, population density, and aesthetic appeal, guides the direction and intensity of interaction. In situations where diversity in roles, beliefs, attitudes, values, perceptions, and language already complicate the communication process (as in interracial settings), a negative environment will increase the impact of that diversity and lead toward the expression of interracial hostility. The street corner of an urban ghetto on a hot summer night is probably not the most conducive setting for open and fruitful interracial communication.

An analysis of the comparative environments of the various races in this country gives some insight into the differential perceptions, attitudes, and affective responses of interracial communicators. Hot (or cold) overcrowded conditions such as those found in many poverty areas, coupled with unpleasant aesthetic surroundings, develop negative predispositions and perceptions in those subjected to such conditions and help to contribute to interracial hostility. Certain whites from middle-class neighborhoods have a "rosier" perception of the world based on the input of a different physical environment. This disparity of physical environments, which results in different mind sets, causes many problems in interracial communication.

This is not to suggest that all nonwhites live under poverty conditions. A significant and unfortunate number do, however, and one cause of the failure of interracial communication is the social force creating the physical conditions; this in turn creates the psychological conditions prohibitive to interracial interaction. There are, of course, intraracial communication problems resulting from a disparity in physical surroundings. Many middle- and upper-class nonwhites, coming from physical environments different than those of certain ghetto dwellers, experience communication breakdown with members of their own race because of the divergence in the psychological set determined by the ambience in which they find themselves. The same can be said of the communication experienced by white of various social classes and different geographical neighborhoods. Those who physically leave economically depressed areas cannot help leaving such areas psychologically as well; the impact of environment on thinking and perception processes is strong.

Proxemics

Proximity, interaction, and friendship. Proxemics refers to the study of "social and personal space and Man's perception of it."[2] A specific area of concentration within proxemics is the relationship between proximity, interaction, and friendship. One theory of "integration" as a means of solving racial problems advances that proximity leads to interaction which in turn leads to the development of interracial friendship. The results of several studies lend support to this theory.

Merton found in his study of a housing project that the majority of friends lived across from each other, that is, within basic sight lines. When the subjects lived side-by-side in a court setting, they did not develop as many friendships because interaction was more difficult.[3] Whyte, in a three-and-a-half-year study of street gangs, found that the individual member's place of residence entirely determined his interaction with others for the rest of his life.[4]

· · ·

The findings and theories of proxemics and interaction have been applied to the study of interracial interaction. Ernest Works comments on his extensive research in this area:

> Research conducted among white tenants in integrated and segregated housing projects validates what may be called a general prejudice-interaction hypothesis, that out-group prejudice is reduced through intimate group contacts of those equal in status. This study investigates the hypothesis from the point of view of the Negro; that anti-white prejudice is

diminished through intimate and interracial contact of persons equal in status. Our data in general supports this hypothesis.[5]

Albert Mehrabian comments further on the same phenomenon:

Some of the classical prejudice studies have shown also that housing projects that permit people of different races to live in close proximity lessen their prejudice toward one another. . . . If increased contact can reduce negative (prejudiced) feelings and even convert them to positive ones, then its effect should be even more profound in cases where the initial attitudes are neutral, as would be the case with two strangers.[6]

Mehrabian also points out, however, the one important exception to this generalization: When hostile groups of persons are placed in close proximity, the increased contact and interaction does not necessarily improve their relationship.

Thus with the exception of cases of extreme hostility, the evidence points to the significance of interracial communication (brought about by increased interracial proximity) as a means of reducing interracial conflict and increasing interracial friendships. Physical segregation precludes interaction and hence inhibits any chance of reconciliation and mutual understanding between the races.

Personal space.   Another concept within the area of proxemics is that of "personal space." Personal space can be viewed "as territory that is carried around with the individual having invisible boundaries. . . ."[7] People have very definite concepts regarding personal space and propriety of behavior. . . .

The concept of personal space is of great importance in interracial communication settings. Society's taboo against interracial sexual contact, coupled with the many sexual stereotypes associated with various races, makes personal space more important in interracial communication than in most interpersonal contact. Researcher Grace Halsell claims that sex is at the base of racism. The theory she advances is that "the white male's fear of the black male's sexual prowess has been exaggerated out of all proportion. . . ."[8] Historically, of course, this syndrome is traced back to the slave period in which white men raped black women, thus creating the fear in themselves that, if given the chance, black men would seek revenge by raping white women. According to Berkeley historian Winthrop D. Jordon:

In our minds interracial sex is not so much a shared activity as it is a dangerous, reprehensible yet fascinating scene of raw lust between "a white" and "a Negro." Lust: we find it hard to think that it could be anything else, anything so personal as love and affection.[9]

Thus, whereas rape is regarded everywhere in the community as an undesirable and ugly offense, interracial rape is viewed in some areas as a capital crime.

This societal taboo against interracial physical mingling, together with interracial sexual stereotypes, has created interesting physical behavior patterns between the races in communication situations. A "touch-don't touch" phenomenon has developed, which is strongly tied to the stereotype held by whites that black and other nonwhites are unclean and have unpleasant odors and textures. Such a physical stereotype explains the strong physical avoidance patterns demonstrated in interracial settings. One black member of an interracial encounter group described his perception of the physical reaction of white women when he sits next to them on buses. The black man reenacted the subtle but observable physical withdrawal of a white woman as she moved ever so close to the window and fixed her eyes in a stare outward so she would not have to confront the black male face to face. In an episode of *All in the Family,* Archie Bunker exemplifies this physical avoidance response when he is so uncomfortably hesitant about drinking out of the same glass from which Sammy Davis, Jr., has also drunk, although he seems to have no reservation about drinking out of the same glass that his white neighbor had used. In the same episode Archie expresses his surprise and disdain on seeing black and white celebrities kissing each other on television. Thus when Sammy Davis kisses Archie at the end of the show, the audience roars with laughter, for they understand that Archie's sense of personal space has been violated.

The "touch-don't touch" phenomenon is a conflict that is characteristically experienced by the white "liberal" who wishes to overcome the physical contact taboo in order to demonstrate overtly his lack of racism. Such a white liberal communicator frequently develops a "touch compulsion," in which he feels compelled to clasp eagerly the hand of a new black acquaintance or to take a bite casually from a black colleague's sandwich. This compulsion becomes evident when the "touching" moves are overdone, when the white is engaged in more hand clasping and embracing with nonwhites than he would normally engage in with whites. In a sense it might be advanced that the white communicator is "protesting too much," that his compulsion to touch is really an attempt on his part to overcome his own strong aversion to touching members of nonwhite racial groups.

The concept of "touch" is thus an enormously strong and subtle force in interracial contact. Sexual myths have imposed taboos on interracial physical contact, and these barriers are based on conscious and unconscious fears and a basic ignorance of the physical features of other racial groups. In interracial settings, attempts to maintain a strong sense of personal space are greater than in ordinary communication settings. The keen awareness of personal space results in self-consciousness and an underlying physical tension which, though subtle, is nevertheless extremely disruptive and serves as one cause of ensuing breakdowns in verbal communication.

The occupation of territory.   This dimension of proxemics is related to personal space, but it embraces a broader physical domain. "The concept of territoriality goes beyond 'staking out' a piece of land for oneself. People possess areas, such as desks, favorite chairs, rooms that are not to be intruded upon, or even particular seats at the eating table.''[10] Thus, even the smallest child in a family soon learns his proper seat for eating and the areas in which he may play. . . .

The occupation of territory has significant implications for interracial communication. It was no accident that much time was spent searching for neutral ground to hold peace negotiations between North Viet Nam and the United States. In order to diminish the territorial advantage of either party, a nonpartisan communication setting had to be found. The same need obtains for interracial communication situations. Territorial considerations explain much interracial conflict. The white society occupies most of the territory in the United States, particularly the most "desirable" territory; hence whites enjoy a higher status. That territory occupied by nonwhites, because it is comparatively so small, is held jealously by its occupants, and any attempt to usurp it is met with extreme hostility. The Black Panthers, for example, view the police as an "invading force," comparable to a hostile foreign army. By this definition they justify resisting the police as a means of protecting and fighting for the "homeland." White social workers in the ghetto also violate nonwhite territory. Their questions and interviews, conducted within nonwhite homes, though mandatory for the welfare bureaucracy, are viewed as invasions of privacy. Further, white "volunteers" who think they are being socially constructive by "going into the ghetto to raise them to our standards" are also enormously resented, for they are coopting already occupied territory. In interracial encounters the subjects of police, social workers, and white community and charity volunteers are extremely volatile, for they represent a threat to the status that accompanies the occupation of one's own territory.

Communicator Appearance

Not only does our general ambience act to determine the course of much of our communication, but our personal appearance, the image we project, also plays an important role. The impression we give through the manner in which we are physically perceived by others communicates to our receivers without necessitating any verbal communication from us and helps determine how others in turn will communicate toward us.

. . .

Clothing is one way in which sub- and contercultures distinguish themselves from the larger dominant culture. These clothing variations may sometimes be regarded as an act of rebellion, as in the case of the refusal of the "hippie" cult to conform to the dress standards of the more conventional society; on the other hand, such divergence in dress may simply be a manifestation of a subcultural pattern, such as in the case of the American Indian dressed in ritual garb. Differences in dress habits are both racial and socioeconomic. The Black Muslims, for example, dress in a simple conservative garb as opposed to the more extravagant costume of a ghetto hustler. The pachuco [a Mexican-American counter-culture youth] contributed his own dress style, which became personified in the "leather jacket" look of the 1950s. The dress styles of social classes differ according to the kind of attire they can afford.

Dress patterns and the stereotypes associated with them have an important impact on interracial communication. Noncomformity to the dress code of the dominant culture is frequently met with scorn on the part of "establishment" members. One need only note the hostility with which many members of the older generation regard the long-haired youth with bare feet and wrinkled war-surplus-type uniforms. Such contracultural dress patterns meet the most resistance, hostility, and distrust from establishment types, because such patterns constitute a symbolic rejection of the values of the dominant culture and a refusal to be controlled by it. The black emphasis on African dress style, for example, demonstrates both a rejection of dominant cultural values and a search for a cultural rebirth stemming from a new and different source than the dominant white culture.

Dress and grooming patterns constitute one of the strongest and easiest bases for stereotyping. A black with an Afro hair style, for example, is automatically labeled a "militant" by certain segments of the society. That hair style comes to suggest an entire series of beliefs, attitudes, and values to the perceiver, which may be positive or negative depending on the values of the perceiver. From the point of view of many in the dominant culture, a youth with long hair, dirty jeans, and no shoes is obviously a drug addict; this assumption is made with no further evidence than dress patterns to support it. Conversely, from the point of view of the contracultural member, a white man with a crew cut and a coat and tie is automatically classified as "establishment."

Working as they do, stereotypes create tendencies to perceive selectively; thus a white person who has stereotyped a black who happens to be wearing an Afro as militant will undoubtedly see only those things suggesting a militant posture; in this manner, the stereotype will be reinforced.

Clothing, then, while it may provide us with some information about a person, also tends to block input of other information by causing us to perceive selectively based on our stereotype of clothing patterns and personality types. In order to overcome this effect, communicators must engage in a dedicated effort to fight consciously the impact of these preconceptions about clothing. . . .

Physical Characteristics

Communicators not only stereotype on the basis of what others wear in terms of clothing and personal decoration. They also form stereotypes based on actual physical characteristics of those interacting. Culture dictates certain standards of beauty and those physical traits deemed desirable; thus members of a culture respond to the physical makeup of each other in the pattern determined by the society. As Barnlund states:

> The size and form of another person's body, along with the various positions it assumes, may affect the inferences we make about his attitudes

and the way we interpret his words. . . . Whether warranted or not, the existence of such physical stereotypes will necessarily affect interpersonal perceptions.[11]

Our perceptions and interactions are very much influenced by these physical stereotypes. In our society, for example, height in a male is highly valued and seen as a source of pride. Height suggests power and strength. On the other hand, height in a female, because of society's role definition of the sexes, is viewed negatively. An overly tall woman is seen as a misfit, in much the same way as is a short man. Stereotypes regarding height in this country demand that to "be normal," a woman should be small and diminutive and appear to need protection and dominance of her tall mate-hero.

. . . .

Secord and others conducted [an] experiment, focusing on racial characteristics. They hypothesized that "there is no difference in the degree of personality stereotyping of Negro photographs varying widely in physiognomic Negroidness. That is, even if he has a Caucasian-like appearance, a Negro will be seen as having in full degree all the stereotyped traits usually attributed to the Negro."[12] Evidence from the experiment supported this hypothesis: "The generally accepted but seldom tested definition of a stereotype as a categorical response to a member of a minority group is thus upheld."[13] In this study researchers also hypothesized that "anti-Negro judges exaggerate the personality stereotype of Negroes, whereas pro-Negro judges de-emphasize it."[14] The experimental results lend significant support to this hypothesis.

Thus physical traits, specifically racial characteristics, provide fuel for personality stereotyping. In our society physical standards of beauty, that which is defined as "beautiful," "attractive," and "desirable," have traditionally been defined through advertising and the media by the dominant white community. Those imbued with such "white" standards of attractiveness frequently experience a type of physiological revulsion at what the white society defines as nonbeautiful. Standards of beauty are not absolute but are culturally induced, so that the tatooed face of an African native woman might be regarded as an exquisite specimen within its own milieu and be judged as nothing more than physical mutilation in this country.

A large part of the racist consciousness in the United States is the aesthetic definition of anything nonwhite as necessarily unattractive and therefore undesirable. Certain black features, for example, have been singled out as targets for disdain, such as hair, skin color, skin texture, nose, lips, and body scent. Racist language is filled with expressions of distaste for these black physical traits, for example, "nigger's wool," "liver lips," or "tar baby." This intense revulsion on the part of many whites to these nonwhite characteristics may be conscious or unconscious; it may be based on a physical fear of nonwhites or may be the product of a natural aversion toward that which is strange or different. Whatever the distinct cause, there is no question that this physical disdain is in part induced and reinforced by the dominant culture.

Much of the personal space orientation and touch aversion occurring in interracial communication settings is based on this physical revulsion and a fear of the unknown physical qualities so exaggerated and fabricated by racist myth. Absurd as it may seem, some whites even fear that somehow a close physical contact with a nonwhite will cause physical darkness to rub off on them. These complex physical avoidance patterns, especially on the part of whites toward nonwhites, are based on aesthetic standards, psychological fear, and conditioned physiological response. The problem is further complicated by the societal taboo that forbids races to come together closely enough so that these myths and fears can be erased.

The effect of this single standard of attractiveness and the physical revulsion demonstrated by whites regarding nonwhites is a tragic and crippling self-hatred on the part of those who are victimized. Before their contemporary efforts to develop their own standards of beauty and desirability, black men and women, attempting to contort themselves into the white man's image of attractiveness, engaged in the very painful process of "conking" their hair by undergoing an agonizing acid rinse in order to straighten and disguise their naturally curly hair. Malcolm X vividly describes this process and its psychological meaning in his autobiography:

> The congolene just felt warm when Shorty started combing it. But then my head caught fire.
> I gritted my teeth and tried to pull the sides of the kitchen table together. The comb felt as if it was raking my skin off.
> My eyes watered, my nose was running. I couldn't stand it any longer; I bolted to the washbasin. I was cursing Shorty with every name I could think of when he got the spray going and started soap-lathering my head.
>
> * * *
>
> This was my first really big step toward self-degradation: when I endured all of that pain, literally burning my flesh with lye, in order to cook my natural hair until it was limp, to have it look like a white man's hair. I had joined that multitude of Negro men and women in America who are brainwashed into believing that the black people are "inferior"—and white people "superior"—that they will even violate and multilate their God-created bodies to try to look "pretty" by white standards.[15]

Blacks are not the only group within our society who have suffered the indignity and self-hatred imposed by a single arbitrary standard of "white beauty." Many Jewish and Italian women, whose noses are larger than that prescribed by the white Anglo-Saxon Protestant value, undergo painful cosmetic surgery in order to make their features conform more to the standards dictated by the dominant culture.

. . . .

These negative physical stereotypes based on arbitrary standards of beauty are not immutable. As the taboos regarding interracial interaction break down, and they can and do, the physical stereotypes and attraction patterns change as well. Prior to World War II, for example, the Oriental, especially the

Japanese, was severely stereotyped on the basis of certain physical traits deemed unattractive. He was described and projected in an exaggerated caricature as a "buck-toothed," "squinty-eyed" devil. After World War II, with American occupation forces in Japan, the physical space between Caucasian Americans and Japanese began to diminish, and some of the physical barriers were removed. Intermarriages took place, and new Japanese war brides had to be taken into American Caucasian homes. To effect this integration, a subtle redefinition of beauty began to take place in order to accommodate Oriental features and values. Caucasian women wanting to be in the vogue began to shape their eyes in a "doe" fashion. (Ironically, and with reference to the previously discussed self-hatred, many brides, wanting to adapt to Caucasian standards, underwent surgery to remove partially the epicanthic folds from their eyes in order more to resemble Caucasian women.) In the United States home decoration styles turned Oriental, and even dress styles tried to copy the mandarin and kimono mode of the Far East. The "China doll" image of the Oriental woman was a far cry from the "Uncle Tojo" stereotype of the prewar years.

Even today standards of attractiveness are changing. Nonwhites have begun to demand that the society recognize multiple standards of beauty. The "natural" hair styles and African garb worn by many blacks are succeeding in changing the white negative stereotype of black features. Some whites are even copying the black standards by allowing hair to grow into "natural" styles and wearing African-type clothing (to the dismay, incidentally, of many blacks who feel their movement is being coopted by such an overly zealous acceptance on the part of the white community).

Standards of physical beauty are thus culturally induced and change through time. Participants in interracial interaction, in order to overcome the physical barriers imposed by arbitrary standards of attractiveness, must begin to realize that previously all-white value patterns have been destructively chauvinistic. Like innocent children we need to rediscover others of different races; we must have the freedom to explore, to touch one another, to encounter real differences and significant similarities, to remove the mystery imposed by forced physical separation. If through interracial encounters we cannot break down these physical barriers, we shall be chained forever to the myths that cause us to run in fright from the unknown.

Nonverbal Behavior

Much of our behavior, though not specifically linguistic, is nonetheless profoundly communicative. The way in which we move, our postural stance, our gestures and facial expressions, and our nonlinguistic vocal traits all communicate a message regarding our thoughts and intentions to receivers.

. . . .

The implications of postural communication for interracial interaction are significant. The lack of trust between the races, the inability of individuals in interracial settings to "turn one's back to another," and the constant state of vigilance observed by participants are expressed in the extreme body tensions present in interracial situations. There is rarely the same degree of total body relaxation in interracial groups as there is in racially homogeneous groups.

Aside from the general posture of tension expressed in interracial settings, the social and sexual taboos that have maintained a relatively segregated society for so long frequently result in a physical and psychological fear and revulsion on the part of all the members of an interracial group. Fear and revulsion are expressed in avoidance postures, as individuals in interracial settings maintain a keen sense of personal space. The avoidance response is cyclical; as the source projects an avoidance message to the receiver, the receiver responds in kind.

Historical role definitions imposed by whites on nonwhites demanded that certain physical postures be assumed by nonwhites in the presence of whites. Given the "power metaphor," by forcing someone to "bow and scrape," one can demean him and strip him of all strength and influence. For many years in the South, for example, it was expected that blacks would physically lower themselves in the presence of whites and that they would always show deference by physically removing themselves from the white man's path. In the modern counterculture, a change in such posture signifies an overt defiance toward those traditional roles. Assuming an expansive size and a special walk enable members of the counterculture to assert their power and authority over their destinies.

Such physical moves can be volatile in terms of communication impact. In one interracial group discussion an elderly white man confessed that when he was driving and saw two young black men "strutting down the street," he became so angry he wanted to run them over with his automobile. So communicative was their physical action that these two pedestrians were able to elicit an extraordinarily violent response from a total stranger without ever saying a word to him or directing an action specifically toward him. Thus much of the tension and hostility felt in interracial settings is not verbally expressed but physically felt and behaviorally transmitted.

Gesture. . . . In his work *Gesture and Environment* David Efron began to study the gestural habits of certain selected ethnic groups. He observed the gestural patterns of eastern Jews and southern Italians living under similar and different environmental conditions in New York City. Efron found:

> . . .gestural behavior, or the absence of it, is, to some extent, at least, conditioned by factors of a socio-psychological nature. . . . They certainly do not bear out the contention that this form of behavior is determined by biological descent.[16]

To verify further the contention that gestural behavioral patterns are culturally induced rather than inherited, Efron found that members of ethnic groups that had been assimilated into the dominant culture demonstrated significantly less gestural behavior than did the members of ethnic groups that had remained within the domain of the traditions of the group.

In interracial settings gesture can reveal the same tension and hostility common to postural communication. Some spontaneous gestures in interracial settings, however, have become codified into a very keen symbolic form of expression. On October 16, 1968, for example, two black Olympic medal winners, while receiving their awards, raised black gloved fists and, with heads bowed, refused to salute the flag of their country (the United States). The clenched fist has become a symbol of defiance and can be found in revolutionary propaganda literature from that of the Black Panthers to messages from the Women's Liberation Movement. This one-time spontaneous gesture has grown into a nonverbal communication of specific significance. The *V* sign, once so familiarly employed by Winston Churchill as the sign of victory in World War II, has in this generation come to symbolize the contemporary struggle for peace. Such a gesture unites all those who use it with a common philosophical bond. The "secret" black handshake also unites members of one racial group in a common cause. This symbolic gesture systematically excludes those outside the racial and ethnic group in much the same way as does a contracultural language code. Gesture is thus also an important form of communication in interracial settings.

Eye contact. . . .   Eye contact and expression play an important role in communication between the races. The famous "glare" expressed so frequently by nonwhites toward whites presents in a moment the entire history of tension and hostility between the races. Such a glance, while mirroring the emotions of the nonwhite communicator, reinforces the feelings of fear and defensiveness in the white receiver. Communication in interracial settings is also often characterized by the actual avoidance of any type of eye contact, suggesting a dislike or distrust among the communicators. People tend to feel that another cannot lie if he is confronted face to face and that, if a communicator can engage in direct eye contact, he most probably has nothing to hide. Direct eye contact, then, must be considered as an essential ingredient in building positive interracial attitudes.

Facial expression. . . .   The communication carried on through facial expression is important in interracial settings, because it reflects directly on the credibility of the communicators. We can lie verbally and consciously control what we say, but our physical behavior, especially our facial expressions, tends to mirror the reality within us. Erving Goffman refers to these two forms of communication:

> The expressiveness of the individual (and therefore his capacity to give impressions) appears to involve two radically different kinds of sign-activity; the expression that he *gives,* and the expression that he *gives off.* The first involves verbal symbols or their substitutes which he uses admittedly and solely to convey information that he and others are known to attach to these symbols. This is communication in the traditional narrow sense. The second involves a wide range of action that others can treat as symptomatic of the actor, the expectation being that the action was performed for reasons other than the information conveyed in this way.[17]

We have less control over the impressions we "give off," because nonverbal behavior is more reflexive in nature. Understanding this, receivers of communication frequently—perhaps unconsciously—look at the body, the face, and the eyes of the communicator to discern the real intent and meaning of a communication message.

The studies cited previously demonstrate that we can interpret meaning from facial expression accurately, consistently, and, to some extent, cross-culturally. They also have shown that we are able to communicate negative attitudes more effectively than positive ones; we thus communicate hostility, tension, and irritation (so frequent in interracial communication) best of all. Unfortunately positive attitudes are not so well or vividly reflected in facial expressions. Given the common hostility inherent in so many interracial settings and the predisposition of individuals in interracial encounters selectively to perceive negativism, these negative facial expressions can come to dominate interracial interaction. Interracial communication can become stifled and strife-ridden through facial expression alone. Such explosive situations are frequently followed by laments such as "What did I say?" or "I didn't say anything!" The communicator may be correct in asserting that he said nothing *verbally*, but he undoubtedly said a great deal through a facial expression that could not be hidden.

Noncommittal facial expressions are not the answer to interracial communication problems resulting from nonverbal conflict. As Feldman suggests:

> The noncommittal facial expression *is* an expression on the face; but *seemingly,* it betrays only that the person does not want anyone to know anything about his feelings. There is no *expression* on the face; *a lack of expression is the expression.* It is a "poker face."[18]

The only meaning that a facial expression such as this projects is that of uninvolvement and aloofness, hardly a remedy for interracial conflict.

Communicators in interracial settings must realize that in hostile or tense communication situations, persons are going to seek all avenues open for interpretation of meaning; these will include the selective observation of bodily and facial expression. Whether or not we verbalize our tensions and anxieties, our bodies express what our words may attempt to hide. Being aware of the communicative power of one's unconscious physical expression, communicators should be better able to deal with the difficulties that arise in interracial settings as a result of unspoken expressions of emotions and attitudes.

NOTES

1. E. T. HALL, *The Hidden Dimension* (Garden City, N.Y.: Doubleday, 1966), p. 1.
2. Ibid., p. 1.
3. ROBERT K. MERTON, "The Social Psychology of Housing," *Current Trends in Social Psychology* (Pittsburgh: University of Pittsburgh Press, 1948), pp. 163–217.

4. WILLIAM FOOTE WHYTE, *Street Corner Society: The Social Structure of an Italian Slum* (Chicago: University of Chicago Press, 1943).

5. ERNEST WORKS, "The Prejudice Interaction Hypothesis from the Point of View of the Negro Minority Group," *Amer. J. Sociol.* 67 (1961): 47.

6. ALBERT MEHRABIAN, *Silent Messages* (Belmont, Calif.: Wadsworth, 1971), p.78.

7. ROBERT SOMMER, "Studies in Personal Space," *Sociometry* 22 (1959): 247–260.

8. GWEN GIBSON, "Problems Facing Interracial Couples," *Los Angeles Times,* 18 August 1972.

9. Ibid.

10. MEHRABIAN, op. cit., p. 36.

11. DEAN BARNLUND, *Interpersonal Communication: Survey and Studies* (Boston: Houghton Mifflin, 1968), p. 520

12. PAUL F. SECORD, WILLIAM BEVAN, and BRENDA KATZ, "The Negro Stereotype and Perceptual Accentuation," *J. Abnorm. Soc. Psychol.* 53 (1956): 78–83.

13. Ibid.

14. Ibid.

15. MALCOM X, *The Autobiography of Malcolm X* (New York: Grove, 1965), pp. 54–55. Reprinted by permission of Grove Press, Inc. Copyright 1965 by Alex Haley and Malcom X; copyright 1965 by Alex Haley and Betty Shabazz.

16. DAVID EFRON, *Gesture and Environment* (New York: King's Crown, 1941), p. 137.

17. ERVING GOFFMAN, *The Presentation of Self in Everyday Life* (Garden City, N.Y.: Doubleday, 1959), p. 2

18. SANDOR S. FELDMAN, *Mannerisms of Speech and Gesture in Everyday Life* (New York: International Universities, 1959), p. 204.

Thirty-Four

Folk-Linguistics: Wishy-Washy Mommy Talk

Cheris Kramer

Men and women speak a different language. According to popular belief, at least, the speech of women is weaker and less effective than the speech of men. Our culture has many jokes about both the quality of women's speech ("If my wife said what she thought, she'd be speechless") and its quantity ("Women need no eulogy; they speak for themselves"). Compared to male speech, the female form is supposed to be emotional, vague, euphemistic, sweetly proper, mindless, endless, high-pitched, and silly.

Such generalizations are not based on carefully controlled research. Although anthropologists have noticed sex-related differences in the languages of other cultures, there have been only a few quantitative studies of the way men and women differ in their use of English. Perhaps this is due to the fact that many researchers view women as peculiar human beings who stand outside the laws governing mankind (i.e., males).

A noted linguist who did devote some attention to sex differences in language had some unflattering things to say about the way women talk. In his 1922 book, *Language,* Otto Jespersen wrote an entire chapter on "The Woman." (There was no parallel chapter on "The Man.") Jespersen made many claims about women's speech, among them that women frequently leave sentences unfinished, and that they are prone to jump from one idea to another when talking. These assertions rested on the author's own observations and examples drawn from literary works.

Until recently, Jespersen's chapter was one of the few published discussions of the topic. But with the emergence of the women's liberation movement, some social scientists and linguists have begun to speculate about how language helps maintain rigid sex-role barriers. Most of these writers have derived hypotheses from their own intuitions as native speakers.

The Folklore of Female Language

In addition to the speculations of linguists, there is also a folk-linguistics of women's speech, a body of folklore about female language that permeates popular jokes and stories. These perceived differences do not necessarily correspond to real ones, but they are important as indicators of cultural attitudes and prejudices.

One way to study folk-linguistics is to examine comic art, which takes much of its material from the relationships between the sexes, including how they talk to each other. Social cartoons are especially useful, since their humor depends on the exaggeration of popular stereotypes of human behavior. In a recent study, I analyzed cartoons containing adult human speech, from three consecutive months (13 issues) of *The New Yorker,* February 17 through May 12, 1973. I chose *The New Yorker* because it is a general-circulation magazine with both male and female readers, and because many cartoonists and critics consider it to be an innovator and leader in the field of social cartooning.

In order to check my own observations and judgments against those of others, I asked 25 male and 25 female students at the University of Illinois to help me identify some of the characteristics of women's and men's speech in the cartoons. I gave each student a list of captions (but not the cartoons themselves) from four consecutive issues, March 17 through April 7. I did not identify the captions as coming from *The New Yorker.* I simply instructed the students to indicate, for each one, whether they thought the words were spoken by a male or female. At the end of the list there was a room for comments about what had guided the student's choices.

For most of the 49 captions, there was a clear consensus (at least 66 percent agreement) that the speaker in the cartoon was of a particular sex. The male students were in unanimous or near-unanimous agreement on 14 captions, while females were in unanimous or near-unanimous agreement on 13.

The Silent Sex

A striking finding that emerged from my analysis was that women did not speak in as many of the cartoons as did men. According to folk-linguistics, women talk too much. But in the 156 cartoons in my sample, men speak 110 times, women only 44. In fact, the number of men goes up to 112 if we assume that a commanding voice from the clouds is that of a masculine God, and that a voice on the phone telling an elephant trainer to "give him two bottles of aspirin and call me in the morning" belongs to a male veterinarian.

There are several possible explanations for the relative silence of women in these cartoons. Most cartoonists are men, and it may be that they depict what they know best and consider most important, i.e., men and male activities. Some students suggested that men try harder to be funny and make more comic statements. Or perhaps the cartoons reflect real life, where men like to have the last, topping word.

Women in these cartoons not only speak less, they speak in fewer places. Men speak in 38 different locations, including a courtroom, doctor's office, psychiatrist's office, police car, massage parlor, press conference, art museum, and floral shop. They are inside a home only 20 of the 110 (or 112) times they speak, excluding cocktail parties. Women, on the other hand, speak in only 16 different places, including the home, store, office and airplane. They are at home on half the occasions when they talk, again excluding cocktail parties. In four of the 13 issues I looked at, women never spoke outside the home at all.

More important, men are in control of language wherever they happen to be, but women, when they do leave home, often seem incapable of handling the language appropriate to the new location. Their speech then becomes the focus of humor. So we have a matron saying to a tight-lipped, barely patient stockbroker, "Now tell me, Mr. Hilbert does Merrill Lynch think utilities are going to keep on being iffy?" And an enthusiastic woman at a cocktail party remarking to a man, "You have no idea how refreshing it is to meet someone raffish in West Hartford." And another woman inquiring of a book salesman, "Do you have any jolly fiction?" These cartoons are funny (subtly, in *The New Yorker* way) because in each case there is a word that does not quite belong at least in that setting.

Politics and Pornography

The women and men who populate *The New Yorker* cartoons discuss different topics. Men hold forth with authority on business, politics, legal matters, taxes, age, household expenses, electronic bugging, chuch collections, kissing, baseball, human relations, health, and—women's speech. Women discuss social life, books, food and drink, pornography, life's troubles, caring for a husband, social work, age, and life-style. Several of the students who rated the cartoon captions said they considered all statements about economics, business or jobs to be male.

We have already seen what happens when a woman steps over these boundaries and tries to discuss a topic like the stock market. In another cartoon, a woman who is listening with her husband to a TV news program and trying to keep up with current events complains, "I keep forgetting. Which is the good guy—Prince Souvanna Phouma or Prince Souphanouvong?" Forty of the 50 students rated this caption as female. A man with a similar question would probably drop the self-deprecating "I keep forgetting," and say something like, "Damm it! How are we supposed to remember which one is Souvanna Phouma and which is Souphanouvong?" This wording would put the blame for confusion on the owner of the difficult name, rather than the memory of the speaker.

In general, women in the cartoons speak less forcefully than men. For instance, they utter exclamations only five times when speaking to another adult, versus 27 times for men. Furthermore, exclamations seem to serve different functions for men and women. Males use them when they are angry or exasperated. A scowling boss yells into his intercom, "Miss Carter! Where's my input?" A husbands says to his wife, "Damn it, Gertrude, Abe Beame isn't *supposed* to turn you on!" But women's exclamations are likely to convey enthusiasm, as when a woman who is admiring a picture says, "Aren't you lucky! Very few people have anything original that's nice."

Freedom to Swear

Since men do not have to be as mild as women, cartoonists let their male characters swear much more freely than their female characters. In *The New Yorker* cartoons, men use swear words (or exclamations with the word "God") 13 times. Women use them only twice, and on one of these occasions there is provocation. A woman says to her husband, who is pouring drinks at their bar, "My God, I mean is that really *all* you can say about me—I've stood the test of time?" Men curse for more trivial reasons. For example, a couple is dining in a restaurant, and the man says, "To hell with what the Sierra Club could do with the cost of a single F-111 fighter plane! Think of what *I* could do with the cost of a single F-111 fighter plane!" With the *hell,* the "masculine" topic, the emphatic *I,* and the exclamation mark, the speaker is clearly recognizable as a man.

Many of the student raters commented on the way profanity, and harsh language in general, distinguish male from female speech. They echoed an observation made by Jespersen half a century ago, when he wrote that women feel an "instinctive shrinking from coarse and gross expressions." Not all modern women agree, however. When I showed Jespersen's remark to some women living in a college dormitory, the spontaneous reaction of several of them was "Shit!"

Another comment by some of the students in the study was that men use a simpler, more direct, more assertive type of language. They are blunt and to the point, whereas women tend to "flower up" their remarks. The caption ratings reflected this view. For example, all but two of the men and two of the women assigned "I'm probably old-fashioned, but I felt much more at home with the Forsytes than I do with the Louds," to a female speaker. One female rater explained, "Women are more likely to preempt their statements with excuses for themselves, 'I may be old-fashioned, but—' ...women are more concerned with a smooth emotional atmosphere." In contrast, men are perceived as self-assured and sometimes condescending. This came out in one of the cartoons, in which a woman complains to a man, "Can't you just say 'Scarlatti' instead of 'Scarlatti, of course'?"

Mommy Talk

Although the people of *The New Yorker* cartoons live in a world that is almost childless, there are some hints of what might be called mommy talk. For example, there is a cartoon portraying two men, one disgusted, the other puzzled, waiting in line for a public telephone. The woman using the phone gushes, "Yes, you are. You're my little snookums. Well, bye-bye for now, Sweetie Pie. Mommy's got to go ... Hi. Was she wagging her tail?"

Finally, according to folk-linguistics, certain adjectives, like "nice" and "pretty," are typical of female speech. In the cartoons, these words sometimes serve to identify a woman as a person with traditional ideas about women's role. At other times, they are the basis for a joke, as when a woman uses them while talking about a "masculine" topic. And occasionally, a man employs them to indicate a role reversal. Unfortunately, sex-linked vocabulary differences are difficult to quantify, but in general, the cartoons do reflect the usual beliefs about feminine adjectives.

These and other findings demonstrate that stereotypical female speech is restricted and wishy-washy. The same picture emerges from other sources. For instance, the *New Seventeen Book of Etiquette and Young Living* contains a section on female speech entitled "Sweet Talk." It warns, "A pretty girl makes a good first impression with her looks, but if the sounds that come out of that pretty face are harsh, the effect is spoiled. She has to be easy on the ears as well as on the eyes."

Mary Ellmann has described the stereotyped formlessness of women's language as it appears in the works of such male writers as James Joyce, Jean-Paul

Sartre, Norman Mailer, and Ernest Hemingway; the Molly Blooms of literature have just let it all flow out. The same looseness of syntax is captured in
a *Saturday Review* cartoon, where a miniskirted coed says to her male professor, "If we don't know how big the whole universe is, then I don't see how
we could be sure how big anything in it is either, like the whole thing might
not be any bigger than maybe an orange would be if if weren't in the universe,
I mean, so I don't think we ought to get too uptight about any of it because
it might be really sort of small and unimportant after all, and until we find out
that everything isn't just some kind of specks and things, why maybe who
needs it?"

A few linguists have tried to pinpoint more precisely the devices women use
to weaken their words. Robin Lakoff has suggested that women use the tag-
question form for this purpose. Instead of a decisive statement, "That house
looks terrible," women are apt to use an indecisive form, "That house looks
terrible, doesn't it?" In this way, they ask for confirmation, and allow themselves to be persuaded otherwise. Lakoff also believes women use intonation
to turn answers into questions, thus communicating subordination and uncertainty: "When will dinner be ready?" "Oh . . . around six o'clock . . .?"

Is Folklore Fact?

Both folk-linguistics and the observations of professional linguists provide
useful clues to popular attitudes, and are rich sources of hypotheses about
language. These hypotheses may or may not fit empirical data about the way
people actually talk. Unfortunately, there have been very few studies on sex-
related differences in actual speech. Some researchers have found that women
are more likely to use standard, "correct" grammar and pronunciation.
Beyond that, we can make few generalizations.

Lately I have begun to explore the problem of perceived versus actual
differences. My work and the work of several others at the University of
Illinois indicates that while it is easy to write statements identifiable as feminine or masculine types, the sex-related cues in such statements appear relatively infrequently in the language of either sex.

In one recent study, I investigated whether men and women differ in their
use of modifiers. Lakoff and others have suggested that some adjectives, like
"adorable," "lovely," "divine" and "sweet," are peculiar to women; their use
by a man could damage his reputation. As I noted earlier, this feature of
women's speech showed up in some of *The New Yorker* cartoons. Women are
also said to use certain kinds of adverbs more often than men. Jespersen wrote
that women have a propensity for hyperbole which leads them to tack *-ly* onto
adjectives, producing phrases like "awfully pretty" and "terribly nice." I
wanted to find out if women really do use more of these forms.

I was also interested in finding out if there is an absolute difference in the
number and variety of modifiers used by males and females. Opinion here is
divided. Jespersen felt that men have a more extensive vocabulary, and in

general take a greater interest in words. In fact, he advised people wanting to learn a foreign tongue to read "many ladies' novels, because they will there continually meet with just those everyday words and combinations which the foreigner is above all in need of, what may be termed the indispensable small-change of a language." If this is true, we might expect a greater variety of descriptive words from men. However, another linguist, Dwight Bolinger, claims that women use more adjectives than men.

Since this was an initial study, I limited my attention to -*ly* adverbs and prenominal adjectives (words that precede and modify nouns, such as "handsome" in "handsome man"). These particular kinds of modifiers, unlike others, are umambiguous and are easy to identify.

Inanimate Objects

I had 17 men and 17 women compose written descriptions of two black-and-white photographs. Since some people have suggested that men are more interested in inanimate objects than they are in people, and the reverse is true for women, I used one photograph showing several people seated around a table, and another showing a large building adorned with pillars and statues. The subjects had 10 minutes in which to write their paragraphs.

I analyzed each paragraph by adding up the number of -*ly* adverbs and prenominal adjectives, and comparing these numbers to the total number of words used. I found none of the differences that are supposed to exist. Statistical analysis showed that women did not differ from men in either the number or variety of -*ly* adverbs or prenominal adjectives they used. Although men tended to use more words overall to describe the photographs, the differences were not statistically significant. And there did not appear to be any sex differences in the kinds of adjectives preferred.

Perhaps the differences are not in the number or variety of modifying words, but in the way they are used. A sensitive person might be able to pick up subtle cues that are not susceptible to statistical analysis. Since middle-class women are supposed to be especially conscious of stylistic variation, I enlisted the aid of 11 female students majoring in English to determine if the sex of the writers could be deduced from internal cues. I gave them 10 typed paragraphs, randomly selected from those written by the participants in the first part of the study. Five had been written by women, five by men; all described the photograph of a building. In only six of the 10 paragraphs was a majority of the English majors able to identify the writer's sex. In all, there were 59 correct guesses and 51 incorrect ones.

Interestingly, none of the English majors questioned the reasonableness of trying to assign paragraphs to male or female authors, and they were all able to give reasons for their choices. Most of these had to do with the number and type of descriptive words used. In *incorrectly* ascribing to female authors paragraphs that were actually written by males, some of the women explained that the passages were graceful, sensitive, and contained a lot of detailed description.

Many questions remain. A greater number of sex differences may exist in spoken than in written language. Differences in written work might show up under other circumstances. For example, an important factor may be whether a woman is writing or speaking to another woman, to a man, or to a general audience. Age and socioeconomic position may affect the writer's style. Since women are individuals, researchers must be careful not to make the error of simply grouping all women together.

Vacant Chambers of the Mind

Words, phrases, and sentence patterns are not inherently strong or weak. They acquire these attributes only in a particular cultural context. If our society views female speech as inferior, it is because of the subordinate role assigned to women. Our culture is biased to interpret sex differences in favor of men.

For example, Jespersen reports an experiment in which male and female subjects had to read a paragraph as quickly as possible, then write down as much as they could remember of it. Women were able to read the passage more quickly and recall more of what they had read. But they lost anyway. Jespersen paraphrases Havelock Ellis' ingenious explanation of the results: " . . .with the quick reader it is as though every statement were admitted immediately and without inspection to fill the vacant chambers of the mind, while with the slow reader every statement undergoes an instinctive process of cross-examination. . . ."

Thus, beliefs about sex-related language differences may be as important as the actual differences. As long as women play a subordinate role, their speech will be stereotyped as separate and unequal.

PART NINE
Intercultural Communication: The Cross-Setting Setting

Experiences and Discussions

1. For each of the eight culturally determined variables discussed by Samovar and Porter, provide one example of how the variable can (positively or negatively) affect intercultural communication.
2. Assume that the United States is one culture (for the purposes of this exercise only). For this "American" culture, give examples of moral, social, political, economic, religious, and individual values that are held to be *absolute* values, as described by Samovar and Porter.

3. Review the various types of nonverbal behavior described by Rich. For your own interactions, which behaviors would you rate as most important for productive and comfortable interracial relationships in work, social, and personal situations?

4. Observe interactions between persons of different ethnic groups. Do you notice any behaviors that differ from those in interactions between persons of the same ethnic group? If so, what are the differences? What suggestions can you offer to people who express feelings of uneasiness when interacting with members of other ethnic groups?

5. Describe a situation that illustrates each of the five stumbling blocks presented by Barna. For each situation, predict the outcome of the interaction.

6. Talk with several Americans who have traveled a great deal. Question them about interpersonal stumbling blocks they have encountered in their travels. What behaviors did they find most strange? What American behaviors would seem peculiar to someone from another country? If possible, talk with people who are visiting the United States for the first time and get their reactions to Americans.

7. Observe a series of cartoons from a major magazine. Do your findings confirm Kramer's? How are other cultural groups depicted?

8. Kramer suggests women may use intonation to indicate indecision. Do your observations and experiences confirm this conclusion? Do men also employ intonation to modify meaning?

For Further Reading

BURLING, ROBBINS. *Man's Many Voices: Language in Its Cultural Context.* New York: Holt, Rinehart and Winston, 1970.

According to the author, the book is "an investigation into the nonlinguistic factors that affect our use of language ... man's use of language is also dependent upon the context in which he speaks and upon his varied personalities." Included are discussions of the setting of language, literal and extended meanings, semantics and syntax, linguistic virtuosity, and language diversification among other topics of interest.

KOCHMAN, THOMAS (ed.). *Rappin' and Stylin' Out.* Urbana, Ill.: University of Illinois Press, 1972.

One of the few collections of readings dealing with black communication, both verbal and nonverbal. Topics examined include the African influence on Afro-American communication, communication in social situations, and the educational implications of distinct ethnic communication styles.

MILGRAM, STANLEY. *The Individual in a Social World: Essays and Experiments.* Reading, Mass.: Addison-Wesley, 1977.

Milgram views the individual as the central focus of social psychology. He examines the role of the individual in terms of the city, authority, groups, and media. The effects of culturally diverse physical environments upon individuals is studied.

RICH, ANDREA L. *Interracial Communication.* New York: Harper and Row, 1974.

An excellent and comprehensive introduction to the principles involved in the process of communication between persons of different ethnic backgrounds, with an emphasis on black-white communication, perceptions, roles, stereotypes, and attitudes.

SAMOVAR, LARRY A., and RICHARD E. PORTER. *Intercultural Communications: A Reader.* 2nd ed. Belmont, Calif.: Wadsworth Publishing, 1976.

This revised edition has an expanded interpretation of "culture" that includes such groups as women, the socially disadvantaged, the poor, and the homosexual population. Ethnic groups given more attention in this edition are the American Indian and Chicano populations. Essays include discussions of the goals of intercultural communication, the influence of culture on perception, international negotiations, and directions in intercultural research.

SITARAM K. S., and ROY T. COGDELL. *Foundations of Intercultural Communication.* Columbus, Ohio: Charles E. Merrill, 1976.

This is one of the first actual "textbooks" to deal solely with intercultural communication. The authors analyze the components of intercultural communication and the role of perceptions and attitudes in effective communication between cultures. Specific attention is given to verbal, nonverbal, and media communication and the ethics of intercultural communication. The authors do a good job of comparing Western and Eastern philosophies and cultures and are sure to provide you with much new information.

	Preliminaries	Verbal	Nonverbal	Intrapersonal	Interpersonal	Group	Public	Mass	Intercultural
Bormann & Bormann	1, 2	3, 6	4, 5		7, 10, 13	11, 12	4, 5, 14, 15	15	
Brooks	Intro.	3	6	1, 2	4, 5, 7, 9, 10, 11	8		12	13, 14
Burgoon & Ruffner	1	3	4	5	2, 6, 10, 11	7	8	9	
DeVito	1–4, 14, 24	19–23	25–31	7–10	5, 6, 11, 12, 13, 15–18, 32–42	32–42	2, 6, 11, 13	4	
Griffin & Patton	1, 2	6	4, 5, 6	3, 8	4, 7, 8 APP. B	5	8		2, 4, 5
McAuley	1	10	9	2	2, 3, 4, 8	APP. A	2, 10		
McCroskey	2, 14	5, 7–10	6		2, 3, 11				
McCroskey et al	1, 2	7, 8	6		3, 4, 5	9, 10	6, 8	11	
McCroskey & Wheeless	1, 2, 8	9, 10	10	5, 7, 11, 14, 15, 19	3, 6, 12, 13, 16, 17	3, 6, 19	9, 10, 16	3, 4	
Myers & Myers	1, 2	3, 4, 5	10	6, 7, 8	9, 11	12	3, 5, 10		10
Scheidel	1	4, 5, 6	6	2, 3	6, 7, 9, 10, 12	8–11	3, 5, 10 APP. A	15	16
Sereno & Bodaken	1, 3	5	5	2, 4, 7	8	9	6, 10		
Tubbs & Moss	1, 2, 3	7	8	6	4, 5, 9, 11, 12	10	11	13	
Wenburg & Wilmot	1, 3, 4	5–10	6	7, 11, 13, 14	8, 9, 12	2			